A MARITIME HIT-AND-RUN OFF THE COAST OF NANTUCKET

– Jennifer N. Sellitti –

4880 Lower Valley Road • Atglen, PA 19310

Other Schiffer books on related subjects

Passenger Liners from Germany: 1816–1990
Clas Broder Hansen
978-0-88740-325-5

Out of the Fog: The Sinking of Andrea Doria
Algot Mattsson
978-0-87033-545-7

Copyright © 2025 by Jennifer N. Sellitti

Library of Congress Control Number: 2023941052

All rights reserved. No part of this work may be reproduced or used in any form or by any means—graphic, electronic, or mechanical, including photocopying or information storage and retrieval systems—without written permission from the publisher.

The scanning, uploading, and distribution of this book or any part thereof via the Internet or any other means without the permission of the publisher is illegal and punishable by law. Please purchase only authorized editions and do not participate in or encourage the electronic piracy of copyrighted materials.

"Schiffer," "Schiffer Publishing, Ltd.," and the pen and inkwell logo are registered trademarks of Schiffer Publishing, Ltd.

Designed by Danielle D. Farmer
Cover design by Chris Bower
Type set in Clarendon URW/American Scribe/LeLick Brush

ISBN: 978-0-7643-6795-3
Ebook: 978-1-5073-0397-9
Printed in India

Published by Schiffer Publishing, Ltd.
4880 Lower Valley Road
Atglen, PA 19310
Phone: (610) 593-1777; Fax: (610) 593-2002
Email: Info@schifferbooks.com
Web: www.schifferbooks.com

For our complete selection of fine books on this and related subjects, please visit our website at www.schifferbooks.com. You may also write for a free catalog.

Schiffer Publishing's titles are available at special discounts for bulk purchases for sales promotions or premiums. Special editions, including personalized covers, corporate imprints, and excerpts, can be created in large quantities for special needs. For more information, contact the publisher.

We are always looking for people to write books on new and related subjcts. If you have an idea for a book, please contact us at proposals@schifferbooks.com.

*To Joe Mazraani
for never letting distance, depth,
or doubt get in the way of a
lifetime of adventure*

⊜   ⊜   ⊜

And the sea gave up the dead which were in it,
and death and Hades gave up the dead which were in them;
and they were judged, every one of them,
according to their deeds.

—REV. 20:13

Foreword	9
Preface	11
Acknowledgments	13

Part I: Choupault | 15

CHAPTER 1	A Wreck in Sight	17
CHAPTER 2	All Ashore!	19
CHAPTER 3	Crossing the Atlantic	27
CHAPTER 4	Franco-Américaine	37
CHAPTER 5	Iron and Steam	45
CHAPTER 6	132 Souls	52
CHAPTER 7	Sailors, Watchmen, Firemen, Passengers	65
CHAPTER 8	Abandon Ship	77
CHAPTER 9	The Dragon	86
CHAPTER 10	Adrift	94
CHAPTER 11	Perils of the Sea	102
CHAPTER 12	Forged in a Storm	108
CHAPTER 13	Purgatory	112
CHAPTER 14	1856	118
CHAPTER 15	Goodbye	125
CHAPTER 16	Laughter	132
CHAPTER 17	Ship!	137
CHAPTER 18	On a Barrel	141
CHAPTER 19	Two Ships *Elise*	146
CHAPTER 20	Gloucester	152
CHAPTER 21	The Phantom Ship	163
CHAPTER 22	Survivors	171

Part II: Durham | 177

CHAPTER 23	Command	179
CHAPTER 24	La Ciotat	182
CHAPTER 25	Mourning	190
CHAPTER 26	Exoneration	196
CHAPTER 27	Notes en Réplique	202
CHAPTER 28	The Marseille Predicament	208
CHAPTER 29	Captain Ward L. Smith	215
CHAPTER 30	Stranded	235
CHAPTER 31	Escape from Marseille	241
CHAPTER 32	The Fog	250
CHAPTER 33	Spezia	253
CHAPTER 34	Friends in High Places	261
CHAPTER 35	Piracy	265
CHAPTER 36	The *Adriatic* Affair	270
CHAPTER 37	Rules of the Road	277
CHAPTER 38	Celebrity	281
CHAPTER 39	Collisions at Sea	288
CHAPTER 40	Fate	298

Epilogue: Everything Is Possible, The 2024 *Le Lyonnais* Discovery   313

Endnotes	353
Bibliography	370
Index	387

There is so much more to shipwreck stories than the circumstances surrounding the event itself. More than anything else, threads of the human element weave in and out, spanning decades and continents. Shipwreck stories are human stories, and the *Lyonnais* disaster is very much a human story.

I became interested in the *Lyonnais* disaster many years ago when researching shipwrecks in the areas surrounding Nantucket Island. Initially, I was investigating the circumstances surrounding the loss of five ships on the same day in 1916, all sunk by a German submarine, the first to cross the Atlantic on a combat mission.

As with most deep dives into history on any subject, additional clues and threads are uncovered. Following these clues and threads will invariably lead in many different directions, much like the branches of a large tree. In doing so, other stories once hidden are uncovered. Often it may be just a paragraph or sentence in a long-since-out-of-print book or document filed away in an obscure archive. These clues emerge and take on lives of their own. In the world of maritime history, the hidden stories are many indeed. For the historian or researcher, the question becomes which path to take, which story to delve into. All of this takes time, an enormous amount of time. Eventually, the historian reaches the point where the end of the voyage is in sight. In the case of unfinished voyages, the torch must be passed, as it were. The research must continue to enable the voyage to be completed and so the story can be shared. Such it is that I have passed the torch to Jennifer.

Jennifer Sellitti has done a masterful job of investigating all the aspects of this event. She has followed leads to the most unlikely of places, from Harvard University to France and back to, of all places, Alabama. In doing so, Jennifer has uncovered twists and turns to this story that have remained dormant for almost two centuries. Backgrounds and lives of both passengers and crew are revealed in extraordinary detail. Unlikely heroes and heroines, as well as the less heroic, are mixed with all walks of society and woven through this story. This is a truly fascinating tale with so many unexpected turns. *The Adriatic Affair* will appeal to readers everywhere.

Captain Eric Takakjian

Fairhaven, Massachusetts, 2022

Preface

The story of the French steamship *Le Lyonnais* is one about the death of many and the survival of a few. It is a true story. A total of 114 people died. Eighteen survived in some of the harshest conditions the North Atlantic can assemble. What makes this story different from other tales of loss at sea is that the rescue of survivors is not where the story ends, but where it begins.

I first heard about *Le Lyonnais* from Captain Eric Takakjian, a wreck hunter and my mentor in shipwreck research. The story of survival drew me in, but I soon became fascinated with the people who lived and died aboard *Le Lyonnais* and others connected to the disaster. The more I dug, the more obsessed I became. This book sprang from a desire to tell their stories as accurately and as vividly and as with as much humanity as possible.

Every author who works in nonfiction encounters the same dilemma: how to make a story come to life while remaining faithful to the historical record. It is a tension not easily resolved. The *Le Lyonnais* disaster took place in 1856. Sources are finite. After conducting almost ten years of research, I am certain there is nothing more to discover about this wreck unless it is buried in some museum basement or someone's personal collection. There are no witnesses to interview for further details. Many of those involved spoke French, German, Dutch, or other languages, so firsthand accounts given to the American press were blunted by poor translation. The era of *Le Lyonnais*'s sinking put up further storytelling barriers. The disaster took place at a time when people were tight-lipped about emotions and not inclined to pour their feelings and experiences into interviews with the press. Those aboard *Le Lyonnais* experienced unimaginable trauma at a time when trauma was not discussed, only borne.

This book aims to remain true to the historical record and, at the same time, to honor the disaster and the people who lived it by telling their stories in detail. To do that, I did my best to understand who the sailors and passengers were and to marry their personalities to their experiences. The effort involved overlapping narratives to separate fact from fiction. Part of the research was weaving each article, account, or narrative together to find points of agreement among survivors and areas where memories differed. Focusing on multiple viewpoints provided more clarity into the thoughts, experiences, and feelings of those involved.

Suffice it to say, none of this book is fiction.

When I am not exploring the ocean, I am a criminal defense attorney. Lawyers are not permitted to make up facts in a courtroom. We are permitted only to argue the facts and reasonable inferences drawn therefrom. I approached this book the same way I approach a jury trial. The story contains facts and reasonable inferences only. There were many times when I wanted to enhance the drama by making up a fact or two, but I restrained myself. There are places where I wish I had more information, but filling in gaps felt like an insult to the people who experienced this disaster and chose what to share and what to keep hidden.

The dialogue in this book comes from documents, articles, transcripts, and other firsthand sources. The rest is created by drawing reasonable conclusions from the documents, statements of others, and overlapping perspectives of those involved.

It has been more than 168 years since *Le Lyonnais* sank below the waves, and yet, so few people know about this incident and its aftereffects. My hope is that this book does justice to the men, women, and children whose lives were forever changed by the simple act of boarding a steamship to France. No person is lost to history while their name is still spoken. We honor them and keep their memories alive by reading, learning, and sharing their stories.

Jennifer N. Gellitti

Acknowledgments

Special thanks to Captain Eric Takakjian, who intrigued and inspired me with the tale of *Le Lyonnais*, passed the torch, and allowed his passion to become my own. Your support and encouragement mean more than I could ever express.

Thank you to the crew and friends of D/V *Tenacious*. You never cease to amaze and inspire me: Captain Joe Mazraani, Becca Boring, Bill Cleary, John Copeland, Bryan Cunningham, Andrew Donn, Mike Dudas, Joel Garcia, Steve Gatto, Dave Hoshauer, Dennis Huber, Tommy Huber, Pete Jawork, David Kennedy, Garry Kozak, Jack Lawniczuk, Darren Lynch, Ben Mahler, François Merle, Kurt Mintell, Harold Moyers, Andrew Nagle, Mark Nix, Chris Ogden, Tom Packer, Pat Rooney, Greg Rosengarten, Chris Shannon, Bradley Sheard, Richard Simon, Joseph St. Amand, Van Strickler, Lori Takakjian, Anthony Tedeschi, Timothy Whitehead, Jennifer Whittaker, Paul Whittaker, and Tom Zajac. To those with us in spirit: Bart Malone and Mr. Jim Lynch.

Rudolph and Barbara Sellitti, my parents, always told me I could be anything I put my mind to—including a book-writing lawyer-pirate. I am thankful to them and to my siblings, Larry and Amy Sellitti, for their steadfast love and support.

No book is possible without colleagues willing to edit with an open mind and a critical eye. Thank you to Tom Belsky, Brynn Giannullo, Joe Mazraani, Tom Packer, Eric Takakjian, and Robyn Veasey for endless hours of assistance. I could not have done this without you.

Thank you to the authors who lent their advice and guidance: Dominic Etzold, Chris Hedges, Charles H. Lagerbom, Kyle Nelson, and Randy Peffer.

The Adriatic Affair

To John Stone, Bob Biondi and the team at Schiffer Publishing, thank you for taking a chance on a new author and guiding me through the process.

Boston Sea Rovers and New Jersey Maritime Museum are two organizations close to my heart. You inspired me to write this book and, in my own small way, contribute to the legacy of stories from beneath the waves. Thank you for all you do and for allowing me to be a part of it. Special thanks to Nick Fazah, Kim Malkoski, Dave Morton, and Patricia Morton of Boston Sea Rovers and to Jim Vogel and Deborah Whitcraft of the New Jersey Maritime Museum.

It takes a village to write a nonfiction book. The village includes historians, curators, family members, and archivists from around the world. From Bob Peck, who opened the Historic Mobile Preservation Society on Mardi Gras just for me, to Martin Cleaver, who worked with me step by step from Birkenhead, England, to reconstruct *Le Lyonnais*, I am grateful to the following individuals and organizations for sharing their time and their collections and for working tirelessly to preserve maritime history for generations to come: Belfast Historical Society & Museum, Megan Pinette, curator; Dorothy Alling, for her friendship and her guided tours of Waldo County, Maine; Florian Lecaer; Historical Mobile Preservation Society, Bob Peck, volunteer archivist; Maine Built Boats, Jon Johansen; New Bedford Whaling Museum; Liverpool Museums, Nathan Pendlebury; P&O Heritage Collection; Penobscot Marine Museum; S. P. Lohia Collection; Steamship Historical Society of America; Ward L. Smith family, Sharon LaDuke, family historian; Wirral Archives, Martin Cleaver, archives and records officer, and William Meredith, archivist.

Last, but certainly not least, thank you to the members of the 2024 *Le Lyonnais* discovery team: Andrew Donn, Joe Mazraani, Kurt Mintell, Tom Packer, Eric Takakjian, and Tim Whitehead. As Herman Melville wrote in *Moby Dick*, "At sea a fellow comes out. Salt water is like wine in that respect." After countless hours spent together—navigating rough conditions and close quarters—I am grateful for the bond that we have forged. It is an honor to share the journey. Here's to the next sea-venture!

Part I

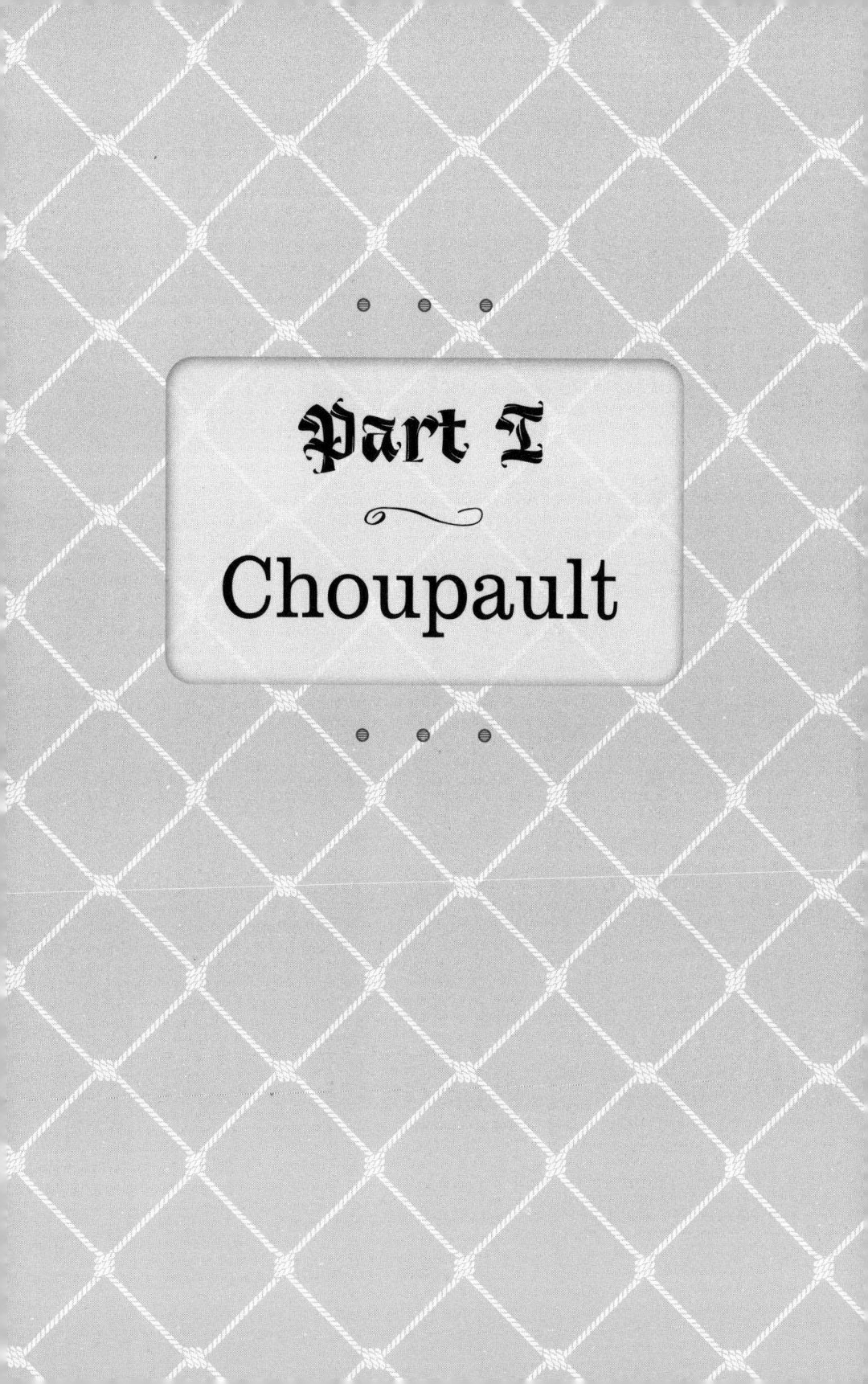

Choupault

CHAPTER 1
A Wreck in Sight

"THERE IS A WRECK IN SIGHT," called the mate to the captain. Captain Enoch Peabody stepped out onto the deck of *Neptune*, a passenger ship from the Chas L. Marshall Line two days out of New York and bound for Liverpool. He looked in the direction his mate pointed and saw something floating in the distance. "Lower a quarter-boat."[1] He spoke with urgency.

He ordered a small party of men into the boat and joined them as they rowed toward the wreckage. Peabody soon realized that the floating object was a small boat adrift, a lifeboat. One of the sailors hollered in the boat's direction. The only answer was the sound of waves lapping against wood.

The men reached the boat and found stillness. They saw no bodies. There was clothing strewn everywhere, which made it impossible to see what lay underneath, but Peabody feared the worst.

The men lashed the boat to theirs and towed it back toward *Neptune*. Some of them sat tall and peered into the lifeboat as they rowed. They reached the ship and secured the boat to it with a thick rope. One by one, the men climbed into the lifeboat to search it. It was stocked with provisions and clothing. The sailors sorted through the items one by one, unsure of what they might find beneath the piles of fabric. They moved methodically toward the center, where a mass of coats and shirts had collected and obscured the bottom. With every jacket the men moved, Peabody expected to find a corpse.

The boat contained six bottles of brandy, two kegs of wine, hams, preserved meats, and a small a quantity of silver and gold coins, amounting to about five hundred dollars. The starboard side had been stoved, or crushed in, and had likely filled with water quickly. The captain surmised she was struck when lowered from a ship. The realization brought him some relief because it meant the boat had never taken on passengers. Two chronometers, instruments used in conjunction with celestial navigation to determine position at sea, were among the items uncovered. They had been deliberately placed in a safe location.

The captain found no bodies. He found no scraps. He found no signs the boat had been used. He was practically certain no living thing had ever occupied it, but, nevertheless, the discovery made him uneasy. After inspecting the lifeboat's contents, he did at last find a clue to the boat's origin and a first step to unraveling the mystery now tethered to his ship—a spyglass engraved with the name "*Cie. Franco-Américaine Steamer Lyonnais*."

The crew hoisted the lifeboat onto *Neptune*'s deck. Peabody took one last look and thought to himself, "There have been hard times very near and very lately."[2] He ordered the crew to hide the lifeboat and all its contents so as not to frighten the passengers.

CHAPTER 2

THE DOCK WAS ALIVE WITH MOVEMENT on November 1, 1856, the day *Le Lyonnais* departed New York. Passengers gathered with their luggage, loved ones wished anxious travelers farewell, and strangers drawn to the excitement of a send-off congregated on the waterfront. The world's most prominent shipping lines sent and received their ships from docks on the Hudson River. Ships bound for Le Havre left from Beach Street, a portion of the Hudson between New York City and northeastern New Jersey, and it was here that *Le Lyonnais* waited her turn to put to sea.

Le Lyonnais was an impressive and somewhat novel sight. It was the first time many in the crowd had seen a steamship with a propeller instead of two paddle wheels. The sleekness of her iron hull, punctuated by iron rivets, conveyed a sense of sturdiness. A reporter from the *New York Weekly Herald* inspected her at the dock and pronounced *Le Lyonnais* "built in the strongest manner" and "fitted and sound in every respect."[1]

The crew readied the ship for launch. *Le Lyonnais*'s cargo, which consisted primarily of wheat and bacon, along with small amounts of other perishable and nonperishable goods, had been loaded the day before along with the trunks that passengers wished to store during the voyage. The crew now turned its attention to cabin baggage. They hoisted smaller pieces on their shoulders and walked them to the passengers' rooms. They used the ship's winches to lift larger trunks from the dock to the ship, where stewards transferred them to passenger cabins. An endless stream of chests and trunks and packages hovered in the air above the crowd and disappeared onto the ship's deck.

Sailors moved with precision and seemed unfazed by the watchful eyes of the onlookers below. They were predominantly French, men of experience and discipline. Many had served in the military during the Crimean War, a gritty conflict in which official designations between naval and ground duties often blurred. Most found their way into merchant service when the war ended in March 1856. The brief interval between the war's end and their employment as merchant seaman showed in their work. There was an earnestness with which they went about their duties which stood in stark contrast to the excitement in the air.

Edward and Edmund Poirier were among those who came to see *Le Lyonnais* depart. Franco-Américaine, a Paris-based company, owned the ship, and the Poirier brothers served as the company's agents in New York. They were responsible for booking passengers and securing cargo contracts from merchants. The agents inspected the ship before her inaugural voyage to Le Havre to ensure that both she and the crew were in good working order.

Safety was personal for the Poiriers. The men lost six family members in September 1854, when the Collins's liner *Arctic* collided with *Vesta* in heavy fog off Cape Race, Newfoundland. Emma Poirier Guynet, her husband, and their four children—ages ten, eight, four, and one—all perished in a disaster that became synonymous with the worst of human nature. *Arctic* did not carry enough lifeboats for the four hundred passengers aboard. The men, most of them crew, prevented women and children from accessing the few boats the ship carried. Sixty-one sailors and twenty-four passengers, all of them male, sacrificed more than three hundred others to save themselves. Not one woman or child survived.

The loss hung heavy on the Poiriers' hearts, and the agents paid utmost attention to preparing *Le Lyonnais* for travel. They had the ship examined by engineers and put a new whistle on board at New York to ensure she would avoid collision in even the densest fog.

The passengers boarded at one o'clock in the afternoon, an hour before the ship's scheduled departure. Men, women, and some children walked up the wooden ramp that connected the ship to the dock. People congregated in small groups once aboard. Moods depended on circumstances. Those traveling with friends and family chatted excitedly, peered over the side of the ship, and waved to those on the dock below. The ones who came aboard with loved ones they would soon leave behind were more somber and held back tears as they awaited a last embrace from a spouse or child. Everyone prepared for the moment the captain called, "All ashore!"—the signal that the ship was about to depart and for anyone without a ticket to return to the dock.

The "All ashore!" came at two o'clock. The crew detached the boarding ramp and cast off *Le Lyonnais*'s lines after the last well-wishers departed.

CHAPTER 2 | *All Ashore!*

Embarkation of a passenger steamship, 1870.
Harper's Weekly Magazine. Author's collection

The captain blew the whistle to signal to the chief engineer that it was time to fire the engines and go. A traveler writing about a steamship's departure from New York for Europe in 1870 described the likely scene: "The engine awakes at once to life and action, the water at the stern begins to be thrown into a whirlpool of boiling surges, and the vast mass, with its hundreds of occupants, gathered from all parts of the country and brought suddenly into close juxtaposition and companionship, begins slowly to creep away from the pier. The parting gun is fired; the waving of handkerchiefs from the long line of passengers leaning over the railing of the promenade deck are answered by similar signals from rows and groups of friends on the pier."[2]

Le Lyonnais left New York on November 1, 1856, with 132 people aboard. The ship had capacity for sixty first-class cabins and thirty second-class but did not sell all its cabin space on its first voyage to Le Havre. She carried thirty-nine cabin passengers and ninety-three crew.[3]

The passengers held sight of the dock for as long as possible. They turned to their own affairs after that. For many, leaving the dock meant exploring the rooms that would serve as their homes for the foreseeable future. Cabins in the mid-1850s were a vast improvement over steerage class but still small. First-class cabins on the 1855 Cunard liner RMS *Persia* were 9 feet long, with two bunk beds and a couch. The beds, called berths, were short and narrow and made from thin mattresses atop hard wooden planks.

First-class passengers in the 1850s did not enjoy rooms to themselves. Cabins accommodated multiple berths, and travelers shared their cabins with other guests. It was not until 1893, when Cunard launched *Lucania*, that the wealthiest steamship passengers could book a single-berth cabin or a suite, which consisted of two single-berth cabins connected by a living room.

The most-luxurious cabins aboard *Le Lyonnais* were in the afterpart of the ship. Second-class passengers occupied the fore cabins, which were less desirable because of the constant noise of waves breaking against the ship's bow. There were two second-class forecabins that accommodated up to fifteen passengers each.

Franco-Américaine hired House of Barbe and Morisse to decorate *Le Lyonnais*. China, fine linens, and glass vases decorated the first-class cabins. Artwork and tapestries adorned the walls. Second-class accommodations were more modest and furnished with drawers, locks, and wall hangars.

The finest cabins were fitted with venetian blinds. What seems like a strange touch for a ship traveling the North Atlantic was a nod to Peninsular & Oriental Steamship Navigation Company's (P&O's) fleet of ships and a feature more important when *Le Lyonnais* traveled to ports in South America. The contract for *Le Lyonnais* referenced P&O, a line that established trade routes to ports in the Far East and Australia, as a benchmark for top quality in construction and decor. P&O used venetian blinds for cross-ventilation to cool its ships in hot climates, so *Le Lyonnais* employed the same.

There was no need to cool *Le Lyonnais* as she left New York in early November. The air was cold, and a breeze blew. Some of the passengers remained in their cabins to unpack their things and get settled, while others took to the deck to enjoy the final sights of land as the ship cruised down the Hudson River. Those in the know went straight to the saloon to select their places for dinner. Dinner was the social center of any transatlantic cruise. One's place at dinner was both a status symbol and a practical matter. The best seats were nearest to the captain and farthest from the noisy engine. End seats were prized because they made it easier to slip away from dinner unnoticed. Seating did not change after the first night's dinner, so savvy travelers prioritized seat selection above other affairs.

A smaller boat approached the ship and landed a pilot, a mariner with specific knowledge of the Hudson River, aboard *Le Lyonnais*. It was the pilot's responsibility to navigate the ship through unfamiliar inland waterways and get her safely to open sea.

Taking the pilot, 1870. *Harper's Weekly Magazine.*
Author's collection

Le Lyonnais snaked down the Hudson. The pilot kept Manhattan to the east and New Jersey to the west. The land masses shielded the ship from harsher winds and kept the waters calm. New York in 1856 was densely populated and dotted with multistory buildings. The outline of the city's bustling streets and skyline soon gave way to the beachside landscapes of the New Jersey shore. The colors faded from shades of gray and black to green and sandy brown.

It took about three hours for *Le Lyonnais* to reach Sandy Hook and make way toward open ocean. The pilot emptied the ship into deeper waters and disembarked at five o'clock. *Le Lyonnais* was now in the hands of her captain, Pierre Stanislas Devaulx.[4] Devaulx handed the pilot a letter to give the Poiriers, in which he spoke highly of the ship and her engines. He had no doubt she would make good time under favorable circumstances.

Le Lyonnais traveled east. The ride continued to be comfortable, with the ship shielded from the winds by Long Island, which was now to the north. Those same winds did not treat the ship as kindly when she met the open ocean, where the winds, with no more land to serve as a buffer, made the water rougher. The smell of the air changed too. There was no more earthiness to it, just the scent of wet salt mixed with engine smoke. *Le Lyonnais* rocked in the waves until the pattern became rhythmic enough to recognize but not quite rhythmic enough to predict.

Many of the passengers became seasick. Seasickness, especially on the first day out, was not uncommon on transatlantic voyages. The weather in the North Atlantic is shaped by the interaction of wind, ocean currents, and contrasting air masses emanating from North America and the Arctic. Weather systems typically move from west to east. Circulation around high-pressure systems follows a clockwise pattern, while low-pressure systems rotate counterclockwise. High-pressure ridges and low-pressure troughs as well as cold and warm fronts have steering effects on systems. Factors such as upper atmospheric weather, the Jetstream, and wind shear further affect weather patterns in the region. These dynamic elements churn up unpredictable storms, swells, and rough seas and contribute to the region's reputation for volatile weather. Most travelers were unaccustomed to such conditions and did not take the early days of these voyages well.

Dr. Jean Clarin, the ship's physician, spoke with some of those who had taken ill, but there was little he could do. The remedies for seasickness in 1856 amounted to nothing more than sage advice passed down by those with experience: lie down. Seasick passengers lay in their berths or in common areas of the ship and prayed for better weather. Most skipped dinner.

The passengers found the conditions difficult, but the crew did not. They were used to the way the sea changed after a ship lost sight of land, and welcomed the feeling of moving with the ocean again. Passengers who escaped their rooms to take in the fresh air watched with envy as the sailors went about their duties oblivious to the sickness that had overtaken so many.

Captain Devaulx did not mind the movement of the ocean. He watched the crew from the quarterdeck and replayed the day's activities in his mind. He stood only 5 feet, 4 inches tall, but his confident air and baritone voice made him seem larger. Devaulx had spent the morning readying the ship for departure and greeting passengers as they boarded. There was a kindness about him, a good nature that comforted those who met him. Although Devaulx enjoyed people, he was glad now to be on the quarterdeck and, for all intents and purposes, alone. He took a deep breath. Inhaling the dense ocean air made him feel at home. His peace was interrupted only by the brief and conscious recognition that he was at ease. It was an ease he had not felt in a long time.

Devaulx was born in Bordeaux, France, to Jean-Baptiste Devaulx and Catherine Jeanne Felicita Chaintal de Laloubie on October 14, 1814. His parents named him after his godfather, Stanislas Ferriere Hant. He came from a family of privilege. His father was a lawyer and deputy judge. Devaulx attended boarding school as a child and entered the navy at eighteen. He served as a pilot aboard the ship *La Louise* and on *Nouvelle Louise* from 1832 to 1834 and traveled to ports in India and the Philippines. The French navy called him to serve from 1835 to 1838. He left the military in 1838 and embarked for the South Seas on *Nouvelle Gabrielle* as a lieutenant and an apprentice captain. He became a captain on May 31, 1841.

Devaulx married Marie Delphine Cantua Gréard, the daughter of a wealthy Bordeaux shipowner, just two months later, on July 14, 1841. His father-in-law gave him a ship, *Amable*, as a wedding dowry. Devaulx took *Amable* to the Indies to engage in trade for his father-in-law's company. He proved to be a good captain but a terrible businessman, who lacked the ability to speculate on the price of goods and to negotiate successful contracts. He lost money on every voyage and was forced to sell the goods he purchased overseas at below cost in Bordeaux. His failures almost bankrupted the Gréard family, and his father-in-law had to sell *Amable* to recoup some of the losses.

Devaulx became a merchant captain for hire. A French company, House of Marsaud, employed him to take their ship *Java* to San Francisco to deliver a cargo of wine barrels and proceed to China for further trade. Devaulx completed the voyage but, instead of heading to China, used the ship as collateral to finance a trip to Sydney, Australia, as well as other business ventures, without Marsaud's permission. The poor decisions resulted in heavy financial losses for Marsaud and kept *Java* in California and entangled in litigation for many years.

This second failure soured Devaulx on the business side of seafaring and ended his career as a merchant captain. Upon his return to France, he asked Jean François Constant Mocquard, a lawyer, politician, and family friend who served as chief of staff to Emperor Napoléon III, to help him secure command of a transatlantic liner engaged in passenger transportation, *Le Lyonnais*.

Devaulx and his wife had three children in the years before he took command of *Le Lyonnais*, a son and two daughters. His son, Stenio, was an aspiring mariner and accompanied his father on *Le Lyonnais*'s maiden voyage to Rio de Janeiro and return voyage to Le Havre in the summer of 1856. Stenio planned to accompany his father again, but the ship's owners redirected *Le Lyonnais* to New York. Devaulx put Stenio on a ship to Bordeaux and left for New York to prepare for *Le Lyonnais*'s November 1856 crossing. The captain wanted no distractions on the ship's first voyage from New York to France.

Devaulx took another deep breath of ocean air and let it out again. Thoughts of the past evaporated as he exhaled. The ship made good way and lost sight of land by dark. The night was black and cloudless. Devaulx ordered the crew to turn on the ship's lights. He was glad to be at the helm and even gladder still the evening's dinner would not be such a grand affair. *Le Lyonnais* was aglow as she glided across the Atlantic under sail and steam.

CHAPTER 3

Crossing the Atlantic

ACHIEVEMENTS IN TRANSPORTATION ON LAND and on the high seas marked the nineteenth century. Transatlantic migration and an increasingly global economy fueled the need to move both people and cargo to places farther and farther throughout the world. Shipping prior to 1800 revolved around freight. Passengers were an afterthought and left port only once a ship's belly was full of goods. They also waited for the weather. A captain's discretion determined when the seas and the winds were suitable for sail. People who wanted to cross the North Atlantic, a body of water notorious for unpredictable seas, could be delayed days or even months until both the weather and the volume of the cargo hold made departure worthwhile.

A group of Quaker textile merchants from New York, led by Jerimiah Thompson, changed passenger travel with an idea they had in 1817. They decided to experiment with a shipping schedule to and from Liverpool. Like many merchants of their day, the men owned the ships they used to transport textiles to buyers. Their idea was to advertise passage aboard their ships on a fixed schedule. Ships would sail on specific dates and times regardless of weather or cargo. Their flag featured a large black circle on it, and their line soon became known as Black Ball. Black Ball, officially owned and operated by Jerimiah Thompson, Francis Thompson, Benjamin Marshall, and Isaac Wright & Son, offered regular service between New York and Liverpool and back again by 1818. They began with four 400-ton ships: *James Monroe*, *Pacific*, *Amity*, and *Courier*. In the years that followed, the line expanded to Boston and Philadelphia and added more ships, some weighing in at more than 500 tons. The public referred to the ships as "packets" because they carried packets of mail in addition to passengers.

Black Ball sailed on schedule and in any weather. The North Atlantic is not an easy crossing. The weather is erratic. Winds from the west made the return trip from Europe particularly grueling. Steering a sailing vessel under such conditions required seamen capable of handling whatever seas the ocean mustered. Black Ball recruited the most-qualified captains for the task, and the line soon earned a reputation for being both punctual and reliable. The fleet averaged twenty-three days to England and forty days westward in the first ten years of operation.

Success bred success, and competitors emerged. Lines such as Red Star and Blue Swallowtail competed with Black Ball out of New York for Liverpool, and similar packets began running from Boston and Philadelphia and to such destinations as London, England, and Le Havre, France.

The need for packets increased as hundreds of thousands of emigrants left Europe for America in search of better lives. Some fled religious or political persecution, famine, and desperate economic conditions in their home countries. Some sought fortune as America expanded to the west and the gold rush boomed. Others came to join family members who left Europe for America in the early 1800s. Regardless of the reason, every person who left Europe in pursuit of the American dream needed to cross an ocean to find it. The packets obliged.

The early packets were sailing ships primarily built and run by Americans. The typical packet had three square-rigged masts and blunted, bluff-bowed hulls, which allowed them to plow through rough North Atlantic seas. The ships were designed not for speed at all costs but for reasonable speed and stability.

Packets transported so many people to the New World that the ships and their captains earned reputations for their abilities and their personalities. Packet captains enjoyed a kind of celebrity status. Shipping lines advertised who would be at the helm for each crossing, and passengers paid premiums to cross the Atlantic with better-known captains.

The ships were reliable but not at all glamorous. Most customers traveled in steerage, dark and cramped quarters located between the main deck and the cargo hold. There were no private rooms or windows. Men and women slept in separate bunk rooms. If a ship carried a full load of cargo or mail, the unfortunate steerage passengers lived among the boxes and the postal bags. There was no hospitality service of any kind. Each traveler received a ration of food and prepared their own meals. They brought their own bedding and cleaned up after themselves.

Conditions varied from ship to ship, but bunk rooms were often damp, foul smelling, and rat infested. Steerage passengers spent most of their time below deck and were allowed little time for fresh air, particularly when the weather was foul. Diseases spread like wildfire and often plagued ships.

Cabin space on packets was available but limited to approximately ten to twenty per ship. Cabins were preferable to steerage, but, before the mid-1820s, they were nothing more than semiprivate rooms where customers shared cramped spaces with strangers. Even cabin passengers prepared their own meals, entertained themselves, and cleaned.

Black Ball's dominance went unchecked until 1836, when Collins Line entered the transatlantic packet business. Edward Knight Collins Jr., the son of a wealthy Massachusetts shipping merchant, joined his father's company in 1821 and began to operate ships to and from New York and Mexico in 1827. His father died in 1831, and Collins sought to turn the company's attention to the more lucrative New York–Liverpool route. Collins launched his Dramatic Line in 1836. Each ship bore the name of a famous literary character. These vessels offered more than on-schedule service to Europe. They boasted "unusually spacious" cabins "furnished with every attention to the comfort of passengers."[1] Maids tended to rooms, and waiters served food in the ships' saloons. The wealthiest passengers purchased cabins above deck and enjoyed an unlimited supply of an amenity theretofore unheard of on packet ships: fresh air. These and other conveniences created a new class of transatlantic travel for those who wanted to arrive on schedule and in style.

Shipping companies advertised cabin amenities, but steerage fares drove profits. Overhead on steerage was low. Most passengers could not afford cabins and continued to cross the Atlantic in insufferable conditions. This meant the fewer days at sea, the better. Speed became the paramount concern for packet lines. Collins was the market leader when it came to luxury but competed with Black Ball and others for the speed that attracted steerage customers.

Collins, a master of public relations, pitted his ships against competitors by sailing on the same dates and promoting the competitions in the press. He stacked the odds in his favor by matching the sailing dates of his newest ships with his competitors' oldest. One such race occurred in 1837, when Collins pit his ship *Sheridan* against Black Ball's *Columbus*. Collins's ship lost the race but, nevertheless, won the publicity. The *New York Herald* reported, "Although [*Columbus*] was successful, it is the general opinion that the *Sheridan* is not inferior as a fast sail."[2] Collins gave the paper a glowing letter written by *Sheridan*'s

Edward Knight Collins, ca. 1845-55.
Photograph by Mathew Brady.

passengers, which was printed in the article. Contests like these became known as "packet races" and reinforced the importance of speed in transatlantic crossings.

Two years after Collins launched the Dramatic Line, a different kind of ship crossed the ocean, one that not only threatened packet competition but transformed the future of shipbuilding. SS *Great Western*, the brainchild of British engineer Isambard Kingdom Brunel and built for Great Western Steamship Company, crossed the Atlantic fueled by a combination of sail and a wondrous innovation, the marine steam engine. American author Daniel Webster, who traveled aboard *Great Western* on her first crossing, toasted her captain with prophetic words: "It is our fortune to live in a new epoch. We behold two continents approaching each other. The skill of your countrymen, sir, and my countrymen, is annihilating space."[3]

Annihilating space was exactly what steamships did. The distance between continents shrank by weeks and no longer depended on fair winds and calm seas. The chief advantage of steam was the ability for men to take over when the winds were not with a ship.

Steamships burned coal to produce heat, converted heat into steam, and used the steam pressure to create a rotational force that generated propulsion. *Great Western* had two side-lever engines that powered giant paddle wheels located on each side of the ship. The furnaces that powered the engines burned below deck. The idea of setting fires in the bellies of wooden ships and crossing an open ocean terrified members of the public and even some titans of shipping. Collins was not one of them. He saw the future in Brunel's achievement. Upon hearing the news that Brunel had made a successful transatlantic steamship voyage, he said, "There is no longer chance for enterprise with sails; it is steam that must win the day."[4] It would be several years before Collins converted his line to steam, but he purchased no new sailing ships after *Great Western* crossed the Atlantic.

Brunel was a prolific civil engineer. He is credited with designing the Great Western Railway, which connected London to the south and west of

England, as well as designing many dockyards, bridges, and tunnels. He understood that adapting the steam engine for maritime use would free ships from the mercy of the wind. He left the railroad business to apply his knowledge of steam to ships, and, in 1838, *Great Western* claimed the title of the first steamship built for regularly scheduled transatlantic crossings.

Brunel was a showman, whose innovative ships and publicity stunts garnered attention. *Great Western* is often credited with being the first steamship to cross the Atlantic, but it was a smaller and less publicized ship, *Sirius*, that beat *Great Western* for that record by one day. She was built in 1837 by Robert Menzies & Sons for St. George Steam Packet Company and put into service running between London and Cork in August of that year.

Isambard Kingdom Brunel with the launching chains of SS *Great Eastern*, January 1857. Photograph by Robert Howlett.

In 1832, American lawyer Junius Smith had the idea for a line of transatlantic steamships to run from New York to Liverpool. He and his British business partners created British and American Steamship Navigation Company (B&A) to build ships for this purpose. Smith's mistake was to publish his idea in the November 1832 issue of *American Railroad Journal*. Shortly thereafter, Brunel began plans to build a ship to do the same. A race began when Smith learned of Brunel's plans. Contract disputes caused construction delays on B&A's first steamship, *British Queen*, but Smith was undeterred. He leased *Sirius* from Ireland's St. George Steam Packet Company and launched her for New York on the same day as *Great Western*. *Sirius* was half the size of her rival, 700 tons compared to *Great Western*'s 1,400, but *Sirius* won the race by arriving one day earlier.

Transatlantic steamship history, however, consists of narrowly sliced categories of "firsts." Because *Sirius* was built for travel between European ports and was leased to win the competition between Brunel and B&A, *Great Western* claimed the title of first ship built for transatlantic travel to make the crossing. She became known as the world's first ocean liner.

Neither *Sirius* nor *Great Western* was the first steamship to cross the ocean. The American paddle wheeler *Savannah* earned that record in 1818, when she traveled to Liverpool from New York powered by a hybrid of sail and steam. Her paddle wheels were more of an auxiliary power source used for a few hours at a time throughout her journey, but she was the first ship to employ steam during a transatlantic crossing.

Savannah belched columns of black smoke as she crossed the Atlantic. Captains of passing vessels, who had never seen a steamship, were alarmed. One, the schooner *Contract*, assumed that *Savannah* was on fire, and pursued her for several hours to assist her, only to discover she was moving under steam. *Savannah* relied on her sails for most of the trip but proved it was possible to harness the power of steam to cross an ocean.

The public was not sold. It was more than the fear of burning fires aboard wooden vessels. Paddle wheels were noisy and smoky. The wheels vibrated when they turned at full speed. Early steamships spewed out funnels of smoke that smelled terrible, especially when the wind was not right. Efficiency, however, won out. Sailing ships moved at the mercy of the wind, and voyages across the Atlantic could take anywhere from six to twelve weeks. The steam engine cut the voyage down to two weeks and forced merchants and would-be passengers to ultimately embrace steam.

Brunel, Collins, and others competed to build the fastest and most-luxurious steamships. The designs were similar, wooden vessels made to look like sailing ships with side wheels for propulsion. Among the emerging competitors to Collins and Brunel was the British-backed line Cunard.

In 1839, Samuel Cunard, a shipowner from Halifax, Nova Scotia, won a lucrative contract to carry the mail from England to North America. The award of the contract to a foreigner incensed British companies such as *Great Western*. Cunard was successful, in part, because he had the backing of Scottish shipbuilder Robert Napier, who supplied engines to the British Royal Navy. Cunard formed British and North American Royal Mail Steam Packet Company and used Napier's company, Napier & Sons, to build ships to fulfill the contract.

Cunard began with a single ship called *Unicorn*. She began service from Boston to Liverpool in June 1840, and her inaugural voyage was the toast of the town. "As soon as the *Unicorn* was announced, by telegraph, the American and British flags were hoisted on City Hall and thrown to the breeze from the masts of vessels in the harbor, and from numerous elevated points along the wharves, and at East Boston."[5]

CHAPTER 3 | *Crossing the Atlantic*

Napier delivered four ships the following year that comprised Cunard's first fleet of paddle wheel steamers: *Acadia*, *Britannia*, *Caledonia*, and *Columbia*. They carried passengers and British mail on the Halifax–Boston–Liverpool route.

Companies such as Great Western and B&A made sensations with their initial voyages, but their ships failed to perform well in the long term. Cunard's only real competition during the 1840s came from the sailing packets.

Cunard built a reputation for sailing the safest ships on the high seas. Its liners were not the most luxurious, but they were well built and endured rigorous inspections before they left port. The line held its captains to high standards and employed only those with long résumés and impressive reputations. Cunard was famous for cautioning his captains to observe safety first. "Your ship is loaded, take her; speed is nothing, follow your own road, deliver her safe, bring her back safe—safety is all that is required," he said.[6] Mark Twain, who traveled aboard the Cunard liner *Gallia* in 1879, quipped "The Cunard people would not take Noah himself as first mate till they had worked him up through all the lower grades and tried him for ten years."[7] The line's market leadership went undisturbed until 1849, when Collins introduced its new fleet of paddle wheel steamers named after some the world's renowned waterways: *Arctic*, *Atlantic*, *Baltic*, and *Pacific*. The introduction of these ships launched one of the greatest rivalries in maritime history, the competition between Cunard and Collins. This rivalry, more than any other, solidified the mid-nineteenth century as the age of steam.

The race between Cunard and Collins was both a point of national pride and an economic boon to both companies. Collins received a contract from the US government to carry mail from New York and Britain. Cunard already had the subsidy from its home country. The lucrative contracts funded both lines, and neither company would have turned a profit without them. Collins and Cunard put the subsidies to use and added ships throughout the 1840s, a competition that led to the development of larger, more-luxurious, and more-powerful vessels.

Speed may not have been of paramount importance to Cunard, but it was important to his customers, and Cunard vessels were no match for Collins's fleet of state-of-the-art steamers. Collins dominated the "Blue Riband," a title given to ships that set speed records for eastbound or westbound crossings, from 1850 to 1854. Cunard briefly seized the title with the launch of a new steamship, RMS *Persia*, in 1855, but the company's position changed in the mid-1850s when the British navy put the line's vessels to service as troopships and supply boats in the Crimean War.

Companies such as Collins and a new group of upstarts rushed to fill the vacuum Cunard's temporary absence created in the market.

Steamships in the 1850s were reserved for customers who could afford first- or second-class tickets. Paddle wheelers were ill equipped to accommodate steerage passengers because of the amount of space the wheels required. The paddles were located amidships, one to port and one to starboard, and extended above and below deck. The two paddles were connected by a bridge that ran across the ship.[8] The amount of space the paddles consumed minimized both the number of above-deck cabins a ship could offer and the capacity for steerage passengers and storage below deck. Thus, steerage customers continued to travel by sailing packet.

Most of the major shipping lines continued to build paddle wheel fleets, but a British engineering company, George Rennie and Sons of London, experimented with a new form of propulsion, the screw propeller.[9] Called a "screw" for short, screw propellers resembled the blade of a fan or an airplane.[10] The screw worked by thrusting a column of water away from the main body of the ship, allowing the reactive force to propel the ship forward.

Captain John Ericsson, a Swedish inventor employed by the British government, tried for five years to convince the British navy to switch from paddle wheels to screws. The government resisted. They were concerned that the propellers would lift out of the water in rough seas, put stress on the engine, and make a vessel difficult to control. Ericsson and inventor Frances Smith founded a company to build a ship to prove the screw propeller's worth. They turned to Rennie & Sons to build the engine and propeller for SS *Archimedes*, the world's first successful screw steamer. The tugboat *Robert F. Stockton*, built by Liverpool shipbuilders Laird & Sons in partnership with Ericsson and American captain Robert Stockton, launched the same year and became the first screw steamship to cross the Atlantic.[11]

Laird began to build ships that employed another innovation, the iron hull. Iron hulls were wooden hulls coated with squares of iron fastened to the ships with rivets. The French military first pioneered "iron clads" as a defense to oncoming artillery, but shipbuilders such as Laird and Brunel realized the broader potential of iron. Iron-hulled ships were stronger, easier to repair, and longer lasting than wooden ones. They were not susceptible to rot or woodworms. Ships made of iron could also be larger than wooden ones because iron was not subject to hogging, a flexing of the hull that occurs when a wooden ship gets too long. Brunel sent his associates to see *Rainbow*, an iron-hulled packet ship built by Laird in 1838 for English Channel voyages.

Seven years later, Brunel revolutionized ocean travel again when, in 1845, he became the first to combine the screw and the iron hull. He had originally planned for his new ship to have paddle wheels and had partially constructed them when Smith and Ericsson loaned him *Archimedes*. He studied the ship and her engine and became convinced his new ship must be propelled by a screw. Converting to screw propulsion required him to redesign the ship's decks and her engine, which set delivery back nine months. The side-lever engines that propelled paddle wheels were incompatible with screws, which required direct-acting engines that applied power directly from the piston rod to the crankshaft.

Brunel eventually delivered. *Great Britain* became the first iron-hulled and screw-propelled steamship to cross the Atlantic. She was the largest ship in the world at the time of her launch and remained so until 1854. Other companies soon followed and opted for a combination of iron and steam.

The screw changed steamship design in two important ways. Eliminating the paddle wheels created space above deck that could be converted to accommodations and entertainment spaces for cabin passengers. Direct-acting engines saved space below deck. They were much smaller and weighed almost 40 percent less than side levers and, as a result, could be placed at a lower point inside a ship.

One industrious shipbuilder sought to capitalize on the newfound roominess above and below deck. A British shipping company, Inman Lines, entered the competition for transatlantic travel in 1852. Unlike Cunard and Collins, Inman was not subsidized by the government. The line's founder and chief engineer, William Inman, leveraged new technologies like those pioneered by Ericsson and Brunel to demonstrate how unsubsidized ocean liners could cross the North Atlantic and make a profit. Inman fortified one of his existing ships, *City of Glasgow*, with iron and replaced her side wheels with a screw. He used the space he saved to accommodate additional steerage passengers. He called the improved steerage quarters "third-class." *City of Glasgow* became the first iron-hulled, single-screw ship to cross the Atlantic with steerage customers in addition to first- and second-class fares.[12] He turned a profit on the crossing by carrying four hundred emigrants in addition to cabin passengers.

Inman grew up in a family of means but, unlike many of his competitors, he did not grow up on the sea. He was from Leicester, a town in the center of England. He sympathized with the plights of those who fled England's interior for better lives. His innovation offered them improvements in the conditions under which they traveled. Inman was also a savvy businessman.

His advances gave steamships ways to make up for the luxury afforded to cabin class and paved the way for shipowners with neither the connections nor the desire to secure government subsidies.

By the mid-1850s, enterprising businessmen across the world sought their share of an exploding market made possible by men such as Inman, Cunard, Collins, and others. Among them were the French brothers Claude-Antoine and Jacques-Victor Gauthier. France had yet to establish a successful steamship line, and the Gauthier brothers dreamed of claiming their slice of maritime firsts by becoming the first French steamship company to conquer the Atlantic.

CHAPTER 4

Franco-Américaine

CLAUDE-ANTOINE GAUTHIER AND JACQUES-VICTOR GAUTHIER formed a transatlantic mail and passenger steamship company in 1855 and procured six ships from renowned British shipbuilders Laird & Sons. One of the most famous yards in England, Laird built more than a thousand ships from 1828 through 1947.[1] William Laird founded the company as Birkenhead Iron Works in 1824 and made boilers from 1824 to 1828. His son, John, recognized that the same principles used to bend and rivet iron to make boilers could be applied to ship construction. He joined his father in the business in 1828, and the pair renamed the company Laird & Son of Birkenhead.[2] Laird & Son began to build ships and applied innovative and sometimes unorthodox advancements in engineering at John's direction. Their shipyard was located on the Mersey River, a small waterway that connects Liverpool to the Atlantic Ocean. Laird owned docks on both sides of the river, in Birkenhead and Liverpool, both of which were prime locations for shipbuilders. Newly minted ships came off the line and slid down the Mersey with regularity in the 1800s.

Fanfare often accompanied the launch of a new ship, especially when she was of an unusual type. Laird's first customer was Irish Inland Lakes Steam Navigation Company, who contracted for four iron-hulled steam packets to carry passengers and cargo between Dublin and Liverpool via the Shannon River. There was much excitement when, on March 6, 1830, the first of these ships carried twenty-nine head of cattle to Liverpool. The *London Guardian* labeled the news an "extraordinary dispatch" and wrote, "This direct intercourse between the interior of Ireland and the port of Liverpool has been accomplished by the Irish Inland Steam Navigation Company and will effect more benefit to the landed, and all the other interests in the country than any legislative measure within the power of Parliament."[3] During the 1830s, while wooden shipbuilding still reigned, the success helped Laird & Sons earn its reputation for high quality and sound construction in iron.

Laird also experimented with new means of propulsion. Like Brunel, Laird recognized the potential for the screw propeller and partnered with John Ericsson on the project for American captain Robert F. Stockton. Although the British navy rejected Ericsson's design, it caught Stockton's attention. The pair came to Laird to build a screw tugboat for river and canal work in the United States that used Ericsson's propeller. Laird completed the ship in 1838, but there was one problem—delivery. The tug had to cross the ocean to get to Stockton in New Jersey. In 1839, *Robert F. Stockton* traveled down the Mersey and crossed the ocean under sail, making it the first screw-propelled ship to technically cross the Atlantic.[4] "Although only 33 tons burthen, 63 ft. 5 in. in length, 10 ft. in breadth, and 7 ft. in depth, she made a voyage from Liverpool to New York under canvas—her propeller having been taken out—with every success. Until he built this vessel, the *Robert F. Stockton*, Mr. Laird had only constructed paddle steamers; and we believe we are correct in saying that, with at the utmost only two or three exceptions, she was the first screw vessel ever built."[5]

Ericsson moved to the US in 1839, and Laird continued to work on vessels that employed his designs. The men constructed the United States Navy's first screw steam warship, USS *Princeton*. Ericsson later helped build the Civil War ironclad USS *Monitor*.

Laird soon earned contracts from the British government. The company delivered HMS *Dover* in 1840, the first iron ship owned by the British, followed by the British navy's first iron-hulled frigate, HMS *Birkenhead*, in 1846. These achievements only increased the company's reputation as purveyors of iron and steam.

Ships such as Brunel's *Great Britain* and Inman's *City of Glasgow* proved to the world the power and economic advantage of the steam engine, but when merchants looked for shipbuilders who could build iron screws, they turned to Laird. Laird prepared to capitalize on a burgeoning market. The company expanded to a yard in South Liverpool to build vessels for the Crimean War between 1854 and 1856 and expanded again in 1857 to a 20-acre, five-dock yard in Birkenhead. It added its own engine works in 1858.

Steamship lines sought ships from companies such as Laird to compete for government-subsidized mail contracts. In 1853, a consortium of merchants with interest in North American trade formed Canadian

Steamship Navigation Company with the intent of establishing steamer service between Great Britain and Canada. They began with the screw steamer *Cleopatra*, chartered an Australian vessel, *Sarah Sands*, and commissioned construction from Laird for three more ships to be named *Huron*, *Eerie*, and *Ontario*. The order was later reduced from three to two ships, and Laird assigned hull numbers 117 and 118. Canadian Steamship acquired additional Laird-built ships for another line and added them to its fleet. It commissioned a third steamer, hull number 121, on February 15, 1854, as a replacement for the third steamer from the 1853 order.

The contract for vessels 117 and 118 was transferred into the name of Canadian Steamship on April 13, 1854, and retained the terms of the October 1853 contract. The document also stipulated, without explanation, that construction of the additional steamer (hull number 121) was to be suspended. This ship was eventually built and sold to a company engaged in Brazilian coastal trade.

Canadian Steamship and Laird drew up an additional contract on May 10, 1854, which authorized an increase in engine power for ships 117 and 118 from 300 horsepower to 370. The ships were to be 270 feet in length and 1,723 tons as laid down. They were delivered in early 1855 and almost ready for launch when John L. Laird, who was a shareholder in Canadian Steamship, allowed the company to cancel the contract without explanation.

Señor Ramon de Zangroniz, of Zangroniz Brothers and Company in Havana, Cuba, stepped in and, acting as agent for the newly formed Spanish Transatlantic Mail Steam Packet Company (Línea de Vapores Españoles Transatlánticos), offered 132,000 pounds for both ships. Spanish Transatlantic had recently established steam service from Liverpool to Havana via the Spanish ports of Vigo and Cádiz and Puerto Rico to deliver and receive mail. Zangroniz was not a new Laird customer. He contracted Laird to build a series of four iron-screw steamships in December 1854. Laird assigned these ships hull numbers 133–136. Laird accepted Zangroniz's offer and, in March 1855, transferred Canadian Steamship's contract to Spanish Transatlantic. Hull numbers 117, 118, 133, 134, 135, and 136 became sisters.[6] The ships were named for ports and regions around the world: *Habana* (117), *Vigo* (118), *Barcelona* (133), *Le Franc Comtois* (134), *Cádiz* (135), and *Le Lyonnais* (136).

The ships were between 260 and 280 feet long, 35 and 37 feet wide, and 25 and 29 feet deep. Gross tonnage ranged from 1,500 to 2,100. They were similar in size to ships in the Inman Line but not as large as Collins's liners. *Habana* was the largest and displaced more than 2,000 gross tons. *Le Lyonnais* and *Cádiz* were identical twins and, at 1,665 tons, were among the smaller ships in the fleet.

Spanish Transatlantic advertised passenger travel as early as the middle of 1855.[7] Laird delivered *Habana* on April 4, 1855. She sailed on her maiden voyage from Liverpool to Cuba on July 23, 1855, under the command of Captain Garcia y Grinda of the Spanish navy. She arrived on August 28, 1855. Her return voyage did not go as planned. She suffered a small fire followed by a total engine failure that damaged the ship's rudder. After three days, enough repairs had been carried out for her to make slow progress, but she ran into a storm that tore away part of her rudder and carried away her main topsail. *Habana* drifted at sea for several days before the passengers were transferred to another ship and she limped to the Azores. The ship was towed to Liverpool for repairs and arrived on January 2, 1856.

Laird delivered *Vigo* on June 2, 1855. She was due to follow *Habana* to Cuba at the end of September, but, due to "a derangement of machinery," her maiden voyage was pushed back to late 1855.[8] That date came and went without *Vigo* ever sailing for Spanish Transatlantic.

Laird completed *Cádiz* on August 30, 1855, and *Barcelona* just days later, on September 1. Spanish Transatlantic was, at the time, still under the mistaken impression that *Habana* would return to Liverpool in time to run to Cuba in late October and *Vigo* would sail in November, so it advertised passenger service and cargo space. The advertisements promised merchants delivery from Liverpool to Cuba within twenty days, and rates equal to sailing vessels and less expensive than competitors. They touted the line's connections to South America and advertised the ease of transfer to boats bound for Puerto Rico and Mexico. Spanish Transatlantic attempted to appeal to first-class customers and boasted cabins with "modern improvements" and "every possible comfort and luxury."[9] The ships employed chefs who served meals à la française, at which diners helped themselves to a variety of dishes brought to their table. A cabin-class ticket to Havana sold for thirty-seven pounds.[10]

Zangroniz had already fallen behind once on his payments to Laird, and *Habana*'s delays and *Vigo*'s mechanical problems only compounded the company's financial difficulties. Work on the remaining four ships was postponed in May 1855 due to nonpayment. Zangroniz paid late and entered into an agreement that allowed Laird to sell the unfinished ships if he fell behind again. The companies arranged a new payment schedule on July 4, 1855. Zangroniz did not meet it. The unexpected delays and repairs to *Habana* and *Vigo* crippled Spanish Transatlantic within its first year of operation and forced the company to cancel its contract with the Spanish government. Plagued by financial woes, on October 2, 1855, Zangroniz allowed Laird to sell Spanish Transatlantic's steamers.

CHAPTER 4 | *Franco-Américaine*

    The Gauthier brothers saw opportunity in Zangroniz's failure. They established Compagnie Franco-Américaine in 1855 with the intention of carrying cargo, passengers, and mail to and from the Americas. Franco-Américaine purchased four existing ships from Spanish Transatlantic and assumed the contract from Laird for the additional ships. They completed the conditions of sale in late January 1856, and Zangroniz became Franco-Américaine's principal agent in Cuba.

Certificate for shares in Franco-Américaine, 1855.
Author's collection

    Franco-Américaine was the second French company to attempt to enter the transatlantic steamship business. The first, Compagnie Generale des Paquebots Transatlantiques (Transatlantic General Steam Packet Company), failed less than a year after its first trip. Paquebots Transatlantiques received a subsidy from the French government in the amount of 16,000 francs and four wooden frigates originally built for the French navy: *Union*, *Philadelphie*, *Missouri*, and *New York*. It started service between Le Havre and New York in July 1847. Complaints of poor seamanship by the line's captains and crew soon followed. The company was accused of fraud for shorting the amount of coal on its ships, which caused the vessels to make inconvenient refueling stops at Halifax before they reached New York. Ships were in constant need of repair both due to construction problems and human error. The string of misfortunes prompted the company to announce, in January 1848, that all four ships would return to the docks for repair. This never happened. Compagnie Generale des Paquebots Transatlantiques collapsed in 1848 and returned the ships to the French navy.

Two American companies established mail and passenger service between New York and Le Havre during this period. Edward Mills, a novice in the shipping business, earned a contract for US mail delivery between New York and Le Havre and Bremen. He founded Ocean Steam Navigation Company with his business partners C. H. Sand, Mortimer Livingston, and John L. Stephens in May 1846. Mills was unable to attract enough capital to carry out his original plan and went under.

New York & Havre Steam Navigation Company carried mail from New York to Le Havre and Southampton via a fleet of paddle wheel steamers including *Arago*, *Franklin*, and *Humboldt* from 1850 to 1861. *Franklin* wrecked in a fog off Long Island in 1854. The company chartered ships until it replaced her with the *Fulton* in 1856. New York & Havre was successful, but it was an American company with no counterpart in France.

The Gauthier brothers filled the void. Their full line included eight ships. The first were *Jacquard* and *François Arago*, 2,000-ton iron steamers built in 1854 and 1855 by Guilbert fils, Nantes.[11] The steamers failed their initial engine trials and inspired the brothers to seek their next ships from a more reliable manufacturer..

The remaining ships came from Laird pursuant to the contract transferred to them from Spanish Transatlantic. Franco-Américaine made slight adjustments to the ships' names to showcase that they were now part of a French line. They changed *Habana*'s name to *Alma* in commemoration of a recent allied victory in the Crimean War and altered the spelling of the others to the French, *Barcelone* and *Cadix*. *Vigo*'s name did not change. Laird delivered the remaining two ships, *Le Franc Comtois* and *Le Lyonnais*, with names unchanged, in January 1856.[12]

Gauthier Frères & Compagnie of Paris and Lyons began to operate Franco-Américaine, its full fleet of steamers between the Port of Le Havre and North and South America, in early 1856. *Barcelone* inaugurated the

CHAPTER 4 | *Franco-Américaine*

SS *Fulton*, built in New York in 1855, pictured in a rare photograph of a paddle wheel steamship. Photograph by Mathew Brady, 1864.
National Archives and Records Administration

line's transatlantic service when she sailed from Le Havre to New York in February. She experienced heavy weather but performed well and made the crossing in nineteen days. She left France the same day as two other screw-propelled steamships, which prompted one newspaper to write, "At this rate[,] sailing vessels must be soon out of fashion in the transatlantic trade."[13] *Alma* and *Vigo* were commissioned by the French government and deployed for several months as troopships in the Crimean War. *Alma* made its first commercial voyage from Le Havre to New York in April 1856. When she returned to France, Napoléon III visited the steamer, an indication of the importance of the new line to France. *Vigo* followed in July. *Cadix*, *Le Lyonnais*, and *Franc-Comtois* began service to Rio de Janeiro the same month.

The new line struggled from the start. British and American shipping lines cut their rates to prevent Franco-Américaine from entering the market. The Gauthier brothers incurred additional costs because France had no drydocks large enough to accommodate their steamers, which forced them to travel to England whenever the ships needed repair or even routine maintenance. The number of competitors flooding the market created additional barriers. Early voyages ran with small numbers of passengers, with profit supplemented by cargo and mail shipments. Franco-Américaine, nevertheless, stayed in business and attempted to compete by offering reliable service with competent captains on ships that boasted the latest in maritime technology. The company was ready to begin regular service on the most competitive passenger route of the day, service to and from New York and Europe, by the fall of 1856.[14]

CHAPTER 5
Iron and Steam

LE LYONNAIS WAS THE LAST OF THE SIX SISTERS delivered to Franco-Américaine by Laird and, by many accounts, the most beautiful. Her bow was pointed and bore a bowsprit that gave her the look of sailing ship, but she was made of iron and, therefore, was stronger than any wooden ship. Her stern was broad and square. Iron hull plates were painted black in contrast to the ship's wooden decks. A line of metal rivets wrapped around the ship several feet below the gunwale and created what looked from afar to be a decorative stripe. Portholes sat below the stripe and indicated rooms where passengers would one day look out to the sea.

The ship had two masts, a mainmast aft and a foremast forward. Each was fitted with two yardarms rigged with square sails made of cotton canvas and off-white in color. The masts were supported by stays and shrouds, wire cables suspended high up on the mast. Shrouds were led to the ship's sides, and stays to the bow and the stern. The wire cables were taut and sturdy but, from a distance, resembled delicate strings of a harp. Sails allowed *Le Lyonnais* to harness the power of the wind, but a large iron smokestack that rose to half the height of the mast signaled that the ship would move by the man-made power of steam.

Le Lyonnais was 260 feet long and 36 feet wide. Laird built her to compete with similarly sized ships of her day. The contract between owner and shipbuilder spelled out specific standards of quality and called for the best available materials and the quality of her iron and her engine and even provided the name of comparable ships to serve as a guide.[1] *Le Lyonnais* was "to be fitted and equal in quality to the ships made by Laird for the Peninsular and Oriental Company (P&O) and to the satisfaction

P. & O. S. N. Co.'s
S.S. "Ellora."

There are no photographs of Le Lyonnais. Her sister, Cadix, is pictured ca. 1859. P&O bought the ship in 1858 and renamed her Ellora. *Courtesy of © P&O Heritage Collection, www.poheritage.com*

---

of Captain Ford."[2] P&O was a British steamship company that operated cargo, passenger, and mail ships to ports in Europe, the Far East, and Australia, and Ford was an inspector hired by Spanish Transatlantic to certify that each ship met its contract specifications before delivery.

Laird constructed *Le Lyonnais* of wood and iron. Her hull plates and reinforcements were metal. Double-riveted iron plates covered the ship. Thick, half-inch plates enclosed the engine room to provide extra protection in the event of collision. Thinner plates covered the surfaces above the waterline.

Additional protection came from watertight compartments, or bulkheads, which were a more recent innovation in steamship design, although the concept dated back to the twelfth century. Watertight bulkheads divided the lower portions of the ship into sections that sealed off from one another so that in the event the ship took on water, only a portion flooded, and the remaining portions kept the ship afloat.

CHAPTER 5 | *Iron and Steam*

An 1869 treatise on iron steamships by chief constructor of the British Royal Navy, E. J. Reed, explained, "There is, probably, no subject on which iron shipbuilders are more generally agreed, than on the desirability, both as regards to safety and structural strength, of the employment of watertight bulkheads. . . . The increased safety resulting from the adoption of these bulkheads proceeds from the fact that a leak or a fire in any compartments can in most cases be prevented from affecting the other compartments."[3]

Le Lyonnais had six watertight bulkheads: two forward of the engine room, two aft, and one in the fore peak, the lower portion of the bow. The remaining one was in the after hold, the narrow portion of the ship at the stern. The thick iron plates that covered the bulkheads were reinforced with angle iron, which was placed twice as close together in the areas around the engine room and the bulkheads than in other parts of the ship to protect the ship's vital organ, the engine, from a breach. Coal bunkers surrounded the engine.

The contract with Spanish Transatlantic called for the engines to be "the best quality equal to any marine engines ever made."[4] *Le Lyonnais*'s engine was 370 horsepower and direct action by gearing. The engines for the *Havana*, *Franc Comtois*, *Barcelone*, and *Vigo* were made by Fawcett & Company. Franco-Américaine changed the contract with Laird to require Rennie & Sons to build *Cadix*'s and *Le Lyonnais*'s engines.

Le Lyonnais had a single screw forged from one piece of iron for optional strength and machined at the ends to fit into place. The shaft was fitted with a mechanism for disconnecting it to allow the screw to revolve freely when *Le Lyonnais* traveled under sail.

The ship boasted another innovation, the tubular boiler. This advancement allowed water to more efficiently circulate around the tubes through which steam passed, yielding higher steam pressure and, in turn, greater speed.[5]

A distilling apparatus connected to the engine produced 500 gallons of fresh water every twenty-four hours. The ship had a donkey engine, a small auxiliary engine used for shipboard functions other than propulsion, such as operating a winch to move cargo or a double-hand pump to remove excess water. The pump could also be worked manually.

The British government in the 1850s had some of the more progressive laws about passenger safety. *Le Lyonnais* followed these specifications, including regulations about the number of lifeboats required. Parliament passed the Passengers' Act of 1849 to govern the minimum number of lifeboats, medical facilities, and provisions that passenger ships had to carry. Clause XVII of the act set forth a scale that determined the number

The Adriatic Affair

PLATE 66

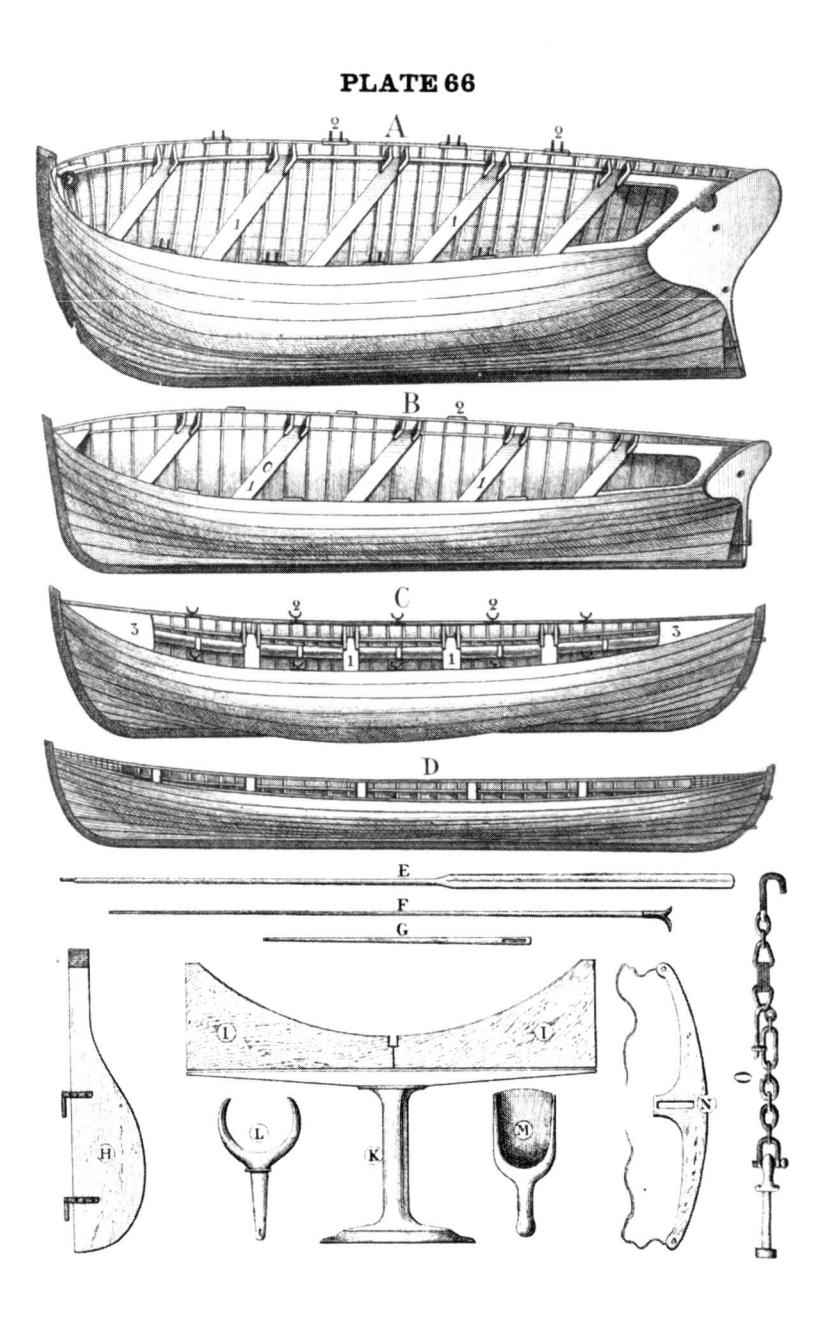

Four styles of lifeboats used in the mid- to late nineteenth century. *From* Illustrated Marine Encyclopedia *by Heinrich Paasch, plate 66*

48

PLATE 66.

Various Boats; and Boat-gear.

A *Longboat; Launch.*

1 Thwarts.
2 Thole-pins.

B *Cutter; Pinnace.*

1 Thwarts.
2 Thole-boards.

C *Life-boat.*

1 Thwarts.
2 Rowlocks.
3 Tanks.

D *Gig.*

E Oar; Boat-oar.

F Boat-hook.

G Tiller; Rudder-tiller.

H Rudder.

I Boat chock.

K Boat-chock-standard.

L Rowlock.

M Bailer; Boat-bailer.

N Yoke; Rudder-yoke.

O Gripe; Boat-gripe.

of lifeboats per ship. The scale measured the number by the ship's net tonnage and not passenger load:

> Two Boats for every Ship of One hundred Tons and upwards;
> Three Boats for every Ship of Two hundred Tons and upwards;
> In case the Number of Passengers shall exceed Fifty:
> Four boats for every Ship of Five hundred Tons and upwards, in case the Number of Passengers shall exceed Two hundred: provided always, that One of such Boats shall in all Cases be a Long Boat, and One shall be a properly fitted Life Boat, and that each of such Boats shall be on a suitable Size, to be approved by the Emigration Officer at the Port of Clearance, and shall be seaworthy, and properly supplied with all Requisites for Use.[6]

Le Lyonnais's net tonnage was close to 1,000, which required four lifeboats.[7] Procurement of the boats was the responsibility of the shipowner and not to be furnished by Laird, but the contract spelled out that she would comply with the "Act of Parliament." *Le Lyonnais* intended to carry more than two hundred passengers, which is why one of her boats was a long boat and one was fitted as a lifeboat.

The Passengers' Act did not call for enough lifeboats for every passenger on board. *Le Lyonnais* was built to carry ninety first- and second-class passengers and accommodate a large crew. Her lifeboats carried approximately twenty people each, depending on type. Four boats were barely enough to accommodate the cabin passengers, let alone crew. This was intentional. Government entities in the 1850s believed that fitting vessels with an adequate number of boats could do more harm than good. Lifeboats were wooden boats affixed to the side or top decks of the ship on davits and took up significant space. In 1870, George Shaw LeFevre, then secretary to the British Board of Trade, participated in a House of Commons inquiry regarding a recent disaster at sea and told the House, "In the opinion of the Board of Trade, it will not be possible to compel passenger steamers running between England and France to have boats sufficient for every passenger they often carry. They would encumber the decks, and rather add to the danger than detract from it."[8]

An 1887 Select Committee of the House of Commons further explained: "Many passenger ships could not, without great inconvenience, carry so many of the ordinary wooden boats as would suffice to carry the whole of the passengers and crew with safety in bad weather."[9] Subsequent acts of Parliament, the Passengers' Acts of 1855 and 1863, altered some of the provisions of the 1849 act, but the lifeboat ratio remained conditioned on net tonnage.[10]

Le Lyonnais had six boats: two lifeboats fitted with oars and sails, two cutters, a yawl to satisfy the "longboat" requirement, and the captain's gig. This was enough to satisfy Parliament, but not enough to accommodate the 132 souls that left New York aboard the ship.

Parliament also governed the use of signals. *Le Lyonnais* had a signal lantern placed at the masthead as required by both French and British law. The ship was equipped with a steam whistle and two bells to signal the watch, to ring for shipboard ceremonies, and to sound the alarm in a moment of danger.

The ship's captain and crew navigated using three binnacles, large stands spaced throughout the ship, each of which contained an adjusted compass. The ship had two winches, one forward and one aft, from which the crew could work the ship's hatchways.

Le Lyonnais launched from Laird's Sefton Street dock in Liverpool on January 9, 1856, and glided down the Mersey River to the open ocean. She passed the other shipyards, riverside docks filled with half-built ships, and shipping-merchant storefronts, whose docks were filled with passengers headed to foreign ports. She left the Mersey, sailed south through the Irish Sea and into the English Channel, and then made way for Le Havre, where she joined the Franco-Américaine fleet.

Le Lyonnais officially launched in the spring of 1856 and made two voyages to Rio de Janeiro prior to heading to New York to fulfill her intended purpose of conveying passengers to and from that port and France. She left New York on November 1, 1856, with cargo, passengers, and crew. She never arrived in Le Havre.

CHAPTER 6

132 Souls

PHILOSOPHER MICHEL FOUCAULT described the ship as "a heterotopia . . . a floating piece of space, a place without a place, that exists by itself, that is closed in on itself and at the same time is given over to the infinity of the sea."[1] A cabin-class ticket on a Victorian-era steamship guaranteed not only passage across the Atlantic but admission into a society that existed for a single voyage and dissolved upon arrival at a ship's port of call. "When the shore disappeared on the horizon, it was as if the vessel and her passengers passed into a solipsistic void where the only reality was themselves."[2]

Le Lyonnais was no exception. She carried passengers from America, France, Spain, Cuba, and England drawn to *Le Lyonnais* for reasons as varied as those countries. Among them were the predictable passengers, people who hailed from wealthy families and the servants who traveled with them. Perhaps more difficult to envision were the individuals who had worked harder to buy cabin passage and did so either out of necessity or reward: the reverend celebrating his redemption from a troubled past, the dutiful son returning home to see his dying father, and the musician in possession of what might have been the world's first great English-language opera. They too folded into the heterotopia that was *Le Lyonnais* and became part of what made the voyage, in its brief existence, unique.

The winds subsided during the evening of November 1 and, in so doing, transformed the rocking of the ship from random to rhythmic. Weary passengers finally got some sleep. They awoke the next morning to fairer weather, and the combination of the sun's warmth and a light breeze enlivened most of them. They dressed in their finest clothes and suppressed any lingering seasickness. Today was the day to make first impressions. Land was long gone, and the men and women spent the day getting acquainted with one another and the ship.

Albert Sumner was perhaps most comfortable in his new surroundings. Although he exuded the upper-class air expected of his first-class ticket, he was no stranger to the sea. He was the son of Charles Pinckney Sumner, a Harvard-educated lawyer, abolitionist, and early proponent of racial integration. Albert's brother was Senator Charles Sumner of Boston, who had become an outspoken advocate for the abolition of slavery in an America on the brink of civil war. Albert was just one year Charles's junior but, rather than follow the family tradition of politics, he signed up for a three-year whaling voyage and sailed from New Bedford to the Pacific. He later served as mate and then as captain on different ships and sailed to ports in South America and Europe. He retired from maritime service in 1840, when, at the age of twenty-eight, he married Catherine Barclay, a wealthy widow who inherited her own father's fortune upon the death of her first husband, Captain Thomas Barclay, Esq., of the British Royal Navy. Catherine was thirty-eight at the time, ten years Sumner's senior. The couple settled in Newport and divided their time between New York and Rhode Island.

Sumner knew the ways of the sea, but this voyage would be different from his others because, this time, he traveled with Catherine and his only child, his fourteen-year-old daughter, Kate. It was Kate who prompted the family's journey to France. She contracted an illness the previous year and suffered from a chronic cough during the winter of 1855 and into 1856. Her parents grew less certain of her recovery as time wore on, and shared deep concerns about her health with her Uncle Charles and mutual family friends. The poet Henry Wadsworth Longfellow, who knew the Sumners through his friendship with Charles, visited with Albert in April 1856. He described him in a letter to his sister, Anne Longfellow Pierce, as a father "in great distress about his daughter's illness."[3] The summer did little to ease Kate's suffering. Her cough persisted until the family's doctor advised the Sumners to take the child to the South of Europe, where the climate promised to be more favorable. Albert booked passage for his family and a servant, Anne Dellamere, aboard *Le Lyonnais*.

Sumner was not the only senator's son aboard the ship. Theodore Armstrong Bailey, the son of Senator Theodoros Bailey, was also a passenger. The elder Bailey served for many years as a senator from New York and later as postmaster general of New York City. His son, who was then forty-six, traveled aboard *Le Lyonnais* with his wife, Julia Strong Bailey, age thirty-one, and her sixty-one-year-old mother, Jeanette Amy Strong.

The Adriatic Affair

There were other men of means aboard *Le Lyonnais*, including John Gardiner Gibson Jr. of the prominent Boston family. John, the son of John Gardiner Gibson and Catherine Hammond Gibson and brother of Charles Gibson, was twenty-one.[4] John Sr. died at sea years earlier when illness broke out aboard the ship on which he was traveling. His wife, Catherine, never recovered from her husband's loss and, in the eighteen years since his passing, kept her sons close. Her heart sank when she learned that John and his wife had booked passage on a steamship bound for Europe.

Women on their way to France without male companions also appeared on the ship's passenger list. Mother and daughter Frances E. Dummer and Cora Adelaide Dummer were among them. Cora, a slight woman with light-brown hair and gray eyes, was twenty years old and not yet married. She and her mother had been preparing for their journey to France for months. Unlike most other American passengers, who applied for passports days before boarding, the Dummers applied for theirs in July.

Frances Dummer, who was fifty at the time of the journey, traveled with one servant, Flora Solomon. Solomon had only recently signed on to work for the family. Her job was to tend to Frances aboard the ship in exchange for cabin-class fare to France. Solomon described her position with the Dummer family by using the European title "lady in waiting to Ms. Frances."[5] It was a phrase typically reserved for servants who waited on royalty, and a sign of the seriousness with which she accepted her duties.

There were no steerage passengers. Early references to Spanish Transatlantic Company's services made it clear their ships were built to operate a prestige passenger, mail, and cargo service, under charter from the Spanish government. Their early advertisements reference only first-class and second-class fares. Franco-Américaine, which later purchased Spanish Transatlantic' s fleet, similarly advertised travel experiences tailored to cabin customers. Initial advertisements indicated that *Habana* and *Vigo* were to carry ninety first-class passengers, fifty second-class, and a "limited number" of third-class, and another advertisement mentions eighty first-class, forty second-class, and thirty third-class. Laird's records describe the passenger accommodations on *Le Lyonnais* and her three sisters as sixty first-class passengers in the cabins in the deckhouse and thirty second-class passengers in the two cabins forward, with bed cabins on the lower deck beneath. The closest thing to steerage passengers on the voyage were two or three men who had agreed to work with the crew in exchange for their fares.

Luxury cabins and the chance to travel with the new, French line may have been the reason that passengers from distinguished East Coast families took a chance on *Le Lyonnais*. The original passenger manifest contained additional travelers of note who changed their plans and booked passage on another ship. Baltimore merchants Henry Lee Higginson, Powell Mason, and Stephen Perkins intended to sail aboard *Le Lyonnais* but transferred to Cunard's *Arabia* at the last moment. *Arabia* departed from Boston on November 4, 1856, bound for Liverpool. Higginson was a patron of the arts and, in 1881, went on to found the Boston Symphony Orchestra.

Giants such as Cunard and Collins feared upstarts such as Franco-Américaine, which threatened to siphon their highest paying customers. They offered discounts to lure passengers away from emerging lines. Franco-Américaine ships made early voyages with as few as fifteen cabin passengers as it struggled to gain traction in the competitive New York market. Perhaps a better fare wooed Higgins and his companions, or perhaps travel plans just changed. Whatever the reason, the decision to rebook passage on *Arabia* might have saved their lives.

There was a good breeze, and *Le Lyonnais* rode on her engine and her sails. By noon, the sky was clear, the weather fine. It was a perfect day for the passengers to explore the ship. *Le Lyonnais* had three decks as well as a raised foredeck and long poop deck aft. Only two decks— main and lower—were accessible to passengers. The rest of the ship was the province of the sailors who worked the ship's sails, firemen who supplied the boilers with coal, and hospitality staff who tended to customers. The lowermost deck contained the ship's engine and boiler rooms. The areas outside these rooms, referred to as the the orlop deck, served as storage space for mail, cargo, food supplies, and shipped luggage.

The main deck was the highest portion of the ship that passengers could access. Crewmen occupied the foredeck and poop deck, on the upper deck at the bow and the stern. The captain or designated helmsman steered the ship from the quarterdeck, located at the forward end of the poop. He took his orders from the officer on watch. The forecastle sat forward of the foremast at the ship's bow and served as sailor's quarters. Fireman, stokers and engineers were berthed further aft, closer to the engine room.[6]

Le Lyonnais operated with a crew of ninety. Although the number of crewmen may seem high for a ship carrying only thirty-nine passengers, the voyage required not only men to work the decks and the sails but a separate crew to maintain the engines and a full complement of men and women to cook, clean, and tend to the passengers' needs. *Vigo*, a larger *Le Lyonnais* sister ship, had berths for one hundred crew members. When *Jeddo*, a ship built by Laird & Sons for P&O in 1858 and approximately the same size as *Le Lyonnais*, wrecked in February 1866, she had on board her captain, five engineers, twenty-eight officers, and 125 seamen, for a total of 159 crew in all.[7] She carried just two passengers at the time.

The forecastle provided sailors easy access to the deck, but its location so high and far forward ensured those who occupied it felt every wave the ocean offered. The sailors did not mind. Most were long accustomed to the sound and the movement of the ocean, even in the foulest weather.

Atop the forecastle rested the bitts sailors used to moor the vessel when it was in port. There was a cathead on each side of the forecastle deck. These were used for stowing the ship's anchors, one on each side. Once an anchor was heaved up as far as the outboard end of the hawse pipe, the sailors rigged a block and tackle from the end of the cathead to the balance rings on the center of the anchor's shank to ease the strain so they could lift the anchor to its stowed position. The catheads also provided good places for sailors to sit during watch as they looked out for obstructions such as debris, icebergs, and oncoming traffic.

The after cabins were located on the main deck level. These rooms were premium because they were better ventilated than those below. Le *Lyonnais*'s main deck was rather long, reaching well forward towards amidships.

The saloon, which served not only as the ship's gathering place for entertainment but as its dining area, sat at the forward most end of the main deck cabin area under the poop.

Passengers mingled and looked out over the ocean as they walked the main deck's expanse. Walking the decks, they saw the ship's masts and sails and her large smokestack. A casing wrapped around the chimney

Passengers walking a steamship's deck, 1870. *Harper's Weekly Magazine.* Author's collection

to 5 feet above the main deck and protected the passengers from the heat created from the rising smoke. The stack pumped black fumes into the air as *Le Lyonnais* moved.

Walking a steamship's deck was not just a way to pass the time. Far from the grand halls and busy thoroughfares of New York, the ship's deck was the place to see and be seen. Women donned the fashion of the day—dresses with tightly cinched waists, drooping shoulders, and voluminous, petticoat-lined skirts. Most kept the colors dark, since darker clothing was less likely to show wear or stains and was, therefore, preferable for travel. Walking dresses, as they were called, featured high necklines and wide collars and lacked trains. Hair was parted down the middle and brushed down on the sides to cover the ears. Women wore bonnets that sat back on the head and tied under the chin, or wide-brimmed hats to keep the sun off their faces. Shawls draped beautifully across large skirts and, at sea, served as preferred outerwear for warding off the chill of an ocean breeze.

Ladies walked on the arms of male companions who also dressed to impress. Men wore cutaway coats, jackets short in the front and long in the back, or sack jackets, a newer fashion, which featured small lapels and a more relaxed fit. Daytime pants, vests, and bow ties were dark in color to highlight the white shirts men typically wore.

The decks proved fitting runways. They were built of wide planks of pine fastened from underneath so no rivets or nail heads would show, an indication of luxury in detail. Copper decoration covered the main rail that protected passengers from falling overboard while they took in the view.

Reverend John B. Cocagne dressed modestly in accordance with his position as a Methodist minister, but he studied the men and women he passed on his walks along the deck with curiosity. He traveled alone on a pilgrimage to see his birthplace for the first time in twenty-five years. Cocagne was born in Roziere in the Franche-Comté, a rural region of France that borders Switzerland. His father sought to better his family's fortune and, in 1831, when Cocagne was just ten, sailed with him for New York. His father was a rough man who chased wealth and fortune in what Cocagne later described as "the wilds of America."[8]

Cocagne did not adjust well to life in his new country and would later tell his congregants about the years he spent mired in "severe struggles with sin, and self, and Satan."[9] He found salvation at Methodist prayer meetings. Salvation transformed into a calling to help others in need of the Lord. Cocagne completed school and entered the ministry. He was received on trial, an apprenticeship required of aspiring Methodist preachers, at the Black River conference in upstate New York in 1846. The church ordained him as a deacon in 1848, at the age of twenty-seven.

He held several posts at churches throughout New York in areas with large populations of French immigrants. Travel was a necessary part of nineteenth-century Methodist ministering, and in Cocagne's ten years as a deacon, he moved once a year from mission to mission. He served seven missions in two states. After a brief stint at the Detroit French Mission in Michigan, he requested a transfer back to New York. The church granted his request and informed him his next post would be at the Black River Mission, the place where he first found his faith. It was a sign to Cocagne that things had come full circle.

His new position in New York would not begin until June 1857, when the Black River Mission held its annual conference. This left an interval of nine months between the end of the Detroit post and the beginning of the new one. He had no desire to spend his break in Jefferson County, where his father now lived. Cocagne was brought to America against his will, and although he loved the ministry, the church had in more recent years dictated where he lived and for how long. He relished the opportunity to choose where he wanted to go. He prayed on it. The answer was his own, but it surprised him. Cocagne yearned to revisit his homeland. The journey was, in some ways, a test, one that required him to spend time once again with people outside the sheltered circles of his Methodist faith. A transatlantic journey seemed the perfect way to satisfy his desires. Cocagne booked cabin passage to Le Havre on *Le Lyonnais*.

Cocagne walked the decks alone. He exchanged polite nods and smiles with those he passed, and treasured in silence the new world in which he found himself, one so different from the ministries and small towns where he had spent the last several years. He was on an exotic journey with people from all corners of the globe. The sounds of passengers speaking French, English, Spanish, and German melted into an orchestral backdrop. Some of the figures Cocagne encountered were larger than life.

A Cuban couple, Don José de Eulate and his young wife, carried themselves like modern-day royalty. Eulate was a colonel in the Spanish service. He had recently married his wife, Antonia, who, at twenty-one years old, was nine years his junior. The newlyweds departed from Havana aboard the steamer *Black Warrior* with Manuel de Eulate, José's brother, and arrived in New York on October 3, 1856. They described the voyage as "charming," and, after a few weeks in New York, their only disagreement was which ship to take to France.[10] Manuel decided to take Cunard's *Persia*. He tried to convince his brother to do the same, but Antonia preferred the French ship, *Le Lyonnais*. José's new father-in-law recommended *Le Lyonnais* because the direct voyage to Le Havre avoided the short transfer from England to France.

The Eulates convinced a fellow Cuban, a young composer from Havana who had also traveled to New York aboard *Black Warrior*, to join them. His name was Don Vicente Díaz y de Comas. Díaz y de Comas was both a musician and a lawyer. He was tall and trim with a long face and small eyes ornamented by wire-rimmed glasses. He had dark hair, a dark complexion, and a bushy mustache fitting of an artist. Díaz y de Comas was on his way to Spain with a copy of a royal album he completed in 1885. *Album Regio* was a compilation of drawings and sheet music published in Havana in 1855 and intended to reflect Spain's cultural influence in Cuba. Díaz y de Comas was traveling to Spain to present a copy of the work to the Spanish royal family. He purchased a ticket for *Persia* but gave it up and booked passage aboard *Le Lyonnais* to travel with his friends. He tucked a copy of *Album Regio* under his arm and carried it aboard the ship.

Theodore Bailey, the son of the New York senator, stood 6 feet tall and cut an imposing figure as he strolled throughout the ship with his wife and mother. His salt-and-pepper hair, high forehead, and confident air announced his privilege long before he introduced himself. Cocagne could not help but smile as he spotted Chas Beaugrand, a good-natured sea captain who had just sold his own vessel, *Marie*, in Cuba.

Beaugrand set out for Hamburg aboard *Marie* on August 22, 1856, but lost his masts along the way. He put into Porto Plata on September 3 under jury masts, masts that have been temporarily rigged after sustaining damage. *Marie* was condemned in port. He sold the vessel there, traveled from Havana to New York aboard the SS *Quaker City* in mid-October, and was making his way back to France as a passenger aboard *Le Lyonnais*. He seemed so at home on the water as he laughed and joked with passengers and members of the ship's crew.

The women retired in the early afternoon either to receive visitors or to rest and prepare for dinner. Victorian fashion dictated multiple dress changes throughout the day and made it unacceptable to wear the same attire from day into evening. Those who planned to meet with visitors in the saloon or in their cabins changed into dresses appropriate for such visits. Others changed into dressing gowns and rested before dinner. Dinner was where the ostentatiousness of 1850s fashion shined. Colors became more vibrant, necklines plunged ever so slightly, and skirts gained volume from multiple layers of petticoats. Men also met the dinner hour with flair. Color adorned vests and bow ties. They donned formal jackets with longer tails and top hats reminiscent of the ones worn by Abraham Lincoln.

Dinner took place in the saloon. One of the largest rooms aboard early steamships, the saloon served both as a dining space and a place for social gatherings. Advertisements for ships promoted the grandness of saloons to attract customers, but, in the mid-1850s, saloons were little more than cavernous dining halls with small decorative touches to create the appearance of luxury. *Le Lyonnais*'s saloon was no exception. It was made of wood and featured windows as well as teak skylights framed by brass guards to provide views to the sky above.

If a ship was a world unto itself, the saloon was its center and dinner its main attraction. There were no private tables that passengers could share with traveling companions or guests of their choice. Instead, men and woman dined at long, banquet-style tables lined on both sides with chairs. Seating in the rows alternated male-female-male-female, so there was a man to keep every woman company in a forced intimacy designed to generate conversation. Cabin passengers were stuck with their dining companions for as long as the meal lasted, and passengers occupied the same place for dinner each evening. Men were expected to dote on ladies, and all were expected to make polite conversation with anyone within immediate speaking distance. Leaving dinner early was not an option. Victorian etiquette forbade getting up from the table unless unavoidable and, even then, required the diner to ask his companions to excuse him. Passengers prayed for good dinner companions, especially to the left and to the right of them.

Diners welcomed men such as Augustus Froelich at the table. He was smart and sociable. His engaging personality, intellect, and quick wit gained him many friends when he first arrived in New York from France in 1851. Froelich served as the French professor at the Troy Female Seminary in Troy, New York, a position he accepted after graduating from the University of France. Froelich's father sent him a letter in October 1856. He was dying. He asked his son to return home to be with him during his final days. Froelich settled his affairs in America and booked a ticket on the next ship leaving for France, *Le Lyonnais*.

George Schedel and his wife were the type of guests who made it a point to find themselves next to the most-important people in the room. Networking was second nature to Schedel. He served as British vice consul to Costa Rica from 1852 to 1853, a post that came with a distinguished title but no pay.[11] Consulates protected British trade interests abroad, and appointments in the 1850s were patronage positions given to those with ties to the British foreign secretary or other governmental officials. "Most nineteenth-century consuls did not have any prior overseas or diplomatic experience and were unsuitable for the job. Most of these men lacked any real knowledge of the culture and traditions of the area to which they were assigned."[12] Schedel's consular service reflected neither a deep understanding of the Costa Rican economy nor the local language and customs. His main motivation for accepting the post was the opportunity to promote Protestantism in the largely Catholic country. In late 1853, after serving only a little more than a year in Costa Rica, Schedel wound up at political odds with the American consul. British officials transferred him to New York, where he held a vice consul post through June 24, 1856. What Schedel may have lacked in his abilities as a political operative, he made up for in his ability to strike up and hold conversation. He was an experienced traveler who knew the importance of shipboard dinners and did his best to reserve a prime location near the better-connected passengers.

The most-coveted seats were near the captain. Captain Devaulx turned the ship over to his mate and dressed in full French uniform to entertain his dinner guests. Devaulx was a short and stocky man with a round chin and oval face. He was amiable and easygoing and lacked the seriousness often associated with steamship captains. His black hair and dark, bushy eyebrows brought out his amber-tinted, hazel eyes. The soft color of his eyes only added to his kind appearance. The passengers liked him immediately.

Devaulx sat with the ship's wealthiest and most-noteworthy guests, those most important to Franco-Américaine's business interests. Their word of mouth in social circles would serve as free advertising for the line, and the Poirier brothers instructed Devaulx to take good care of them.

Sumner was one of the ship's most important passengers because of both his immense wealth and political connections. He and his family occupied choice seats at the captain's table. Devaulx soon realized, however, that dining with Sumner was a privilege, not a chore. He was a man who attracted attention first by his name but kept it with his good humor and generosity. He was short and stout with dark hair and blue eyes. The plumpness of his face and of his body only enhanced his cheerful personality. He had experienced much in his forty-four years and possessed the charm, fine tastes, and mannerisms of a man from an affluent family, and the ability to connect with the sailors and servants who earned their livings on voyages like this one.

Sumner enjoyed good company. He and his wife spent the summer of 1856 planning the trip to Europe and shared the details of their travels with friends on many occasions. One summer day, he visited his friends Dr. Stanley Gridley Howe and American sculptor Thomas Crawford in Boston.[13] The men took a walk to the shore of a nearby bay. They passed the time telling stories to one another and making small talk while tossing sticks and stones into the water. Sumner spoke about his family's upcoming journey to France. Crawford asked Sumner if he was at all concerned about crossing the Atlantic in November. Before he could answer, Dr. Howe quipped, "Albert's got nothing to worry about. Fat people make good swimmers."[14] The men laughed, Sumner the hardest of all. They continued to skip stones and whiled away the afternoon in one another's company. Perhaps it is a story Sumner shared with his dinner companions aboard *Le Lyonnais* without ever knowing the profundity of the joke.

The captain made his exit after dinner and returned to the quarterdeck. The men and women separated, and the saloon transformed into a sitting room. The men played cards, smoked cigars, and enjoyed after-dinner drinks while the ladies became acquainted with one another. Frances and Cora Dummer struck up a conversation with a woman named Margaret Bassford. Margaret was twenty-one and had given birth to her first child, a son she called Francis, just two months before she set out for France. She planned to bring Francis with her and her husband on the voyage but, at the last moment, decided to leave the infant with her mother so her husband could concentrate on his business in France. She missed Francis terribly and wondered aloud if she had made the right decision. Frances and Cora reassured her that a steamship crossing the Atlantic in late autumn was no place for a child so young. Flora Solomon, Frances's lady in waiting, joined the conversation. The company brightened Margaret's spirits, and the ladies began to discuss their lives in New York and their plans for France.

There was a piano in the saloon, and, as the evening wore on, there was music and singing. Devaulx could hear the music from the deck, and the sound of it pleased him. He was quite fond of music. He played the violin, the piano, and the flute when he was not at sea. Devaulx was an amateur, but Margaret's husband, celebrated American pianist and composer Thomas Franklin Bassford, was a professional who delighted the audience by playing a tune or two.

The past few years had been successful for Bassford, but it was the May 12, 1854, performance he gave at L. J. Descombes's Rooms at 585 Broadway in New York City that changed his life and inspired his journey to France. Critics recognized Thomas's talent not merely as a pianist but as a composer. "Although Bassford played well, his forte was obviously composition. If the opportunity be afforded to him, he will doubtless distinguish himself in a higher department of the art than he has yet essayed."[15] He was then just twenty years old.

He achieved his first success as a songwriter in his teens and made a name for himself as a rising star by the age of nineteen. In his early years, he published several songs that were sold by Horace Waters of New York. They included instrumental polkas and serenades with lyrics. Songs such as "Banjo Dance," "Bignores Polka," and "Sweet Lady Do Not Stay" made him popular at concert rooms in New York City, where people would gather to hear performers play for one dollar a ticket.

Critical acclaim followed the reviews of the 1854 concert. Bassford moved up from a day job of working in a piano store to opening his own piano-and-sheet-music store, Bassford and Brower, located at 603 Broadway. He married Margaret Alberta Clayton of New York in June 1855 and continued to work, perform, and compose. His wife gave birth to their son, Louis Franklin "Francis" Bassford, in August 1856.

One of Bassford's dreams was to create an English-speaking opera worthy of acclaim, a work that would rival European masterpieces. In his review of Bassford's May 12, 1854, performance, one critic pointed out, "The new Academy of Music should open a more ample field for the native artist. By its charter, it pledged to present an English Opera—and that definition includes of course all works in which the English language is used as the spoken medium."[16] The inclusion of this endorsement in an article about the young composer's performance referred to Bassford's aspirations.

Bassford played before audiences at larger venues after his debut at Descombes, including a grand concert at Hartford City Hall. In 1856, he was invited to perform at a four-part series of soirees, or small concerts, in New York. Bassford was a devotee of pianist Louis Morceau Gottschalk, who traveled the soiree circuit at the same time. Born in New Orleans, Gottschalk spent most of his time working outside the US and traveled the world performing his own romantic piano compositions. He sought new influences and inspiration for his music abroad. Bassford dedicated his composition "Banjo Dance" to Gottschalk, who responded in kind with a similar composition. Bassford was held in greater regard as a composer, and Gottschalk was recognized for his technical playing skills and is mentioned by critics alongside Franz Liszt and Sigismond Thalberg as a virtuoso on the piano.

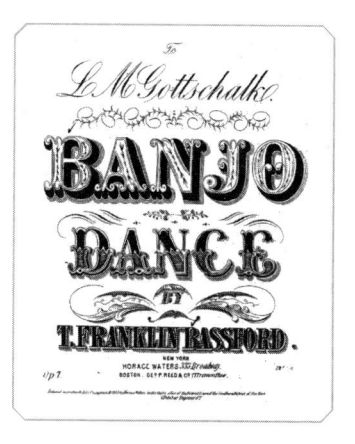

"Banjo Dance" sheet music with dedication to Gottschalk. *Library of Congress, Music Division*

The Adriatic Affair

Gottschalk and Bassford knew one another and played to audiences on Broadway during the spring and summer of 1856. It was Gottschalk who insisted Bassford complete his musical studies at the Paris Conservatory of Music, and Bassford did not give a second thought to following his mentor's advice. He applied for a passport on October 22, 1856, and planned to spend the next three years studying his art at the epicenter of nineteenth-century music composition. He booked passage to Le Havre for himself and his family aboard *Le Lyonnais*.

The piano played on in the saloon. Darkness fell. The passengers sang and danced and laughed and talked as *Le Lyonnais* moved forward into the night. Their bellies were full, and they were at last able to enjoy one another's company. The evening was so pleasant they scarcely noticed that the ocean's swells had gotten stronger and a haze had crept its way across the starlight.

CHAPTER 7
Sailors, Watchmen, Firemen, Passengers

Sailors

Most of the sailors were fast asleep by ten o'clock in the evening. They took rest when they could get it, since every man knew he could be called upon to stand watch or otherwise assist his captain or crewmates anytime during the day or night. Jean-Louis-Marie Choupault, Julias Dublic, and Alexis Cauvin were among the men fast asleep in their bunks.[1] It felt good to rest. The waking hours for sailors aboard ships such as *Le Lyonnais* were difficult. The labor was constant, and it required muscle. Sailors hoisted and adjusted sails on officers' commands. The tasks required them not only to pull heavy ropes, chains, and cables but to climb tall masts to fine-tune the ship's rigging. The men maintained the ship when they were not sailing by repairing rigging, oiling the masts, and washing the decks. Their muscles grew tired not just from chores but from bracing their bodies against the movement of a vessel on an always-churning ocean. Climbing into a bunk at the end of a day and closing one's eyes was a simple pleasure.

Steward's Mate Stanislaus Thillaye was lying in bed waiting for sleep to come to him. He checked his pocket watch and noted that the time was just before eleven o'clock. Thillaye was responsible for tending to passengers' needs. The earliest days of a voyage were the busiest for him because it was during this time that the passengers became oriented with the ship, readied their cabins, and settled into their new surroundings. His work may not have been as physically punishing as the sailors', but he was grateful to be off his feet and away from the passengers' stream of questions and requests. He savored the silence. The fairer weather pleased him, and he hoped for a good night's rest.

Not long after Thillaye checked his watch, a heavy concussion rocked the ship. It came without warning. The blow did not feel as powerful as it did substantial—a dull, heavy, crash. Thillaye knew it was not the waves or a storm that had rocked *Le Lyonnais*, but an impact of some kind. The vibrations woke all the men. Cauvin bolted out of his bunk and ran to the deck. Dublic opened his eyes but closed them again and fell back to sleep. Choupault awoke but did not get up. He hoped he was wrong about the noise he had just heard. Deep inside, he knew he was not. He hesitated. It was as if some part of him knew that once he started moving, it would be a long time before he would stop. He postponed the inevitable for a few more seconds until the boatswain ran into the bunk room and roused the deck crew. "My boys, get up! We're run into!"[1] Choupault moved, now with deliberate speed.

The chief engineer and chief steward sent men to the firemen's and stewards' quarters to rouse their crews. The first fireman ordered his men, Dublic among them, to head to the engine room. He did not speak about what struck the ship. The men moved on the urgency of his orders alone. One of Thillaye's fellow steward's mates came into his quarters and delivered the news out loud: "The ship is sinking!"[2]

Cauvin got on deck just after the collision. He was standing on *Le Lyonnais*'s starboard side and could see onto the offending ship's deck. He saw no one aboard save the helmsman. Thillaye also ran straight to the deck, where he found Cauvin speaking to a fireman named Pierre Bienaimée. Bienaimée had been working in the engine room at the time of the collision. The chief engineer sent him to the deck to give a report to the officers and to relay any orders from them. Thillaye listened as Cauvin and Bienaimée traded information and observations about what had so violently shaken the ship. It was a collision with another vessel. "The ship that hit us had no lights,"[3] Bienaimée told the others. Cauvin agreed. He was one of the first to arrive on deck and saw the ship as she cleared and passed. He added, "There was not one man aboard on lookout."[4]

Most of the sailors were already assembled when Choupault approached. "She ought to have carried a light at the mizzen," he said as he joined them. He went to the rail and looked out to sea. The mystery ship was ahead of them and, by now, at some distance. Choupault could see her stern. It was square. Her mizzen, the aftmost mast on a sailing vessel, was rigged with the sail pointing fore and aft while her other masts were square-rigged and cut across the ship. She was a barque, a type of sailing ship with sails rigged in such formation.[5] She was too far away for Choupault to read her name, but he knew what she was by her shape and her size and her style. "American," he muttered.

The men could no longer see the ship that hit them, but they heard the cries of distress from those on board. The shouting was loud at first but dissipated as time and distance separated the two vessels. The screams from those aboard the barque lasted no more than ten minutes. The ocean was then quiet.

No one spoke. The men strained to catch any glimpse of the ship or signs of life from those aboard her. "She must have gone down," Bienaimée concluded.[6] The others nodded agreement. They paused briefly until their silence was broken by the collective realization that there was no more to be gained by staring into the gaping darkness. They had work to do. Choupault and Thillaye sought out their officers for orders. Bienaimée descended back to the engine room to deliver the grim news to the men below: there was no help coming.

Watchmen

The night was dark and hazy at the time of the collision. Darkness at sea is a different sort of dark. It is deep and ink-like. It does not come quickly. When the sun sets on the open ocean, the darkness yawns until both sky and sea become opaque. It is then that the water seems bottomless, the sky cavernous. The vastness of a dark ocean makes objective measures of space, such as distance and speed and direction, difficult to judge even for men of experience and makes the night watch vital.

Le Lyonnais was running at 11 knots per hour under sail and steam in such darkness on the evening of the collision. She displayed lights according to French regulation, a wise precaution in the blackness, but a precaution that depended on someone from an approaching vessel to see those lights.

Sailors aboard *Le Lyonnais* kept watch around the clock. The men took turns staring both into the daylight and into the darkness for signs of other ships, changes in the wind and weather, and dangerous natural phenomena such as ice or drifting debris.

There were twenty-seven people on the deck at or immediately after the collision: three officers, fourteen crew, and ten passengers. The captain was on the poop. First Lieutenant Jean-Marie Mathieu, the officer on watch, stood on the quarterdeck. The first mate, Pierre Roussel, was at the helm. Twelve deck sailors looked out from their posts around the ship, and two more stood watch at the cathead.

The haze on the evening of the collision made the watch more difficult than it would have been on a clearer night, but the men were aided by some light from the stars. One of the cathead watchmen saw a glimpse of something unnatural off *Le Lyonnais*'s starboard side. The object was a shadow at first but morphed like a ghost materializing from a mist.

"Ship!" the watchman shouted. "Ship to starboard, bearing down us under full sail!"[7]

Someone rang the bell. It clinged and clanged and sent out into the air a warning that would have sounded joyful under different circumstances. The captain rushed to the helm. He ordered the crew to blow the whistle, which had been put aboard in New York. It was loud, so loud the sound reverberated not only through the ears but through the body. The men held their ears and shrugged their shoulders as she blew. The sound could be heard for 10 miles, but it had no visible impact on the approaching vessel.

The men on deck were powerless. The other ship was already too close. All they could do was watch and hope the captain could evade her in time. The ship grew nearer and nearer. She was made of wood—a sailing ship. The men counted three masts, but only the foremost and main mast were square-rigged—a barque for certain. Her long, pointed bowsprit, a spar that extended forward from the ship's bow, stretched out over the water. Her anchor was affixed to her bow. As she grew even closer, the men saw a decoration on the front of the ship at the prow, the bow's highest point. It was a figurehead of some kind made of elaborately carved and painted wood. The figurehead's colors became clearer as she neared—black and gold and red.

The ship moved with all her sails on the wind. There was no sign she was making any effort to get their attention, let alone to avoid a collision. She blew no horn, sounded no alarm, and made no evasive movements. The men saw no one on deck. *Le Lyonnais*'s sailors yelled and screamed and waved their arms, but the stranger ship kept coming. Her bowsprit pointed at them like a sword.

Devaulx knew that if each ship continued her course, the bow of the oncoming vessel would strike *Le Lyonnais* amidships on the starboard side in a T-shaped collision. Devaulx turned the ship to port and hoped he could avoid an accident by creating enough space for the oncoming vessel to pass him on the starboard side.

The decision came too late. The barque struck *Le Lyonnais* across the companionway amidships as she turned. The bowsprit struck first. It cleft with the sound of breaking timber like a large tree limb cracking in a storm. Splintered pieces of wood fell like rain and landed onto *Le Lyonnais*'s deck in intermittent thumps. The thud of the sailing ship's bow making full contact with the steamer's starboard side followed. The blow was thunderous, and it crushed *Le Lyonnais* from the companionway as far as the shrouds.

The barque's anchor struck *Le Lyonnais* high at the iron plates protecting her coal bunkers. One of the flukes caught a plate and, as the two ships crossed one another, yanked it off. The barque, in clearing away, made one last sound. It was the noise of her figurehead ripping from her bow and smashing onto *Le Lyonnais*'s deck. The ship shook and the figurehead rolled across the deck, banging and bumping with the tempo of the waves. The barque left so much of her fore works on *Le Lyonnais*'s deck that the damage later convinced the men beyond a shadow of a doubt that the barque had gone down.

Illustrated Times of London's depiction of the
Adriatic and *Le Lyonnais* collision, December 27, 1856.
Author's collection

Second Mate Adolphe Luguiere was asleep at the time of the collision, but the shock roused him. He ran straight to the deck to find the captain at the helm and a barque disengaging from *Le Lyonnais*. He looked at the ship that was, for a moment, locked onto his. There was no one on deck. She had no lights. She was at full sail. It was only when she pulled away that Luguiere saw any light coming from her. It was the light of her compass binnacle, a stand fixed at the stern. The binnacle light grew dimmer and dimmer as she left them.

Luguiere and Mathieu ran to *Le Lyonnais*'s starboard side to inspect the collision site. One of the lifeboats, the one of English design, was crushed. They hoped the boat had taken the brunt of the impact. The men looked to their captain. He was perfectly cool. Perhaps he believed the worst was over. Perhaps he was concentrating on the task at hand. Perhaps it was just his nature. Whatever the reason, his disposition gave them some relief as they took leave of him and ordered the boatswain and steward's mate to the forecastle to rally the men.

Not long after, Luguiere saw some men gathered on the deck, among them a fireman and some sailors. They appeared to be exchanging information. He thought one of them might have seen something useful. He hurried toward them but stopped when he almost tripped over something in his path. He looked down, expecting to find wood or metal or some other debris from the collision. What he found was part of the figurehead that had been torn from the other ship when she broke away. It was the head of a dragon, black with a gold mane, and piercing red eyes. A gilt-darted tongue stuck out from the dragon's open mouth. Luguiere watched for a few moments as the piece of the dragon's head rolled from side to side, wagging its tongue as it knocked back and forth with the movement of the ship. It felt like a warning. He stared back into the dragon's shifting eyes and thought about the figurehead's unique design, "At least there is a way to identify the barque that hit us." He stepped over the dragon carefully, so as not to further offend him, and continued to move toward the men.

Firemen

The engine room was a dusty, dark, and dirty place hidden in the bowels of a steamship. There, sailors called firemen or stokers shoveled coal into the furnaces that kept the boilers producing steam to fuel the engines. "Stokers" and "firemen" are interchangeable terms for the same job. A "stoker" referred to someone who worked on military ships, particularly in the Royal British Navy, while "firemen" were merchant sailors. By the early 1900s, some referred to firemen and stokers collectively as a ship's "Black Gang" because the constant exposure to hot coal painted the firemen's clothing and skin with a thick black grease.

Scooping coal into furnace boxes was backbreaking work. In addition to burns, muscle pain, and heat exhaustion—the obvious hazards of shoveling heavy loads into blazing fires on always-shifting ground—firemen frequently suffered lacerations, hernias, and dehydration. Exposure to coal dust caused respiratory ailments. Responsible captains ensured that firemen stayed hydrated, got plenty of rest, and worked no more than eight hours at a time, which required three redundant shifts to work an engine room. The total number of men required to keep a steam engine moving depended on the number of furnaces. Each furnace had to be manned around the clock, and even ships with a single smokestack like *Le Lyonnais* had multiple furnaces. Each furnace required approximately six men to manage the necessary shifts on a voyage.

Another hazard for firemen was their position in the ship. Engine rooms were buried in the depths below the waterline and among the lowest steamship compartments. They were fully enclosed, with no portholes, and in the 1850s there was no mechanism for the men to communicate with sailors or passengers on deck unless a messenger went above to exchange information. Collisions usually took the engine room by surprise. A ship's lower compartments were often the first to flood, leaving those inside with little chance of escape.

Steam was new to captains in the 1850s. Captains such as Devaulx had spent their careers on sailing ships and, although they knew their vessels, deferred to chief engineers on mechanical matters. This created an almost parallel structure between the deck crew and the engine crew. Chief engineer Gigneux commanded *Le Lyonnais*'s engine crew. He supervised personnel, oversaw the equipment, managed engine room operations, and handled all engine-related aspects of the voyage. Devaulx was the ship's ultimate authority, but the world below deck belonged to Gigneux, who led a complement of men with different backgrounds and training than most of the other sailors.

Firemen Pierre Bienaimée, Fabian Nestor, and Victor Poirreaux were feeding coal into *Le Lyonnais*'s hungry furnaces on the evening of November 2, 1856. The men used large iron shovels to move heaping scoops of coal from piles on the floor next to them into fireboxes beneath the ship's boilers. The task was endless, the senses familiar: the crackling of the fire, the clouds of swirling dust, the smell of charred earth. The men counted the hours until they could surface for some much-needed rest.

None of them saw the barque approaching. They first knew something terrible had happened when they felt a blow against the ship that rocked some of them off their feet. The blow was followed by the sound all firemen prayed they would never hear: the sound of rushing water. Gigneux ordered Bienaimée above deck to learn what he could, apprise the captain of the situation below, and seek orders.

The collision broke away the iron plates that reinforced the coal bunkers and kept the coal dry. It was not long before water seeped through the bunkers and made its way toward the engine room. It put out the furnace fires almost instantaneously. *Le Lyonnais* stayed her course, but the water soon extinguished the fires. With each passing moment, the ship moved less by the force of her own steam and more by the inertia of a heavy object in forward motion.

Bienaimée found the captain, who ordered those below to get the pumps going and make all attempts to save the engine. Bienaimée stopped to exchange bits of information with some sailors as he made his way back down below. Water was pouring into the engine room by the time he returned. As he walked past his fellow firemen in search of Gigneux, the ocean soaked his boots and his pants. Bienaimée looked down. The water was not clear. It carried with it chunks of black rocks he immediately recognized as coal and ash and cinders that the incoming seawater had swept up and carried along as it moved through the bunkers and into the ship.

Bienaimée found Gigneux and told him what he had learned above deck. "Get the pumps going," Gigneux yelled. The effort was short lived. Coal and ash choked up the valves and rendered them useless. Despite their best efforts, it took only ten minutes for the engine to stop.

It was now Gigneux who ascended to find Devaulx. "Water is pouring into the coal bunkers."[8] Devaulx could tell by the expression on Gigneux's face that it was coming in at a rate too devastating to be stopped. Gigneux, who was always thorough, added what Devaulx already knew: "The ship is sinking."[9] The men locked eyes for a moment, but there was nothing more to say. Gigneux turned and descended back into the bowels of the ship.

Passengers

Most of the passengers retired early, Flora Solomon among them. She changed into her nightdress, climbed into her berth, and replayed the evening's events in her mind. She had hardly known the Dummers when she signed on for this journey, but the kindness they showed her and the new acquaintance she had made in Margaret Bassford set her at ease. "It will be a fine voyage," she told herself. The sound of the evening's music and of her new friends' laughter rang in her ears as she tried to sleep.

She was still awake at the time of crash. The first she knew of the collision was the "tremendous shock."[11] A loud, dull noise came with it. Close behind the crash came the sound of water. Solomon froze. It took her several moments to realize what was happening. The sounds of people screaming jolted her back to the present. The cries came from all parts of the ship. Solomon sprang out of bed and walked out of her room, still wearing nothing but her sleeping dress. The moment she stepped outside she saw passengers running around in confusion and panic.

She tried to stop a man for answers, but he ran past her. She managed to flag down someone else. "The ship struck another vessel!" was all he told her.[9] Another passenger told her an oncoming vessel hit them. The information was inconsistent, but the panic in the eyes of those to whom she spoke was the same. It seemed that everyone she met was afraid they would soon drown.

Solomon found the second mate, Luguiere. He was running somewhere and had only a moment to speak with her. He looked not at her but in the direction in which he was moving as he answered her question and moved on. "A vessel hit us and went down. We heard screams and a noise that sounded like the sinking of a ship."[10] That was what he said. What she heard was, "We are on our own."

It was chaos on deck. Passengers emerged from their rooms to find the once-pristine decks littered with debris. They ran in all directions, tripping over pieces of splintered wood. Some screamed. Some cried. Some ran back to their rooms to hide. There was no order in the moments that followed the collision. Sailors were not immune to the panic. Several of them were seized with fear when they first left the forecastle and assembled.

Solomon walked to the starboard side of the ship and looked out into the night. It was too foggy to see any signs of the vessel that hit them, or any other vessel, for that matter. She looked down to find the ship crushed in and taking on water. There was a 2-foot-square opening at the waterline on the ship's starboard side in the shape of a diamond, where the collision had stripped away one of the iron plates that had looked so strong to her just two days ago. Water poured in through the hole every time a passing wave dipped the ship to starboard. Solomon was afraid but determined not to let it show.

Devaulx's assessment of the damage was more optimistic. The position of the hole was precarious but not impossible to reach. He believed that the crew might be able repair the ship and stop the flow of water if they worked both from outside and inside. He formed a plan, but to execute it he would first have to organize every able-bodied man and woman aboard the ship.

"Gather round," the captain called as he gestured for people to come closer. The crew immediately heeded the order, but even though they had all assembled, the captain kept calling out and waving his hand. The passengers looked at one another and soon realized he was talking to them as well.

When Devaulx finally mustered the group, he paused for a moment before he spoke. Every pair of eyes upon him was wide with fear. He felt enormous compassion for them. People were scared, and he knew it. He was scared too but did not let it show. There was work to be done.

Devaulx did his best to exude calmness. That, in and of itself, eased the crowd a bit. Then he spoke. First, he issued orders to any firemen still on deck and to all the sailors. He sent the firemen and the carpenters to the engine room to try to locate the leak and stop the flow of water coming through it into the ship. He pointed to some of the sailors and instructed them to work together to cover the hole from the outside. He noticed that his crew calmed considerably once he gave them orders, and realized the passengers might be less anxious if they had something to do. He needed all the help he could get. He knew he had not one but two sea captains in his midst, Beaugrand and Sumner, and they were both among the crowd. He asked them to remain on deck and work with the crew to repair the hole from the outside. The men obliged without a moment's hesitation.

Devaulx ordered the remaining crewmen and willing passengers to move items from starboard to port. There was no damage on *Le Lyonnais*'s port side. The idea was to weigh the ship down on the port side and cause her to list. This would lift the hole in the starboard side above the waterline and stop the flow of water long enough for those above and below deck to repair it. Choupault was among the sailors assigned to move objects from one side of the ship to the other. He dragged some items and carried others. He moved everything he could find—chairs, tables, debris, rigging. The sea was running rough as he worked, which made moving the objects to expose the breach more difficult than it might have been in calmer weather.

Choupault and the others' perseverance paid off. The ship began to tilt, and soon she listed just enough to give Beaugrand, Sumner, and the men on the starboard side clearance to work. They grabbed a large, studded sail, draped it over the side of the ship, and covered the hole. They strapped a rope to one of the smaller sailors and lowered him over the side with two pieces of wood, a hammer, and some nails. He placed one wooden board diagonally across the sail and nailed it into place. He crossed the other board over it to make a large "X" and nailed that into place as well.

While sailors worked above, Gigneux led the remaining carpenters to the engine room. The hole was small enough to convince them they could stop the flow of water by propping objects against the inside wall. Those above sent mattresses, quilts, and other items down to them—anything to plug the hole or absorb water.

The plan seemed to work. Those above deck watched the flow of water into the hole. It slowly subsided, and the crowd erupted in cheers. Passengers embraced one another and, for a moment, believed that the ship might survive the disaster. The joy was short lived. Although there was less water coming through the hole, the ship continued to fill with water at the same rate below deck.

The captain formed a bailing party. The crew rigged a cable down to the engine room so water could be removed, lifted to the deck, and sent over the side. The passengers and crew passed buckets of water from one person to another and another until the person at the end of the line dumped it overboard. They used whatever they could find to hold water, including pails, large casks, and hogsheads or 5-gallon buckets. The officers and the captain helped whenever one of them had a moment during which they were unoccupied by other tasks. Dublic and Choupault were among those who worked with the passengers. Once it started, the bailing never ceased.

Solomon found comfort in heeding the captain's orders. The coolness of his demeanor made her feel a bit better, and although she was a lady, she was strong and no stranger to hard work. She grabbed an empty container, joined her fellow passengers, and set to work on the bailing. She did what she could to help, but the sea was rough, and the water just kept coming.

The passengers and crew worked heroically, but the water gained on them at too fast a pace. Devaulx ordered the men to throw cargo overboard to lighten the ship as much as possible and keep the hole above the waterline. Choupault and the other sailors now went from moving items from starboard to port to dumping them over the side. They dragged heavy tables, chairs, sacks of grain, furniture, and whatever else they could find to the side of the ship, heaved them over the rail, and tossed them into the waves.

Despite their best efforts, the hole that had once teetered on the waterline sank below it. Choupault and the others hurled items overboard at a furious pace. Those below pressed more than a dozen mattresses against the wall. It was no use. The water just kept coming.

While the passengers and deckhands worked above, the firemen worked below. When they could no longer pump, they bailed and sent water up and out to be thrown back to the sea by the chain of passengers and crew above. The process was tedious. Incoming water replaced every bucket they sent out. They retreated to the deck when the water threatened to overwhelm them.

Fabian Nestor crawled out of the engine room. He was on duty at the time of the crash and had shoveled coal into the fires for several hours before the collision. He never heard the ship that hit them, and had not surfaced from the engine room since. After the collision, he helped his fellow firemen first by pumping water, then by carrying mattresses to the hole, and then by lifting buckets of water. He was exhausted. He was soaking wet when he emerged from below, but his face and hands were still black from the coal that perpetually stained them. He found the captain. Devaulx smiled at him the way a father smiles at a son who has tried his best at something but, nevertheless, faced defeat. He spared Nestor from the burden of speaking. "My poor fellow," the captain said, "the water is gaining upon us."[12] A sigh was all Nestor could rally in response.

Nestor saw Choupault and Thillaye together on deck. He knew Choupault to be a reliable man and sought him out in an effort to find out more about what had happened while he was below. He joined a conversation in progress. Choupault told Thillaye, "The ship that hit us fired twice after the collision."[13] Nestor asked where the ship was from, and Choupault responded, "American." Nestor wondered out loud if the Americans would return to save them. He looked out at the open ocean and saw nothing. "She must have gone down."[14] Thillaye, confident in the unwritten code that any seaman able to save the lives of others would do so if they could, nodded his head in agreement.

CHAPTER 8

Abandon Ship

THE PASSENGERS AND CREW BAILED all night and most of the following morning, but their efforts made no appreciable difference. Devaulx was now convinced that there existed a second hole beneath the waterline, one they could not reach.

The experienced sailors realized hours ago that there was no hope in trying to save the vessel, but they did as they were told and removed bucket after bucket of water from the ship, with little change in their pace or their demeanor. It was around noon when the passengers began to grasp the state of things. They had labored all evening, their spirits buoyed by joining forces with the crew to save the ship, but their work slowed as the day wore on, until it no longer served even the collateral purpose of keeping them occupied. It was just a waste of energy.

The captain did the math. He had six boats in all: two cutters, two longboats, and two lifeboats (one of English and one of American design). The American lifeboat would hold about twenty people, and the cutters, maybe, twenty-five. The yawls could take only six people each for a total of eighty-two spaces. The English lifeboat had been damaged in the collision, but after a brief inspection and with no alternatives, Devaulx decided to use it. It would hold twenty more.

Le Lyonnais's stern was heavy, but she was holding for now. "We've got some time," he thought to himself. He could save everyone, or at least give everyone a fighting chance, but to do so he needed space on lifeboats for at least thirty more people. He ordered some men, most of them sailors, to help him build a raft. They stripped *Le Lyonnais* of any building materials they could find—wooden spars from sails, topmasts, cabin doors, boards, debris, and even ornamental woodwork. They grabbed chicken coops, hogsheads, and empty wine kegs and lashed the materials together with rope to construct a raft large enough to accommodate fifty people and lowered it into the water. To say it floated would be an overstatement, but the basic structure of the raft proved workable. Some of the men climbed onto it and continued construction while others stayed on deck with the captain and lowered building materials down.

Nestor was among those who remained on the ship with the captain and passed items into the waiting arms of the men below. The sea had been swollen all morning, but the weather was fine enough to work. Winds increased as the day wore on, and around the time the raft hit the water, a light rain fell. The waves lifted the makeshift raft with a deceptively soft rise and fall, but Nestor heard the hushed whispers of the veteran sailors. They knew what the swells and intermittent rain foretold; a distant storm was drawing closer.

Devaulx, now satisfied there was a place for everyone, assembled the passengers and most of the crew on the quarterdeck. The remaining crewmen finished the raft. "We will abandon ship," he announced. He did not make the decision lightly. They were fortunate that *Le Lyonnais* was still afloat, but there was no telling how long she would last. The plan was to stand by the sinking vessel as long as possible and hope another ship passed and rescued them.

The captain prepared the crew for embarkation of the boats. There was no panic. The ship was not in any immediate danger of sinking, and the crew assured the passengers there was enough space for everyone. Devaulx ordered passengers into specific vessels and made sure each had a commander and some crewmen with knowledge of the sea. There was no difficulty assigning each of the thirty-nine paying passengers into a boat with a complement of capable sailors.

Devaulx assigned one of the cutters to Roussel. Inside, he placed a compass, charts, chronometers, and a sextant. The boat also had a complete set of new sails and was well provisioned with enough food and water for two weeks.

The captain approached Sumner and Beaugrand and asked them to assume command of the second cutter. The pair had been invaluable to the repairs of the hole at *Le Lyonnais*'s waterline, and Devaulx was short of men with leadership experience at sea. The men accepted without hesitation. "May I speak with you for a moment," Sumner asked Beaugrand before Devaulx could show them to their boat. Sumner welcomed responsibility for the safety of his own wife and daughter, but his concern extended to strangers as well. He had been a great comfort to the female passengers throughout the chaos following the collision. He asked Beaugrand if he was willing take a larger share of the female passengers and children into their boat. Beaugrand understood. "Of course," he responded. They informed Devaulx, who embraced the help.

Devaulx made sure the sea captains' boat was well provisioned. It had sails, oars, and navigational equipment and was well stocked with wine, brandy, preserves, and meats. The captains placed a spyglass and two chronometers, one of which belonged to Beaugrand, inside the boat. One chronometer was marked "David Jne Barre, 576," and the other, "Arnold and Dent, 84 Strand, London, No. 998." Beaugrand placed papers inside the boat. These included the ratings on the chronometers, and a memoranda book regarding the sale of his ship, *Marie*, which he sold in Havana prior to his arrival in New York. The last thing the Baugrand placed inside the lifeboat was about $500 in coins, a portion of the proceeds of *Marie*'s sale.

Responsibility for the remaining lifeboats fell to Devaulx's third lieutenant, René Dublot, and his second mate, Luguiere. The captain and his men decided to stay with one of the yawls and accompany the raft. Purser Gustave Baumstarck and his staff were assigned to the other.

Devaulx personally assigned the passengers to the lifeboats. The boats hung from davits, sets of large, crescent-shaped arms, located both amidships and on the poop. The boats were suspended from the davits by ropes that ran through blocks, pulleys used to lift heavy objects, on each side. It took two men working in concert, one on each rope, to lower a boat into the water. The sailors were keenly aware of stories about lifeboats being demolished when lowered too quickly in a panic, or swamped when released into stormy seas. Each boat was precious. The sailors lowered them like their lives depended on it.

A swell rocked *Le Lyonnais* as the crew lowered Sumner and Beaugrand's boat into the water. The force knocked the boat loose, and the waves swept it away. The spyglass, chromometers, Beaugrand's personal papers, and enough food and water to sustain twenty people for a fortnight were swept away with it.

The remaining boats waited in the water. The crew lowered rope ladders over the side of the ship, and the commanders and a small amount of crew stepped down to each boat. Boats took turns waiting beneath ladders as sailors both on the ship and in the boats guided passengers into the waiting vessels. All hands not involved in assisting passengers or commanding lifeboats stood by the wreck and continued to work as custom and order demanded.

The Bailey/Strong family waited on deck for their assignments. Devaulx approached, pointed to the boat commanded by Second Mate

Luguiere, and said, "This one." Theodore and his mother-in-law, Jeanette, moved toward the ladder, but Theodore's wife, Julia, hesitated. The ship felt sturdier to her than a boat being tossed about by ocean waves, and Devaulx's presence gave her great comfort. She begged her husband and her mother to stay on the ship with him. "But the captain is the one ordering us into the boats," replied Jeanette. Julia could not be moved. "Wherever the captain goes, I go," she insisted.[1] The family remained on the ship.

The passengers assigned to Sumner and Beaugrand's vessel now searched for spaces on the remaining boats. The captain oversaw the reassignment of the stranded passengers himself, but there was, nonetheless, confusion. The boats were neither uniform in design nor equally outfitted. Passengers jockeyed for position in what they perceived to be the best-equipped and most-comfortable vessels. Some boats were overcrowded, which required the crew to shift passengers to others. The captain also wanted to balance the number of men and women aboard each vessel. Survival in the boats depended not only on the mercy of the waves but on the ability of those aboard to bail water, row, keep watch, and steer. The balance of men and women was an important concern. Sumner's group had a larger number of women in it than others. Devaulx ordered his crew to transfer passengers from one boat to another to make space for those from Sumner and Beaugrand's boat and to distribute the women more evenly.

Devaulx had initially ordered George Schedel and his wife into Roussel's cutter. They were among the last to board it and were surprised to find it overloaded with more people than the captain had assigned. There were twenty-eight passengers in a space meant for twenty to twenty-five.

Third Lieutenant Dublot commanded the English lifeboat. Solomon's new employers, the Dummers, and her new acquaintances, the Bassfords, were among the first to board it. Solomon waited her turn to step inside.

Devaulx paced the deck. He assessed who was on what boat, and noted the ratio of passengers to crew and men to women on each vessel. "There are too many ladies in these boats." He pointed to the cutter and the English lifeboat.[2]

Solomon was just stepping from the ladder into the English lifeboat when the captain yelled his orders. A sailor directed her to switch to the American lifeboat, which was floating nearby and under the command of Luguiere. Luguiere rowed toward her. Solomon was nervous about leaving her acquaintances but moved without complaint.

Mr. and Mrs. Schedel had not yet taken their seats on the cutter and, although they heard the captain's orders, ignored them. Mr. Schedel felt great confidence in the boat because of its condition, the social standing of the passengers in it, and the high rank of its commanding officer. The boat was crowded, but it was sturdy and dry. Roussel's men put their oars in the water and began to move away from *Le Lyonnais* with the Schedels aboard. The cutter soon found itself near the American lifeboat.

Mr. Schedel did not like the looks of its commander, Luguiere. Unlike Roussel, who held a place of importance as the man next in line to the captain, Luguiere was only the second mate—a sort of hybrid of a sailor and an officer. He took orders from the first officer and managed the sailors as they worked, but he still ate, drank, and slept in the forecastle alongside fellow sailors. Luguiere was a young man of only twenty-eight years old, but despite his youthful appearance, he was a man of experience. He served in the French navy during some of the bloodiest battles of the Crimean War. War had made him brash and impulsive but had also left him with survival skills. Schedel neither knew nor cared about Luguiere's background. To him, Luguiere was just a simple sailor who got command of a boat by nothing more than fate. He was glad he and his wife were safe aboard the cutter.

The cutter moved closer to the American lifeboat, and Luguiere and Schedel locked eyes. "Come into my boat," he called to Schedel with a bit more authority than required under the circumstances.[3] Schedel declined. He disliked both the second mate's appearance and his gruff tone. Luguiere issued his order again, only this time with more energy. Schedel persisted in his refusal in part because he found the way the young sailor spoke to him offensive and in part because Luguiere's boat was not as solid looking as the cutter.

Luguiere had met men like Schedel before, educated and arrogant, men who thought they were too good for the likes of him. He turned to his men and roared, "If they don't come willingly, bring them by force."[4] He emphasized the word "force" with enough delight to give Schedel pause. Schedel tried to reason with him. "Your boat looks unsafe," he said almost apologetically. Luguiere's tone softened: "The boat is safe. I swear it!"[5] There was a pause. Luguiere filled it with a reminder that although he was willing to offer the Schedels reassurance, he was unwilling to ignore the captain's orders, "If you don't come, my men will bring you by force."[6] This time, he emphasized the "will." Schedel sat in the cutter, and Luguiere sat in the lifeboat. The two men stared at one another, neither willing to put an end to the impasse.

Schedel broke first. He turned from Luguiere and called to a cabin boy who was working nearby. The boy was the lowest-ranking sailor aboard *Le Lyonnais*, a position filled by a child who wished to become an able seaman. The boy looked in his direction. Schedel pointed to Luguiere's boat and asked, "Is this boat safe?" The boy answered, "Yes, sir."[7] Luguiere smirked. He elected to ignore the condescension and accept victory. He started to make space for Schedel and his wife on his boat, but before the boy could get back to work, Schedel called out to him again: "One more question." The boy stopped and looked at him. So did Luguiere. Schedel pointed at Luguiere and asked, "Is this man an able mariner?"[8] Luguiere stood up with a mind to move toward Schedel, but when the boy answered, "Yes," Schedel and his wife stepped into Luguiere's lifeboat.

Schedel immediately regretted that step. The sting of cold water cut right through his shoe. He looked down to find a pool of water collecting in the center of the boat. Keeping the vessel afloat would require constant bailing. He tried to turn around and go back to his former place on the cutter before he put his second foot down, but Luguiere's men grabbed him with the force they had promised and shoved him in his place. Schedel pleaded for his wife to be returned to the other boat. Luguiere refused after letting him beg just a little longer than necessary.

The reassignment of the Schedels to Luguiere's boat satisfied the captain that there was enough room in the cutter. There were now more than twenty-five passengers commanded by Roussel, among them the first and second engineers, the steward, his nephew, and all ten of the cabin servants.

The two small yawls were moored to the wreck and reserved for the captain and purser. The captain remained on deck, but the first officer, the purser, and some others stepped into their boat. Nestor stayed with the captain and helped put the finishing touches on the raft. He finished at about two o'clock in the afternoon. The men placed on the raft two barrels of wine, two puncheons of water, and enough food to last fifty people at least a month. Devaulx assigned Nestor to the boat commanded by Luguiere and made additional assignments of his most-trustworthy sailors. Anyone not assigned to a lifeboat would take refuge on the ship and later the raft.

The boat in which Luguiere, the Schedels, Solomon, and Nestor found themselves contained twelve others. Most of the men were members of the crew. They included Third Engineer Desfour, Steward's mate Thillaye, a baker named Lambert, a crewman by the name of Joste, Julias Dublic, Alexis Cauvin, Victor Poirreaux, Pierre Bienaimée, and a fireman the crew referred to as "Father François." Other passengers included an Italian named Mr. Domenigo, a Spanish passenger, and Ernestine Bellet of France, for a total of fourteen men and three women. The boat had no navigational instruments. Schedel was right. Judging by the rank of its commander and crew and the social position of the passengers on board, the American lifeboat did not take highest priority. He did little to hide his contempt for those around him, especially the sailors.

Work aboard *Le Lyonnais* finished at about five o'clock in the evening. The lifeboats were full. The raft was complete. Any passengers or crew who were still aboard *Le Lyonnais* left the ship, save for the captain and a few officers. Thirty-six hours had passed since the collision. The weather was cool. The sky was dark and covered with clouds. The wind blew in force. The rain was light, but from time to time the sky opened and poured upon them. The darkness and a tumultuous ocean made it impossible for the small boats to navigate. Devaulx hoped the light of day would bring at least some clarity to the weather if not to their predicament, so he ordered the boats to remain by the wreck all night.

There was still reason to hope. *Le Lyonnais* had been traveling on a major transatlantic route. The steamer fired a cannon the entire time they were building the raft and loading the boats, to attract anyone within earshot to come to their aid. They would continue to fire the cannon all night. Passengers and crew, especially Devaulx, remained optimistic a passing ship would save them.

Luguiere's boat left the steamer and remained nearby as instructed. All the men and women in the boat slept that night except Luguiere, Mr. Schedel, and his wife. The winds carried the lifeboat on the waves. The boat was sometimes driven far away from the steamer. Other times it came so near Schedel feared it would crash into *Le Lyonnais* and sink.

Schedel watched Luguiere and critiqued his every move out loud. "Remain alert!" Schedel yelled. "Watch the waves!" "Don't crash into the ship!" He took every chance he got to remind the young sailor of how much danger they were in. "It's none of your business," Luguiere snapped; nevertheless, he woke the crew and ordered them to stand by for the rest of the night to help keep the boat steady and near the ship.[9]

Twice, the Schedels thought they were saved. The lifeboats were floating at some distance from the ship when the steamer's cannon fired. People in the other boats shouted as the rockets rose into the air. Schedel asked, "What's happening?" Luguiere exclaimed, "A ship! There is a ship in sight!" Schedel woke his wife to tell her that a rescue ship had arrived. Luguiere laughed. "I'm only joking."[10] The crestfallen Schedels settled back into their seats.

The cries that Schedel misinterpreted as cries of joy came from the raft and one of the other boats. The English lifeboat, commanded by Dublot, was floating near the wreck when a heavy wind blew it into the raft and caused people aboard both vessels to scream for help. Planks and loose boards from the raft cracked and sank, and the waves washed

Dublot's boat away. Passengers tumbled into the water. Some were rescued by the raft. Others were never seen again. Later in the evening, a wave crashed a boat into *Le Lyonnais* with such force that people were tossed out and drowned.

The night went on like that, filled with few sights but many sounds: the sound of a cannon steadily firing, the sound of ocean waves cresting and then collapsing on themselves, and the sounds of people screaming. Sometimes the sounds would come all at once, but more often they came one by one.

Sunrise was sobering. The sights it revealed put the sounds in grim context. Many people were tossed from boats during the night. Dublot's lifeboat was long gone. The men and woman lucky enough to survive now clung to the raft, which was overcrowded, damaged, and in danger of falling apart.

Devaulx called all hands to return to *Le Lyonnais*. The Schedels hoped the captain planned to reorganize boats. Luguiere was one of the only boat commanders who did not lose anyone during the night, but, despite his performance, the Schedels welcomed an opportunity to rid themselves of him. Devaulx clarified his order when Luguiere's boat got closer. It pertained only to those aboard the raft. He needed the people on the raft to come aboard the ship so the men could repair, rebuild, and reboard it. Luguiere headed away from *Le Lyonnais*, and, with him, the Schedels' last hope of leaving the lifeboat into which they had been forced vanished.

The boats remained near the wreck. Waves drove two boats into the raft, and the people on them were tossed into an ocean running rough with large swells. Devaulx ordered the boats to pick up anyone struggling in the water. Luguiere tried to reach them, but the condition of the sea and of his boat made precise navigation impossible. Many drowned. Those who did not drown swam to the raft, which was itself at the point of going to pieces. Luguiere had no choice but to leave those in the water to their fates. Approximately two-thirds of the people who had been placed in boats drowned the first night.

Devaulx could no longer wait. He called his officers back to the deckhouse one last time. It was approximately seven o'clock in the morning on November 4. He spread out a map, showed them where they were, and drew a line with his finger to the nearest land. "Pull for Montauk Point," he told them.[11] The captain made one thing clear before he parted ways with his officers, "I will remain here, with the ship, until she sinks." He wished each of his officers Godspeed as they left *Le Lyonnais* for the last time.

CHAPTER 8 | *Abandon Ship*

Frank Leslie's Illustrated News depiction of the passengers standing by the wreck, December 6, 1856. *Author's collection*

CHAPTER 9
The Dragon

THE BARQUE THAT PUNCHED TWO HOLES IN *Le Lyonnais* was long gone. The survivors assumed she had gone down, because she never answered the call of their cannons or circled back to check on the steamship's welfare.

Steamships were still in their infancy in 1856, but sailing ships were a different matter. They had been evolving for thousands of years. The first known ships with sails dated back to 3000 BCE, when the Egyptians added masts to vessels powered by oarsmen. By 1000 BCE, the Phoenicians, Greeks, and Romans traveled the Mediterranean on ships powered by square sails, supplemented with oarsmen when the winds were unfavorable.

Austronesians used catamarans from 3000 to 1500 BCE to establish trade routes in the South China Sea. Routes forged by these ships in the years that followed extended as far as Japan and the western coast of Africa, and vessels became larger to accommodate longer journeys.

By the time of the Han dynasty, 200 BCE to 200 CE, fleets included vessels with as many as four sails. Ships transported cargo and people to and from ports in the area that now encompasses Taiwan, Micronesia, and the islands lying in between mainland Taiwan and mainland East Asia.

Song-dynasty shipbuilders revolutionized sailing in the tenth century with the invention of the junk, a ship with multiple masts and large, square-shaped sails fortified with bamboo battens. The horizontal battens across square sails gave them the texture of crinkled paper lanterns. Junks employed two maritime innovations: rudders and watertight compartments. Wooden rudders attached to the ship's stern used the water's pressure to stabilize steering. Watertight compartments partitioned the ship, so if one compartment flooded, the others kept it afloat. The innovations would later inspire nineteenth-century steamship shipbuilders such as Brunel, who sought to maximize maneuverability and minimize risk of loss in Atlantic crossings.

In 1795, a British ship designer named Sir Samuel Bentham argued to the Royal Navy for his new ships to use watertight compartments based on the junk boat's design. "His idea was not adopted. Bentham had been in China in 1782, and he acknowledged that he had got the idea of watertight compartments by looking at Chinese junks there. Bentham was a friend of Isambard Brunel, so it is possible that he had some influence on Brunel's adoption of longitudinal, strengthening bulkheads in the lower deck of the *Great Britain*."[1]

Junks were primarily used in coastal trade. As time marched on and merchants needed to transport goods farther away, they turned to the dhow, a vessel with origins in East Africa. Dhows are distinct-looking boats with slender wooden hulls and one enormous triangular, "lateen" sail that runs with the keel. Thirteenth-century dhows ranged in size from 100 to 500 tons. Larger ships typically had a mizzenmast with a second lateen sail that was far smaller than the mainsail and gave the vessel additional stability. The ships also featured center-mounted tillers to control the ship's rudder. Fishermen and merchants used dhows for coastal trade and on voyages in the Indian Ocean.

Exploration of the world's oceans marked the fifteenth century as the age of discovery. Sailors turned from commerce to loftier pursuits and set out not only to transport goods but to conquer new continents, earn the favor of kings and queens, and expand empires. Men set sail without knowing where or when their voyage might end. The ships in which they traveled had to be large enough to hold years' worth of supplies, and strong enough to survive a variety of weather conditions and climates. The journeys inspired a new kind of ship, the carrack. The precursor to the Spanish galleon, carracks were wide, three-masted ships with rounded sterns and pointed bows. They were large enough to carry provisions and strong enough to be stable in heavy seas. Carracks were developed by Portuguese shipbuilders, but later Spanish and French shipbuilders created their own versions. Christopher Columbus, Vasco de Gama, and Ferdinand Magellan sailed carracks on their expeditions. Both the forecastle and the aftercastle on carracks rose high and gave the ships the "U" shape for which they are known.

Shipbuilders elongated masts, added sails, and improved hull designs in the centuries that followed, to produce sailing vessels that were larger, faster, and more reliable than before. Ships dominated everything from trade to exploration to warfare and marked the period between the late sixteenth century and mid-nineteenth century as the golden age of sail.

America embraced the age of sail and became a world leader in the production of sailing ships. Three co-occurring events fueled the country's prolific shipbuilding. First, American fishermen and whalers earned their living at sea, and exploding population growth in coastal towns increased demand for fish and whale oil in the early part of the nineteenth century. Second, immigration to the US from Europe required ships large and stable enough to carry passengers across the Atlantic. Third was the Industrial Revolution.

The invention of mechanized manufacturing processes transformed the American economy from an agricultural to an industrial one. Advancements introduced in the late eighteenth century quickened the speed at which cotton could be spun into textiles and, in the decades that followed, spawned the opening of mills and factories across the country. Merchants located their business on the coast for easy access to the ocean, their only practical distribution channel at the time. Populations exploded along the Eastern Seaboard as people came from more-rural areas to the coast in search of work. Merchants needed vessels to move the goods produced in their factories to ports around the world.

The term "sailing ship" was and is still used to describe any vessel that moves on the wind, but classes of ships depend on the purpose to which the ship is suited. In the eighteenth and nineteenth centuries, brigs, schooners, and barques ruled the seas, and each played a specific role in maritime commerce.

A ship's sail plan distinguished one type of ship from another. Sails could be rigged square or fore and aft. Square-rigged sails ran perpendicular to the keel, cutting across the ship. Fore- and aft-rigged sails ran with the keel. Square-rigged sails required more rigging—the ropes, cables, and chains that support the mast—and, thus, more crew to manage them.

Brigs had two masts with square-rigged sails. The fast and maneuverable sail plan made them well suited to serve as merchant vessels and warships. Schooners, smaller vessels that bore two or more masts, all with fore- and aft-rigged sails, were largely reserved for coastal trades such as fishing and short cargo runs.

Full-rigged ships and barques became the vessels of choice for merchants looking to send goods across the world's oceans, but it was the clipper that became the classic American sailing ship. These tall ships had pronounced V-shaped bows, elongated masts, and sleek appearances.

Clippers were square-rigged with a minimum of three masts, but larger ships usually had more than three. Sails covered every available space on masts that often stretched more than 100 feet into the air. Their rigs could be extreme, and clippers often carried additional sails such as royals, skysails, and studding sails, which required manpower to maneuver. More sails required more crew, which made clippers expensive to operate, but merchants made up the difference by moving at a fast "clip" and "clipping" days from a journey's usual length. Soon, shipbuilders up and down America's Eastern Seaboard produced clippers, and the epicenter of construction moved from medium-sized maritime cities such as Baltimore to larger cities such as Boston and New York.

Clippers carried high-value cargo with time-sensitive delivery from the East Coast to far-flung ports in Europe and the Orient. The ships carried tea and exotic goods from the Far East and served as the backbone of the opium trade. Clippers also carried men and supplies to the California gold rush. Top speeds for steamships in the 1850s reached 12 to 13 knots, while a clipper could travel 16 or more.

Maritime historians date the clipper ship era between 1845 and 1869, with the bulk of construction taking place between 1850 and 1856.[2] Production was both explosive and short lived. Clipper sail plans made them less suited for the unpredictable winds encountered in transatlantic travel. Steamships soon eclipsed the clipper's speed, and railways west offered cheaper and less arduous alternatives to cross country travel. These innovations were the death knell for clippers and rendered them extinct.

Clippers received the glory, but barques were the workhorses of the merchant economy in the mid-1850s. The barque was a more enduring vessel designed to achieve decent speed with larger holds. Barque hulls were broader and deeper than clipper hulls and capable of swallowing higher volumes of cargo. The ships often had a single deck and devoted the rest of their space to goods carried.

Barques featured three or more masts, but what made the barque different from other sailing ships was the aftmost mast, the "mizzenmast," which was fore- and aft-rigged. This made it easier to handle than a ship with square-rigged sails. A barque of the same length and tonnage required fewer crew than a clipper ship. For example, a four-masted clipper required a crew of thirty or more, but a four-masted barque could sail with as few as ten men and, for the cost of a few extra days of travel time, saved owners enormous sums in salaries. Barques were also better suited to the challenging North Atlantic winds than their full-rigged counterparts. A full-rigged clipper was faster in perfect winds, but fore- and aft-rigged sails performed better when heading into the wind. The barque's combined sail plan also gave captains more options for adjusting sails in difficult weather. Shipbuilders who wished to combine the aesthetic virtues of the clipper and the utility of the barque created ships that combined the barque's sail plan and high-volume hold with pointed bowsprits and ornate decorations.

Maine produced more wooden sailing vessels in the nineteenth century than any other state. A long coastline nestled on the Penobscot Bay and a forested interior with a healthy supply of timber made it a perfect place to build ships. Shipbuilding became the Maine's primary industry and attracted a workforce from surrounding states. One-third of the state's male population worked for the maritime industry in the mid-nineteenth century.

Maine was known for building fishing schooners in the 1840s but soon turned to building clippers. Maine shipyards built eighty-nine clippers between 1850 and 1856. Many achieved records for speed, including *Snow Squall*, which made a round-trip voyage to Rio de Janeiro in a record fifty-three days; *Red Jacket*, which earned the record for reaching Liverpool in thirteen days; and *Flying Scud*, which reached Marseille, France, in just nineteen days. Bath, Maine, was the fourth-largest port in the United States by 1856, and the port of Waldboro, Maine, was the seventh largest.

Maine shipyards designed to capitalize on the clipper market adapted to build other types of ships, including barques. After the Civil War ended in April 1865, Maine became synonymous with a type of ship called the Downeaster. Downeasters were square-rigged and fuller in size than the clipper but had pointed bows and sleek lines for fast sailing. The ships balanced speed and tonnage, which enabled merchants to deliver large shipments on schedule. The mid-1850s was a period of transition, during which Maine shipbuilders began building more-versatile ships designed to combine the finer attributes of the clipper with larger cargo capacity. Maine earned a reputation for high-quality construction, and builders approached their work as both businessmen and craftsman.

Local merchants used Maine-built coastal ships to carry goods to and from the South in the years before the Civil War. Barques carried loads of lime, hay, fish, timber, ice, and other goods to destined ports and returned with bellies full of cotton bound for northern textile mills. They also carried loads of cotton to England.

The demand for barques resulted in an explosion of new shipyards in Maine. Some sold all their ships to merchants, but others retained interests in some or all their vessels. This not only alleviated some of the costs to buyers but provided shipbuilders with a steady stream of income to finance expansion of their yards or investments in future ships. "Mainers kept a financial interest in these ships, frequently providing captains and officers, and Maine ships were recognized in most ports of the world. Investing in them resulted in the wealth that created the attractive towns surrounding the [Penobscot] Bay."[3]

Columbia Perkins Carter of Belfast, Maine, was one the most prolific shipbuilders of the period. He is credited with constructing more than a hundred vessels in Belfast from 1841, when he opened his shipyard, to his death in 1876. Carter moved to Belfast from Montville, Maine, at the age of nineteen and found work in the shipyards. "[He] appears to have been a natural at his profession, for in 1839, just seven years after his initial baptism into the craft of wooden boats, he served as master workman for the brig *Democrat* . . . built by J. Y. McClintock in 1840."[4]

Throughout the years, Carter took on a series of partners to build ships and created a complex legacy of connections to prominent Belfast businessmen. Carter, like other Maine builders, produced mostly schooners in the early 1840s. In the latter part of the 1840s and early 1850s, his yard built schooners, brigs, and barques. He was a perfectionist. He spared no pains in acquiring material for his ships and became known for his attention to detail, structural innovations, and sound construction. His reputation soon proceeded him not just in the Northeast but as far as the East Indies and Australia.

Carter Shipyard, Belfast, Maine. *Courtesy of Belfast Historical Society & Museum*

Belfast was the perfect location for a shipbuilder. The city sits at the mouth of the Passagassawakeag River estuary on Belfast Bay and Penobscot Bay, with easy access to the Atlantic. It was only 30 miles from Bangor and 40 miles from Augusta by land, and close to the ports of Boston and Portland. Farther inland, Maine farmers grew the timber used in shipbuilding throughout the world, including white pine prized for ships' masts. Neighboring Bangor was the lumber capital of the world by the mid-nineteenth century and shipped more than 200,000 board feet of lumber annually.[5] Mills floated the logs in ships downriver to cities such as Belfast and to shipyards such as Carter's.

Carter entered into a partnership with a group of local businessmen in 1855, including Patterson, J. Havener, Jonathan Durham, Charles Durham, and others. The newly formed company, called Patterson & Carter, constructed a new yard on the waterfront in Upper Steamboat Wharf for building ships and erected a building on the site to house the firm's offices. Newspapers put great stock in the new venture, "From what we know of the skill and energy of the members of the firm, we are warranted in saying they are bound to take front rank among the shipbuilders of Maine."[6] Carter retained an interest in Patterson & Carter, but it operated independently from Carter & Company's existing operations.

The first ship produced from the partnership was a three-masted wooden barque called *Adriatic*. Designed for transatlantic travel, she had one deck and a large hold for cargo. She was of average size for a barque of her day: 400 tons, 123 feet long, 30 feet wide, and 12 feet deep. The barque had a pointed bow and a square stern. One of her most impressive features was a long, decorative bowsprit.

The firm spared no expense on *Adriatic* and hoped to use her to distinguish itself among Maine shipbuilders. A reporter called the barque, "in model, material, and workmanship [a ship] that would bear comparison with any vessel of the class launched here."[7]

Jonathan Durham Sr., one of the investors in *Adriatic*, was a farmer and former ship captain who owned land in Belfast, Maine. His ancestors were among the men who founded the city. His father, John Durham, had invested in land throughout Waldo County, Maine, which Jonathan Sr. inherited. Durham knew Carter from local business and political circles and owned a shop on Miller Street next to the Carter shipyard.

Jonathan Durham Sr. entered the partnership with Carter not necessarily for himself but for the benefit of his two sons, Charles and Jonathan Jr. Charles was an aspiring lumber dealer, and the partnership with Carter provided lucrative business opportunities for him. Durham's other son, Jonathan Barnet Durham, was a sailor, and the partners hired him to command the vessel.

Captain Jonathan Barnet Durham left Belfast in his new ship on October 31, 1856, along with a crew of nine sailors. He set out for Savannah, Georgia, carrying a load of lime and hay. From there, he planned to pick up a load of timber and head to La Ciotat, France. To get there, he would sail southeast, clear the Nantucket Shoals and proceed southwest to Georgia. The Durham family had high hopes for the journey. Jonathan Durham Sr. had invested a significant sum of money in the venture with Carter.

Adriatic could fit the general description of many Maine-built barques of the day, save for one remarkable characteristic—her billet head, a decorative piece of woodwork that adorned the bow, and a figurehead at the point of the bow. Figureheads themselves were not uncommon, especially in Maine, where woodcarving was an art. The most popular were images of women with flowing gowns and hair to mimic the impact of an ocean breeze. Shipbuilders also chose nautical or patriotic themes such as mermaids, Neptune, sailors, and bald eagles with open wings. The carvings were intricate and painted in bright colors. They served both as a focal point for the ship and as a means of identification. *Adriatic*'s billet carving was as unique as it was intricate. There could be no mistaking her for another barque. She was adorned with a dragon, painted black with a gilt mane, red piercing eyes, an open mouth, and a gold dart for a tongue.

CHAPTER 10

Adrift

CAPTAIN DEVAULX HAD HOPED the daylight would bring his weary passengers and crew some clarity. It did, but it was not the clarity he wanted. In the daylight, those aboard the lifeboats could see the vastness of the ocean. They could see the horizon. It stretched out in all directions, yet, at every place, the sky met nothing but water. They could also see *Le Lyonnais*. Her bow was higher now. Her stern hung heavier beneath the waves. Yesterday, the passengers and crew felt some safety in her shadow, but it was now clear that their only hope of rescue lay in sailing small and damaged boats across miles of open ocean. The daylight amplified their fears.

Luguiere turned the American lifeboat over to another sailor while he met Devaulx on the ship to receive his final orders. He bid the captain and his fellow sailors goodbye and started down the rope ladder to the waiting boat. There was no time for sentiment. He admired Devaulx and hoped he would see him again one day soon but turned his thoughts to what was next. He looked down and saw the faces of those now in his charge. He took his duties seriously but was not necessarily overwhelmed with compassion for his comrades or by the sudden realization that their fate now rested in his hands. He was, if truth be told, excited about the prospect of navigating their small boat to safety. Luguiere was twenty-eight years old—old enough to lead but not quite old enough to understand what leadership meant to those who had no choice but to follow.

Luguiere's thirst for adventure was not new. He volunteered for dangerous duty during the Crimean War. He requested assignment aboard the steamship *L'Aigle* and fought in the 1854 Battle of Bomarsund, when British and French forces attacked an uncompleted fortress in the Baltic Sea. The Russians chose the location of the fortress, the Aland Islands, because they believed that large ships would not be able to pass through the narrow waters surrounding it. This was true for sailing ships but not steamships, which required less draft. British forces bombed the fortress using steamships in June 1854, and in a battle that lasted from the end of July to the beginning of August, British and French forces succeeded. Luguiere also served at Sebastopol, aboard *Mogador*, and in the fall of 1854, participated in a series of battles to capture and destroy a strategic Russian military stronghold in the Black Sea. Luguiere engaged not only in naval operations but in field battery onshore. He was fresh from the war when he found work on *Le Lyonnais*.

Luguiere was glad to have so many sailors in his boat. He knew some better than others. Joste and Cauvin served on the deck crew and had been under his command all along. He was less acquainted with the firemen who labored below deck unseen, but he knew firemen were a hardy sort and was glad to have them aboard. Besides, every crew member in the boat had proven himself worthy when working with the captain to save the ship.

The passengers were a different matter. George Schedel, for whom he had no use, was the only able-bodied man among them. The rest were either women or old men. Luguiere doubted any of them would be able to carry their weight. To make matters worse, only the sailors and the Schedels, who had taken their coats and hats with them when they left their cabin, were dressed for the weather, and the growing swells foretold of storms.

Flora Solomon and Ernestine Bellet were naked by Victorian standards. Solomon sprang from bed after the collision wearing nothing but her nightgown. Bellet was similarly dressed. The sailors brought five coverlids into the boat. These quilted pieces of canvas were not waterproof, but water resistant enough to protect the boat from the elements. The sailors kept two for that purpose and gave the remaining coverlids to the women to keep them warm. Bellet wrapped the material around her body and relished the warmth it provided. Solomon did the same but felt a tinge of guilt deriving benefit from something the group might need.

Everyone was in their places and as comfortable as possible under the circumstances. Solomon looked around. There were only three lifeboats left: Luguiere's, Roussel's cutter, and the purser's yawl. The thought gave her chill. It must have done the same to the captain. "Keep together," he cautioned as the boats set off.

The sailors set their oars in the water and started to row, but before the boat got too far from *Le Lyonnais*, Luguiere noticed another boat coming toward him. It was Purser Baumstarck's yawl. He thought at first that Devaulx was sending a new group of passengers to join his party, but he soon realized that the yawl contained only an officer and one occupant. The occupant looked like a man he knew. Luguiere held his hand to his forehead to block the wind and squinted to get a better look. When he saw he was correct, his hand fell from his head, and he sighed with relief. Just for a second, a smile curled in the corners of his mouth.

The passengers exchanged glances, anxious to know why the captain had sent two men out to them. The yawl pulled alongside. "This sailor was once assigned to your boat," said the officer. "He ought to be with you still."[1] The officer's words got the passengers' attention. They were miserable from a night spent in too-close quarters and met the arrival of an eighteenth person with skepticism. They whispered to one another, but Luguiere had no time for any of it. He stretched his hand out to help the man aboard.

Schedel asked what the passengers were thinking: "Who is this man?" Luguiere was so pleased by the new sailor's arrival that he dispensed with the bitter tone he reserved for Schedel. "Choupault."[2] He answered with certainty as if the name itself were a sentence with a beginning, a middle, and an end.

Jean-Louis-Marie Choupault was a deck sailor. He too had served his country in Crimea, although he did not speak much about his exploits there. Luguiere had always liked him. He was a good seaman, capable and strong, with a jovial nature that would serve them well on a journey into the unknown. "I am glad of it," announced Luguiere. "He is a clever man."[3] Dublic, Cauvin, and the other sailors smiled. They too were happy to see Choupault and greeted him with open arms. The newly formed group of eighteen passengers and crew parted from the ship for good.

Luguiere's boat joined the others, and together they made way northwest. Unlike the other boats, which were fully provisioned, Luguiere's boat had no compass.[4] They intended to stay with the other boats not only for safety, but so they could follow for navigation.

Choupault took the helm of the boat to which he was assigned. "American," he muttered to himself, this time referring to the lifeboat's design. He went to work straightaway and inspected the boat to ensure she was as seaworthy as possible under the circumstances. The lifeboat was made of wood and similar in appearance to a rowboat. Unlike the cutters, which had broader sterns, this lifeboat was pointed on both ends. It had wooden planks, or thwarts, that sat perpendicularly to the bow with enough room for about eighteen to twenty people. It was adequate for their numbers, but there was not much room to spare. The lifeboat had a small mast and sail at the bow to catch the wind, and a rudder and tiller to maneuver it from side to side.

A strong breeze blew. Small waves began to form, and white rolls of foam floated on top of them. "North wind," Choupault noted. The thought ignited in him the same uneasiness it does in all sailors. Bitter cold and stormy weather almost always accompany the north wind, especially in late autumn. Mythology from Greek to Norse to Inuit proves this has been true for generations. While the myths depicted other winds as benevolent deities, the north wind was always the vengeful, angry god with the short fuse. Choupault could not help but laugh to himself at their misfortune, "It has to be the north wind."

Steering the boat would be difficult. The direction of the wind left little doubt the storm would grow as the day wore on, and sweep the swells into larger waves. Even now, the waves rocked the boat from time to time, a troubling prospect in heavy seas. Choupault knew the passengers would be at risk every time the boat met a decent-sized wave. One pitch could send a man overboard. He inspected the rudder and tiller to ensure they were in good working order. They were not. He used an oar to alter the steering mechanism and did not stop adjusting until he was sure he could maneuver the boat in any weather.

The boat took on water during the night, which had not receded during the day. "The boat has a leak," Choupault thought to himself. He suggested to Luguiere that they organize the crew to bail the water with whatever was available, including one of the canvases and empty containers. They stretched the remaining canvas across the boat to keep out some of the water in the likely event a large wave washed up and over them. The crewmen took turns bailing and resigned themselves to the fact that this routine would have to go on incessantly if they were to survive the journey.

The boat moved away from *Le Lyonnais*. Some of the passengers turned to take one last look at the dying ship as Choupault worked, Solomon among them. The ship seemed to her to be sliding into the water in an act that was at once graceful and terrifying. She looked away. She preferred to concentrate on where she was going rather than where she had been.

Luguiere's eyes searched not for his ship but for his captain. He saw Devaulx in the distance with some of his men in one of his yawls. They floated near the raft. The captain was a good man. Luguiere took in the scene for a moment. He wished Devaulx well but knew what standing by the wreck meant. "In the end," he thought to himself, "the water always wins."[5]

George Schedel was the last to turn back. *Le Lyonnais* was still high out of the water, and the captain's yawl and the raft were still tethered to the ship. He expected to watch the raft break loose and set upon the waves. Instead, he saw something strange. The captain's yawl left. This was peculiar, considering it was both custom and the captain's stated intention to stand by the wreck until the end. The raft was still moored to *Le Lyonnais*'s hull with a thick rope. A man stood ready to cut her loose with an ax when the ship sank, but there were still many men aboard the ship.

The raft was crowded. Passengers and crew huddled together. Women and children, whose boats broke and sank during the night, now found themselves among them. They clung to one another and to what little structure there was as the ocean tossed the raft about. It was strapped together and had no oars or sails. Once those aboard cut her loose, the raft would drift at the mercy of the waves. It would be a miracle if it survived one night.

Schedel's heart bled with the sight of the unhappy people left behind. He could no longer make out individual people in the distance. The passengers were now just a thick swarm. They cried out as the lifeboats pulled away. He did not know whether they had fallen victim to yet another wave or if they were crying from despair as those in the boats abandoned them to an obvious fate.

Choupault was the only one who did not look back. He focused on the task at hand. Although he was not in command, he had assumed the responsibility both of navigating at pace with the other lifeboats and preventing their boat from capsizing. He took the first shift at the helm.

The survivors were hungry. They had little food or water since whatever they had eaten on the evening of November 1, approximately sixty hours before. Those sixty hours were grueling, particularly for the sailors, who spent them bailing the ship, throwing heavy objects overboard, and assisting with the lifeboats. No one slept. The crew and passengers suffered from the effects of hunger, thirst, and fatigue before their boat even set to sea.

Devaulx told his men that each boat had been supplied with enough food for fifteen days. The main source of nutrition was a bag of ship biscuits, an inexpensive and long-lasting cracker made from flour, water, and salt, meant for survival. The biscuits were left to dry after baking to prevent spoilage, which made them hard and almost impossible to chew in their raw form. Sailors called them "molar breakers" or "sheet iron." Soldiers called them "hardtack." What hardtack lacked in taste it made up for in calories, a vital source of energy in a survival situation. The boat's supply also included one saucisson de Lyon, some preserves, and six bottles of wine. There was no water. The supply had been spoiled during the collision, and the only available puncheons had not been allocated to Luguiere's vessel. The remaining water and food stores could not be reached because they were in holds in the ship's stern.

One of the sailors opened the bag of ship biscuits. He reached in expecting to feel the familiar, cardboard-like texture he had so often eaten at sea. The bag instead felt like wet sand. The stream of waves washing over the boat had turned the biscuits into salty paste. Lambert, the baker, sighed when he saw they were ruined. The sailor set the biscuits aside for the moment and turned to the sausage and preserves. He handed out equal amounts to each man and woman.

Solomon was starving. She placed the food in her mouth only to find it so dry she could barely chew. It was even more difficult to swallow. The food caked to the sides of her throat and clung there. The sailor rationed two bottles of wine. Each person's share amounted to about one-third of a cup when divided among eighteen. Solomon waited for the wine. The small sip did little good and only served as a reminder of how much more she wanted to drink. She attempted to eat one of the pasty ship's biscuits, but it was so salty it only increased her thirst.

Choupault ate what was offered but had no time to despair over its sufficiency or taste. The storm increased in size and strength, as he knew it would. Staying afloat in the rough seas would be no easy feat. It required skill, strength, and, most importantly, the ability to read the direction of the wind and waves. He started to get a feel for the vessel and made mental notes of how she moved on the open ocean, the best way to steer her, and how she confronted the oncoming waves.

Moving perpendicularly into a wave risked being swept up as it crested, and injuring either the boat or its occupants as the boat crashed down on the other side. A wave from the side could swamp the boat with water or, worse, capsize it. Choupault approached each large wave at a slight angle, so the boat rose and fell on its longest axis. This allowed it to pitch and roll, which decreased the amount of stress both on the passengers and the boat.

Steering in the rough water was grueling. Choupault used the full weight of his body against the oar to create the resistance required to turn the boat as each wave approached. When the waves crested, they swirled with white foam and sent spray toward the boat that blinded him as he steered. He mopped his eyes and kept a watch on the size, shape, and direction of approaching waves and shouted out when it was time for the passengers to brace for large ones. He monitored the skies for changes in the wind and the weather. He checked the other boats in the event that they needed assistance, or the opposite became true. His eyes were ever scanning for a vessel that might save them. Choupault thought about the moment of the collision, about his suspicion that once he got to work it would be a long time until he could rest, and he laughed silently to himself.

He had been awake since the collision. He too had lifted heavy objects from *Le Lyonnais*'s deck and thrown them overboard, bailed water in an effort to save her, and helped load the lifeboats. During the night, however, when his companions rested in the lifeboat, he worked aboard *Le Lyonnais*, fortified the raft, and assisted the captain. Now that he was assigned to a boat, it was Choupault who saw to it she was as prepared as possible. When he was not making repairs, rowing, or steering, he helped the others with the bailing. The other men assisted, but the responsibility for keeping the boat afloat, for keeping them alive from moment to moment, had become his.

It was now late afternoon. Choupault's body was breaking. He surveyed the boat and the passengers. The bailing was working. The water in the bottom of the boat came up to their ankles but seemed to stay at that level. The passengers settled down. They were growing accustomed to the constant movement of the boat. The weather was awful but holding. The waves were high, but there was a predictable rhythm to their rise and fall. The passengers were getting better about seeing the big waves coming, and bracing themselves as they struck. The night would be difficult. Worst-case scenario was that the storm would grow stronger. Even if it did not, the waves would feel stronger and more frightening because no one would be able to see them coming. Choupault knew. Darkness can break even the strongest man at sea.

Things were stable. It seemed like as good a time as any to get some rest. Choupault asked one of the other sailors to relieve him and gave the boat one last look before he took his place on a bench. He reminded the sailor of the many tasks at hand, "Keep up the bailing. Watch the waves. Steer into them." He gave the sailor explicit instructions: "We have no compass. Above all else, stay with the other boats." Choupault sat down on the bench and fell fast asleep.

Choupault's replacement was not as capable an oarsman. He allowed the boat to fall leeward, pushed away from the others by the force of the wind. Rather than wake Choupault, the sailor followed in the general direction of the other boats and did his best to keep them on the horizon. The distance between the boats grew in a span of less than an hour. A thick fog set in. Now lost, the sailor woke Choupault, but it was too late. The other boats were impossible to see. Their boat was now alone, without a compass, and drifting on the wind. Choupault, once again, took the helm.

The fog lifted in the late afternoon. The twilight was clear and somewhat calm. Choupault used the position of the dying sun to set a course northwest.

Night fell.

Choupault remained at the helm for hours, and found himself there long after nightfall. His muscles now burned each time he forced the oar against a wave. His bones ached. His eyelids hung heavy. His eyes, long accustomed to seeing for miles in the dead of night, now blurred the sea, the sky, and the waves into an open field of bluish black. The storm had not changed much in the few hours that had passed since they lost sight of the other boats, but the waves seemed to come at him much faster now. He feared he might miss one or, worse, fall asleep where he sat. He turned the boat over to Luguiere and took a seat on one of the thwarts. He fell asleep only seconds later. Luguiere was at the helm no more than five minutes before he turned the boat over to another sailor.

CHAPTER 11

Perils of the Sea

Water, water, everywhere,
And all the boards did shrink;
Water, water, everywhere,
Nor any drop to drink.[1]

—"Rime of the Ancient Mariner,"
Samuel Taylor Coleridge, 1798

THE PARADOX OF BEING STRANDED AT SEA is dying slowly of thirst while surrounded by water. Winter in the North Atlantic, however, presents dangers beyond the lack of fresh water. The cold can kill a man even more quickly, and the combination of frigid temperatures, the lack of potable water, and extreme fatigue magnifies the chances of death when stranded at sea.

Water is a crucial ingredient to the chemistry of the human body. It helps the brain think, maintains blood flow, transports nutrients throughout the body, lubricates joints, supports cell structure, facilitates muscle movement, and flushes waste. Total body water comprises anywhere from 45 to 75 percent of a person's body weight. Muscle mass is 70 to 75 percent water, while water in tissue can vary between 10 and 40 percent. It is impossible to know exactly how long a person can survive without fresh water, because biological and situational factors determine an individual's ability to go for long periods without it.

The body retains moisture when water is lacking. Cells shrink as the body diverts water from them into the bloodstream to defend vital organs. The first signs of dehydration include dizziness and headaches. Motor skills and strength decrease as dehydration sets in. Thirst and dry mouth follow, signals sent by the brain to remind the body to rehydrate. Even in the earliest stage of dehydration, the body is unable to produce tears or perform any function that requires the unnecessary expenditure of water.

The kidneys receive less water as dehydration continues, which thickens the blood. Urine output decreases, and any urine produced is dark, yellow, and concentrated until the body stops producing it. The heart rate increases to maintain oxygen levels. Breathing becomes rapid as the body tries to compensate by taking in more oxygen. The skin, once devoid of moisture, starts to shrivel and lose elasticity. It will remain in place for few seconds when pinched and slowly sink back to normal. A dehydrated person's eyes may become sunken and hollow as the skin tightens from lack of water. Once the blood becomes too concentrated, blood pressure drops and leads to listlessness and lack of consciousness.

The brain and heart are approximately 73 percent water.[2] Brain cells, like the other cells in the body, shrink when deprived of it. The cell constriction can cause abnormal brain function that manifests as episodes of delirium, violence, or confusion.

British neurologist MacDonald Critchley studied the effects of dehydration on shipwrecked sailors in the 1940s and 1950s. He reviewed records and survival stories and concluded that few sailors died of dehydration alone. It was first the cold and then drinking seawater to combat the early stages of dehydration that caused the deaths of the shipwreck victims he studied. He wrote, "As dehydration increases, the victim's will to resist the desire to drink sea water weakens until finally he succumbs to the temptation and death is caused by the ingestion of sea water. Sea water poisoning must be accounted, after cold, the commonest cause of death in shipwrecked sailors."[3]

Salt is the enemy at sea, and the impact of drinking seawater is well documented. The salinity of human blood is 9 percent. Seawater is a hypertonic fluid, meaning it has greater salinity than blood. Seawater, at 35 percent, has almost four times more salt than the human body can process through the kidneys and expel through the urine. Tissues in the body contain some fresh water that, as part of an ordinary diet, is used to dilute salt. The body steals from the organs when there is not enough fresh water available. The process increases dehydration and thirst. Because the body cannot urinate enough to compensate for the intake of salt, it craves more water. This leads to a cycle of drinking more seawater, which accelerates dehydration and leads to organ failure. The brain is one of the organs that shuts down. Drinking salt water hastens the hallucinations, violent outbursts, confusion, listlessness, and loss of consciousness that are the hallmarks of death by dehydration.

Critchley tells what happens when a very dehydrated person drinks seawater. There is "immediate slaking, followed quite soon by an exacerbation of the thirst, which will require still more copious draughts. The victim then becomes silent and apathetic, with a peculiar fixed and glassy expression in the eyes. The condition of the lips, mouth, and tongue worsens, and a peculiarly offensive odour has been described in the breath. Within an hour or two, delirium sets in, quiet at first but later violent and unrestrained; consciousness is gradually lost; the color of the face changes and froth appears at the corners of the lips. Death may take place quietly: more often it is a noisy termination, and not infrequently the victim goes over the side in his delirium and is lost."[4]

There are countless tales of sailors who went mad from drinking seawater. In 1859, a sailor named Brown from the crew of *Florence Nightingale* drank seawater after a shipwreck. His behavior became so erratic that the fellow occupants of his lifeboat drew straws to choose who would kill him. Brown got a short reprieve when the captain caught a fish, but died shortly afterward and was thrown overboard. Passengers in a lifeboat from *Evening Star*, a ship that wrecked in a storm off Cape Hatteras in 1866, began drinking seawater after seventy-two hours in the boats. They became so mad they "lost their reason."[5] The seamen in command "were compelled to threaten any person who drank seawater should be thrown overboard before the terrible evil could be checked."[6]

John Rutledge, a packet steamer out of Liverpool bound for New York, struck ice and sank in 1856. She took 150 passengers and crew with her. Thirteen people drifted in a lifeboat for nine days. They died one by one, each succumbing to their own private combination of cold, exhaustion, and thirst.

One deckhand, Thomas W. Nye, a descendant of the famous New Bedford and Fairhaven whaling family, survived to tell the tale. Provisioned with only 6 pounds of biscuits, 1 gallon of water, and one bottle of brandy, the *John Rutledge* survivors fought over food. All the passengers except Nye turned to drinking seawater when the food was gone, a mistake that drove most of them mad before it accelerated their deaths. He described his experience as being "trapped with twelve lunatics" and the final moments of those who perished as "an old story of delirium and death."[7] One man, who had been quiet all day, suddenly turned to his wife and ripped her hair from her head in clumps. He died with bloody chunks of her scalp in his hands. Another crew member became so insane that he bit into a woman's arm. The boatswain tried to throw the oars overboard just twelve hours after he started drinking seawater, and when Nye prevented him, he struck Nye in the head with a bucket and split open his chin. Nye bore the scar for the rest of his life.

Those in the safety of a lifeboat may dive inexplicably into the sea. In 1872, survivors of *Missouri*, which caught fire and sank near the Bahamas, reported that two in their boat became "very crazy."[8] The men kept jumping from the lifeboat into shark-infested waters, only to be dragged back by their companions. "Several times they jumped overboard, but we succeeded in rescuing them from a horrible death, as the sharks were all around us; we could see their fins, but they did not molest us in the boat. The same men jumped overboard again, and we stopped pulling at the oars, but the poor fellows disappeared. This had a terrible effect on us. Two of them died on board, and we heaved their bodies overboard.... The men all ran mad before they died, and several times made an attack on us and some of them even bit us."[9]

Cold is another lethal enemy. Exposure produces effects similar to dehydration, but for different reasons. Hypothermia occurs when body temperature drops to an abnormally low level. It can kill quickly or slowly. Falling into cold ocean water can kill a person in minutes, while prolonged exposure to extreme temperatures can cause a person to lose consciousness and expire.

The human brain is sensitive to even small changes in temperature. The hypothalamus, the part of the brain that recognizes changes in body temperature, initiates physical responses to bring the temperature back in line. The body shivers to generate heat; however, if the body loses heat faster than it can make it, the core temperature falls. The body withdraws blood from the skin as the body temperature falls, to reduce the amount of heat that escapes, and redirects blood to protect the vital organs, such as the heart, lungs, kidney, and brain. The heart and brain are most sensitive to lower temperatures. A decrease in brain function occurs in direct relationship to the decrease in body temperature and stops altogether when the body reaches a core temperature of approximately 93 degrees Fahrenheit. Electrical activity in the brain slows down as the body becomes colder, making it difficult to think or even move. The interference with brain activity is dangerous because it often prevents a person from recognizing that something is wrong and asking for help. Individuals suffering from hypothermia are at great risk of lying down, falling asleep, and dying, with no one noticing until it is too late.

A person may do or say strange things as the body shuts down. Climbers experiencing hypothermia have been known to strip off items of clothing or remove clothing all together. This happens because brain has shut down certain areas of the body and signals that these areas are no longer cold.

Early symptoms of hypothermia include loss of coordination and numbness in the extremities. What may begin as an increase in appetite gives way to apathy as the core temperature drops. A person may experience slurred speech and skin that is pale and cold to the touch as symptoms progress. Shivering is a sign that the body's core temperature has dropped below 93 degrees. Decreasing consciousness, a slowed heart rate, and difficulty breathing follow. The person may then go in and out of consciousness and become unable to respond to communication. Breathing and pulse become faint and difficult to detect. Just prior to death, the muscles in the body become rigid, almost as if in rigor mortis, and the pupils will no longer dilate. The symptoms can make a person appear dead even though they may not yet be. Loss of consciousness followed by organ failure ultimately causes death.

Frostbite is a close companion to hypothermia. Another condition caused by the cold; it alone can cause anything from discomfort to death. In the early stages of hypothermia, the body draws blood away from the limbs to protect the vital organs, leaving the extremities—typically hands, feet, ears, and lips—vulnerable. A condition called the hunter's response begins as the extremities farthest from the heart become cold. Blood vessels intermittently dilate and constrict to preserve as much extremity function as possible. When the brain senses a danger of hypothermia, however, it permanently constricts the blood vessels to prevent them from returning cold blood to the internal organs, and frostbite begins.

It starts as frost nip, a numbing of the skin caused by the constriction of blood vessels, a condition that warming up indoors cures. When exposure to the cold continues, second-degree frostbite sets in. The skin becomes white, blue, or blotchy, and the skin feels hard and cold to the touch as the layers of tissue below the surface begin to freeze. Tiny blood clots might occur as circulation decreases. The limbs may begin to swell and even feel warm. Severe (or third-degree) frostbite occurs as time wears on and as the damage goes deep enough to reach the tendons, muscles, nerves, and even bones. Severe frostbite usually causes some permanent tissue death.

November in the North Atlantic is a perfect host for life-threatening conditions. Cold and lack of water affect both the brain and the body in a myriad of ways. The extent to which these conditions might affect a person is controlled not only by the temperature and the availability of provisions but by a person's health going into a survival situation. Age and fatigue and improper nourishment are risk factors for dehydration and hypothermia. Someone who is young or healthy or well hydrated going into a lifeboat on the open sea will fare better than a person who is old or sickly or fatigued.

Extreme fatigue is an overexertion without sleep or nourishment, and it too can be fatal. Exertion depletes the body's resources. Fatigue brought on by physical exertion has an impact both on the body and the mind unless those resources are replenished by food and rest. Mental acuity decreases. It can happen quickly and lead to, among other symptoms, confusion and problems with coordination. A simple task such as walking a straight line can easily confuse a person who is physically exhausted. Extreme fatigue also causes apathy, depression, and feelings of hopelessness.

CHAPTER 12
Forged in a Storm

THE MOON ROSE AT ABOUT NINE O'CLOCK IN THE EVENING. The wind rose with it. It came from the north and brought with it an intense power and a biting chill. Choupault was still asleep in his place on the thwarts, slumped between the side of the boat and a neighboring sailor. His body was limp and lifeless. Only his head moved. It snapped and rolled as the boat lurched and swayed in the waves.

Luguiere stood by as Choupault's replacement steered. He did not steer well. The boat pitched in waves that increased in both size and strength, and the sailor did little to control it. Choupault slept. The boat's violent movements shook everyone but him.

It was blowing a gale. The waves crested and broke in whirls of white foam. Some exceeded 20 feet. Those that did crashed with such force they threw off spindrifts. The spray flew on the wind toward the passengers and pelted their faces with salt and bitter cold as they strained to keep their eyes open.

Luguiere shot disapproving glances and barked occasional orders at the sailor at the helm but never assumed command of the lifeboat himself. It was as if he knew he could do no better under the circumstances and wished to save himself the embarrassment. The passengers already knew. They looked at one another and, in those desperate glances, agreed they would be dead before morning if their fate rested in the hands of the sailor now at the helm. The same thought crossed everyone's mind. Choupault was the only man with the skill, the knowledge, and the strength to steer the boat in these conditions.

CHAPTER 12 | *Forged in a Storm*

Schedel was usually quick to point out Luguiere's imperfections, but he too was silent. He resisted the urge to speak lest Luguiere dig in and insist on keeping this new sailor in his place. All Schedel and the others could do was pray that Luguiere would realize on his own that he needed to wake Choupault and get him to take over.

The winds grew stronger. The sea rose higher. More of the waves grew tall, folded over onto themselves, and sent the boat on chaotic rides. Luguiere finally moved to wake Choupault when the waves swelled to a size that disturbed even him.

The passengers breathed a collective sigh of relief when Luguiere called Choupault's name, but it was short lived. Choupault did not move. "Wake up!" Luguiere shook him by the arm. Still nothing. Luguiere shook the sailor more violently now. "Get up!" Choupault did not stir. Luguiere grabbed the sailor's body with both of his hands and shook him again.

Choupault finally moved his head. "I'm sick," he groaned. "I want to sleep."[1] His speech was so slurred they could barely make out the words. Luguiere tried to rouse Choupault one more time, but he no longer moved. He slumped in his space on the bench in a lifeless hulk.

Choupault's eyes were closed. They had melted into their sockets and dissolved into a black void. Opening them was an impossible task. His body burned. His back was broken. His resolve gone. The very idea of moving seemed abstract to him. Part of him was still there. That part wanted to get up—to do his duty—but it was a command his body simply could not follow. Both the soldier and the sailor in him had never refused an order, but now, refusal was his only option, and it was so much easier than he thought. Once he refused to get up, the duel inside his mind ended. Refusing released him.

"No," uttered Choupault. This single syllable took effort to pronounce, but speaking it put him at peace. Luguiere's voice went distant. The darkness opened into a light he yearned to follow. Not one of Choupault's muscles was tense. He floated away. He no longer cared about being a sailor or obeying orders or saving lives or the wind or the rain or the waves or the goddamn boat. He traded it all for some rest. "I won't get up." He slid into a peaceful dream. "I will stay here. I won't get up. I won't . . . will." His voice trailed off into a hush until his lips moved but made no sound at all.

"You are the only man who can steer this boat!"[2] It was Luguiere who screamed. His own words surprised him as they leapt from his mouth. He did not expect to say it. To do so was to admit that although he was the man who was in charge, he was not the man they needed. The truth hung in the air for just a moment before one of the passengers spoke.

George Schedel broke the silence. He did not address Luguiere but, instead, moved closer to Choupault. He leaned over the man now wilted on the wooden board beside them and put his lips next to his ear. "Help us," Schedel whispered. There was a moment's pause before the others joined, each pleading with Choupault to get up. Luguiere spoke again. He repeated the same words as before, only this time he committed to their truth. "You are the only one who can steer this boat." Choupault's friend Dublic joined the other voices. "Get up, my friend," he said gently. "Get up, and I will help you."

Choupault was in a faraway place on the other end of their prayers. The pleas of the passengers and sailors overlapped one another and washed over him like discordant music. He heard the words ever so faintly at first. It took what seemed like an eternity for him to latch on—to reach for the meaning and allow the sounds to bring him back. The darkness filled in behind his eyes, and he felt again the cold sting of the north wind. He clenched his fists and once again felt the ache in his hands and as he crunched his frozen fingers. He took in a shallow breath and then a deeper one, before letting it out. It seemed to the passengers like hours before his eyes fluttered open and he looked up at them. Dublic extended his arm to his friend. Choupault took it and used all his might to steady himself as he rose and crept back to the oar.

The sea state forced him back. He sat near the makeshift helm and took stock of what had transpired in his absence. It was the dead of night. The sky was black and sunk down over the water. The winds blew in force, and the waves roared around them. They could rise as high as 30 feet if the wind continued to blow this way. If it was difficult to navigate the wind and the waves during the day, it would be almost impossible to do so now. The wind came from the north, so there was no point in trying to head in that direction. Sails were no good. They were a liability in such weather. The singular goal that evening would be to stay afloat.

"I need you here," said Choupault to Dublic as he pointed to the space on the bench beside him. His coherence alone comforted the passengers. Dublic moved next to him to act as a lookout for oncoming waves. He was a much-needed second pair of eyes on what promised to be an impossible night.

The storm tossed the boat like a plaything. Choupault and Dublic struggled to keep it pointed in any direction, but even with their best efforts, it pitched and rolled beneath them. It took everything in Choupault's power to keep the boat from capsizing and to keep himself from going back to sleep.

Ernestine Bellet and Ms. Schedel shrieked every time an unexpected movement took the boat. Solomon was just as frightened as the others,

CHAPTER 12 | *Forged in a Storm*

but she braced herself in her seat and tried not to let it show. Fear was a liability that only made it harder for the men to do their jobs. She watched as Choupault strained his body and his mind to stay focused on the task at hand. Their lives depended on this poor man, who had already endured so much for them, surviving until dawn. She knew that the night could very well kill him.

Helplessness was not in Solomon's nature. Watching Choupault suffer through just a few rough waves was enough for her. The sailor was just a few feet away, but it seemed like miles. The state of the water made it impossible to stand up without being swept overboard. She gripped the bench beneath her, lifted her hips, swung them to the side, and followed with her feet and inched her way toward the helm until she found herself next to Choupault. He had not noticed Solomon moving toward him until she arrived. He was curious about why she changed places, but not enough to ask. She leaned over and stretched her body across his knees. No one asked her to do it, but instinct told her to steady him.

Solomon startled Choupault, but he was soon grateful. The small amount of extra weight holding him down in his seat made an appreciable difference in his ability to brace himself against the raging ocean. The warmth from Solomon's body eased some of his pain, but it was her courage that truly enlivened him.

The sky opened without warning and poured a violent rain. It did not much matter. The waves had already drenched them to the bone. The consequence of the rain to the boat was another matter. It now leaked at a rate of eight barrels per hour. The passengers and crew bailed as fast as they could. One huge wave escaped Dublic's eye and struck against the boat with such force that it threw the passengers from their seats and filled the bottom of the boat with a dangerous amount of water. Choupault, with Solomon still bracing him, turned the boat in just enough time so that only the top of the wave went over them. No one was tossed overboard, but it was a reminder that the next time they might not be so lucky.

Bellet and Ms. Schedel cried out every time the boat moved. Only Solomon, occupied with her task of steadying Choupault, kept her fear to herself. It was a simple act, but Choupault admired it. "She is the bravest of them all," he thought to himself.[3]

CHAPTER 13

Purgatory

THE SEA HAD NOT YET SWALLOWED *LE LYONNAIS*. Those who remained by her, by choice or by chance, waited out the storm and hoped the morning would give them an opportunity to escape. After the captain directed the three lifeboats to leave the ship, he ordered all remaining hands to assist the struggling raft. The sailors assigned to stay with the ship worked together to fortify it enough to support the swarm of people who now clung to it so desperately. Some worked from the raft while others passed tools and materials to and from the raft and the ship. They tried to reinforce it by adding more wood and shifting passengers to distribute weight. The rising storm made the situation bleaker and only increased the difficulty. Nothing worked. The men were exhausted. *Le Lyonnais* was sinking rapidly by the stern.

Devaulx sat in his yawl with Dr. Clarin and five other sailors. The small boat remained tied to *Le Lyonnais* and drifted with her. The other sailors, about twenty-five of them, remained on the raft with the passengers. They tried to keep it from capsizing while they worked.

The men had been working for two straight days. Just that morning, they watched Luguiere and the others set sail in the ship's only lifeboats. They knew by now that the ship would sink. It was only a matter of when. Their survival now rested entirely on their ability to fortify the raft.

Adrenaline kept the men working in the aftermath of the collision. Desperation motivated them for many hours after that. When fatigue and hunger and the reality of their circumstances set in, it was loyalty to their captain that kept them going. It was the only thing.

CHAPTER 13 | *Purgatory*

It was midmorning when one of the sailors looked up from his work and saw something odd. The captain's yawl departed. He gave no warning. Some said the captain spotted a sail and went for help. Others claimed he could not control his yawl in rough seas. Still others suggested he prematurely abandoned ship. The nobility of his reasons for leaving mattered less and less as the distance between captain and crew grew wider. The sailors respected Devaulx and trusted him with their lives. Not only had he maintained order on the ship in better times, but, after the collision, he had given them hope and inspired them to work long after their bodies were broken. The sailors now watched as he became smaller and smaller, until the man who had once loomed so large a figure in this tragedy was but a speck on the horizon. They lost sight of him at eleven o'clock in the morning. Their captain left them.

Order dissolved instantaneously. The first sailor to give up put down his tools, climbed off the raft, and returned to the ship. Another followed. One after another followed until approximately twenty sailors who had been assigned to stay with the raft quit and crawled back to *Le Lyonnais*.

Many of them, weary from nearly sixty hours of backbreaking work and now free from incessant orders, attacked the ship's remaining provisions, including the liquor. They ate and drank, some for the first time in days. The men became less inclined to work with each bite of food and every swallow of wine.

A fireman, Tongard, dragged himself back on board the ship. Although he too abandoned the raft, he did so with different ideas than those of his companions. He returned to *Le Lyonnais* with a mind to regroup the men and devise a new plan to save those on the raft and escape the sinking ship.

Tongard had no time for food or drink. He looked over the ship's side from the deck and saw that the raft was in a terrible state. Almost fifty people swarmed over a space meant for no more than thirty. Tongard saw from his new vantage point how hastily the raft had been strapped together. Those on board both the raft and the ship were doomed if the sailors took no action. They had to start over. He implored the men to start building a new raft. The sailors, consumed by the lack of resolve that comes from being both exhausted and intoxicated, were unimpressed. "I'd rather die with the ship,"[1] shouted one in response.

Tongard's impassioned pleas for help managed to convince a small group of like-minded men to join him, among them the chief cook, Cayolle; the first stoker, Romain; and a passenger named Cedas, who was a blacksmith by trade, and four or five others. They devised a plan to build two smaller rafts to ferry building supplies back and forth from the ship to the main raft. They planned to make the necessary repairs to the main raft and attach the two smaller ones to create a more spacious platform to accommodate the passengers and additional sailors.

Those who did not want to go down with the ship set to work constructing the two new rafts, using the only materials still available—cords, wooden planks, and cabin doors. Thanks to the sailors who refused to join in, they were also able to make use of a few empty wine kegs.

A storm gathered. The winds picked up so much by evening that they had no choice but to the lower the first of two new rafts into the water. The small raft, under the direction of Romain, Cayolle, and a handful of others, made several trips to and from the main one, carrying food and other supplies. The small raft had not yet been connected to the main raft and stayed tied to the ship with a rope while the men worked. The small raft broke from its mooring at about eleven o'clock in the evening and floated out to sea. It carried the men away with it.

The night set in stormy and terrible. The second raft would have to wait until morning or until the weather calmed. Tongard and the few remaining sailors in his company stayed aboard *Le Lyonnais* and waited for the right time to lower their raft and connect it to the main one. The main raft remained fastened to the ship by a thick rope while they waited out the storm.

Tongard had four men left: the ship's steward, the second stoker, a fireman named Leguit, and Cedas. He knew that their little raft would never get them to safety. Connecting to the main raft was their only hope, their last means of escape. It was the only way off the ship. There was no other boat. There were no building materials left. The ship was filling with water, and there was little time. The sailors who refused to join Tongard had long ago decided to go down with the ship. Tongard and his four friends were the only men aboard *Le Lyonnais* who still cared enough to live. They were now forced to wait out the evening between the living, who waited for them in the water, and the near dead, who slumbered on deck. The night would prove to be a strange kind of purgatory.

The sea was as merciless and the night as black as the last. *Le Lyonnais*'s bow now extended high out of the water. She was almost upright and shook back and forth violently in the waves. Each pitch gave a shock to the raft. The motion of the waves jerked the rope tight, pulled the raft to the ship, and then let it out again. Several times the raft crashed into the side of *Le Lyonnais*, causing passengers to scream. Pieces of the raft splintered and broke into the ocean each time it struck the ship.

Tongard barely slept. Fear kept him up. He heard the passengers screaming over the sounds of the storm. Their cries were pure terror. He knew that at any moment the large raft would break into pieces, and all those upon it would be lost, but the raft was his last chance. He needed that raft to hold. He needed that raft.

The rope binding the raft to *Le Lyonnais* was heavy and connected to it from below the waterline, making it impossible for anyone on it to reach under, find their end of the rope, and cut it, particularly in the weather and the darkness. Aboard *Le Lyonnais*, on the other hand, any one of the sailors could have cut the rope and allowed the raft to take its chances on the waves.

The people on the raft screamed. Their voices rang out over the sounds of the storm, the creaking ship, and the crashing waves. They pleaded with the sailors to cut the rope and end the constant yanking of the raft into the ship. The fear in their voices became more and more immediate as the night wore on, because each time the raft collided with the ship, more of the raft and more of the people on it were lost. Those on the raft had only one chance—to get free of the ship that kept dragging them back to her.

Tongard knew it too. "The unfortunates who were on it uttered heart-rending cries, begging for aid, imploring that someone would cut the hawser which fastened the raft to the ship, which they could not do themselves because their end of the rope was under water."[2] All he had to do was cut the line, but the raft was his only way off *Le Lyonnais*. The rope was his lifeline, and cutting it meant seeing his only means of escape drift away in the rolling waves.

Tongard tried to ignore the passengers' pleas by covering his ears to muffle the noises they made. "How can I let the raft go?" he thought to himself. "It is our only chance of safety."[3] He found Cedas and the others. They justified their inaction by convincing one another that the raft would hold. "The night is too dark and [it's] too violent a time to act," said one. They vowed to throw themselves into the water at daybreak to recover and repair the damaged raft. They agreed, "We will wait until dawn."[4] The men told themselves their only option was to make their way in what they hoped would be the light and the calm of morning.

Tongard knew in his heart that by dawn it would be too late, but the group eased the burden of his decision. He found a spot to sit down and rest. "I can't do anything now," he lied to himself as he drifted off to sleep. "It has been decided."

Sailors often feel the movement of the sea in their bodies before they awaken, and it was that way for Tongard the next morning. The sea was calmer than the night before but still swollen from nearby storms. Whether the storms were coming or going he could not tell. His ship rose and fell as the swells passed. There, in the space between sleeping and waking, Tongard hoped the whole ordeal had been just a bad dream. He opened his eyes just enough to let in the light. The sky was gray. The waves were quieter. The ship was quiet too. A light rain fell.

Tongard propped himself up and opened his eyes wide. The state of the ship once again became real. He rose with resolve to find and wake the other men but soon remembered something that stopped him where he stood. The raft! He walked across a deck littered with drunken sailors who remained passed out where they fell. He stepped over them carefully, the way a surviving soldier moves over corpses on a battlefield. He reached the port rail and held it. The copper felt cool beneath his hands. He took a deep breath and peered over the side and into the water.

The raft was gone. All that remained was the rope and a single piece of wood that had been fastened to it. The rest had fallen to pieces during the night. The people had disappeared one by one while he slept, and the cries of the passengers had long since ceased. Tongard shuddered as it occurred to him that the screams he heard before he drifted off to sleep were not just cries for help but last gasps of life. Not one of the forty-nine men and women and children aboard the raft survived.

He stared at what remained. The piece of wood glided gently in the ocean. It bobbed up and down with the waves as if relieved to be rid of the weight that had once overwhelmed it. It was light and free. Tongard felt sick. He turned away and went to wake the others.

He once again stepped over the minefield of drunken companions. They were all over the deck, their limbs sprawled out and their bodies half immersed in rising water. He was less careful this time and ran from man to man yelling and shaking them awake. "In a few hours the ship will sink!" he cried as he shook one. The man did not even stir. He tried another: "We may still save ourselves by building a new raft!" Those who did wake up were indifferent. Tongard kept trying. One of the sailors, annoyed by the interruption, opened his eyes, lifted his head, and turned in Tongard's direction. "Me?" he snapped. "I don't work when it rains."[5]

The ship continued her slide into the ocean. Tongard and his four remaining men set to work on making a new raft. The water came faster now, and there was not a moment to lose. They strapped together two empty wine barrels and some cabin doors with a piece of cord. The water soon overtook *Le Lyonnais*'s deck.

The men feared that the ship would sink before they could launch the raft, so they got on it with no provisions and no navigational equipment of any kind. Some of the men were barely clothed, and all of them were thoroughly drenched by salt water and rain.

CHAPTER 13 | *Purgatory*

Despite their best intentions to build a raft that was safe and spacious, Tongard and his men set out on nothing more than some wine barrels and cabin doors lashed together in their final moments aboard *Le Lyonnais*. They launched at six in the morning of November 5, 1856, one day after the lifeboats had departed and three days after the collision. Only five of their original group remained: Tongard, Cedas, the ship's steward, the second cook, and Leguit.

The five men watched as fifteen sailors who remained aboard the ship took refuge in the forepart as water rose in the after part. They were not sleeping now. It took about an hour for the water to drive them forward up the deck and into the bow until there was no place left to go.

Tongard and the others held on to the raft with their hands and dangled their feet in the water. They kicked away from the ship as fast as their legs could take them. When they had gotten about four lengths away, they turned and saw it. *Le Lyonnais* plunged endways, stern first, her bow raising itself perpendicularly and entirely out of the water. She hung there for a second with her bow to the sky in a final heave of existence. She did not stay long. Soon after, she capsized to starboard and disappeared in a midst of boiling water and a whirl of foam with a noise like an explosion.

After that, it was quiet.

CHAPTER 14

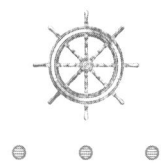

1856

LE LYONNAIS WAS NOT THE ONLY SHIP THAT MET HER END in the Atlantic Ocean in the mid-1850s. Far from it. Competition for transatlantic travel was fierce. Ocean liners competed for high-end customers by promising to make the fastest crossings. Packet steamships competed to sell tickets to eager immigrants looking for reliable passage to America. The lines prided themselves on keeping a schedule, which meant making the crossing in all seasons and all weather. It is difficult to know the exact number of vessels that sank during transatlantic crossings in the 1850s. There was no American organization that kept track of such numbers. The regularity with which stories of shipwrecks and macabre tales of survival appeared in the daily papers is a testament to how many ships went down.

The winters of 1854, 1855, and 1856 were particularly difficult. Storms were frequent—the cold, relentless. *City of Glasgow*, a passenger steamship from the Inman Line, set out for Philadelphia from Liverpool on March 1, 1854, carrying 480 passengers and crew. She vanished. Local newspapers began posting her description after sixty-four days lost, so passing ships would remain on the lookout out for news, survivors, or wreckage. A month later, the vessel *Briton's Pride* described an eerie scene from her voyage across the Atlantic. "Aug. 12 passed a chest painted green, and lettered 'G.B., City of Glasgow,' in a gilt ornamental wreath, and a few minutes after passed a headboard, about twelve feet long with letters on it, but could not make them out. These were doubtless the remnants of the ill-fated ship *City of Glasgow*."[1]

CHAPTER 14 | *1856*

SS *City of Glasgow*. Author unknown.
National Maritime Museum

Inman Line replaced *City of Glasgow* just six months later with a new steamship, *City of Philadelphia*. She wrecked on her maiden voyage when she grounded close to shore in a fog off Cape Race, Newfoundland. The passengers swam to safety, and much of the cargo was saved. The disaster nevertheless struck a chord with shipowners and those who planned to cross the Atlantic. "During the winter, the loss of one of [the Inman Line's] fine ships created a painful sensation on the mind of everyone here, and the same feeling was now produced yesterday by the intelligence that the new ship *City of Philadelphia* was wrecked also."[2]

Earlier in 1854, *Franklin* ran aground off Long Island, approximately 50 miles from Montauk Point. The fog was also the backdrop for *Vesta*'s 1854 collision with *Arctic*. The story of "women and children last" was so salacious it headlined newspapers for months to follow, and reporters compared the crew's behavior in later shipwrecks, such as the *Le Lyonnais* disaster, to the bar set by *Arctic*'s crew.

Another great peril, one made famous by *Titanic*'s sinking, was ice. *Titanic* was by no means alone in owing her fate to an iceberg. Ice made winter crossings from Europe to New York particularly dangerous. The year 1856 was one of the deadliest on record for ice in the region. Much of this was due to a perilous crossing of Ice Alley, a stretch of water that passed over the Grand Banks of Newfoundland that was home to ever-shifting glaciers.

Ice Alley claimed *Titanic* more than fifty years later, but long before that, captains feared the dangers waiting there. Captains relied on word of mouth, sharp eyes of sailors on watch, and dumb luck to make it to their ports of call.

The luxury steamship SS *Pacific* left Liverpool bound for New York in January 1856. She was both the pride and hope of the Collins Line, which was reeling from the devastating loss of the *Arctic* in 1854. *Pacific* was never heard from again. Five years later, a message in a bottle washed up on the shore of Uist, one of six Scottish Islands in the Outer Hebrides. It read in part, "On board the Pacific from L'pool to N. York. Ship going down. [Great] confusion on board. Icebergs around us on every side. I know I cannot escape."[3] The note confirmed what everyone suspected: the ice had claimed her.

Detail from an 1853 lithograph by Day & Son (England) of SS *Pacific* in a storm in 1852. *Library of Congress Prints and Photographs Division*

It was also in January 1856 that the crew of the ship *Germania* found Thomas W. Nye, the sole survivor of *John Rutledge*'s sinking, semiconscious and floating in a lifeboat with four frozen and dead bodies he had been too weak to commit to the sea. His account of a harrowing journey and struggle for survival with twelve passengers who had gone mad from drinking seawater was published in newspapers in the United States and Europe and whispered about by sailors in New York.

Driver, a clipper ship carrying immigrants for the Red Cross Line, vanished after she left Liverpool with 344 passengers and twenty-eight crew members bound for New York in February 1856. Her true end is a mystery, but the presumption is that she too was lost in the ice fields. A similar fate befell *Ocean Queen*, a 1,000-ton packet ship carrying eighty-five emigrants and a crew of seventy-five from London to New York. She left London on February 8, 1856. She passed the Isle of Wight one week later, signaled all was well, and was never seen again. An American ship, *G. B. Lamer*, left from England for New York the same day and narrowly survived treacherous ice fields, leading her owners to believe that *Ocean Queen*'s occupants encountered the same obstacle but met a different end.

The storms that ravaged the Atlantic in the winters of 1854 and 1855, and the bitter cold they brought with them, continued into the following year. By March 1856, more than 830 men, women, and children met their end crossing the Atlantic, and by midyear that number rose to more than three thousand.

The loss of life, vessels, and cargo had a tremendous effect on the insurance industry and forced smaller insurers to close when they could not pay the losses. A maritime affairs writer reflected on the previous year in a January 4, 1857, column. He wrote of the impact the storms of 1856 had not only on the maritime insurance industry but on friends and colleagues:

> The continued accounts of disasters at sea are winding up a sad year to our insurance companies, whose losses have been enormous. The storms during the year were awfully destructive, and the crashing of timbers of the strong ships wrecked at the same time several of our insurance companies who had taken risks on them. Those who escaped a similar fate are still flourishing, and with good management they may even weather another year as calamitous as the one just closing. It has, too, been a fleeting year; to me it seems but yesterday that the congratulations of friends were heard, whereas the year has fled and the tongues of many who joyously uttered those congratulations lie silent in the tomb. . . . Time has very rarely hung heavy with me; nor can it with anyone who is truly alive to the calls of duty and humanity.[4]

On January 1, 1856, the same year *Le Lyonnais* collided with the *Adriatic*, the packet sailing ship *St. Denis* set out from New York bound for the same port, Le Havre. She encountered a hurricane. A surviving sailor described it as the worst he had seen in more than twelve years at sea, "with the wind blowing furiously and sea running wild and high."[5] The force of the wind was so violent that it ripped her sails from her masts, knocked the ship over, and filled her deck and cabins with water. The crew righted the ship by cutting the masts, but she sprang a leak. The captain gave the order to abandon ship. Most of the passengers drowned when the ship capsized, and both the steerage area and cabins filled with seawater. The few who remained could not be coaxed into leaving the ship and boarding the lifeboats in such a ferocious storm. Eleven crew members made it into the only lifeboat that survived, some by jumping over the side of the ship and swimming for it. They begged their captain to join them. They reminded him that he had a wife and seven children waiting for him in Brooklyn. His eyes filled with tears, but the captain, who had commanded the vessel for nearly twelve years, refused to go. "When last seen, and just previously to the vessel going down, he was observed on the quarterdeck, winding up his watch."[6] The two officers and nine crew drifted on a raging sea for two days until they were rescued by a passing schooner. They had little food and no fresh water and suffered from cold and thirst. The New York papers published accounts of the incidents and statements of the survivors.

March 1856 saw the demise of the British barque *Blake*. A violent snowstorm demasted and waterlogged the ship. The captain's account of the gruesome days that followed were summarized by the *Buffalo Evening Post*:

> During a snowstorm, she was capsized; seven were washed overboard, the decks burst open, all the hatches washed off and every morsel of provisions carried away. The remainder of those on board were without food or drink for five days; on the eight[h] day a small cask of water was got at, and a half-drowned rat was caught and devoured; afterwards a man died and his body was reserved to be eaten and was actually eaten in part when on the ninth day after the disaster, the schooner *Pigeon* of St. Johns, N.F.[,] hove into sight and rescued the sufferers. Eight persons were washed overboard; two died of cold and starvation; and seven were saved.[7]

Notices about overdue ships were even more common than reports of disasters. Newspaper shipping columns provided anxious shipping agents, merchants, and family members with daily reports about vessels that had not reached their ports on schedule. The reports sometimes contained sightings by other ships whose captains provided reasons for the delay. In March 1856, the *New York Daily Herald* published a disturbing list of sixty vessels bound from eastern ports for New York that never arrived. The article summarized the state of Atlantic Ocean travel in the winter of 1855 into 1856:

> The past winter had been terribly prolific of disasters on sea and land, and particularly so on the former. Never before have we been called upon to record so many shipwrecks during one brief season, or such fearful destruction of human life; but fearful as that destruction has been, we fear our sad duty is not yet ended, and that we will have still more to chronicle. A large number of vessels bound to this and other ports in the United States have not yet been heard from, although mostly all of them have been out from one to two months beyond the time of their expected arrival period from the list of these which we subjoined, and which we have compiled with great care, it appears that there are 60 altogether which have not been heard of up to the present date.
>
> Excessive severity of the weather, the intense, protracted cold, the violent gales, and the great snowstorms, with the obstructions caused to navigation by the immense field of ice and icebergs which have been seen as far South as latitude 12 deg., 43 min. North, latitude 50 deg., 28 minutes West—all these will account to some extent for the detention of the missing vessels. Old and experience[d] sea captains have told us they never saw the ocean so much obstructed with snow below a certain latitude as it has been during the past winter, and at so early a period of the season. They found it utterly impossible to avoid it and have been in it for several days before they could extricate their ships. The steamships have encountered strong westerly gales on the passage and have been more or less detained by icebergs. Every vessel that arrives brings confirmation of the reports we have published from time to time in regard to the dangers which have attended navigators during the last two or three months, and which have signaled this year particularly as a year of disasters and calamities on the high seas.
>
> During [a] storm, the schooner *Pacific*, the Spanish bark *Duke de Braganza*, and an unknown brig were wrecked on the Jersey coast, over thirty lives lost. The *Duke de Braganza* went to pieces and no trace was ever found of her officers, passengers, or crew. To these were soon added over a dozen other vessels which were wrecked along, or in the immediate vicinity of, our coast.
>
> These were succeeded by accounts of others which had gone down out in the middle of the ocean, among which was that of New York packet ship *Saint Denis*, which foundered on the 6th of January last. Of those on board the vessel, numbering forty-two persons, thirteen of whom were

passengers, only eleven were saved, and these were all members of the crew. The greatest suffering was caused by the cold and a large number were literally frozen to death, while others were so affected by it as to render amputation of the feet and hands necessary to preserve their lives.

The only shipwreck which so far we have yet heard of as having been actually caused by the ice, was the *John Rutledge*, which was lost on the 20th of February by coming in collision with an iceberg. Her crew and passengers to the number of one-hundred-and-twenty, took to the boats, but only one was saved, and the story of his sufferings during a period of nine days, in an open boat, surrounded by ice, and four days of which he was without food or water, is one of the most painful recorded in the history of maritime disasters. We trust that this is the only ship which has been wrecked in the ice, but it would be vain to imagine that all have passed through it uninjured. To it we must in the absence of the positive—in the absence of any—information on the subject, attribute any disaster that has happened to the missing steamship *Pacific*.[8]

There is little doubt that the crew and passengers of *Le Lyonnais* read some of the articles or heard at least some of these accounts. Newspapers reported the disappearance of ships with regularity, not only to inform but to encourage ships traveling the same route to keep an eye out for survivors. Some survivors lived to tell their tales. The details of the sinkings were widely publicized in the years and months leading up to *Le Lyonnais*'s departure, and the stories were similar. Whether sunk by ice, storm, or collision, there were too many passengers for too few lifeboats on these ships, lone boats were forced to survive adrift at sea in punishing conditions, and, perhaps more importantly to those in Luguiere's boat, who had ample time to reflect on stories from the year, an overwhelming number of those who took to the lifeboats or remained with sinking ships were forever lost to the sea.

CHAPTER 15

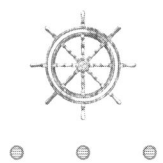

Goodbye

DAWN CAME. It did not bring fairer weather, but at least it came. Those aboard Luguiere's lifeboat were grateful simply to be alive. The wind still blew from the north. The sea was stormy, the waves high, the intermittent rainstorms relentless. The group's meager food supply was gone, and they began to suffer from thirst. They groaned for just one drop of seawater.

Every sailor knew the perils of drinking it. All of them had heard the tales of men and women who had gone mad from drinking from the ocean. The crew swore they would not succumb to the temptation at the beginning of their journey and warned the passengers of the same. Now, thirst beckoned—not just the desire to replenish the body with fluid but real thirst, a primal and unfathomable urge. Luguiere felt it. His throat constricted. It was difficult to speak and even breathe at times. His lips were cracked and dry—his mouth, cotton. The dull pain in his head that used to come and go now gathered in a constant ache behind his eyes. "I am strong," he told himself. "I can endure it." The recognition helped, but he felt sorry for his companions and tried to ease their suffering.

He suggested an alternative. They would collect and drink their own urine. Physicians in the 1850s knew both the chemical composition of urine and how drinking it could affect the body, but it was not common knowledge outside the medical profession. Myths persisted that drinking urine was a better alternative to seawater in a survival situation. Newspapers in the 1830s reported stories of prisoners and soldiers who survived harsh conditions by drinking their own waste. A decade after the *Le Lyonnais* disaster, five survivors of the wreck of *Van Capellan* drank both urine and the blood of those who died before them during a harrowing fifteen days adrift on the Indian Ocean.[1] "Thinking our own urine was fresher than the salt water, we took to drinking it," one survivor explained.[2]

Le Lyonnais's crew and passengers suffered from the same misapprehension. Drinking urine is much like drinking seawater. Small amounts are harmless to a person who has access to fresh water and other fluids, because their urine is mostly water. It is different for a person who is already suffering from dehydration. Concentrated urine consists of minerals, salt, and trace amounts of toxins from the liver. It can also contain harmful bacteria. Urine is not sterile. Any bacteria expelled from the body are returned to the body in a more concentrated form when urine is ingested. The more dehydrated a person is, the higher the concentration of salt and pollutants. In cases of extreme dehydration, such as that experienced by *Le Lyonnais*'s passengers and crew, the concentration of toxins would have been very high. Just like salt water, the more a urine a person drinks, the faster it dehydrates them and the thirstier they become.

All the passengers and crew of *Le Lyonnais* urinated into a stone jar. The eighteen men and women passed the jar around and took turns drinking their share. They refilled the jar when they could, a task that proved more and more difficult as the hours wore on. Drinking urine served only to worsen their thirst.

The wind brought with it cold from farther north and caused the temperature to drop. Rain turned to hail. The men and women tried to catch it on their tongues and in any container not being used for bailing, but the constant rolling of the waves made it difficult to collect fresh water in any fashion. The wind cut right through them, and as it did, small beads of ice lashed their skin.

Two among their party were older men: Father François and a Spanish passenger whose name no one knew. The Spaniard now shivered from the wet and the cold. He crossed his arms and curled forward in his seat as if trying to hold the warmth in the center of his body. Father François trembled too. The man was nearly sixty. He wore little clothing but had passed at the opportunity to use one of the coverlids and gave it to one of the women during the first storm. The thought of asking for it now did not even occur to him.

Father François was the oldest of the group, but he was strong for a man his age. He worked as a fireman and shoveled coal into *Le Lyonnais*'s furnace boxes, a task that required both strength and endurance. He moved much slower now. Luguiere relieved him of his responsibilities in the lifeboat to give him the chance to recoup his energy. Father François moved less after being discharged from his duties. Now, he rarely moved at all. He closed his eyes from time to time, and the others had no cause to wake him.

Toward the evening, the group spotted a ship. It was the first one they had seen since they left *Le Lyonnais*. The vessel was just a speck on the edge of the horizon, but it was a sign of life. George Schedel immediately rose. He waved his arms and screamed at the dot on the horizon. "We're here! Save us!" The rocking of the boat knocked him down, but he rose again and kept going. "We're here!" Some of the others joined him, and soon a small group hollered into the distance. Luguiere encouraged them and soon found himself waving his arms in excitement.

Choupault remained in his seat. "She is too far away," he thought to himself. "Especially in this storm." He did not tell the others. Solomon took Choupault's lead. She followed his eyes to the horizon but did not waste her breath. Father François was a different story. If he noticed the ship in the distance, it did not register in his eyes or in his body. The vessel soon vanished. The passengers quieted. The ship was too far away, but the mere prospect of rescue heartened some of them.

Solomon saw it differently. The passing ship, which was likely impressive up close, looked so small in the distance. Rescue required a ship like that to pass close enough not only for the survivors to see it but for those aboard the ship to see them. The weather, the time of day, the waves, the competence of the watch, and so many other obstacles competed with the prospect of a ship spotting them. Their lifeboat was not just small, it was less than a speck—a piece of driftwood floating barely above the surface of a vast sea. Solomon kept her thoughts to herself. She forced a smile at the others and nestled down into her seat.

The passengers readied themselves for bed, a practice that consisted of moving around in their seats until they reached a position comfortable enough to sleep but not so comfortable to put them at risk when the boat jumped. They had fallen into a steady pattern of sleeping and waking in organic shifts and trusted their colleagues to wake them in the face of any new or imminent danger. Sleep, in general, was easier now. They were exhausted, and riding the waves during the night no longer frightened them as much as it had in the beginning of their ordeal. There was little change in the weather, and those aboard the lifeboat now knew what to expect in the hours ahead.

Choupault was in his usual place at the helm when the passengers readied themselves for rest. "Good night," he said to Solomon as she settled into place. "Goodbye," she answered.[3] The response should have startled Choupault, but it did not. It was too perfect for the circumstances in which they found themselves. The others chimed in, and so began a grim practice among the passengers of bidding one another "goodbye" instead of "good night" before they turned in.

Their second full night at sea in the open boat was as cold and stormy as the first, but they survived it. The morning sky was dark and gray and showed no signs of improvement. Waves washed over them night and day in an endless stream. They were unpredictable. The passengers were already drenched to the bone, yet somehow the icy sting of each wave felt new. Wind always came between the waves. It continued to blow from the north and brought with it a cold worthy of its origin. The morning was even colder than the previous night had been. "Dry" was a concept they no longer recognized. Icy waves and intense cold followed bitter winds in a cycle that repeated itself without end.

Sunrise was one of the few things to which the passengers look forward, if for no other reason than it meant they had survived another night. The simple act of opening their eyes astonished most of them. Father François took much longer than usual to wake up on the morning of November 6. Relief from his duties the day before meant there was no one depending on him to take a shift or complete a task. The others did not notice how long it took him to open his eyes or how blankly he stared at the horizon once he did.

Luguiere, in his way, managed to ensure order on the boat. He spent most of his time barking at the sailors. The sailors did the lion's share of the work, kept the watch, maintained responsibility for steering, and monitored the boat's seaworthiness. Choupault spent most of his time at the helm. The other sailors—Cauvin, Dublic, and Joste—did their best to assist him. Desfour, the third engineer, supervised firemen Nestor, Poirreaux, and Bienaimée as they tended to the bailing. The remaining crew, including steward's mate Thillaye and Lambert the baker, did as Luguiere commanded, and pitched in where they could.

The passengers assisted the men with the work as much as possible, but as time wore on and falling temperatures got the better of them, they took solace in their status as paying customers. They tucked their hands inside their clothes or the coverlids to keep themselves warm and passed the time by stretching their arms and legs to maintain the feeling in their limbs. The Italian passenger, Mr. Domenigo, suffered greatly from hunger, thirst, and exhaustion. No one else in the lifeboat spoke his language. He learned early on that communication would be difficult, and gave up on it. He sat in his place, huddled for warmth, and moved only when it was his turn to claim a share of the stone jar's contents.

CHAPTER 15 | *Goodbye*

Those who spent the days at work had neither the time nor the luxury of trying to keep warm. Choupault could no longer feel his hands or his left forearm. Each time he grasped the oar the bones in his knuckles snapped. The color in his fingertips was gone. He examined them, holding them a few inches from his face as if they were not his own. The skin pulled tight across the tips and faded from pale white to an intense red and turned back to the color of flesh only when it reached the palms. He ran his thumb across his fingertips and felt the strange sensation of touching someone else. He made fists with his hands and let them in and out again and again and again to force back a feeling that never quite came.

The day wore on. There was little room on the boat. Everyone had a place to sit but not enough room to lie down. The weary passengers shifted in their seats, but to stand was to risk being swept away by a wave. Water collected in the bottom of the boat. It was always above their ankles and sometimes reached their shins. The wind chilled that too and kept the passengers' feet immersed in a frozen trench. The men bailed nonstop. Whoever was not at the helm or on watch dipped empty bottles and jars and buckets into the water, filled them up, and tossed the water overboard in yet another cycle without end.

The passengers passed around the stone jar of urine and took reluctant sips when thirst became intolerable. Father François now refused his share. He had not said much all day. He closed his eyes more often now and for longer periods of time. He barely stirred when the boat rocked in a strong wave.

Evening closed in. It was twilight once again, and soon it would be dark. Rain-laden clouds covered the sky and gave no indication the storm would break. The light struggled against the clouds and spun bands of deep gray and navy blue that clung to the horizon and grew darker and darker until they faded into black. The sight would have been quite beautiful under other circumstances, but for the passengers, twilight was nothing more than a promise of another night of cold and waves and riotous seas.

Father François died before the last swirls of light left the sky. He did not go quietly. Said one who watched him pass, "To imagine the agony of an old gentleman of sixty years struggling with death in its most harrowing aspect will fail to realize the scene."[4]

No one disturbed the dead man. Perhaps this first death paralyzed them. Perhaps there was some debate about what to do with him. Perhaps a wild ocean made it too dangerous to do anything in that moment. If there was ever talk of more-disturbing plans for the use of his body, no one ever spoke of it. Father François's body remained in his place on the boat until long after dark.

Hours passed in silence. The passengers saw a schooner windward. She was much too far away, and the state of the sea made it impossible to signal her. The same as the day before, some yelled and screamed and moved their hands and hoped someone would spot them, but this time it took them longer to stop. Their pleas were more desperate than they were the night before.

Temperatures dropped precipitously after sunset. The men and women tried to sleep, but most could not. It was not the cold that kept them up; it was Father François. He remained in his seat. His skin was now the whitest shade of blue, and so long deprived of water, it shriveled around his bones as his body cooled. The effect sank in his cheeks and pulled the skin away from his eyes until they bulged from their sockets. His body, frozen in its final moments of agony, became a monument to their misfortune.

Choupault was once again at the helm. This time, Luguiere stayed up with him to keep a lookout and to look out for Choupault. Something about Choupault had changed. He had returned from his illness the day before and had steered the boat capably since then but, from time to time, uttered an odd phrase or responded inappropriately to something said. Luguiere was not alarmed but thought it best to keep an eye on him.

Luguiere kept an eye on the other passengers as well. They made small movements in their sleep. What looked like smoke came from their mouths when their hot breath hit the cold air. It was one of the only ways to distinguish the sleeping from the dead. The Spaniard had not moved in a long time. Luguiere watched him closely for a few minutes and saw no signs of breath leaving his body. He moved closer to the man and leaned his ear over his mouth. Nothing. He shook him. Nothing. The Spaniard was dead. There was no violence in it. He just went to sleep and never woke up.

The second death so closely on the heels of the first unsettled even those passengers who had come to terms with Father François's passing. Luguiere was glad he stayed awake. He knew he needed to work alongside Choupault to steer the boat in the storm and to keep up everyone's spirits. Choupault regretted he never learned the Spaniard's name.

Solomon had not even tried to sleep. She studied the two dead men and thought about how much more they had suffered than she. They had been at work and had refused the very blanket that now kept her warm. She felt a sharp and sudden guilt knowing the men died not of the cold but of the costs incurred in keeping her alive. She wanted to throw the blanket off her body, as if doing so would rid her of the shame she felt, but she could not. She was too cold for a sudden burst of emotion, and that only worsened her guilt.

    She could not cry. Her body was no longer capable of making tears, but Choupault could see from her expression that she was crying just the same. He positioned himself between her and the dead men. "Look away," he whispered to her as he put up his hand to block her view. He turned and moved toward Father François. Solomon buried her eyes in her hands. Luguiere and Choupault grunted as they lifted Father François's frozen body from its place. Solomon heard a small splash as they set the dead man loose on the waves. She heard the sound a second time when the sailors lowered the Spaniard into the sea. No one spoke or said any last words. Each of them said a silent prayer that they would not be next.

CHAPTER 16

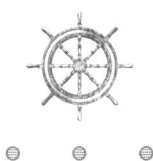

Laughter

LUGUIERE AND CHOUPAULT STAYED AWAKE ALL NIGHT. They found it difficult to keep the passengers alive, not because of the storm but because they had begun to abandon hope. Each of them knew it was only a matter of time before death took one of them, but death had been an abstraction. Now it had a face. Father François's anguish gave it one. Luguiere, for the first time since their journey began, took turns with Choupault steering the vessel and trying to console the passengers. Through their exertion and their resolve, they did not lose anyone else that night.

The sea remained tempestuous through the evening of November 6 and into the early-morning hours of the seventh, but it moderated as time wore on and gave the passengers their first respite from a storm in more than five days. The waves no longer washed over them, but calmer seas brought with them a new challenge: the bitter cold. Temperatures plummeted as the storm faded. Rain turned to snow. Wet turned to cold. Waterlogged clothing did not dry; it turned to ice on their backs.

It snowed all day. The passengers curled up and warmed their hands and feet by rubbing them together and blowing hot air into them. Bellet shivered. She had been nearly naked when she came aboard and had only the coverlid to keep her warm. The Schedels seemed to fare the best in the cold. Mrs. Schedel, who wore a coat and hat, was better clothed than the other women, and her husband had not done as much work as the other men. Mr. Schedel, however, suffered from insatiable thirst. His throat was hoarse. The chill of cold air made the very act of breathing an effort. He took shallow breaths to avoid the pain that always followed the deeper ones.

CHAPTER 16 | Laughter

The sailors in charge had now given up even the pretense they were sailing in a direction. Everyone knew they were lost. The storms blew them God knows where, and without food and water and warmth, the men no longer had the strength to sail and steer the boat toward land. There was nothing left to do but to drift and to pray they crossed paths with a ship.

Luguiere and Choupault worked throughout the day with the other sailors. It was easier to bail now that it was only the leak and not the waves or the rain filling the boat with water. Choupault was no longer forced to spend every waking moment at the helm. He turned his attention to his companions and tried to entertain them. He was at his best now. When he noticed pain in one of his comrades' eyes, he cracked a joke or engaged them in one of his stories until they managed some kind of recognition.

The sailors kept one another company by telling tales of their adventures in the war and at sea. They talked like sailors. Schedel found their colorful language and off-color remarks revolting and indecent. At the beginning of their journey, Schedel regretted that his wife neither spoke French nor understood much of it. Now he was grateful. "Luguiere is the worst of them," he thought to himself.[1] "He was supposed to be our leader but has proven capable neither of leadership nor labor. Now he makes it worse with this vulgar conversation."

Luguiere reminded Schedel of a man he once knew: Captain Lawrence, the foul-mouthed master of a ship called *Saint Mary*. His encounter with Lawrence in November 1853 resulted in Schedel's transfer from his vice consul post in Costa Rica to a lesser post in New York.

Schedel served as British vice consul to Costa Rica in 1853 and lived in the country's capital, San José. He received some disturbing information from a resident in the port city of Puntarenas in mid-November. A British subject who served as boy on the American barque *Saint Mary* claimed he had been beaten by the captain's mate without provocation. Schedel believed it was his duty to intervene because the incident occurred inside a shop on land rather than aboard the ship. He launched an investigation, which revealed that the boy was in fear for his life. The boy told the investigator he would rather drown himself in the ocean than return to the ship.

San José, located on Costa Rica's interior, was far from the western port city of Puntarenas, and the American consul at the port did not take kindly to Schedel's interference or share his belief that this was a matter in which consuls from either country should intervene. In a letter "unworthy of a gentleman," he appealed to the British consul directly and demanded the sailor boy be thrown in jail.[2] Lawrence was similarly incensed by Schedel's interference and petitioned the consul as well. His letter was even less diplomatic than the American consul's response. Lawrence threatened Schedel's life and pledged to come to San José to "knock him down" for attempting to interfere with discipline aboard his ship.[3]

The captain kept his promise. He traveled more than 80 miles from Puntarenas to Costa Rica's rugged interior. He endured horrendous weather, mountainous terrain, and roads so rough they were almost impassible, all to give Schedel "a good whip."[4] The British and the Americans were engaged in a political struggle for influence in Central America, so the Costa Ricans took an even-handed approach. They warned Schedel that Lawrence was coming for him, but did not try to stop him. Lawrence arrived in San José in late November armed with a pistol. He treated himself to a good dinner, got rip-roaring drunk, and went looking for Schedel. A well-respected American doctor in San José convinced Lawrence to leave the weapon behind while he did. Lawrence barged into the British consul's office, screaming and threatening Schedel's life. The consul threw him out, but the drunken captain took to the streets of San José, where he shouted profanities and vowed to all within earshot to "cowhide" Schedel at the first opportunity.[5]

Schedel did not deign to respond to a man as uncouth and unhinged as Lawrence directly. Instead, he asked the Costa Rican authorities to intervene and warned that if they did not, he would shoot the American captain down in the street "like a dog."[6] Their advice to Schedel was to stay at home in his room, where Lawrence could not find him, and wait until the captain returned to his ship. Schedel never went looking for Captain Lawrence but defied the Costa Ricans by taking daily walks through town. Five days later, the British government transferred Schedel to New York.

Luguiere was not American. Schedel judged his temper to be distinctively French, but his foul language and belligerence reminded him of Lawrence just the same. Schedel thought Luguiere picked on some in their party, particularly Solomon, and treated them poorly throughout their journey. If that was true, Solomon either never noticed or never complained. Neither did anyone else. Schedel was the only person bothered by Luguiere's tone and the tenor of his stories. Just the ability to hear a conversation, especially one punctuated by laughter, was a blessing to everyone else.

Choupault's limbs, which up until now had been frozen solid, began to tingle. They felt warm and swelledl until he could feel his heart beating softly through his fingers. He knew from his days in the war how easily a solider could be felled by the cold. Warmth was not a good a sign. Choupault was not sure exactly why, but warmth in frostbitten limbs always brought the field doctors, who treated the wounds by covering them in grease and wrapping blackened hands and feet with bandages. Choupault tuned the war out of his thoughts. He did not care. Survival depended on the moment, and in that moment, he welcomed the warmth in his fingers and his toes and the comfort it brought him.

His thirst was unbearable. The urine was disgusting and now in short supply. The water, now calmer, looked more like a lake than an ocean. The sunlight glinted upon it and revealed a clear, almost Mediterranean blue. It called to Choupault. He caught a glimpse of his reflection on its surface. He barely recognized the man in the water. The man beckoned him to drink. "Just a drop won't hurt."

Choupault's conscience had no time to answer. He cupped his hands, plunged them over the side, and splashed a cup of seawater to his lips. He restrained himself for the first sip but soon gulped mouthful after mouthful. It did little to quench his thirst, but Choupault did not care. The mere illusion of drinking was more important to him than its effect. Others followed his example throughout the day. Almost all the passengers and crew had stolen the occasional sip, but Choupault's indulgence gave them permission to do so without shame. Even Luguiere began to drink from the sea.

Father François's and the Spaniard's passing had left more room on the boat. Space was not unlimited, but passengers could change positions and spread out a bit. A few people at a time could lie down on the benches, and the passengers spent the day taking turns doing so. It felt good to stretch without fear of disturbing someone else or being swept away by a wave.

The sun dipped ever so slightly toward the horizon. The afternoon would soon give way to twilight. George Schedel shifted some of his clothing to prepare for his wife a little couch on one of the thwarts. She leaned against his arm as he embraced her, and was soon fast asleep. Schedel, with his wife in his arms, sat close to Choupault and talked with him. Choupault could be just as bawdy as the other sailors, but Schedel could not help but like him. He was genuine, a man comfortable in his own skin. Schedel envied that part of him. Choupault absorbed Schedel in stories about the past. He talked about his childhood, his time in the French navy, Crimea, and his adventures at sea and jumped from topic to topic without waiting for reply.

Schedel glanced at the horizon. Clouds still littered the sky, but for the first time since the collision, he could see the light of sun radiating behind them. The sun was so round it looked as though it would burst, a vivid egg yolk balanced on the edge of the world. Choupault talked until the yolk snuck below the horizon. It hung there before it flattened and sank below the waves. Schedel was, for one moment, at peace.

Choupault told stories well into the evening. Schedel rarely got a word in, but truth be told, he did not care. His throat hurt too much to speak, and Choupault's voice was a welcomed change from the crashing waves and howling winds that hallmarked the first three days of their journey. Choupault was in the middle of yet another story when he stopped in midsentence and shot to his feet. Schedel followed the path made by Choupault's eyes and saw a faint light. The light grew dimmer and disappeared. Soon, it appeared again in the same spot. It was a ship so far out it danced on the horizon, disappearing and reappearing again depending on the lifeboat's relationship to the movement of the ocean and the horizon. She was far, but with the calmer sea state and a little luck, they might just reach her. The boat sprang to life and movement. Choupault searched the boat for flares. He tried to send them up, but they were still too wet to catch fire.

The crew moved toward the light both by oar and sail. They followed in the same direction until they saw the light no more. It was dark by the time the light vanished and they were, once again, alone.

It was quiet. The passengers slumped in their seats and tried to absorb this latest setback. Choupault, still at the helm, broke the silence. He laughed. He laughed loud and at nothing in particular. The sound of Choupault laughing made Luguiere laugh too, until both of them were laughing so hard that the lack of cause for the laughter no longer mattered. This latest miss was just a minor setback to Luguiere. He always believed they would be rescued, and the sight of so many passing ships only strengthened his resolve. Schedel never cared much about what Luguiere did or said or thought. What worried him was that Choupault, the only man on board he trusted, did not seem quite right.

Schedel once again prepared a place for himself and his wife. No matter how much he fidgeted, he could not get comfortable. The peace he had found only a little while ago had been snatched from him by the ship, the horizon, and the laughter, and he could not get it back. He would never get it back. He settled in for the night. Choupault turned to his new friend and said, "Goodbye." Schedel let the words reverberate through him before he closed his eyes and tried to get some sleep.

CHAPTER 17

Ship!

"SHIP!"

Choupault was screaming, or at least it felt that way. His throat was so dry it took the weary passengers some time to recognize the sounds he made as an alarm. "Ship in sight," he said as he pointed to the horizon.[1]

It was almost dawn on the morning of November 8. The storms had passed, and the morning was calm. The sun had just begun to light the sky when Choupault spotted a three-masted vessel on the horizon. She was close, less than 5 miles away. "A gunshot," in his estimation.[2]

The passengers awoke and saw the same. There was no need to suppress their excitement this time. The ship was too close. "We are saved!" one of them yelled as the others erupted in cheers.[3] Luguiere gathered the men. They were frozen and tired, but their first real chance at rescue sprang most of them to life. The sailors got ready. The ship was going north, and, as luck would have it, there was a small breeze in their favor.

They put up the sail but used a combination of sail and oars for maximum speed. Cauvin and Choupault manned the oars. The men rowed with all their strength. Their muscles burned. They treated each pull as though it was their last. The others cheered them on. The sailors were closing the distance, and it did not take long before everyone in their party understood that it was not a matter of if, but when, the passing ship rescued them. Even the sailors, who had been reserved throughout the journey, laughed and cried with joy as the ship on the horizon grew larger and larger. Only Schedel was nervous. "Calm down," he begged the others. He feared that premature celebration might divert the crew from the task at hand. "We aren't yet saved," he admonished them. He paused. It was difficult to catch his breath in all the excitement.

"How many bottles of wine do we have left?" Luguiere called to Schedel, who had somehow become the keeper of the boat's only remaining provisions, four bottles of wine.[4] No one ever said how or why these had been placed under his protection and for what purpose they had been reserved. He held up four fingers. Luguiere acted as though they had already been saved and were relaxing on the ship's deck. "Open them up," he howled. "Drink them all out!" Schedel wanted to oblige, but his pessimism got the better of him. He proposed, "We will drink two now and save the others for when we are safely aboard the ship."[5] Luguiere grunted, but he was happy Schedel had agreed to open any wine at all. Schedel opened two bottles and monitored the shares. The passengers, who had drunk nothing but urine and salt water since their first evening at sea, gulped their small portions down to nothing.

Choupault and Cauvin had no time for drink. They rowed with all their might toward the ship, which was now in full view. The sailors could see her features. She was American with square-rigged masts and the body of a clipper. They drew nearer. Choupault saw sailors on deck. He could almost made out the ship's name. "S. The ship's name begins with an 'S.'"[6] "Any moment now," he told himself. "One of the men on deck will see us and all of this will be done."

Cauvin saw the men move toward the sails and watched for movements consistent with the ship slowing or changing direction. "At last," he thought, "they will turn the mainsail to slow her." Just then, the men on deck turned the ship's sails not against the wind but in search of it. The clipper bolted forward and headed north at full speed with all her sails on the wind. She traveled much faster than their small boat could follow. "After her!" Luguiere commanded. Choupault or Cauvin pulled the oars with even more energy. The men and woman yelled and screamed. Dublic waved a white distress flag, but the clipper ignored their signals. It was not long before she was out of sight.

"No!" Schedel cried. "Come back!" Luguiere lamented their luck. "She did not see our signals!" Choupault and Cauvin glanced at one another. "They did . . ." Cauvin started to speak, but one sharp glance from Choupault silenced him. They agreed in that moment not to tell the others what they knew; the men aboard the clipper had seen their boat and deliberately left them.

Moments before the clipper changed course, Cauvin saw the men on deck take a large studding sail and hang it over the side of the ship to cover the vessel's name. Choupault saw it too. Those aboard wanted to make sure the people in the lifeboat could never identify them. Choupault thought it best to keep the information from his companions. Rotten luck was one thing, but deliberate coldheartedness was more than the group could bear.

"Follow her!" Luguiere ordered. The desperate survivors encouraged the men to carry on, hoping they might catch the clipper yet. Choupault and Cauvin rowed with less fervor than before, but they rowed and hoped someone aboard the clipper might have a change of heart. They caught brief sights of her at times, which only reraised peoples' spirits and compelled the men to row faster. The clipper disappeared for good after a four-hour chase. Dublic let go of the white handkerchief he had been waving. No one watched as it flapped away like a bird on the breeze. "Stop rowing," Luguiere ordered. Choupault and Cauvin dropped the oars on command. The lifeboat hurtled forward for a few seconds before it began to drift, once again, by the will of the ocean.

Ms. Schedel let out a scream. It came not from her lungs but from deep within her body. It held her up for a moment, but once it escaped, she collapsed into the bottom of the boat, threw her face on her hands, and wept. Others wept too. No one spoke for more than an hour. Choupault too was silent. The chase cost him precious energy, but his companions' despair reassured him he made the right decision in keeping from the group what he and Cauvin knew.

The little boat drifted. There were no more sails that day. The men and women did not move as they floated on calm waters. The day passed with them going through the motions and completing the tasks to which they had grown accustomed in mindless routine. No one spoke one word more than necessary.

They drank the remaining two bottles of wine. Schedel did not even try to stop them. There was no longer any point. His condition had gotten worse. He could barely breathe, let alone speak. The wine inspired in Dublic an insatiable thirst. When it was gone, he gulped down cup after cup of seawater. It only made him thirstier. Everyone in their party had now succumbed to drinking it. Choupault had drunk the most. He suffered momentary lapses of reason. He was a capable sailor and had few problems steering the ship. It was as though his body had separated from his mind and was doing what it had been doing all his life. Despite Choupault's unwavering qualities as a sailor, Luguiere now assigned someone to stay with him when he was at the helm. He decided that Dublic, who had proven to be the second-best sailor among them, now warranted the same attention.

Schedel looked at his wife. She had not made a sound since they lost the clipper. Her blank expression scared him far more than either

her tears or her screams. She was empty. Whether it was from drinking seawater or from exhaustion, he could not tell. She abandoned more hope each time they missed a passing ship, and this most recent failure broke her. Making a place for her on a bench and holding her in the crook of his arm was the only thing he could do to comfort her. He pulled her close. Her body responded, but her expression did not change as her head fell onto his shoulder. There was nothing more he could do. There was no more any of them could do. There were no provisions left. There were no grand plans. There was no destination within reach. Whatever happened next would be a matter of fate. Either some ship would come along, or they would die one by one of madness or cold or starvation or all three.

Schedel was the only person on the boat responsible not just for himself but for someone he loved. It was an incredible burden, and the weight of it suffocated him. He nudged his wife away from his arm. "It is not fair," he told himself. "It's not right." His heart beat faster and his chest constricted. It was hard to breathe. He felt a sudden urge to sleep not because he was tired but because he sensed his own weakness.

He lay down on the bottom of the boat in the pool of frozen water that had once again collected there. At one time the mere sting of the water through his shoe was an unacceptable indignity. Now, he submersed his entire body in it without care. No one stopped him, not even his wife. He was too determined, and they were too despondent. It felt so good to lie down that Schedel did not feel the cold. He tried to tell them, but he no longer had a voice, just two shriveled vocal cords scraping against one another. It did not much matter. No one could understand the sounds he made. He spoke complete gibberish.

His breath was shallow, and his chest labored with every inhalation. He sometimes gasped for breath so violently that his torso heaved up and his eyes opened wide. His wife leaned over him. Her expression was blank. He looked into her eyes and felt overwhelmed by the sense that he had failed her—that he had failed them both. "It's not fair," he tried to tell her, but she did not understand. He felt heavy, so heavy he might just fall through the bottom of the boat and melt into the ocean. Melting. The thought comforted him.

Mrs. Schedel still wore her wide-brimmed hat. She tied it in a bow at the base of her neck, and the brim made a kind of halo around her face. Schedel looked up but no longer recognized her. She appeared to him a monk who had come to give the last consolation to a dying sinner. "I am forgiven," he murmured as he let go and dissolved into peaceful sleep.[7]

CHAPTER 18

On a Barrel

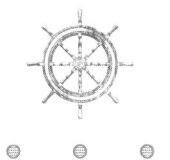

TONGARD, CEDAS, THE SHIP'S STEWARD, the second cook, and Leguit, clung to the raft they had formed from planks and empty wine barrels. Its surface area was less than 30 feet. The proper lifeboats had been gone for more than a day. *Le Lyonnais* was beneath the waves. The sailors who had chosen to stay with the ship were sucked into the sea when *Le Lyonnais* took her fatal plunge.

The ocean raged. Some waves reached heights of close to 20 feet. The men had no sails or oars to even attempt to point their raft at an appropriate angle to the waves. They tried to use their legs to turn themselves, but the wind, waves, and currents were far stronger than they were. The waves alone moved them. It did not take long for the men to realize that all they could do was hang on.

There were times when large waves lifted their raft and sent it crashing down on the other side. Other times, the men got caught at the bottom of a wave and watched the water stand up, lurch, and crash down on top of them. The sensation of drowning repeated itself over and over again.

November 5 passed with the men doing nothing but rising and falling on the open ocean. It took all their power to endure it. They had no food or water, and their clothing was useless in the wet and the cold. The temperature dropped when day slid into evening. The sky opened and pelted the men with sleet and snow.

They tried to take turns resting at night, but there was no such thing as sleep in their circumstances. The sea state made it impossible to get on top of the raft for long. There was no place to sit. There was no moment to lie down or rest. Falling asleep in such high seas, even for a moment, meant certain death.

The men were surprised to find themselves alive when the sun came up on the morning of November 6. The violent seas continued. The rise and fall of the ocean seemed heavier than the day before, but it was quite possible that the seas remained the same and the men were just more exhausted. Staying awake became a far-crueler punishment than the wind and the cold and the waves.

Heavy seas jolted the raft and threw it into the air. It pitched and fell and washed the second cook away. The man kicked his legs and waved his arms to keep his head above water. His companions tried to reach him, but the ocean pulled him away until he disappeared.

Leguit was in deep despair. A short time after the second cook's death and without warning, he threw himself from the raft into the water. He did nothing to resist the waves that swirled and broke around him. The others had no way to get to him without putting themselves in grave danger. His expression was calm and his body limp when the waves engulfed him.

The steward watched Leguit disappear, and followed his example by letting go of the raft and launching himself into the ocean. Tongard and Cedas grabbed him in time to pull him back to the raft before the sea could take him. It was a small victory for the two sailors but not for the steward. "Let me go," he begged. Tongard shook the man. "We can't give up!" They had already lost two men. Allowing the steward to choose his own fate marked to Tongard some invisible line he could not cross. Again, the steward dove into the water and again Tongard and Cedas prevented him from drowning. They dragged him back to the raft for a second time. The steward kicked and screamed and begged them to let go, but he was no match for two men who pulled him through the water. Tongard and Cedas brought him back to the raft and held him until he stopped struggling.

The three men held on. The afternoon provided no respite from the waves. Survival meant more than staying afloat. The men gripped the boards, kicked their legs, and used all their strength to stay with it. They did their best to work together, but it was every man for himself. To sleep, to lose one's grip, to give in even for a moment meant certain death.

The men held on to the raft through the afternoon, until a huge wave washed over them and caused it to capsize a second time. The steward disappeared. Tongard did not know if the waves swept the steward away or if the man, once again, let go. It did not matter. The ocean had claimed a third man in a single day. Only Tongard and Cedas remained.

Tongard was not like the other men. He saw no romance in the idea of sailor surrendering to the sea. He did not join the sailors who chose to go down with the ship. He had been one of the few who refused to let go of the raft and sacrificed the lives of the forty-nine passengers on it. Tongard had led the small group of men to find another way off the ship. He never resigned himself to the idea that five men were no match for a gale on the open ocean, and he certainly did not have the constitution for suicide. He clung on by nothing more than the sheer force of his will to a few fragile pieces of wood lashed with a cord. It was not so much that he wanted to live; he was just too afraid to die.

His will kept him going. He was otherwise powerless. Hour after hour after hour, Tongard and his companion faced the combination of two ferocious elements: the wind and the water. It had tumbled and stirred and tossed the men for more than thirty-six straight hours. Their limbs had long since gone numb. They could no longer feel their fingers clench the raft and knew only that they were still holding on because they had not been pitched into the sea. They fought the sleep and the cold and starvation and knew that any moment could be their last.

On November 7, their third day on the open sea, the waves capsized their raft a third time. The men held their breath, swam beneath the raft, and flipped it right side up again. They clenched it with all their might as the storm continued into the evening and through the next morning.

The weather calmed a little by dawn. The respite from the storm gave Tongard and Cedas the chance to contemplate their misery. They had only seawater to drink and had not eaten anything since their final night aboard *Le Lyonnais*, which now seemed a lifetime away. They had been beaten with rain and snow and immersed in frigid water for two days. Their hands were frozen, and their legs were exhausted from kicking. Their limbs were no more than heavy wooden logs. It was more difficult to move them with each passing hour. The worst was the struggle against the constant urge to sleep.

The deprivation dulled their reflexes and made it even more difficult to maneuver in the storm. The urge to sleep sometimes overcame them and caused one of the men to slip from the raft. The other was there to save him. Cedas looked at Tongard. There was no doubt their luck would soon run out. They would either fall asleep and not wake up soon enough to catch the raft, or they would freeze to death clutching it. He did not have to say what they both knew. They would not survive another day.

The storm moderated that evening. The small change in the weather eased Tongard's and Cedas's suffering just enough to make it possible to endure the night; nevertheless, it felt like a miracle when the sun came up. The weather was much calmer. Tongard grabbed the wooden planks and pulled his chest on top of the raft. He used his arms and legs to crawl across the planks until he stretched his body on top of them. Cedas did the same, and for the first time since they left the sinking ship, the men were able to float atop the raft. The muscles in their arms and legs were so tight and numb that their bodies denied them even the reward of relaxation.

The pair floated for a few hours in the safety of calmer weather. Tongard spotted a vessel at about eight o'clock in the morning. She was just a cannon's shot away. He woke Cedas. The two screamed and tried to wave their frozen arms, but they were a speck on the horizon. They dropped back into the water and kicked in the direction of the ship with all their might. It was no use. The vessel continued her course and disappeared.

The men crawled back onto the raft and floated the rest of the day in miserable silence. The waves no longer washed over them. This only caused their tattered clothes to freeze to their skin. Their limbs were frozen too. The longer they rested, the harder it was to move. Even if the seas stayed calm, it would be difficult to hail a ship without flares or flags or even the ability to stand, move, or shout. Without oars, they would not be able to move themselves closer to a passing ship. Their only chance of rescue was for a ship to pass close enough to see them, or for a watchman with a keen eye to spot them on an empty ocean. Cedas looked at the horizon. It was empty. He laid his head down on the raft and prayed for sleep. Tongard did his best to stay awake and scan the horizon.

It was four o'clock in the afternoon when Tongard saw another vessel, or, rather, another vessel saw him. The ship grew larger and larger until they could see she was an American barque. Tongard grunted to Cedas to wake him up. The men did their best to move so those aboard the barque would know they were alive—at least they thought they were moving. They moved so little that the men aboard the barque believed they were dead. The ship came straight toward them. She was *Essex*, then three days out of Boston and bound for Rio de Janeiro with a cargo full of ice.

The crew of the barque was almost correct. Tongard and Cedas were almost dead when *Essex* found them. They were too frozen to move from the raft to the barque or to assist with their own rescue in any way. *Essex* sailors descended onto the raft. Tongard's and Cedas's bodies were so frozen that the sailors had to pry them from the wooden planks. They tied ropes around the men, slung them over their shoulders, and hoisted them aboard their ship.

The captain, Ray, took the kindest care. Merchant ship captains in the 1850s sometimes brought their wives with them to cook and care for sailors on board. Ray was one of them. His wife lavished the men with attention and nursed their frozen limbs back to health on the journey to Rio.

CHAPTER 18 | *On a Barrel*

The men told the tale of *Le Lyonnais* and her sinking to Ray and his crew but did not arrive in Rio de Janeiro until late December. It took much longer for word of their survival to reach New York. When *Essex* was twenty-five days out of Boston, the captain stopped in Pernambuco, Brazil. There, he spoke to Captain Sparrow of the barque *Cambridge* and sent word that he had picked up two *Le Lyonnais* survivors. The news reached Boston on January 29, 1857, and, with it, the end of any hope that those aboard the raft survived.

The report about the raft was grim. When Tongard and Cedas last saw it, on it were Richard and Voisin, the two principal stokers; Remeur, the coal man; a French girl who had served as a chambermaid to the passengers; and three American women passengers, one of whom was a girl aged ten to twelve. No women or children should have been on the raft. They came from Dublot's boat, which had capsized before leaving the wreck, or from those boats that crashed into *Le Lyonnais* the night they stood by the ship. Tongard reported the names of some of the sailors he saw aboard the ship on the evening of the fourth, the night before the ship sank: Brimot and Louis, two coal men, and others. He also mentioned the men who had worked with him to build the smaller raft that was lost on its way to the main raft with supplies, including the first stoker, Romain, and Cayolle, the chief cook.

The men arrived in Rio on Christmas Day 1856 and proceeded straight to the American consul, who received them with open arms. Questions from the press abounded. They said sixty were drowned following the collision and before the boats departed. They saw other vessels nearby at the time they were picked up, a fact that gave hope that other survivors had been rescued.

Ray communicated what the men told him via letter to Boston. Most of it centered on their efforts to fortify the raft. "Capt. Ray of the *Essex* says that he learned from them that a large raft was made and fastened by a rope to the crippled steamer, on which a large number of people got. A small raft was made to take provisions; but night came on, and the large raft, with her load of human beings, was either cut or broke adrift in the night, and what has become of the people these men have no knowledge."[1]

Tongard never mentioned that he and the four men determined to leave the ship refused to cut the raft loose. He never spoke of refusing to cut the line. He never told them he ignored the pleas of the forty-nine men, women, and children. He had no reason. He and his companion were the only people who had survived *Le Lyonnais*'s final moments. Tongard was alive, and that was all that mattered now.

CHAPTER 19

Two Ships Elise

GEORGE SCHEDEL LAY IN THE BOTTOM OF THE BOAT. He was neither dead nor alive. He had breathed just enough throughout the evening to prevent the others from throwing him overboard. He suffered from starvation, dehydration, and bitter cold, but most of all hopelessness. The passengers did their best to keep from touching him. Despair was now contagious.

Those aboard the lifeboat were still adrift in the Atlantic. They were far from land, where the water met the Gulf Stream, a current that moves north from the Southern Hemisphere, bringing with it warm and clear water. There were times when the surface was as blue and calm as an inland lake.

Luguiere spotted a sail on the horizon at eight o'clock in the morning. The ship was far away, but the breeze was favorable to them. He ordered the men to set up a sail and head in the ship's direction. Many of the passengers were still asleep when Luguiere saw the ship. They slept more often now and exerted themselves only when necessary. Strange movements were one of the few things that woke them in their weakened states. Their little lifeboat had become a part of them. Subtle shifts in her movement that just days ago would have been imperceptible now evoked in them visceral responses. Everyone woke up when the boat turned to move toward the ship on the horizon. They were glad to see a ship but had learned from previous chases to temper their enthusiasm. This ship was too far away to excite them, but too rich a prospect to ignore.

Schedel woke too. The sensation of the boat moving with purpose restored his will. He opened his eyes, pulled his body out of the frozen trench in which he had spent the night, and slid up onto the bench beside his wife. She looked at him. She was glad he was conscious but did not have the energy to celebrate the occasion with more than a faint smile.

The breeze picked up, but the ship they were chasing was going in the same direction, so the same breeze that moved them moved her. Her sails were so much bigger and stronger that the more the wind blew, the greater the distance grew between them.

The wind died down and gave the men an opportunity to catch up. They turned to the oars. Choupault and Dublic rowed toward the ship. Dublic had consumed so much seawater the previous evening that he grew madder and madder as he rowed. The faster he pulled, the quicker the salt water pumped through his body and poisoned him. Everyone feared he would somehow ruin the chase. Cauvin took over for him, and he and Choupault strained with all their might to reach the ship.

The firemen tended to Dublic. It took great effort to keep him still and in place, but he calmed in time. The passengers signaled the ship for help. They lost their white signal flag the day before. One of the men now made a flag of his red flannel undershirt and waved it in the air, moving his arms up and down in distress. It was no use. Both ships were moving in the same direction, and the renewal of the breeze gave her too much gain on them. They would never get close to her, and it would be unlikely that a man on watch would spot them from such a distance.

They gave up. Reserving energy was now as important as finding rescue. They could not afford to engage in fruitless labor. It was disappointing, but the group had grown accustomed to disappointment. Events that would have dashed their hopes the day before washed over them now like the water, the wind, and the waves.

Solomon sat upright in the lifeboat. It was difficult to move. It was not only from the cold. Her skin squeezed her like a corset tied too tight. A lifelessness crept over her limbs. The paralysis in her body only made louder the thoughts in her head. She was at a turning point. She knew it. She had spent the last week in constant fear of drowning, but today was different. She drifted in and out of hazy thoughts and felt so "stupid" from her sufferings that she no longer cared if she lived or died.[1] The indifference did not frighten her. It felt like freedom.

She was lucid enough to know she would soon lose her mind. She wondered why she could not always remember what had happened a few days or even a few hours ago. How did so much time go missing? Watching Dublic and Choupault in the throes of their delusions provided some answers. She wondered what strange things she had said or done in hers. Choupault was more like her. He was often in a normal frame of mind but occasionally not. Dublic was different. Dublic had crossed over. Madness consumed him. The other sailors took turns watching him. They held him down during outbursts and kept him from leaping into the waves. The day before, Solomon was too scared to make eye contact with him. Today, she was unafraid. She caught Dublic's glance for a moment and, for the first time, understood the person staring back at her. The sailor was gone but, in his delirium, he was far from this place. He was happy. The pity that Solomon once had for him now turned to envy. "It will be dark again soon," she reminded herself. She knew she would not survive the night.

The day wore on. Passengers languished in the boat and did their best to perform their duties while conserving their energy. The day gave way to the afternoon, and the sun began to drop into the sea. Luguiere spotted another sail on the horizon. She too appeared to be going in the same direction as the wind. Luguiere ordered the men to chase her anyway. They sailed, but the ship grew no larger or smaller. She stayed the same size as they both moved in the same direction. The men rowed and sailed for more than an hour. They were not gaining on the ship, but they were not losing her either. With a little luck, the breeze would drop out and they could row to her.

Choupault saw something out of the corner of his eye. It was another ship so far on the horizon that it was but a particle. It was on their port side and much farther away than the ship they were chasing, but Choupault thought she was moving in their direction. Choupault pointed it out to Luguiere, but Luguiere insisted they follow the first ship. "It is closer," he yelled. "We must not give up!"

The men rowed with all their might and changed places when exhaustion got the better of them. Choupault followed the first ship as commanded but kept a close eye on the other. The second ship had grown ever so slightly larger, which confirmed his suspicion she was moving toward them. He said nothing. It would be impossible to chase them both. They would have to sacrifice the closer ship to chase the new one. He had to be sure. Minutes later, he saw the second ship make a small, almost-imperceptible shift. "She just altered course," he said under his breath. He looked around. The only reason a ship's captain would alter her course on a day as clear and calm and on an ocean as empty as this one was if he saw something on the water. It was enough to convince Choupault that the ship to port had seen them. "She just altered course." His voice was louder and firmer now.

"Change direction!" Choupault called out to his fellow sailors without even looking at Luguiere for his consent. They stopped rowing, looked at Choupault, and looked back to Luguiere. Luguiere hesitated. "To port," said Choupault. The confidence in his voice was all the assurance the others needed.[1] They did not wait for Luguiere's agreement before they changed direction and rowed toward the new ship.

The men had long ago reached their physical limits. They knew this was their last chance. They heaved the oars in the water and broke their backs on every stroke. Frozen limbs now throbbed as the blood tried to circulate to them. The men took turns at the oars to combine the pieces of strength each had left in him.

The rest of the group assumed the worst as the men rowed. They waved their red flannel flag but reserved the strength it took to wave their arms or scream out. Concern about the decision to give up Luguiere's ship for Choupault's weighed on them. More than an hour had passed. The first ship was gone. The new ship did not appear much larger. The passengers wondered if the decision to follow Choupault, a man increasingly prone to delusion, was the right one. He was the only sailor among them who claimed to see the ship change course. "What if it was all in his mind?" Schedel wondered. Choupault had proven to be the ablest sailor, but Luguiere was the only sailor with his wits about him.

The men rowed. A sharp sensation fired from their backs to their shoulders, to their arms, and into their fingertips each time they plunked the oars into the water and pulled. It was the last real effort left in them. The knowledge both frightened them and made them pull faster. The ship was closer on the horizon after two hours of rowing. It was still difficult to judge whether she had seen them or whether she was just vaguely headed in their direction, but she was growing larger rather than smaller, which was a good sign. Anxiety overtook the group. The passengers screamed, shouted, and waved the red flannel flag with genuine enthusiasm.

Choupault rowed with the most energy. Since he saw the ship make the small shift in course, he had been certain she was coming for them. The ship grew larger on the horizon until a third hour passed, and most of the passengers were convinced of it too. The ship confirmed their suspicions a little past the third hour, when she signaled. Choupault clutched the oars as he sighed with relief, "It is done."

There was no longer any point in rowing, but the men took no chances and continued to do so until they reached the ship. The barque *Elise* towered over them in the water approximately one hour later. She was returning to Bremen, Germany, from Baltimore with a load of passengers and cargo under the command of Captain George Nordenholt. The survivors of *Le Lyonnais* shouted to the captain and sailors on deck that they were alive and in need of rescue. *Elise*'s crew helped lift each of the passengers on board. They began with the women and the passengers and finished with the crew. Some laughed. Some cried. Others stared in stunned disbelief, but they all, in one way or another, celebrated their survival on the ship's deck.

Schedel later wrote: "At 4 o'clock in the afternoon, on Sunday, 9th November, after six days and nights of danger and suffering, and when the eleventh hour had sounded and an apparently unavoidable death stared in our face, we were saved."[2]

Luguiere was the last sailor to land on *Elise*'s deck. There was the matter of their lifeboat. Nordenholt did not want it. It leaked, had no steering, and contained no provisions or equipment of any kind. The passengers could not bear the thought of letting the boat go. They begged the captain to take it with them. The little boat had become a part of them, a seventeenth survivor. It had kept them alert to changes in the winds and the waves and kept them afloat against all odds. In the end, it delivered them to *Elise*. The captain did not have the heart to refuse such a passionate plea and ordered his crew to hoist the boat aboard and stow it away.

The survivors told Nordenholt about both the circumstances of their sinking and their suffering in the days that followed. He, in turn, told them he spotted their boat on the watch three hours earlier, when they were scarcely visible on the horizon. Some small movements in the lifeboat convinced him they were alive and in bad condition. The movement Choupault saw was the captain adjusting *Elise*'s course to come to their aid.

Nordenholt treated the survivors with the utmost kindness. *Elise*'s doctor tended to the injured. The ship still had a long journey to Bremen, and Nordenholt feared not only for the health of some survivors but also that his small ship did not have enough water for sixteen additional passengers, especially some who needed more than a daily ration to restore their health. The next day, Nordenholt hailed another ship, which was carrying German immigrants to New York. In a startling coincidence, the other ship was also named *Elise*.[3] The New York–bound *Elise*, captained by Adolph Neilson, had greater capacity, more provisions, and was better suited to take on additional passengers.

Nordenholt offered the survivors the choice to remain on his vessel and go to Germany or to return to New York. Luguiere and his crew decided to go to New York so they could report *Le Lyonnais*'s loss to Franco-Américaine's agents. Most of the other passengers had no desire for a long journey to an unplanned destination and elected to return to America as well. Only the Schedels continued to Bremen.

The two ships *Elise* met at sea. The Schedels bid their companions farewell as they transferred to the New York–bound vessel. "Goodbye," said

Solomon as she embraced Mr. Schedel. "Good night," he whispered back.

The names of those saved by *Elise*:

Ernestine Bellet, passenger

Mr. Domenigo, passenger

George Schedel, passenger

Mrs. Schedel, passenger

Flora Solomon, passenger

Pierre Bienaimée, fireman

Jean-Marie-Louis Choupault, sailor

Alexis Cauvin, sailor

Desfour, third engineer

Julius Dublic, sailor

Joste, sailor

Adolphe Luguiere, second mate

Lambert, baker

Fabian Nestor, fireman

Victor Poirreaux, fireman

Stanislaus Thillaye, steward's mate

CHAPTER 20

Gloucester

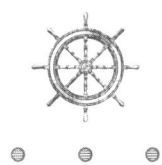

EVERY PASSENGER AND SEAMAN ABOARD *LE LYONNAIS* believed that the ship that hit her went down. The sound of *Le Lyonnais*'s cannon, the gloss of her lights, and the cries of her passengers would have been too loud and too bright to overlook even in the starry haze and rolling waves. Those who survived the wreck believed that if the men aboard the ship that hit them had not been in peril themselves, they would have come to their aid.

Steward's Mate Stanislaus Thillaye was a man of few words. He had little to say when he reached New York. His comments related only to the fate of the ship that struck his own. "She must have gone down because had she floated, we would have seen her the next morning and if she was not seriously hurt, she would have come to our assistance, as we kept firing a cannon into the night."[1]

Other survivors made similar mention; the ship that hit them went down. It was as if they took some measure of comfort in the knowledge their further suffering could not have been prevented because their only hope of immediate rescue had met the same fate they did. What Thillaye and the others did not know when they touched land in New York was that although the collision damaged the ship that hit them, it did not cripple her. She did not sink, and, after the collision, her captain never even thought of assisting them.

Captain Jonathan Barnet Durham of the barque *Adriatic* moved only forward. He passed the steamer heading east with the wind in his sails. He assessed the damage to his own ship, made repairs, and set sail for the nearest port without doubling back to check on the steamship's welfare.

He saw *Le Lyonnais* off his leeward bow for twenty minutes before her lights disappeared, and then she was out of sight. If his behavior in the days ahead told any tale, she was also out of mind.

Durham estimated the nearest port to be the seafaring town of Gloucester, Massachusetts. He arrived in that place on November 4 at eleven o'clock, less than forty-eight hours after the collision. He anchored *Adriatic* in the harbor and rested for the evening. He went to the customhouse, a place where ships registered when entering and exiting the port, the next morning and provided a list of repairs he sought for his ship. Most of the damage to *Adriatic* was cosmetic. There was no damage done to her main timbers or the fastenings. Her body, sails, and masts remained intact. She lost her bowsprit and jibboom, forward bulwarks, and head gear—the debris that wound up strewn across *Le Lyonnais*'s deck. She also lost a dragon figurehead.

Durham detailed the damages but remained silent as to the cause. He made no mention about a collision with a steamer. He sent a letter to his father and the owners of his vessel and informed them of the need for repairs. Durham made no report to any authority about the accident or informed anyone that there may be a steamer in peril less than two days away and in need of assistance.

Repairs to *Adriatic* began on November 6. Durham ventured to Belfast, Maine, to meet with *Adriatic*'s owners and agents during that time. He arrived on November 11, 1856, but even after his meeting with *Adriatic*'s shareholders said nothing publicly about the accident.

News of *Le Lyonnais*'s sinking and that a small group of survivors had been picked up by *Elise* and were bound for New York Harbor reached port late on the evening of November 14, 1856. The New York papers did not carry the story until the following morning, but the shipping community was small, and the newspapers and merchants who earned their livelihood in the industry had information exchanges in major port towns such as New York, Boston, and Gloucester that shared the information via telegraph. Word of *Elise*'s arrival spread. Word the ship that hit her lost a dragon figurehead with red eyes and gilt dart for a tongue spread with it and prompted reporters and nosy merchants to speculate about the identity of the offending vessel. Durham had, by then, kept his secret for nine days. It was only a matter of time before the survivors reached land and told their side of the story. The captain chose November 14, the day *Elise* arrived, to make his first public report about a collision with "a steamer, her name is not known."[2]

He reported the story to the *Belfast Republican Journal*, his hometown newspaper. The paper's owner and editor, George Moore, was an ally to local merchants, including Durham's brother Charles, and sought to position *Adriatic* in the best possible light. Durham gave Moore's paper his first published account of the collision. Moore buried the one-paragraph story on the paper's second-to-last page. Publication allowed Durham to claim he reported the matter, but placement in the back of the paper among the advertisements ensured that the story would not garner much attention. The report was so small it went unnoticed for several days by the New York papers:

> Disasters—Barque Adriatic Durham of and from Belfast for Savannah, was run into on the night of the 2d inst., by a steamer, her name is not known; those on board the barque put up lights, etc., to attract attention, but no notice was taken by the steamer which came steadily on striking the barque forward, carrying away bowsprit and forward bulwarks, and doing other damage. The steamer passed on without rendering any assistance; the barque was put to Gloucester for repairs.[3]

The first public statement made by the captain of the ship that collided with *Le Lyonnais* would have been front-page news in any other newspaper.

The New York and Massachusetts media soon put two and two together and surmised that the steamer was *Le Lyonnais*. Any reservations about the barque's identity were settled by the fact that the dragon figurehead Luguiere remembered from *Le Lyonnais*'s deck matched the one severed from *Adriatic*'s bow.

Media and local shipping officials, including those from the Gloucester Merchants Exchange, approached *Adriatic*'s crew in Durham's absence and took a closer interest in the ship. The exchange served as a collection of insurers for the shipping business, and its agents represented shipowners' interests. The insurance companies insured ships against losses and investigated claims on behalf of their clients. The Board of Underwriters wrote those insurance policies.

John T. Smith was a member of the Merchants Exchange at Gloucester. He spoke with one of *Adriatic*'s sailors on November 17, 1856. The sailor told Smith that Durham and the second mate were on deck at the time of the collision and saw the steamer's lights twenty minutes in advance. The sailor said nothing about *Adriatic* hoisting a light, but echoed his captain's assertion that those aboard *Adriatic* were unaware of any damage done to the steamer. *Adriatic* sustained little damage, "except the loss of her head gear," the sailor confirmed.[4] He supposed the steamer stood her course. The sailor first told Smith that *Adriatic* arrived in Gloucester the day before, on November 16. He communicated the information he obtained to Edward and Edmund Poirier, *Le Lyonnais*'s New York agents, and to the *Brooklyn Daily Eagle* via telegraph.

Later, after learning of the report made by Durham to the *Belfast Republican Journal*, Smith discovered that *Adriatic* had arrived in Gloucester much sooner than the sailor claimed. He sent a second telegraph to the Poiriers: "The barque *Adriatic* arrived at Gloucester November 4 (not yesterday 16th) and made no report beyond putting in for repairs."[5]

The same day, Mr. George H. Rogers, one of Gloucester's most enterprising citizens, boarded the barque. Rogers ventured into the Surinam trade with great success in the 1830s and, with the money he earned, bought a wharf in Gloucester where he could bring smaller vessels with cargo from Boston. He conducted substantial business in the port.

Rogers spoke with Durham's first and second mates. The officers explained that the barque was heading southwest on the wind and saw the steamer about fifteen to twenty minutes before the collision. They endeavored to tack to avoid the ship but struck her abaft in what they referred to as "the paddle boxes."[6] *Le Lyonnais* did not have paddle boxes, but many steamers of the day did, and they were located abaft between the stern and center of the ship.[7] The officers either used the term to denote the area of the ship they struck, or they were not watching closely enough to see the paddle boxes and assumed the steamer had them. The officers further indicated that they hailed the ship and requested her to stand by and render assistance, but her lights disappeared within twenty minutes. They believed that the steamer must have seen the barque some time prior to the collision, because the steamer blew a horn.

When ships collide at sea, answering the question "Who hit whom?" is largely a matter of perspective. This reality did not prevent everyone from experienced sailors to landlubbers from opining about the *Le Lyonnais* tragedy within days of *Adriatic*'s identification and the arrival of survivors in New York. Everyone had an opinion on the cause of the sinking and the conduct of the captains, and local newspapers stoked the debate to sell papers.

Moore, the editor of the *Belfast Republican Journal*, was known for his ability to describe events in ways that made them accessible to the everyday reader. He was unafraid of interjecting personal opinion into "news" articles. He was also unafraid of wading into political debates. "He was an antagonist to be feared in a political controversy, for he comprehended at once his adversary's situation, he perceived his weak points, and he possessed the dangerous faculty of overwhelming with wit and ridicule those he could not confound by argument."[8] He mounted a staunch defense of Durham that employed this strategy.

The *Belfast Republican Journal* declared in its small, November 14 article that "the steamer ran into the barque."[9] The declaration prompted reaction from writers in New York and Massachusetts. The editor of the *Boston Traveler* called the *Belfast Republican Journal*'s take on the collision "evidently absurd from the manner of her sinking" and noted the delay in reporting and the circumstances under which *Adriatic* sought repairs as reasons to be suspicious of information provided by Durham and his crew.[10]

Moore's paper defended its position. "The report published in our paper came through the officers of the barque, it is true; but we do not see that it differs from statements published in Boston papers. In cases of collision, it might naturally occur that each vessel would report that they were run into. It is not for newspapers to settle such questions."[11]

That is exactly what happened. Newspapers decided to settle the open questions, and a war between the *Belfast Republican Journal* and New York and Massachusetts newspapers began over who was to blame for more than one hundred lost lives.

Early questions about the sinking centered on three duties inherent to captaining a vessel: (1) the duty to yield, (2) the duty to signal, and (3) the duty to aid. Resolving the first debate was not as simple as it might seem. Steamships and sailing vessels were just beginning to share the world's oceans. Customs existed, but no established rules required a vessel to behave in a certain way when it encountered another. This became even more problematic when vessels from two different countries, each with their own customs, met. Some captains suggested establishing different routes for inbound and outbound vessels, while others argued for universal rules for meetings at sea.[12] Rules governing conduct would develop in time, but in 1856, captains of sailing ships and steamships used instinct, custom, and common sense to avoid collision.

Critics chastised Captain Devaulx for not slowing down to allow the barque to cross his bow, and *Adriatic* for not changing course when it appeared the steamer could not turn fast enough. Sailing ships are far more difficult to navigate than steamships, which is why a modern sailing ship has the right of way over a motorized vessel regardless of most circumstances. It was customary, even in 1856, for a steamship to give way to a sailing ship moving on the wind. All ships, however, had a duty to take evasive action to avoid collision. Questions abounded about why Durham continued to move toward *Le Lyonnais* at full sail when she showed no signs of turning:

Now, Mr. Editor, I do not intend to question Capt. Durham's seamanship, but why did he not put his vessel about sooner? Why try it when it was evidently too late? Why not throw the topsails aback and check the barque's headway whilst she still had steerage on her way? Why wait until the collision became unavoidable and then order the helm to be put down? The officers informed [the authorities in Gloucester] that their topsails were shaking when they struck the steamer. It is well known that while a ship is in stays she is forging ahead; had her topsails been thrown aback she would not have had headway on her. But, as you say, let us hear from Captain Durham.[13]

Some of the most spirited debates about the collision occurred between anonymous critics, who used the pseudonyms Ringbolt and Eyebolt. Eyebolt was a staunch supporter of Durham, while Ringbolt stood behind Devaulx. Both wrote letters to papers in New York, Boston, and Belfast. Ringbolt and Eyebolt never disclosed their identities, but each had knowledge of seamanship and of maritime regulations.

Eyebolt framed the counterargument in a letter to the editor of the *Boston Republican Journal* dated December 5, 1856:

[Your correspondents] say that it was gross carelessness on the part of the officers of the barque. Let us see. Had the steamer kept her course, she would have gone past her stern; but instead of continuing on her course, when within two cables' length, they attempted to cross the barque's bow—and hence the collision. Now, to put the most favorable construction we can on the matter, is that they could not determine which way the barque was standing. Under such circumstances, what should have been their duty? I should say the steamer should have been stopped till they had ascertained which way the barque was going; but no such thing was done.

Every seaman understands that a sail vessel is to keep her course, not to alter it for a steamer; and all steamers advertise for them to do so; and the barque's course was not altered till it was found a collision was inevitable. Capt. Durham then did what every prudent master should do; he ordered the helm put down, which brought her to the wind, receiving the blow stem on; which had he not done, the steamer would have struck the barque amidships, passing over her, and burying barque and crew in the depths of the ocean. That there was recklessness, no one can deny, but not where Ringbolt sees it.

He says, 'that through fright or bad seamanship the barque attempted to cross the steamer's bow'; not so, the steamer attempted to cross the barque's bow, and learned when too late that the battle is not always to the strong.[14]

Luguiere gave a detailed, sworn statement before the counsel general of France in the United States before the Imperial Order of the Legion of Honor in New York on November 15. It was published in full by the New York papers and did not bode well for *Adriatic*'s captain and crew. Durham added details to his scant first account only after newspapers published Luguiere's testimony. Reporters, particularly those in Boston, had become critical of Durham's conduct by this time. Durham released a statement on or around November 20 in response. It read:

> On Sunday night Nov. 2d, before 11 o'clock, the barque steering by the wind heading WNW, discovered a steamer about three or four points off the weather bow, supposed to be steering ENE. The night was starlight but hazy; should think we saw the light 20 minutes or more before we struck. The steamer continued her course, which would have carried her by our stern, if not altered, but upon nearing us she suddenly changed her course, which rendered a collision inevitable. We endeavored to save ourselves by tacking, but it was too late, and in a few minutes, we were afoul, striking the steamer abaft the wheelhouse[,] carrying away of jibboom, bowsprit, ripping up the topgallant forecastle and starting the whole starboard bow from the deck frame, and the wood ends forward. We then hailed the steamer and requested them not to leave us but received no answer. We then kept away before the wind to prevent losing our masts and to ascertain the extent of our damage. Saw the steamer's lights about four points on our lee bow, and kept in view for ten or fifteen minutes, until lost in the distance. Supposed that she had received little damage and had continued on her course. We secured our masts and repaired the damage as well as possible and shaped our course for the nearest port, and arrived at Gloucester November 4th at 11:00 p.m., and reported myself to the Custom House and to the Reading Room, stating the full particulars. The statement with regard to the weather being foggy is entirely incorrect, as it was starlight, with a slight haze in the atmosphere.
> —J. B. Durham[15]

It was the first time Durham alleged that the steamer changed course, and a departure from his earlier statement that she came steadily on. Had the steamer continued, he now argued, she would have passed him at the stern. It was because she shifted course that he was forced to turn his ship. He also claimed he kept away from the steamer after the collision to prevent losing his masts. The amendments directly addressed the complaints that had begun to surface against him.

Another important factor in the early debates about the collision between *Adriatic* and *Le Lyonnais* was the duty to signal. French law required a vessel to carry a lantern on the mizzenmast to serve as a visual indicator in darkness or hazy weather. There was no corresponding regulation in the US; however, steamships and sailing vessels routinely carried such lights.

Adriatic claimed to have seen the steamer's light a full twenty minutes before the collision but did act until the last possible moment. Those aboard *Le Lyonnais* insisted that there was no one on deck aboard *Adriatic* save the helmsman. In the years to come, much would be made of who was at fault for the collision. The visibility of the steamer's lights as well as questions about whether *Adriatic* hoisted a light at all would figure prominently in that debate. The only reports taken from *Adriatic*'s crew were made at Gloucester, and they are conflicting. Neither the crewman nor the officers mentioned that *Adriatic* raised a light. None of the crew participated in subsequent interviews about what transpired at sea. After Gloucester, the only person who spoke publicly on behalf of *Adriatic* was the captain himself, and he asserted he hoisted a light that should have been visible to *Le Lyonnais*. No other person in his crew mentioned this light in the weeks following the collision, and not one person aboard *Le Lyonnais* claimed to have seen it. Durham's supporters dismissed the issue as insignificant because the night was bright enough to make *Adriatic* visible to passing ships even without a signal light. "It was a starlight night, and a vessel could be seen from the steamer at a mile's distance, at least," wrote Eyebolt in one of the columns.[16]

The insurmountable obstacle for Durham was his decision to leave the scene of the collision without ever checking on the steamship. Those who inspected *Adriatic* at Gloucester noted she was barely injured. "Trifling" was how one reporter summarized her damage.[17] *Adriatic*'s repairs amounted to $2,000, a small fraction of the value of the ship. The barque sustained no structural damage, and while she needed repairs before making a transatlantic voyage, she could have surveyed the area for the steamer. Some, including the publication *Nautical Magazine and Naval Chronicle*, which reported only on subjects connected to maritime affairs, insisted that it was the captain's duty to go in search of the steamer. Another paper put it more bluntly, calling such action Durham's imperative duty "as a sailor and a man."[18]

Durham's supporters ignored Luguiere's assertion that *Le Lyonnais* blew her whistle and fired her cannons into the night. As Eyebolt put it:

> The second mate of the steamer also states, "that the barque kept away without offering any assistance," while at the same time he forgot to say that none was asked. Not a gun was fired, nor signal given of any kind by the steamer. Capt. Durham kept away before the wind, to keep his masts from going by the board, and was running about the same course as the

steamer but saw nor heard nothing of her and supposed that she was uninjured. He says, "that had they made a signal, he would have gone to their assistance, and done all in his power to rescue them." I have the statement of the officers and crew of the barque, that the steamer, although hailed by the mate, and requested to lay by, made no reply but kept on her course.[19]

Eyebolt's conclusion placed extraordinary faith in Durham's claim that *Le Lyonnais*, a sinking steamship with a disabled engine and holes in her hull, never used her cannons or brand-new steam whistle to call for help. He went on to blame Devaulx for launching Luguiere's lifeboat when it was ill equipped, and suggested they would not have needed rescue had the lifeboats been sufficient. "[Luguiere] leaves without provisions . . . while we see it stated by some of those picked up in [his] boat, that the other boats were well provisioned, and had on the raft provisions for 40 days, and were comfortably clothed."[20] It never occurred to Eyebolt that the lifeboat's amenities proved irrelevant in determining who survived and who did not in days of ferocious storms.

Finally, there was the matter of Durham's silence. "It is a singular circumstance," wrote the *Boston Evening Traveler*, "that Durham, of the *Adriatic*, should have been in port so long without having [his report] previously published."[21] Durham's claim that he reported the "full particulars" "to the Custom House and to the Reading Room" was a clever use of language. What he reported was the damage to his own ship.[22] No one in Gloucester knew of an accident before word of *Elise*'s return reached town.

Public scrutiny wore away at Durham's position:

> The collision broke away the iron plates of the coal bunkers, letting in the water and in 10 minutes the fires were extinguished. Could all this injury be done without the knowledge of those in command of the *Adriatic*? It is impossible. And what does Captain Durham report to the *Belfast Journal*? That he had been run into by a steamer which passed without rendering any assistance! The public may decide who was it that rendered no assistance. Shipmasters too often show the grossest selfishness and inhumanity in neglecting signals of distress, and rigid investigation is required to know how far the *Adriatic* is obnoxious to the charge.[23]

It was not just his silence that was at issue; it was the length of his silence. The Merchant's Exchange was more than just a network between

CHAPTER 20 | *Gloucester*

shipping agents and insurers. It facilitated search-and-rescue efforts. These were not acts of benevolence but ones that reduced insurance liability. Rescues and even partial salvages were far less expensive to insurers than total losses. Agents could have instructed ships going to and from the area of the collision to be on the lookout for the wreck or survivors. Had an immediate report been made of a steamer in distress, the Board of Underwriters for the exchange would have sent a steamer to the area to check on her condition and to search the area for survivors in the event she had gone down.

People talked not only about the culpability in Durham's silence but about what the length of his silence meant to those drifting in the Atlantic for days after *Le Lyonnais* went down, to the sailors who at the moment Durham arrived in Gloucester were still struggling aboard a ship that would not sink for two more days, and to those in New York and France still clinging to the miracle that their loved ones might return to them. "It appears that [Captain Durham] reached port on the 4th. Fully ten days—an age in such an emergency—elapsed in which knowledge of the occurrence has been smothered. If the lives of those unheard from have been sacrificed, a large share of the responsibility will rest upon Captain Durham and the agents of the vessel. The bare fact that a collision had occurred should have been heralded far and wide, with all possible dispatch."[24]

The *New York Herald* called upon the captain for answers: "Let us hear what Captain Durham has to say for not lying to, after the collision, to see how much damage he had done, and what assistance was required by the unfortunate passengers and crew of *Le Lyonnais*."[25]

The Massachusetts papers soon pivoted from defending Durham's conduct to reporting rumors that *Le Lyonnais* had survived. A few ships from Maine claimed to have seen steamers matching *Le Lyonnais*'s description on the ocean in December. Discovery of the French ship would have vindicated Durham, and the paper reported such sightings with reckless earnest. One report noted, "If [*Le Lyonnais* is found], the anathema against Captain Durham by land sailors will not amount to much."[26]

Days turned to weeks. There was no sign of *Le Lyonnais*. The best efforts of the *Belfast Republican Journal*, Durham's father's friends, and anonymous supporters such as Eyebolt were no match for an obvious truth: Durham left 132 men, women, and children to die at sea. *The London Guardian* published a poignant analysis of Durham's failure to act in the wake of the collision. "It was the duty of the captain to go in search of the steamer. Had he done so, every soul might have been saved."[27]

The public turned against Durham. The Gloucester customhouse investigation continued. Rumors spread from Belfast to as far as New Orleans that the Board of Underwriters themselves would soon call Durham before them to explain his decision to leave the scene without checking on the steamer's welfare.

Durham realized it was high time to leave Gloucester. He and his crew departed with *Adriatic* on November 29, 1856, and arrived at their original destination, Savannah, Georgia, on December 9. They dropped off a cargo of lime and hay and picked up a load of timber bound for Europe. *Adriatic* sat in port until the last day of 1856, when she was cleared for passage to La Ciotat, France. Durham supposed it would be a quick run to France and back, and that during the time he was gone, the fervor over *Le Lyonnais* would settle down.

The new year turned, and with it, any chance that additional survivors had been picked up by a passing vessel vanished. Durham's last defense, that *Le Lyonnais* had somehow survived, vanished with it. *The London Guardian* put it plainly: "It seems scarcely probable that [the passengers] will ever be heard from [until] the sea gives up its dead."[28] The last line was a biblical reference, a warning to Durham that he would one day face judgment about his conduct during the disaster. It came from Revelation 20:

> And the sea gave up the dead which were in it,
>
> and death and Hades gave up the dead which were in them;
>
> and they were judged, every one of them, according to their deeds.
>
> —Rev. 20:13

CHAPTER 21
The Phantom Ship

NOVEMBER 15, 1856, WAS A SATURDAY. Senator Charles Sumner and his friends Henry Wadsworth Longfellow, George Hillard, and Cornelius Felton gathered as they had tried to do each Saturday since 1837. It was in 1837 that Longfellow and Felton, professors at Harvard University, met author Henry Russell Cleveland and Charles Sumner and his law partner, George Hillard, and formed an informal social and literary association Longfellow dubbed the "Five of Clubs."[1] In the late 1830s and early 1840s, the young men met almost every Saturday at Longfellow's home on Harvard's campus in Cambridge, Massachusetts, to discuss their lives, their plans, and their futures. They met less often as they grew older, and when they did, their talks turned to philosophy, literature, and tumultuous times in an America on the brink of civil war.

Longfellow and Sumner arrived early to the Five of Clubs dinner on November 15, 1856. The closest friends among the group, their bond had been forged in the club's early days and strengthened throughout the years as Longfellow supported Sumner in his efforts to abolish slavery and Sumner supported Longfellow's transition from literary professor to full-time poet. Tonight, however, they would not speak of such things. Longfellow and Sumner sat down before the others arrived and discussed Sumner's health.

Sumner had given a powerful speech in Washington, DC, just months before, in May 1856. Immediately following the speech and in direct response to it, South Carolina congressman Preston Brooks struck Sumner with a metal-topped cane and beat him to bloody unconsciousness on the Senate floor. The speech, titled "The Crimes against Kansas," was an unrelenting rejection of American slavery and would later be hailed as one of Sumner's best orations. Longfellow called his friend's address "the greatest words, on the greatest subject, that has been uttered since we became a nation."[2]

Sumner almost paid for his words with his life. His injuries were so severe that he was still recovering six months later. Hillard and Felton disagreed with some of Sumner's more liberal political positions, so Longfellow thought it best not to discuss the matter when they arrived. His dear friend was doing better but still not well. Longfellow feared he had "a long and weary road before him."[3] He hoped, for his friend's sake, that the evening would be one full of laughter and pleasant conversation.

Charles Sumner (left) and Henry Wadsworth Longfellow. *The Politics and Poetry of New England*, photograph by Alexander Gardner. Washington, DC, 1863. *Library of Congress*

Hillard and Felton rushed in a short time later. Longfellow could tell by the looks on his friends' faces that he would not get his wish. "It's your brother," one of them said. "His ship has been run down at sea." Sumner said nothing.[4] The report was a great shock to him. He feared not only for Albert but for the lives of his sister-in-law, Catherine, and his niece, Kate. He left at once to go to Boston, where those who worked in the customhouse and the newspaper would no doubt have more information.

Sumner was not the only family member who sought information about survivors in the days following the news of the collision. *Elise* arrived so late in the evening of November 14 that only four newspapers, three in New York and one in Connecticut, reported on the disaster the next day. The short reports were based on a sparse account provided by Captain Neilson, commander of the New York–bound *Elise*. Only one published a partial list of the survivors' names. The list came from Neilson's report, and the spellings of the names, most of which consisted of only a first name or a sailor's title, were too butchered to provide a trustworthy account to family members seeking confirmation. Farther north, in Massachusetts, news of the disaster had not yet reached a single paper. The only information available was whatever rumors leaked out of the customhouse in Gloucester or from newsroom telegraphs in New York.

News of the disaster and rescue of sixteen survivors made front-page headlines on November 16, 1856. The reports included passenger lists, but because the fourteen survivors who chose to go to New York remained on *Elise*, it would not be until November 18, when Franco-Américaine transferred the survivors to a New York boardinghouse, that the newspapers learned and published their names. Information took even longer to reach France, where most of the crew's friends and loved ones lived. Rumors filled the spaces in between and taunted desperate families with hope.

Sumner used his connections to learn what he could about his brother's fate. It was inconclusive. Albert was not aboard *Elise*, but the last time anyone saw him, his wife, or his daughter, they were still alive and in one of the lifeboats. There remained hope that the boat was rescued by a passing ship. Six years earlier, in 1850, Charles received the news that his brother Horace drowned in the shipwreck of *Elizabeth*. It seemed like yesterday. Sumner told himself that this time it would be different. Albert was strong and no stranger to the sea. If anyone could survive a wreck, it would be him.

Catherine Gibson and Charles Gibson anxiously awaited news about their son and brother, John Gardiner Gibson. Like Sumner, Catherine had suffered such pain before. Eighteen years earlier, she waited to learn that her husband was one of many who died of illness aboard a ship. When newspapers first published the names of *Le Lyonnais*'s missing, T. G. Gibson, a person unknown to Catherine and Charles, appeared on the list but not John. Catherine breathed a sigh of relief, but it was only temporary. The following day, the papers printed a retraction and added John's name to the lost. The death of a child is unbearable for any parent, but losing both her husband and her son to the sea was too much for Catherine. Her niece later wrote that she "never ceased to mourn inordinately" over the loss of her eldest son.[5]

Papers published reports and revised them as new information came in. The original passenger manifest listed "Basseford," his lady, a servant, and "children" as passengers on the ship. Because of Margaret's last-minute change of heart, her only child, one-year-old Louis Franklin, did not join her on the journey to France. He stayed behind with his grandmother in New York.[6]

The public strained to connect strange occurrences to the disaster. A body washed ashore on Siasconset Beach, Nantucket, in mid-November. The coroner pronounced that the body had been in the water for several weeks, and the New York Times speculated the man was a victim of the *Le Lyonnais* disaster. The man's clothing suggested he was a passenger as opposed to a sailor, and a comb found in the breast pocket of his vest revealed the initials "W. N. L." No one on the passenger manifest matched that name.

People on both sides of the Atlantic awaited news of lost loved ones. On November 26, a rumor arose that *William L. Burroughs* had taken *Le Lyonnais* passengers on board. The next day, newspapers called the rumor unfounded. As the year wore on, many still hoped that more survivors had been picked up by passing ships that either could not or did not communicate word to port. It was not uncommon for crossings to take weeks, and with so many ships traveling similar routes as *Le Lyonnais*, hope for rescue was still possible even as November turned to December.

Hopes rose and diminished again with the discovery of empty lifeboats. Captain Peabody of *Neptune* discovered the cutter commanded by Sumner and Beaugrand in November, but news of it did not reach New York until mid-December. The discovery led some to believe that Sumner and his party had been picked up by a ship. The rumor was soon quashed by Solomon and Schedel, both of whom remembered the boat. It had broken away from *Le Lyonnais* after the provisions, chronometers, etc. had been placed in it, but before any person climbed aboard. Luguiere's boat took it in tow for a short time but could not manage to keep it in the violent weather. Solomon watched as the boat "drifted away at the mercy of the waves."[7]

Neptune's agents transmitted news of the boat's discovery to *Le Lyonnais*'s owners in Le Havre. A French newspaper, the *Bordeaux Journal*, confused the telegraph about the boat with the discovery of more survivors and reported on December 8 that Captain Devaulx and fifteen others had been rescued and delivered to Bordeaux. The steamship *Canada* brought the same news from Liverpool to Halifax later in December. The story morphed into a report that Mrs. Jeanette Strong; her daughter, Julia; and her son-in-law, Theodore Bailey, were among the saved. The Halifax port communicated the news to Mrs. Strong's brother, Leonard Bailey, who received the telegraph on Christmas Eve 1856. Through Christmas and the three days that followed, Leonard believed that his sister, his niece, and her husband were alive, only to later learn the rumor was false.

Similar events occurred in Cuba. On Christmas Day 1856, *L'Aborada*, a Cuban journal, reported that Don José de Eulate and his wife, both passengers aboard *Le Lyonnais*, had been picked up by a British vessel bound for Jamaica just one day after the sinking, on November 3. This time, the newspapers were skeptical. The report claimed the couple and some other survivors had been rescued on November 3, yet no ship had brought such news to New York. The report turned out to be false, but only in part. A British brig, *Beauty*, picked up one of *Le Lyonnais*'s boats on its outbound voyage to Jamaica, but there was no one in it. It was just the opposite. The boat discovered by *Beauty* was white with a square stern, likely the cutter commanded by Roussel. It was bottom up and stoved in on the starboard side. The boat's oars were lashed to the thwarts, and its lugsail and mast floated alongside it. Inside was a cask of water and a life buoy marked *Le Lyonnais*.[8] The condition of the boat was proof of how unlikely it was that any of the others survived the storms, wind, and waves that had so plagued the known survivors.

Rumors taunted the public for a time but eventually ceased. Discovery of the boats by *Beauty* and *Neptune* meant there were no other lifeboats left to find, and it was unlikely that survivors would have been picked up and not yet reported. Every lifeboat had been accounted for except for the small yawls commanded by the captain and purser, and only one had endured.

Five passengers survived. Those who did were lucky to be alive. Recovery from the disaster was another matter. Solomon lost everything she owned on *Le Lyonnais* but felt fortunate to escape the disaster with her life. Some who perished left substantial fortunes behind. Once the final list of the dead had been named, families endured the difficult task of distributing property to their heirs. Family members both of the Sumners and the Bassfords contested their wills, and lawyers emerged and called upon survivors such as Solomon to testify at court proceedings.

Sumner's wife was extremely wealthy. She inherited upward of one million dollars when her first husband died.[9] She also had children from her previous marriage. The law at the time dictated that if Mrs. Sumner outlived her husband, her fortune passed to her children from the previous marriage. If her husband outlived her, it passed to his heirs. The last time Solomon saw the Sumners, they and their daughter were alive and in a lifeboat. The facts of the case presented a novel issue in American law about who is deemed heir when a family dies but there is no way to determine the exact order of their deaths.

The court ruled that the child died first, the wife second, and the husband last, a holding based on the assumption that men were stronger than women or children. The husband or his heirs inherited marital property in the absence of testimony to prove a wife outlived her husband.

The lawsuit was the talk of Newport. The Sumners were wealthy people, and although they prevailed in court, they gave a substantial share of Mrs. Sumner's fortune to her children. Longfellow wrote, "The Sumners were not the sort of people to take advantage of any such legal quibble. They pressed the claim on principle but then gave Charles' share of his wife's fortune back to her heirs."[10]

The loss of his family members devastated Charles Sumner. "During the winter, although physically much better, his brain refused the slightest draft upon it, and notwithstanding his repeated determination to begin his labours anew, a single day in the Senate—the last of his old term—was all his broken nerves allowed."[11] He took the oath of office and sailed to France, where he began a recovery both from his physical injuries and mental anguish that took almost two years.

Margaret Clayton Bassford's will went to probate. The issue there was not intestate succession but whether the will, which was written on a small piece of torn paper, was valid. Solomon was again called to testify. She could not opine about a piece of paper written long before she met Mrs. Bassford, but was called as a witness to the Bassfords' presence aboard *Le Lyonnais*. She testified that the Bassfords were alive and on a boat containing about twenty people when she last saw them. Her life was saved, she told the court, when she was forced to step out of the boat they were in and into another.[12]

The loss of life on *Le Lyonnais* was catastrophic, but there were also material possessions, some noteworthy, aboard the ship. Peabody discovered a small amount of gold and silver coins aboard Beaugrand's lifeboat, which led some to believe that *Le Lyonnais* was carrying a large cache of gold and silver. This was not the case, and the rumors were dismissed. The money found inside the boat corresponds to the sum he received for selling his ship in Cuba. He placed the coins in the boat along with his other personal possession, such as his notebook and personal chronometer.

Composer and artist Don Vicente Díaz y de Comas carried with him a copy of *Album Regio*, a rare work of art designed to demonstrate Spain's influence on Cuban culture. *Album Regio* was approximately 103 pages long and contained lithographs of the coats of arms of the territories of Spain, complemented by sheet music adorned with allegorical figures such as lions, fortresses, musical instruments, ships, and other emblems. It included sheet music for contradanzas, habaneras, zapateados, waltzes, polkas, hymns, and marches. The musical pieces and drawings were arranged under the coats of arms they represented. Each coat of arms was drawn and painted by hand in vibrant colors. Reds, blues, yellows, and gilt adornments predominated. All the musical works were composed by Díaz y de Comas except for the Royal March that appears under the coat of arms of Castile. Spanish painter Patricio de Landaluze created the engravings. The book ends with a family tree of the Spanish royal family.

Díaz y de Comas was traveling to Spain via France so he could deliver a copy of the album to the queen of Spain, Isabel II, to whom he dedicated the work. Díaz y de Comas produced only a handful of copies of *Album Regio*, and one of them went down with the ship.

The other material possession of note belonged to Thomas Bassford, the other young composer aboard *Le Lyonnais*. Bassford's most significant composition to date was an opera he had written. It represented an important personal advancement in his work from a composer of individual songs to a composer of larger and more-complex pieces. It was also an opportunity to honor his country by presenting what was hailed by many critics as the first well-composed opera by an American to be sung in the English language.

Bassford based the opera on the legend of a seventeenth-century ship captain named Hendrick van der Decken. Captain van der Decken loved the sea. He loved it more than most. The sea called to him, and he preferred to sail than to do anything or be anywhere else. The captain undertook a voyage from his native Holland to East India and planned to return with spices. His ship reached the Cape of Good Hope, a rocky headland on South Africa's Atlantic coast. A huge gale swept up and a storm came upon them as the captain and crew rounded the cape, and the storm grew in strength and in fury. Thunderous waves clapped. The wind headed them and tore their sails to pieces. The crew begged Captain van der Decken to seek the safety of the bay, but he refused. He walked the deck and swore at the wind in defiance of heaven itself. He forced his men to sail on in the merciless storm. First the men prayed. Then they threatened mutiny. When those efforts were unsuccessful, they once again begged him to change course, but the captain was as unrelenting as the ocean. A bolt of lightning struck the ship's deck and splintered it in two with smoke and fire. The crew, on hands and knees, pleaded with their captain to change course. He looked at the sky and cried, "I will never stop. May I be eternally damned if I do. We will sail until Doomsday!" The moment the captain uttered those words, the ship, captain, and crew disappeared.

Legend has it that Captain van der Decken's ghost ship forever haunts the Cape of Good Hope. In the four centuries since his ill-fated voyage, sailors, beachgoers, and lighthouse keepers have reported seeing a gloomy barque making great speed on windless seas beneath tattered sails. She exhibits a bright glow, appears suddenly, and then, just as suddenly, disappears in the mist. A sighting of the ghost ship portends foul weather. The legend says that any person who sets eyes on her will soon die at sea. Those who handed down the stories dubbed it the curse of the *Flying Dutchman*.

The *Dutchman* legend inspired Bassford's opera "The Phantom Ship." It was a composition on which he had worked passionately but had not yet completed leading up to his voyage to Paris. The only known performances of a portion of the opera were at Bassford's soirees in April and May 1856. On April 3, 1856, baritone Allan Irving performed "Thou Gazest Deep and Earnest" (from unpublished opera *Phantom Ship*)." Although the next soiree program, from May 12, 1856, is unpublished, critics mentioned the importance of English-sung opera in their reviews.

Thomas Franklin Bassford did not make a living on the sea. He did not keep a lighthouse. He never saw the *Dutchman* floating in the mist off the Cape of Good Hope. He did, however, make his only known performances of an opera devoted to a legendary ghost ship that heralds doom just five months before *Le Lyonnais* set sail. After those performances, the ocean swallowed both the budding composer and his unfinished masterpiece to the deep.

CHAPTER 22

Survivors

REACHING THE DECK OF THE RESCUE SHIP ALLOWED *Le Lyonnais*'s survivors to succumb to the madness of their minds and the exhaustion of their bodies. The early days aboard *Elise* were a blur for many, particularly those who labored the hardest in the boats. Solomon spent the return trip to New York in and out of consciousness. Dublic climbed back from delirium as his body purged itself of seawater. Choupault's fingers were so frozen that they balled into fists no matter how hard he tried to straighten them. His feet were so damaged that he could not walk, and he spent the trip to New York confined to bed. Captain Neilson provided the survivors whatever he could. He gave the sailors his clothes to wear and allowed passengers to use his quarters as their own, but medical capabilities aboard his ship were limited.

Elise arrived in New York late on the evening November 14, 1856, carrying German immigrants and fourteen shipwreck survivors. Throngs of people lined up outside Franco-Américaine's New York office the next morning. Some went in search of information about their loved ones. Others went to gawk. Newspaper reporters clamored to catch a glimpse of the men and women who survived. They were disappointed when only the German immigrants departed the ship. The survivors remained aboard *Elise* due to their dire medical conditions while Edmund and Edward Poirier arranged for their care and shelter.

There was one exception. The morning after *Elise*'s arrival, Luguiere left the ship and went straight to the French consulate in New York. He was *Le Lyonnais*'s highest-ranking survivor and represented his employer at a meeting with the consul. Luguiere fared the best during the disaster and was the only survivor who did not require medical attention. French law required the highest-ranking survivor of a shipwreck to make a report to the nearest authority within twenty-fours. He spoke to Charles Marquis du Montholon, France's consul general at New York, and Consulate Chancellor Louis Borg within that time frame. The Du Montholons were a powerful French family with ties to Napoléon III, and Du Montholon served both as consul general to the US and an officer in France's Imperial Order of the Legion of Honor.[1] Interest from the highest levels of French government signaled France's concern about the collision from the outset. Luguiere spent the entire day with Du Montholon and Borg and described to them the details of the collision as well as their ordeal in the lifeboats. The officials were so moved by Luguiere's account that they pledged to assist the surviving sailors, all of whom were French, in their recovery. A summary of Luguiere's statement, which was provided by the consul to the local papers, caused both hope that other boats may have been picked up by passing ships and concern that some boats might still be adrift on the Atlantic.

The Poiriers sent the surgeon from *Le Lyonnais*'s sister ship, *Vigo*, to visit the sailors and surviving passengers aboard *Elise*. Frostbite had blackened the fingers and toes of all but a few of them. Large blotches appeared on some, indicating places where bodies were most affected by the cold. Walking was difficult. The survivors' feet had been submerged for more than a week in the frozen seawater. Once they lost feeling in their feet, they did not even try to keep them dry or warm, which only made the situation worse. Choupault, Cauvin, Fabian, and Solomon could not walk on their own. Dublic's left big toe was frozen solid.

The process of reviving the dying tissue was a slow and painful one that required the gradual rewarming of the tissue. The doctor submersed the passengers' frozen feet in salty water that was only slightly warmer than the temperature of seawater and increased the warmth of the water over time. Long-dulled nerves sent signals to the survivors' brains that something was not right as the dying tissues warmed. The signal came in the form of intense pain. "My feet are in a terrible state, and I suffer at times from the greatest pain" is how Solomon described it.[2] The doctors slathered her feet with an oily substance to keep the wounds moist and then wrapped them to allow them to heal. Both Choupault and Dublic spent several days in bed before becoming well enough to walk on their own.

Fingers and arms also succumbed to the cold. Cauvin's right wrist was frozen, as was Nestor's arm. Choupault's left arm was frozen from the wrist all the way to the elbow. Dublic's left wrist and hand were swollen from saltwater poisoning and, as they thawed, bled from large contusions that crossed his skin like lashes. Treatment for frozen limbs was much the same as frozen feet. Doctors soaked them in warm water, coated them with medicine, and wrapped them. The wounds were ghastly and ranged from large black spots on the skin to bursting, puss-filled blisters. The doctors checked the men and women from time to time and changed the wrappings.

The Poiriers arranged for the sailors to stay in Mr. Chatillon's boardinghouse at 79 Leonard Street in New York City, where they would remain until they could board a ship home. *Vigo*'s surgeon treated them there. The French consul and Franco-Américaine provided each sailor with money to buy new clothing.

Solomon returned to her parents' home in the bowery section of New York City. The bottoms of her feet were frozen, and she could barely walk. Bellet suffered from frostbite. She went to stay with friends. The Poiriers did not disclose to reporters where the remaining passenger, Domenigo, recovered from his injuries, but at the time of his arrival in New York, he was so frostbitten they feared for his life. It was only after the crew transferred to the boardinghouse and the passengers returned to their loved ones that Franco-Américaine released the names of the saved.

A reporter from the *New York Herald* visited the boardinghouse on November 17. It had been more than a week since the crew's rescue, but many of the men were still recovering from frozen limbs and contusions. Those who spoke about their experiences were tight-lipped about the details of the collision and their survival at sea.

Luguiere stepped into the vacuum left by their silence, and the press became enamored with him. He gave his own account to a reporter, who described the twenty-eight-year-old as "the perfect specimen of a frank and gentlemanly sailor."[3] Luguiere projected the image of a young, confident, level-headed hero. He refused the five-hundred-franc sum allotted to him from a charitable fund taken up New York, and asked for his share to be donated to the poorer members of the surviving crew. He dismissed their nine days at sea and told reporters that his capable men could have survived at least four more days in the open boat. He further claimed that despite devastating storms that blew them far from shore, he could have reached land if he had a compass. His assertions strained credibility, but the papers ate them up. "Now that [Luguiere] has shared in a shipwreck and in field battery, he only wants to experience an earthquake to render his catalogue of sightseeing complete. He assured the consul Saturday in a modest, unassuming manner, that from the first to the last he felt certain of being saved and laughed heartily at the extraordinary demonstrations of delight displayed by his companions when they found themselves aboard the *Elise*."[4]

Luguiere had no intention of resting at the boardinghouse. He was about to board another ship. Franco-Américaine leased *Marion*, a paddle wheel steamship from the Charleston line, for a ten-day cruise to search of *Le Lyonnais*'s survivors. Luguiere's participation in the search only furthered his favor with the consul and the press. "That he is a perfect stranger to fear is proved by his desiring to return immediately to the scene of the disaster," the *New York Herald* wrote.[5]

Captain Foster of *Marion*, Luguiere, and an officer of the *Vigo* all boarded *Marion* on November 19. Their trip was fruitless. *Marion* returned to New York within nine days with no sign of the steamship and with news of more gales and foul weather. The only remaining hope was that some ship bound for a foreign port had picked up survivors and had yet to send word.

Those first few days in New York gave survivors time to reflect on the collision and its consequences. They were lucky to be alive, but someone was responsible not just for their misery but for the deaths of their fellow sailors and so many others. They described the ship that hit them in detail, and asked shipowners to take notice of any sailing vessels with dragon figureheads. Poirreaux remembered a ship with a similar figurehead, called "*Bragonne* or something like it," lying in port in the East River.[6] Reporters sought to confirm the sighting, but to no avail. The men were certain the ship that hit them had gone down. Even Captain Sharpe of the *Vigo* was of the opinion that the barque must have gone down within minutes, on the basis of the nature of the collision and the relative size of the two ships.

It was in the boardinghouse on Leonard Street where the sailors first learned they were wrong. The morning paper arrived on November 15. None of the French sailors spoke much English, but it was not long before others translated the news that a ship matching the description of the one that struck them had made its way to Gloucester, Massachusetts, uninjured. *Adriatic*.

Thillaye froze. He sounded out the name. *Adriatic*. His mouth went dry. He tried to swallow, but the act only caused the feeling of emptiness to settle in his stomach. It was impossible. "How much misery could have been avoided if only they came back for us?" He remembered those who died—Father François, the Spaniard, and all those who had drowned or starved to death adrift at sea. The image of Father François's face, blue and twisted in the torture of his final moments, blinded Thillaye with anger. Neither Choupault nor the others could find the words to comfort him.

The sailors recovered and waited at the boardinghouse for news of additional survivors and of how and when their employers would facilitate their return to France. Their opportunity to return home came in December 1856. Franco-Américaine, the consul, and a charitable organization in New York arranged for the remaining members of *Le Lyonnais*'s crew to travel aboard *Mercury*, a packet ship from Boyd & Hincken's Le Havre Line. The ship arrived in New York on November 13, 1856, and departed for France again on December 13, 1856.

CHAPTER 22 | *Survivors*

Mercury was a clipper with two decks and a gross tonnage of approximately 1,100. She was more than twice *Adriatic*'s size, but she was a sailing ship. Choupault used his return voyage to Le Havre as an opportunity to learn how American sailing vessels operated. He peppered *Mercury*'s captain, Thomas Stetson, like a curious child about all aspects of American maritime customs and regulations. "Why do you raise the light?" "When are you required to hoist the light?" "How many lights do you carry aboard this ship?" He was a man obsessed. Choupault spoke to *Mercury*'s crew about their experiences at sea and on watch and studied the way the captain and crew handled encounters with steamships and other sailing vessels.

Le Lyonnais left New York with a crew of ninety-three. Only nine of her crew survived. They arrived in Le Havre weeks later. The port city appeared at first as a skyline and then emerged into view. Her stone buildings and wide thoroughfares were a sight for sore eyes.

Mercury reached the mouth of the port. The men adjusted the sails, and the captain took the ship through a narrow waterway lined on both sides by wide docks that faded into cobblestone streets. Wooden pylons that separated boats from one another dotted their path. Seagulls swooped and squawked and shrieked. Some perched upon the columns and welcomed them home.

"Lines on!" Stetson cried when the ship at last reached its resting place. The men attended their stations and tied the ship to bollards in what felt like an instant. One by one, nine *Le Lyonnais* survivors stepped off *Mercury* and onto the dock.

Le Havre, where the Seine River estuary met the English Channel, was a French gateway to the world. Choupault took it all in. Rows of multistory merchant buildings lined the harbor. Horse-drawn carriages moved passengers and luggage to ships bound for ports unknown. Small markets sold the day's catch. The air smelled of salt and fish and steamship smoke. Choupault took in a deep breath and let it out again. There were so many times he thought he would never see this place again.

He stepped away from the ship and onto the main street that lined the water. People went about their daily business, passengers walked to and from the ticket offices, and sailors rushed to waiting vessels. They nodded their heads in polite greeting as they passed. Choupault nodded back. They had absolutely no idea where he had been or what he had experienced. He smiled to himself. He was, once again, an anonymous sailor in a lively port city. It suited him just fine.

Luguiere received most of the attention in the days and even years that followed the collision. He was the highest-ranking survivor and would serve as *Le Lyonnais*'s voice in statements to follow. There was,

Le Havre, France. Steel engraving of a drawing by Joseph Mallord William Turner, 1857.

however, no question among the survivors about to whom they owed their lives: Choupault.

Survivors spoke his name with reverence. It was Choupault who steered them through storms for days on end, Choupault who kept spirits up when things were darkest, Choupault who sacrificed his body and his mind so they could carry on. In the end, it was Choupault who found their rescue ship and saw them saved.

A German newspaper published George Schedel's account in February 1857, more than three months after the collision. Schedel, who had not spoken to any of the others since the rescue, wrote, "Choupault, I declare it with all emphasis, saved our lives. During the days and nights, when we were struggling for existence against the waves which raged around our weak boat, next to God, he, as a clever pilot, saved us from sinking. . . . Without [Choupault] all of us were buried long ago in the ocean."[7]

Choupault bid farewell to his shipmates and soon found himself alone for the first time in months. He walked to the water's edge and stood there for a time with his feet planted beneath him and his arms crossed in front of his chest. His stance was sturdy, but he could still feel the sway of waves within his body. It was just one of the consequences of crossing an ocean. A ship passed. She unfurled her sails and caught the wind. Her tall, dark figure cut against bright-blue skies. Choupault wished the sailors a safe journey. He watched the ship set to sea and did not move again until she dissolved into the horizon. "Tout est fini," he said to himself. "It is finished." He took one last look at the water, turned away, and vanished into the bustling city of Le Havre.

Cunard line poster, 1874. Design by
George H. Fergus.

Etching of the Carter Shipyard in Belfast,
Maine. Etching by E. M. Woodford.
Courtesy of Penobscot Marine Museum

Two pages from "Album Regio." A polka decorated to commemorate Santander, Spain (*left*). Queen Isabel II of Spain's family tree (*right*). *Courtesy of S. P. Lohia collection*

Illustrated Times of London's colorized depiction
Le Lyonnais's passengers with the sinking ship,
December 27, 1856. *Author's collection*

Old Harbor (Vieux-Port), Marseille, France, between
ca. 1890 and 1900. *Library of Congress*

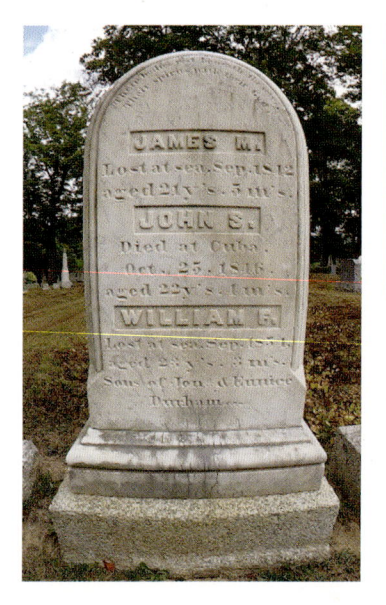

Durham family gravesite, Belfast, Maine. *Photos by and courtesy of Charles H. Lagerbom*

Jonathan B. Durham's grave, Malden, Massachusetts. *Photo by author*

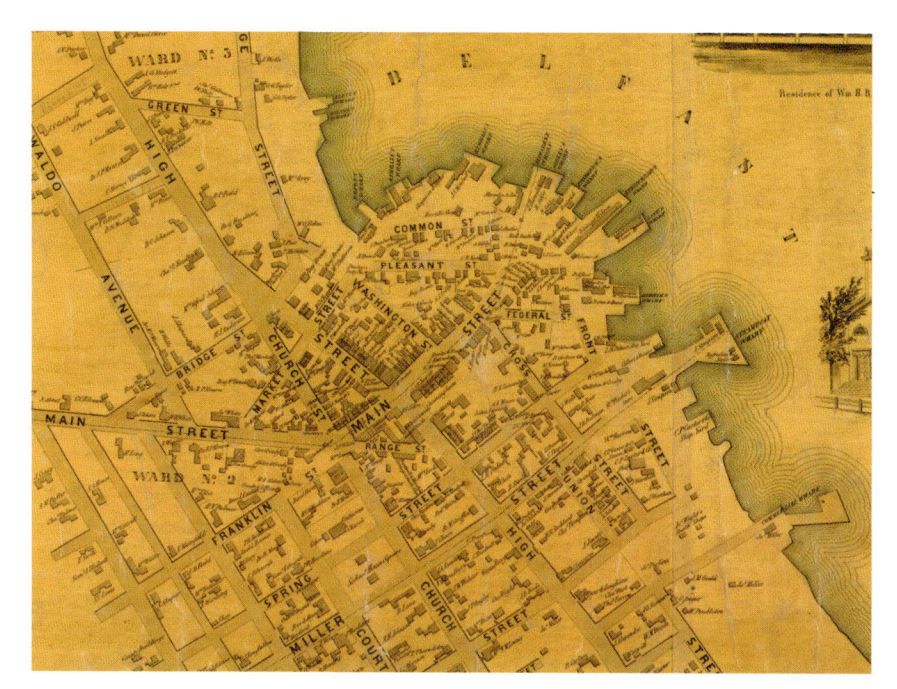

Portion of a map of the city of Belfast, Waldo County, Maine, including Durham's Wharf and C. P. Carter Shipyard. Lithograph by E. M. Woodford, published by E. M. Woodford, Philadelphia, 1855. *Library of Congress, Geography and Map Division*

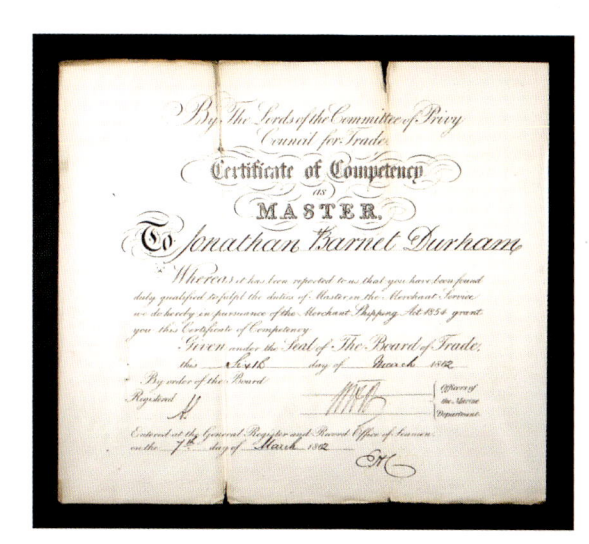

Master Mariner certificate awarded to Captain Durham by the British Board of Trade. *Digitized from the National Archives in Greenwich, England, by Ancestry.com*

The Church Street house Captain Durham purchased for his family in Belfast in the mid- to late 1870s. It was previously owned by Captain Asa A. Howes. Durham lived in the home during the late 1870s and early 1880s before returning to Massachusetts. *Photos by author*

Captain Eric Takakjian pointing out Georges Bank to Rick Simon on a chart at the beginning of the 2023 expedition. *Photo by author*

The 2023 *Le Lyonnais* expedition team. *Left to right*: Kurt Mintell, Rick Simon, Andrew Donn, Eric Takakjian, Jennifer Sellitti, Joe Mazraani, François Merle. *Photo courtesy of Atlantic Wreck Salvage*

Divers suiting up on August 22, 2024. *Left to right*: Tim Whitehead, Tom Packer, Eric Takakjian, Jennifer Sellitti, Joe Mazraani, Andrew Donn. *Photo courtesy of Atlantic Wreck Salvage*

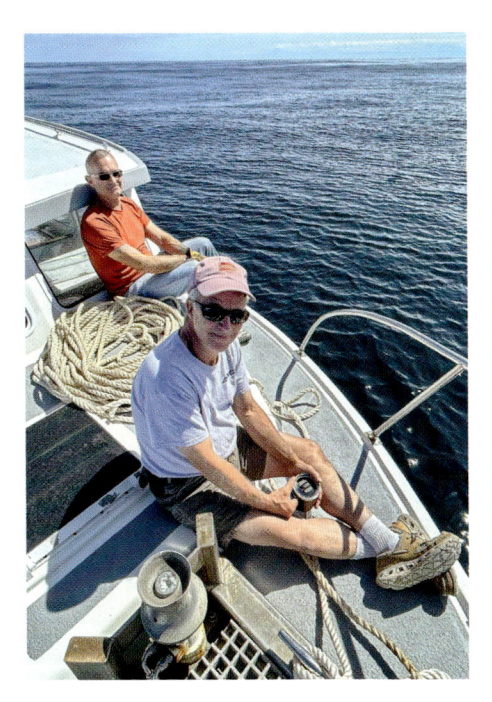

Kurt Mintell and Eric Takakjian getting ready to throw the hook at the first dive site on the morning of August 22, 2024. *Photo by author*

Divers Tom Packer, Tim Whitehead, and Joe Mazraani reviewing photos of *Le Lyonnais*'s sister ship, *Cadix*, during the 2024 expedition. *Photo by author*

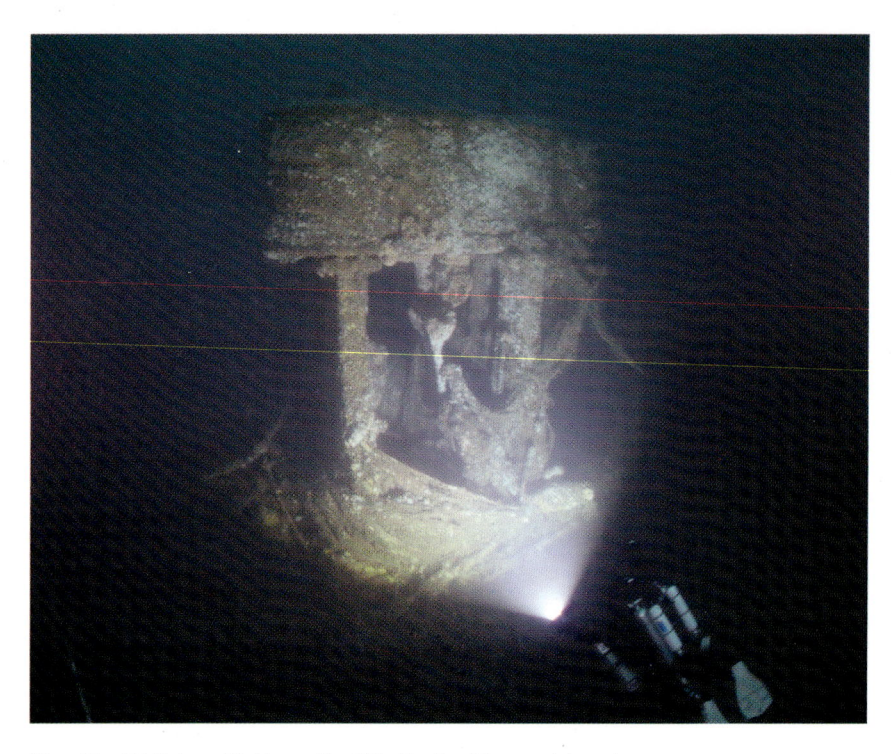

Diver Tim Whitehead lights up the "Big Engine Steamer's" engine.
Photo by and courtesy of Andrew Donn

The "Big Engine Steamer's" boilers.
Photo by and courtesy of Joe Mazraani

Another view of the "Big Engine Steamer's" elongated boilers.
Photo by and courtesy of Joe Mazraani

The "Big Engine Steamer's" engine standing tall on the ocean floor. *Photo by and courtesy of Andrew Donn*

Joe Mazraani surfacing from a dive on *Le Lyonnais* on August 23, 2024. *Photo by author*

Andrew Donn completing his decompression in a roaring current on August 22, 2024. *Photo by author*

Kurt Mintell (*seated*) and Andrew Donn talking during a break between dives on August 24, 2024. *Photo by author*

Joe Mazraani, Eric Takakjian, and Tom Packer reviewing video footage of *Le Lyonnais*'s engine on the afternoon of August 23, 2024, in preparation for the next day's dives. *Photo by author*

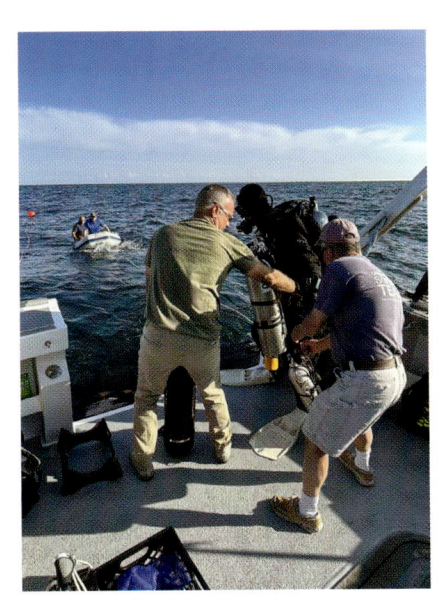

Tim Whitehead on the afternoon of August 23, 2024, preparing to splash on the wreck to retrieve portholes. *Photo by author*

Tim Whitehead surfacing after successfully recovering the portholes for the team. *Photo by author*

Tom Packer preparing for a dive on *Le Lyonnais* on August 23, 2024. *Photo by author*

Tom Packer and Joe Mazraani splashing on *Le Lyonnais* to measure her engine cylinder. Jennifer Sellitti and Eric Takakjian are assisting Tom Packer on deck while he waits for Joe Mazraani, who is in the water, to begin his descent. *Photo courtesy of Atlantic Wreck Savage*

Le Lyonnais's sternpost.
Photo by and courtesy of Andrew Donn

A clam dredge wrapped around *Le Lyonnais*'s capstan. Fishing gear such as dredges and nets pose threats to shipwrecks in the North Atlantic. *Photo by and courtesy of Anrew Donn*

One of *Le Lyonnais*'s engine cylinders. *Photo by and courtesy of Andrew Donn*

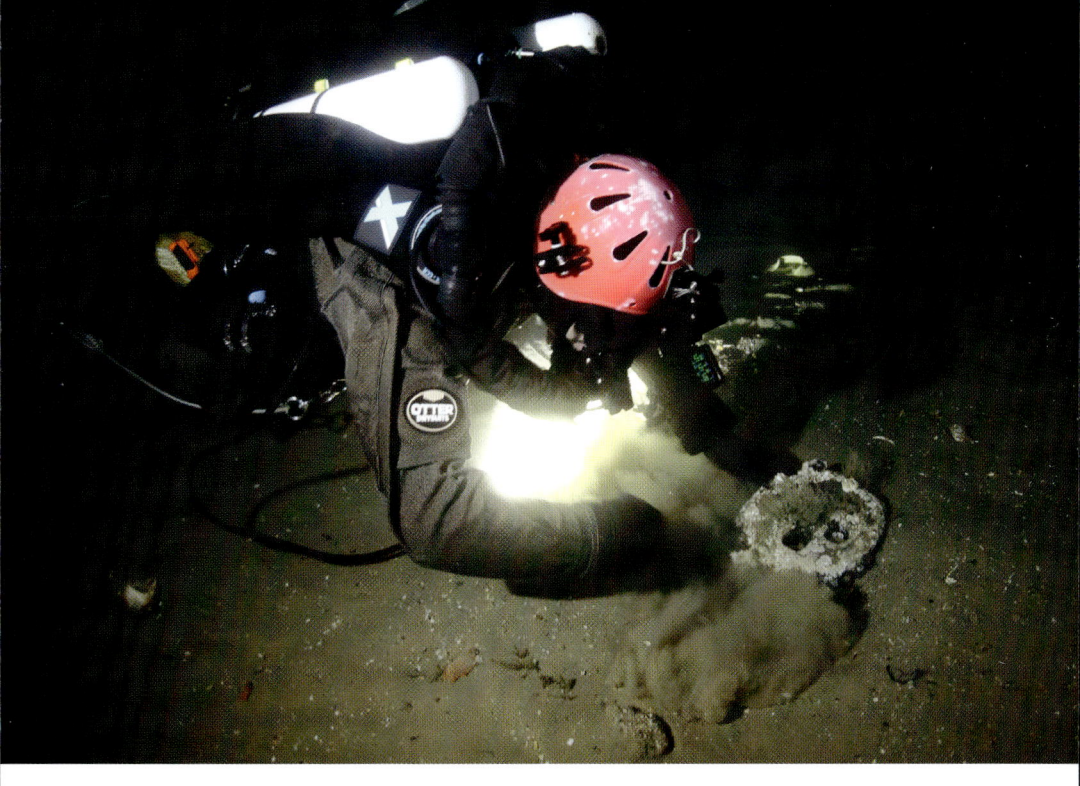

Joe Mazraani, fanning away the sand to reveal a deadeye used as part of *Le Lyonnais*'s sail rigging during a dive on the wreck on Saturday, August 24, 2024. *Photo by and courtesy of Andrew Donn*

Square-shaped containers believed to be tanks that were part of *Le Lyonnais*'s water distilling apparatus.. *Photo by and courtesy of Andrew Donn*

The team, safely back at Fleet Marina in New Bedford, with portholes recovered from *Le Lyonnais*. *Left to right* (back): Andrew Donn, Kurt Mintell, Joe Mazraani, Tom Packer; (front) Tim Whitehead, Eric Takakjian, Jennifer Sellitti. *Photo courtesy of Atlantic Wreck Salvage*

Part II

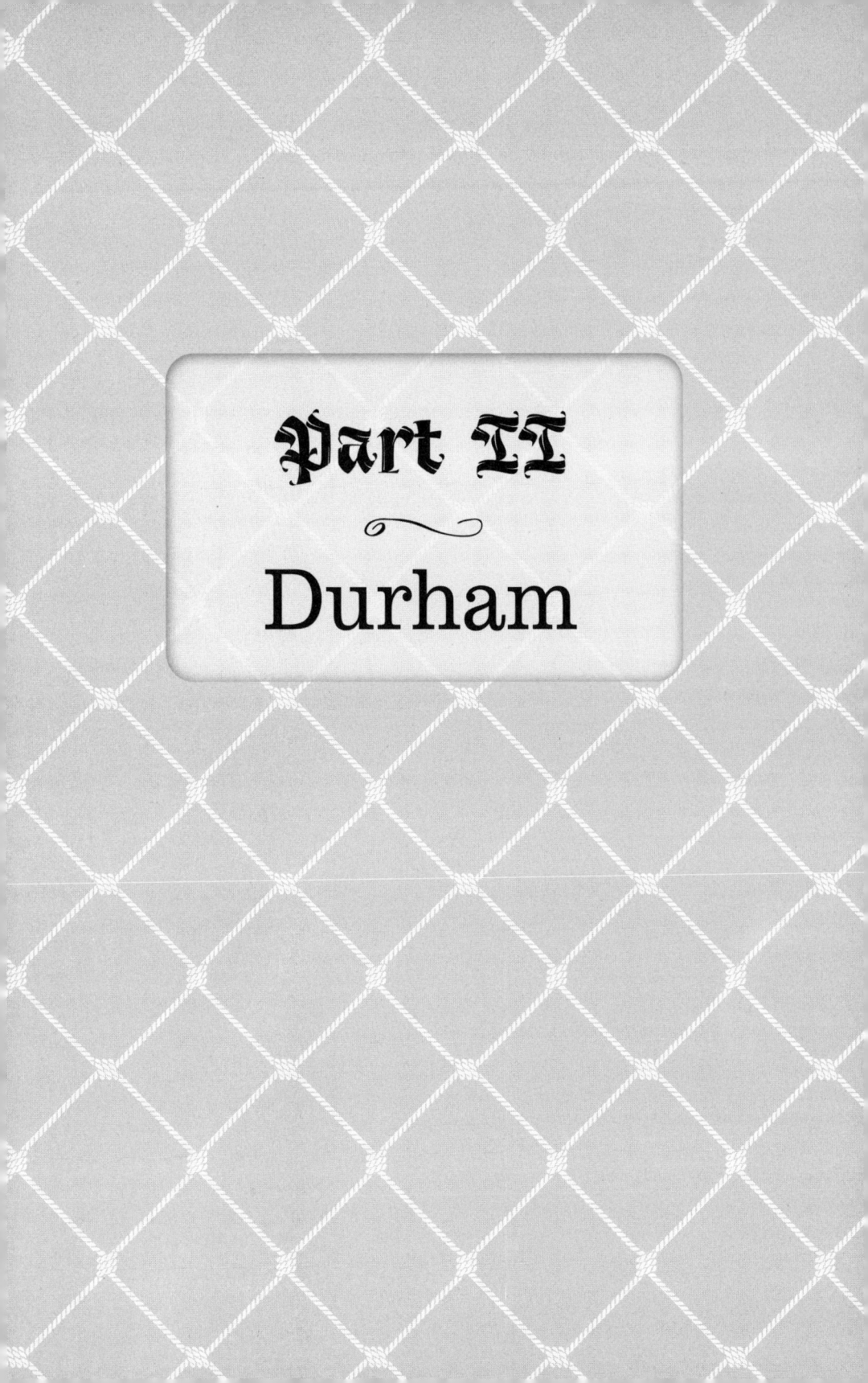

Durham

CHAPTER 23

Command

CAPTAIN JONATHAN BARNET DURHAM stood at *Adriatic*'s helm and spun it casually beneath his fingers. The ship's deck splayed out before him. Long wooden planks made pathways that parted at the middle and met again at the pointed bow. Durham followed the lines with his eyes. He loved this view. The sails rose high and flapped in the crispness of the breeze. Men darted about the ship upon his orders. They climbed the rigging, adjusted the sails, and readied the vessel as she made way toward land. Moments like these made Durham believe the world lay at his feet.

The sailor's life came naturally to Durham. He was born in the seafaring town of Belfast, Maine, to Jonathan Durham Sr. and his wife, Eunice, on March 11, 1827. Jonathan Barnet, "Barney" to his friends and family, was the second youngest of eight children, two girls and six boys. Eunice gave birth to all eight between 1818 and 1831, a span of thirteen years.

Barney's grandfather John Durham was a sea captain, merchant, and landowner. He was also one of Belfast's original sons, a group of thirty-five men who divided Waldo County, Maine, into shares in 1768. Barney's father, Jonathan Sr., inherited both John's land and his livelihood.

Barney was not the only Durham to follow his ancestors' footsteps. His older brothers George Anson, James Monroe, and John Sergeant and younger brother William also became sailors. Older brother Charles was the only one of the six who chose a different path. He became a lumber dealer.

Barney was eighteen when he first set to sea professionally as a boy aboard the Belfast brig *Topliff*. Although the ship's boy was usually a young teenager, "boy" was a job title used to describe a person new to the occupation of sailing. An older teen such as Durham sometimes signed on as a boy to learn the job. He spent five months aboard *Topliff* in the summer of 1845. The ship, a coastal trade vessel with two masts and square-rigged sails, stopped briefly in New York, bound for New Orleans. She visited ports in Delaware and Philadelphia in between. Durham learned to work the sails, stood watch, and ran errands for the captain.

He took to sailor's work and sought out as much of it as possible aboard the merchant vessels that called Maine's busy ports home. He served as an ordinary seaman aboard the schooner *Mary Farrow* and left Bangor on May 3, 1845, on a voyage that took him from Charleston, South Carolina, to Frankfurt, Germany. It was the first time Durham crossed the ocean aboard a ship, and the adventure captivated him. He returned to Bangor six months later, on November 1, 1845, a man of the world. He set sail again in March 1846 to England with Captain Edward Colby aboard the Newburyport brig *Salisbury*. Colby often took his crews on long voyages, sometimes up to two years. The 1846 voyage lasted a little less than a year, but it took Durham from ports in Europe to Matanzas, Cuba, and home again.

After *Salisbury*, Durham earned a promotion from ordinary seaman to seaman. Ordinary seamen spliced lines, worked the sails, and handled the masts and yards. Once an ordinary seamen mastered the basics and "knew the ropes," he advanced to seamen, a distinction that came with increased pay and responsibility. Durham took his first voyage as a seaman aboard *Essex* in the winter of 1846, followed by a stint on *St. Petersburg* and a second voyage aboard *Mary Farrow*.[1] The year 1848 presented new ships and new destinations with work aboard the barques *Harriet Martha* and *Acadia*. Most of these vessels carried goods from Boston to southern ports such as Charleston, Savannah, and New Orleans.

Durham became chief mate aboard the Belfast brig *General Marshall* in the fall of 1848. He was responsible for making sure the crew carried out the captain's orders. The turn at sea lasted almost a year, from October 1848 to September 1849, his longest yet. Durham subsequently became first mate aboard the Boston brig *Ottawa* and then *Shammer* out of Kennebunkport, Maine.

While Durham's maritime career advanced, his father's wound down. Durham Sr. transitioned from captain to farmer and, by 1850, abandoned the mariner's life. He spent the latter part of the 1840s engaged in real estate and in building up both a workshop near Belfast Harbor and the family farm. He became involved in local politics and served on boards and committees in Belfast throughout the 1850s.

CHAPTER 23 | Command

It took Barney only five years to work his way from boy to captain. He got his first command at the age of twenty-thee aboard the Boston brig *Napoleon*. His time with *Napoleon* was brief, from October 1850 to March 1851, but it gave him a taste of what it meant to take charge of a vessel. His next command lasted much longer.

Barney's rise through the ranks coincided with the expansion of one of Belfast's most renowned shipbuilders, Carter & Company. Owner Columbia Perkins Carter built his first ship, *Tonquin*, in 1841 and earned a reputation as a reliable man and the respect of community members such as Jonathan Durham Sr. "As an employer, and in all business relations, Mr. Carter was scrupulously just, and every obligation was met promptly and fully. There was rarely, if ever, a business so large carried on with so little flourish or display. He believed in work and achievement, not in red tape. He never forgot the respect that belonged to men[,] and gave to the humblest person in his employ a hearing as attentive as to the merchant whose ship he contracted to build."[2]

Barney's older brother, John Sergeant, worked as *Tonquin*'s second mate in 1841 and 1842. Carter built a new schooner, *Siam*, in 1850. Barney served both as captain and consignee of the vessel, which meant he was responsible for securing cargo and commanding the ship. He spent the better part of three years at *Siam*'s helm, running a coastal route from Belfast to Savannah. The voyage became routine for him, and Savannah like a second home. He made business connections with local merchants, captains, and shipping agents in the port.

Carter's reputation for building high-quality ships was warranted. *Siam* did not disappoint. Durham went on to captain Carter's schooner *Malabar* and eventually, along with his father and brother and their partners, chose Carter to build *Adriatic*. They built a yard on Upper Steamboat Wharf in Belfast to accommodate her construction. The yard and the ship were Jonathan Durham Sr.'s legacy, a venture that would provide his sons, the captain and the lumber dealer, with the means to prosper in businesses of their own.

Adriatic was everything young Barney wanted in a ship. He worked with his father and brother on her plans. He knew every line, every detail. She was the culmination of all he had learned both from his ancestors and his years at sea. *Adriatic* was also the young captain's freedom. It was the freedom to travel where he wanted, to do what he pleased, and to make his own destiny—the freedom of having command not just of a ship but from the whims of shipowners. *Adriatic* was an investment for his father and brother, but, for him, she was a dream come true. When he was behind the helm on the open sea, *Adriatic* did not belong to his father or his brother or their partners. She belonged only to him.

CHAPTER 24

La Ciotat

IT HAD BEEN MORE THAN TWO MONTHS since *Adriatic* left Savannah. The journey took longer than expected due to foul weather and unfavorable winds. None of that mattered now that Durham's destination was in reach. He saw land in the distance. It came in the form of a vast limestone plateau that rose high above the sea and stretched out like an open hand into the ocean. La Ciotat. The landscape here was unmistakable.

The city of La Ciotat is home to the Soubeyranes cliffs, the highest cliffs in France and among the highest maritime cliffs in all of Europe. Ciotat means "city" and dates to fifth-century navigators who found the area a convenient launching point for trade routes. The town sits at the bottom of a crescent-shaped bay and faces the sea. La Ciotat's back nestles against Bec de l'Aigle, "the Eagle's Beak," a rock formation that resembles an enormous bird's beak and juts out over the ocean at the bay's southernmost tip.

Merchants built the first shipyards in the early 1600s, but competition from the nearby ports of Marseille and Toulon kept the city from becoming a preferred destination for seafarers. That changed in the mid-1830s, when La Ciotat saw a small renaissance. A new pier built in 1835 doubled the city's harbor capacity. In 1836, Louis Benet, the son of a wealthy La Ciotat shipowner, bought a shipyard and modernized it. He brought engineers and shipbuilders from all over Europe, who introduced new propulsion systems such as the steam engine and modern methods of construction.

La Ciotat's geographical advantage was that it rested between the cities of Marseille and Toulon. Benet's advancements caught the attention of larger shipbuilders in the neighboring cities, who outsourced contracts to him to keep up with their own production demands. Benet built ships throughout the 1840s and earned lucrative contracts from Marseille- and Toulon-based companies. An 1848–51 economic crisis in the region caused a temporary decline in the shipping business. Larger shipbuilders went back to doing their own work; smaller ones went under. Benet was unable to keep up with construction advancements, and his venture soon deteriorated. He liquidated the businesses in 1851 and sold the assets to a new company, Compagnie des Messageries Nationales. Messageries Nationales ushered in a period of industrialization in the region, which earned La Ciotat recognition as a thriving shipbuilding community and a gateway to France for mid-nineteenth-century merchants.

The Durham family sought to cash in on La Ciotat's revival. Durham arranged with Georgia lumber dealers Muller & Michaels to deliver a load of lumber to buyers in the city. The delays at Gloucester cost him two months in delivering on the contract. *Adriatic* at last set sail for France from Savannah on the morning of January 1, 1857. Durham wanted to put distance between himself and New York at the time, but, in hindsight, he viewed both the hour of his departure and his destination as symbolic. It was a new year. *Adriatic* carried lumber and almost 200,000 feet of timber in her belly. Durham was on his way to meet customers in a Mediterranean city brimming with promise.

The barque arrived in the Old Port of La Ciotat on February 10, 1857. Durham planned a short turn, a little more than one week. It would give the men enough time to rest before offloading cargo, restocking provisions, and preparing the ship for the next leg of the journey. La Ciotat was a picturesque fishing village dotted with seventeenth-century homes. Durham thought it a pleasant enough place to lay over for a short time, but he did not come for the scenery. He had other business—securing new cargo. An empty ship on the voyage home was a floating business expense. He met with local merchants in the hopes of finding someone looking to ship something to America or another destination in Europe. One eventually hired him to bring a small amount of freight to Sicily. It was not enough to fill *Adriatic*'s hold, but the contract promised enough additional income to make the trip worthwhile and gave him a foothold for further business in the region.

Durham reported to the La Ciotat customhouse on February 20, discharged his cargo of timber, paid his custom dues, and cleared for Sicily. He arranged with the customs authorities to pay the duties on his outbound freight at five o'clock in the evening the following day and to begin his voyage to Sicily on February 22.

The men spent most of February 21 filling *Adriatic* with ballast, a method by which ships shifted the weight balance of their cargo for sailing. Without ballast, a ship carrying little to no cargo would pop out of the water like a cork. Moving ballast was grueling work. The men shoveled rocks and sand into the holds until the ship reached the weight and stability required for travel. The crew had about half the ballast loaded by four o'clock in the afternoon, an hour before Durham was to pay his freight, when a customs officer boarded *Adriatic* and asked to see the captain.

Durham greeted the officer with a smile, asked if there was a problem, and added, "I will be there in an hour to pay my freight." "I'm sorry," said the officer. "There has been a mistake in your clearance. Proceed to the customhouse immediately to rectify the matter."[1] Durham obliged.

The customhouse was an official building where civilian authorities collected import and export taxes, conducted port business, and provided ships with clearance to sail. The officer opened the door and motioned for Durham to step inside. The mood chilled the moment he did. Another officer, whose stature suggested that he outranked the others, approached. "An order has come from Le Havre by telegraph from the owners of *Le Lyonnais*," he said. "We are seizing your freight and your vessel."[2] The officer informed him that his clearance to Sicily or any other port had been rescinded. He added, with more formality than the situation required, "By order of the French government, you may not leave France until the *Le Lyonnais* matter is settled."[3]

France required ship captains to present clearance paperwork before leaving any port. Without papers, Durham would be stuck in La Ciotat until the matter was resolved. He tried to reason with the officer, but it was no use. The orders came from a higher authority than anyone in La Ciotat possessed.

"I demand to see the consul," said Durham. The American consul could provide guidance on navigating French law and marshal political resources in support of his interests. The officer replied, "There is no consul here," and directed him 30 miles northwest to Marseille. Durham returned to his vessel to inform his crew and departed for the neighboring city with haste.

The morning after Durham's departure, his crew awoke to the sound of footsteps coming from the ship's deck. They jolted from their bunks and ran out of the forecastle to investigate. French officers surrounded them. "Who here is in command?" asked one. Joseph Shaw Thombs, *Adriatic*'s first mate, stepped forward. "I am."

Thombs was twenty-two years old. He was born in Castine, Maine, a town located across the Penobscot Bay from Belfast. Castine's prosperity, like Belfast's, came from fishing and shipbuilding. Local ropewalks, sail lofts, and ship chandlers provided goods and services for the maritime trade. Thombs's older brother, Charles R. Thombs, was a sailmaker who moved to Belfast and opened a sail loft there. Thombs joined him. He learned to sail first from his brother and then as a seaman on ships coming to and from Belfast Harbor, including those operated by Carter & Company. It was there that he met Durham. Despite Thombs's youth, he soon became the captain's most trusted man and earned the first-mate position aboard *Adriatic* on her maiden voyage. It was up to Thombs to ensure the crew followed the captain's orders at sea. Now it was up to him to fill Durham's shoes in his absence.

Thombs was a newlywed. He married Ella Nancy Osbourne on October 12, 1856, just two weeks before *Adriatic* set sail. He hoped to use the money earned from Durham's new venture to build a future with his wife. He approached the situation in which he now found himself with the boldness that Durham expected of him as a leader and the caution that his wife expected of him as a husband.

"We are seizing your cargo," said the officer. Thombs let them take it. They had legal cause, and he saw no value in fighting a losing battle. The officer in charge remained on deck and shouted orders to Thombs's men. "Unbend these sails!"[4] The crew froze. Thombs stared at the officer for a moment and took a step closer to him. He held his hands out to the sides of his body as if to keep his men back and said, "Stay where you are." The words were for his crew, but he looked at the officer when he spoke. The officer was unmoved. "You can do as I say or I can take all of you to prison."[5]

Thombs decided it was better to comply, and let the captain sort it out. His arms fell to the sides of his body. "Unbend the sails," he said. The men unfroze upon his orders. They began untying the knots that fastened the sails to the spars and lowering them. The officers left while the men worked. It was early evening, and they did not get much work done before the light faded.

They continued their work the next day. Unbending the sails on a ship of *Adriatic*'s size took at least twelve to fourteen hours. The crew worked slowly to stretch the time, both out of loyalty to their captain and because they believed that the misunderstanding would soon be rectified, and that they would have to raise the sails all over again.

The customs officers returned the next day and the day after that to assess the crew's progress. Once the officer in charge was satisfied that *Adriatic* could not sail, he found Thombs again and ordered him to unhang the rudder. This time, Thombs refused. Sails were easy enough to reraise, but unhanging the rudder was a more complicated process. Removing and replacing it could compromise *Adriatic*'s ability to steer when the time came. The officer showed Thombs nothing to suggest that French authorities had ordered the rudder removed. Thombs pressed, and the officer backed down. Thombs kept watch over the ship for the next week, and French authorities kept watch over him.

Durham remained in Marseille, a city far larger and more cosmopolitan than La Ciotat.[6] France's oldest city and one of Europe's longest continuously inhabited settlements, Marseille rests on the sea in a sheltered depression surrounded by limestone hills and became a natural home to explorers, fishermen, and merchants. Open access to the Mediterranean made it a strategic port from when the Phoenicians settled the area as a trading outpost around 600 BCE. It became a staging port for trade expeditions to Africa and northern Europe by the fourth century.

Marseille emerged as a center of business and government in the eighteenth century, when France improved the ports for naval use. The city's strategic importance grew in the nineteenth century, along with advancements in shipping and industry, and its port became the fifth largest in the world by the 1830s, behind only New York, Liverpool, Hamburg, and London. The French expanded the port in the 1840s to accommodate the influx of vessels and the increased size and capacity of steam-powered ships. Bureaucracy followed. Marseille's Office of the General Consul of the United States represented America's interests in the region and provided guidance to American businessmen.

Durham reported to the consul's office as soon as he arrived in Marseille. The consul himself, George Washington Morgan, greeted him. He was a large man with a strong stature and firm handshake. He had light skin and light-brown hair parted far on the left side of his head near his ear and blended into a bushy pork-chop beard that stopped at his lower jaw. He had small eyes and bushy eyebrows that made him appear as though he was squinting in concentration. The outer corners of his eyebrows pointed downward and lent a seriousness to his appearance. Morgan was rugged. Neither his fine clothes nor his tasteful French office could disguise it. Durham was not sure what to make of such a man.

He soon learned that Morgan was not motivated by impulse but by duty. Patriotism ran in his blood. His father named him after President George Washington. His grandfather, also named George Washington Morgan, was the first to inform President Thomas Jefferson of Aaron Burr's conspiracy. It was not politics, however, but the battlefield that called to Morgan in his youth. He dropped out of college at the age of sixteen and followed his older brother to the US Army. They traveled

George W. Morgan, ca. 1860-75. Photograph by Mathew Brady. *Library of Congress, Manuscript Division, Brady-Handy collection*

from Pennsylvania to Texas, where they served during the War of Independence. Morgan rose to the rank of lieutenant and then captain and assumed command at Galveston. He served as a Texas Ranger until 1839, when he resigned and returned to Pennsylvania. He entered the United States Military Academy in 1841 but left before he completed his degree. He moved to Ohio, became an attorney, and served as prosecutor of Knox County from 1845 until 1847, the outbreak of the Mexican-American War. Morgan was appointed colonel of the Second Regiment of Ohio Volunteers and left for the front lines. He was commissioned as colonel of the 15th US Infantry in March 1847 and served under General Winfield Scott.

Pragmatism also ran in Morgan's blood. He exhibited a no-nonsense approach to conflict. In 1846, when Mexican troops found themselves overmatched by American forces in the war, they engaged in guerrilla warfare. Morgan kidnapped several prominent Mexican citizens in response and proclaimed he would execute one of them for every American soldier the guerrillas killed. The guerrillas stopped their attacks. Morgan was wounded in battle in October 1847 and returned to Ohio, where he resumed his law practice. President James Buchanan appointed him consul to Marseille in 1856. He was thirty-six years old.

The Marseille post was Morgan's first political appointment, but it was an important one. France's leader, Louis Napoléon Bonaparte (Napoléon III), had been a popular president from 1848 to 1851. A newly-enacted French law prevented him for running a second term, so he assumed power in an 1851 coup d'état. He sought to reestablish France's dominance around the world, which made diplomatic relations with the US delicate. Morgan was tasked with maintaining the balance with an audacious French leader while representing American interests in the strategic stronghold that was Marseille.

Durham launched into the story of how and why he was stranded in La Ciotat. Morgan waived his hand as if to say, "Save your breath." The consulate office was the epicenter of business, politics, and gossip in the city. He already knew all about *Adriatic*'s seizure. He told Durham that the Gauthier brothers had sued him in the French Tribunal of Commerce for *Le Lyonnais*'s total loss. Durham insisted he was not at fault and attempted to tell Morgan the story from the beginning. He did not get far before Morgan interrupted: "I will demand to have your ship returned to you but not until you provide a formal statement attesting the facts of the collision."[7] The finality in the colonel's voice crushed any hope the US government would jump in and pledge support to Durham without fully vetting his claims.

Durham agreed to prepare the sworn statement. Morgan gave him one piece of advice in parting: "Hire an attorney to protect your interests." He emphasized the "your." Durham took the advice and selected a young, American-born attorney living in France named Albert Aicard.

The captain remained in Marseille and insisted that Thombs, another mate, and two sailors who were on board *Adriatic* at the time of the collision come to the city to sign the statement he prepared for Morgan. The consul promised to send the letter to the American minister at Paris when they did. Durham was hopeful, for the first time, that Morgan would come to his aid and demand the French government release his vessel.

Durham met with Aicard about the lawsuit, and they zeroed in on two threshold legal issues. Both were jurisdictional in nature. The first was whether the French government was within its rights to seize an American vessel and Italian-bound cargo in a French port. The second was whether France had jurisdiction over *Adriatic*'s collision with *Le Lyonnais*, an American vessel that collided with a French steamer in international waters. Aicard petitioned the court with respect to these matters in late February 1857 and argued for a change of venue to the American Tribunal of Commerce, on the basis of Durham's nationality and the location of the collision.

The unprecedented seizure of a foreign vessel for acts committed outside French territorial waters unnerved business merchants in Marseille, who sent a flood of letters home to inform American newspapers of *Adriatic*'s predicament. Many of the letters reached elected officials in Washington, DC. One businessman went so far as to suggest that the US government seize the next Franco-Américaine ship to reach an American port and hold it for ransom until the French released *Adriatic*.[8]

Durham met several of his countrymen in Marseille, all of whom offered support. Some were traveling through, while others were committed to ships that had been seized and lying in French ports for debts unpaid. American ship chandler John Stephen Martin and a group of American captains became Durham's closest allies. These men realized that any one of them could be in Durham's position and rallied their support and their friendship.

His new friends called the charges absurd. They could not recollect another instance of a foreign government attaching the property of another for an incident that occurred on the open ocean. Their indignation fueled Durham. His frustration grew stronger each day as he, a man with a penchant for taking matters into his own hands, waited for politicians, lawyers, and diplomats to negotiate on his behalf.

His compatriots' reaction provided Durham with some reassurance that the events would resolve in his favor, but in the back of his mind there was the nagging sensation that comes with being put for too long in harm's way. What if he lost? It would be impossible for him or his business partners to make *Le Lyonnais*'s owners whole. He wrote to his father in Maine. "I do not know what the owners of the *Lyonnais* expect us to do, unless it is to pay for the ship; for if she is insured, as the papers state, I should think they would think they stood a better chance of getting their money from the underwriters."[9]

The French Tribunal du Commerce issued its decision on the jurisdictional issues on March 17, 1857, and denied Durham's request to try the case in an American court. The judges based the ruling on an 1841 decision by the Court de Rouen. There, the court held that under the Napoleonic code, "Every French citizen has a right to demand justice in the tribunal of his country, and that this right is a consequence of the protection owed by the public power to [its] lives."[10] The court relied on the expansive nature of the Napoleonic code and noted that Durham failed to point to any treaties that exempt French courts from hearing disputes between French and American citizens.

The decision was a blow to the Americans. Observers criticized the ruling and opined that the case would now be difficult for Durham to win. They contrasted the French court's behavior with America's reaction to the collision between the ships *Vesta* and *Arctic*. "It is certainly a very hard case for the master and owners of the *Adriatic*. The French steamer *Vesta* ran her iron bow into the unhappy *Arctic*, of the Collins Line, and sunk her, with a large number of valuable lives, and not a thought of retaliation was ever breathed; yet now we hear of this singular and ungenerous movement against the master of a vessel which was so badly injured by the collision that he supposed for many hours that she was in a sinking condition."[11]

The French Tribunal du Commerce scheduled a hearing date for March 24, 1857, at which it would hear legal arguments, review documents, and receive testimony. The court instructed each of the parties' attorneys to summon their witnesses to Marseille.

CHAPTER 25

Mourning

MOTIVE IS THE ENEMY OF TRUTH. It clouds judgment. It fills in gaps. It molds memories in a manner so authentic that it becomes difficult to call the product lies. To say that the witnesses to the collision between *Adriatic* and *Le Lyonnais* converged upon Marseille with motives to paint the facts in the light most beneficial to their respective sides is an understatement. The question of whether some deliberately lied is more complicated.

It had been almost five months since *Adriatic* collided with *Le Lyonnais* on the open ocean. One hundred forty-three days since the men and women who survived the disaster experienced it. During those days, they spoke to one another, read newspaper accounts, and turned the events of November 2 over and over in their minds. Some testified at hearings. Some spoke to the press. Others learned more about the disaster from those accounts. Newspapers across the world published details of the collision and offered opinions as to who was at fault and why. By March 24, 1857, it was difficult to separate what survivors from both sides knew from personal experience and what they had learned from published accounts, conversations, and rumors. The witnesses carried with them not just their memories of November 2, but all their experiences in the wake of that night when they gathered in Marseille.

There, lawyers prepared them for the trial ahead.

> In any case of unintentional collision it will be found, and most naturally, that each party will present the strongest testimony in its own justification; even when the rules, ordinarily applicable to such cases, may have been departed from, strong, if not sufficient, reasons are adduced for it. In

CHAPTER 25 | *Mourning*

many cases of departure from the rules, although the collision may not have been avoided, had the rules been strictly observed the consequences might have resulted more fatally. And it is not at all improbable that collision cases are frequently improperly decided by a skillful management of witnesses, or by a theory (rather than the precise facts) of the case formed after the danger was past, and the minds of men had become calm and reflective.[1]

Luguiere wasted no time after *Mercury* returned him to his home country. The French minister of marine had not yet declared Devaulx dead, but both the government and Franco-Américaine recognized Luguiere as the highest-ranking survivor of his ship's disaster. Luguiere spent his days working with his employer to provide information necessary for corporate attorneys, insurance companies, and the families of those lost. Luguiere traveled from Le Havre to Paris and then to Marseille, prepared to do whatever was necessary to see Franco-Américaine made whole.

Luguiere's stories about the crew's heroic efforts inspired the government to act. The commissioner of the Port of Le Havre recommended honoring Luguiere with the Knights Cross of the Legion of Honor, Choupault with a gold medal, and the other surviving crew members with statements of recognition. A few days later, on January 14, 1857, the minister of the navy and the colonies appointed both Luguiere and Choupault as Knights of the Imperial Order of the Legion of Honor, "for the fine conduct they [showed] following the sinking of the transatlantic liner *Le Lyonnais*."[2] They proceeded to Marseille, and the Tribunal du Commerce, shortly thereafter.

The tribunal had jurisdiction over disputes between merchants and matters of corporate law. Judges were not former attorneys or legal scholars, but businessmen elected to short terms to preside over trade disputes. The tribunal's primary goal was to protect business interests, not legal ones. Panels of three judges decided cases.[3]

Durham's attorney advised him not to testify at the hearing. He planned to introduce his sworn statement at Marseille and his original statement to the Belfast newspaper instead. *Adriatic*'s first mate, Thombs, and sailors Thomas Warrer and William Koller would testify at the hearing.[4] Other than the informal statements Thombs made as part of the Gloucester Customs Exchange inquiry, none of these sailors had ever spoken publicly about the collision. Alexis Cauvin joined Jean-Marie-Louis Choupault and Adolphe Luguiere in Marseille to round out the list of Franco-Américaine's witnesses.

The months following the collision had been difficult for Choupault. His left arm suffered from frostbite damage so severe that he no longer had the full use of his hand and could not work. His doctor told him that he might never be able to do a sailor's job again. He had spent his entire life aboard ships. He knew nothing else. Choupault still moved through the world moment by moment, but his approach to life was no longer a product of his good nature; it was a product of fear. Thoughts of the future terrified him.

Choupault arrived at the courthouse on the morning of March 24, anxious about the trial ahead. He removed his hat and stepped inside. He had worn his finest clothes, but inside the formal halls of the Tribunal du Commerce de Marseille, they somehow felt like a costume. He looked down and patted his lapels and pants to make sure everything was in its proper place, just like he used to do back in the navy when he knew his uniform was subject to inspection.

Attorneys, businessmen, and court officials gathered for the hearing. The witnesses gathered too. Luguiere huddled with Mr. Clappier, Franco-Américaine's agent, who represented the company's interest in the tribunal proceeding. Choupault looked in the corresponding place across the room and saw a man talking just as intimately to his attorney. He had not been introduced but knew who the man was both from his position and the way he carried himself: Captain Jonathan Barnet Durham.

It was the first time he had ever laid eyes on him. Choupault had heard the name a thousand times. He had prepared himself for this moment, but when it finally happened, it was not what he anticipated. He thought he had buried the past at sea, pushed it away, and moved on. What was once acceptance of the disaster and all it had wrought dissolved into rage the second his eyes met Durham's. The feeling flooded over him until he thought he might drown in it. There was no similar recognition in Durham's face, which made the sensation that overwhelmed Choupault even more painful. He did not expect Durham to admit fault, but he did expect some sign of contrition. Durham did not notice Choupault's intense stare. He did not seem to notice Choupault at all. He went about his business as though the gravity of what they experienced was nothing more than inconvenience or a bad dream.

Choupault found a seat and tried to collect himself. He could not. He saw instead a dark ocean alive with howling winds and massive waves. He felt the sting of the frostbite that ruined his arm. He remembered the morning at the boardinghouse when he finally put a name to the man who left him for dead. Captain Jonathan Barnet Durham. He wondered how the lawyers would answer for that—how they would answer for him.

CHAPTER 25 | *Mourning*

Choupault was ready to deliver all he knew to the tribunal, not for himself or for some faceless steamship company, but for all those he could not save at sea.

What Choupault did not know, what he could not know, is that Durham was not immune to the punishment of loss. The sea had taken from him too. She had not done it all at once, but slowly and methodically, piece by piece, throughout the years. What Choupault did not know was that in the years before *Adriatic* and *Le Lyonnais* met in the Atlantic, four of Durham's five brothers died, three of them at sea.

Durham was fourteen years old when his second-eldest brother, James Monroe, became second mate aboard the Massachusetts barque *Wyandot*. Just a year later, on August 13, 1842, *Wyandot* left Campeche, Mexico, bound for Bremen, carrying a cargo of logwood. Another ship spotted her on September 15 in the Bay of Mexico, the day before a hurricane struck. She traveled in the company of other vessels, only one of which was ever heard from again. Chance did not favor *Wyandot*. Neither she nor her crew survived the storm.

Four years later, in 1846, Durham's older brother John Sergeant was second mate aboard Carter's brig *Tonquin* when it stopped in Braga, Cuba, to load a cargo of molasses. John was overseeing the crew on October 15 when a crane fell and crushed him. He died nine days later in a Cuban hospital.

Captain George Anson Durham, Durham's oldest brother, died in 1849 at the age of twenty-nine.[5] Tragedy struck the family again just six years later, in 1854, when the youngest member of the Durham family, William, was lost at sea.

William was the family's youngest child and more like a son than a brother to his older siblings. Durham was four years his senior, and by 1850 they were the only children who still lived at their parents' home in Belfast. William died while Durham was captaining voyages from Boston to the ports of Charleston and Bonaire aboard the Boston brig *Martha Hill*. He returned to Maine for a few months in the winter of 1854 to mourn the loss with his parents, his brother Charles, and his two sisters. They were all the family he had left.

The Durhams never recovered James's, Jonathan's, or William's bodies. They erected a tall, pale, gray marble headstone at the family plot in Belfast's Grove Cemetery that bore the inscription "Their bodies rest beneath the waves. Their spirits with their God." They engraved on it each child's first name, middle initial, year of death, and age at death and identified them as "Sons of Jon. & Eunice Durham." None of them lived long enough to father children of their own.

The timing of the deaths was cruel. They almost perfectly punctuated a span of twelve years and forced young Barney to spend his early adulthood marinating in grief. Even if time could have healed the wounds, there was never enough of it before the next death. His family's brokenness was one that could never be repaired, only borne. The damage hardened Durham. He was quite affable in public, but those closest to him described him as introverted, quiet, and prone to bouts of depression.

Durham's stay in Belfast after his youngest brother's death was brief. In January 1855, he set sail on *Martha Hill* for Charleston, South Carolina, where he loaded logwood and coffee bound for Aux Cayes, Haiti. The magnitude of William's recent loss weighed upon him during the voyage. He felt both a responsibility to his family and the burden that came with being alive.

His father and brother felt it too. They had spoken in recent years about building their own ship. Jonathan Sr. had already sold off some of the family land to raise capital, but William's death lit the fire to turn the idea into reality. Charles came from Bangor to Belfast to work with his father on the endeavor. The two did not have enough money to build the ship they wanted, so they approached local businessmen who, along with Carter himself, became their partners. The new firm, Patterson & Carter, set to work on plans both for the new company and the new vessel. Barney left *Martha Hill* a few months later and spent the remainder of 1855 in Belfast working with his father and brother on *Adriatic*. He took one final turn at sea aboard *Malabar*, from December 1855 through May 1856, to pass the time and earn some money during *Adriatic*'s final construction.

Jonathan Durham Sr. sank everything he had into the new venture. He gave Patterson & Carter some Durham family land on Upper Steamboat Wharf to accommodate a new shipyard and office building and invested his last $20,000 in the ship's construction. He spared no expense in the materials or the workmanship and vowed to make the new company's first ship the finest and best-constructed vessel ever built in Maine. He went into debt to see the dream fulfilled, and expected the money that *Adriatic* earned would soon make him whole again.

To the public, Patterson & Carter was yet another business venture for the enterprising Jonathan Durham Sr., but privately, Jonathan told those closest to him that he was building *Adriatic* for Barney. It was as if building a ship of his own would somehow immunize his son against his brothers' fates.

Barney returned to Maine in the summer of 1856 to join his father in business. He participated in sea trials with *Adriatic* and helped prepare the ship for her inaugural voyage, which was scheduled for October.

CHAPTER 25 | Mourning

Adriatic was not just a business venture but a new beginning. When the ship launched on October 31, 1856, carrying a load of hay and lime bound for Savannah, an entire family's hope for a better future launched with her.

The lessons that life had taught Jonathan Barnet Durham launched with her too. He had learned the hard way what happened when sailors tempted fate. He had watched his father console his mother each time she lost a son. He had seen the devastation on her face not once, not twice, but four times. His father abandoned the sea and became a farmer to spare his mother the risk of losing him too. Now his father had poured every penny, every favor, and every ounce of energy he had left into building *Adriatic*—for him.

The dream lasted three days. Just three days after *Adriatic* left Belfast Harbor on her first voyage, she struck *Le Lyonnais* amidships. Her bowsprit hit first and snapped like a twig in a storm. Her bow thudded into the steamer's side and clung there briefly before tearing away. The ships separated, and *Adriatic*'s dragon figurehead tore from her prow and tumbled onto the steamer's deck the moment they parted. Parts of *Adriatic*'s fore works cracked and sank straight into the waves. The steamer never slowed and soon disappeared, leaving *Adriatic* damaged and alone.

Durham was on deck. He saw fractured wood and dead sails ahead and, beyond that, an empty ocean. The sounds of screaming men and splintering timber soon came to an end until all he could hear was the collapse of waves folding onto themselves. The night was too dark to assess the extent of the damage, and the sounds of the waves were too quiet to drown out the voices in his head. He was the only sailor left in his family. He was the only brother left to Charles. He was his father's only hope. He had to come home.

Durham never spoke about his brothers. No one outside Belfast ever learned about his family's history or the way it might have affected him in the aftermath of the collision with *Le Lyonnais*. Choupault never learned that Durham seemed so devoid of empathy not because he did not recognize the need for it but because he had none left to give.

The Marseille courtroom bustled with men preparing for the formal proceedings to begin. Lawyers greeted one another with broad smiles and firm handshakes. Clerks carrying stacks of documents scurried around the room. Noises of rustling papers and small talk filled the air. Amid the chatter and the flow, Choupault and Durham locked eyes for just a moment and just as quickly looked away. Neither man would find what he was looking for in the other. They were each on their own.

CHAPTER 26

Exoneration

THE PUBLIC REACTED STRONGLY TO DURHAM'S DECISION to leave the scene without checking on *Le Lyonnais*'s welfare. People sympathized with the passengers' plights and vilified Durham for leaving them to die. Debate existed about who was at fault for the collision, but it was difficult even for Durham's staunchest supporters to defend his choice to leave the scene. All of that changed the moment the French seized *Adriatic*.

Marseille had become one of the premier ports in Europe. Port traffic more than doubled between 1821 and 1851, and the city's population doubled with it. Marseille was an epicenter of commerce by 1857. The seizure of an American vessel for a collision that occurred in international waters sent a chill through the collective spine of the maritime community. Every merchant who sought to do business on the ocean feared repercussions. Success for the French meant opening the floodgates for other nations to impose their laws on American merchant vessels any time there was an accident anywhere in the world. What was once great sympathy for those who suffered or died aboard *Le Lyonnais* turned into a matter of life or death for American business interests abroad. Newspapers, many of which were owned or supported by businessmen with strong ties to merchants who made their livings on the sea, were quick to rally to *Adriatic*'s cause. Even the New York papers, which had once chastised Durham, now sided with *Adriatic*. "The American ship *Adriatic*, which was the ship that came in collision with the French steamship [*Le*] *Lyonnais*, was libelled [*sic*] recently at Marseilles. The cause has come before the courts; and the captain of the *Adriatic* alleged the French courts had no jurisdiction in the case and

CHAPTER 26 | *Exoneration*

craved its dismissal to the American Courts. The Court overruled this plea and continued the case until yesterday, when its merits were to the entered. The survivors of the crew have been subpoenaed as witnesses for the plaintiffs."[1]

It was against this backdrop that the witnesses testified.

Luguiere, Choupault, and Cauvin testified that the ship made way under sail and steam with her lights on. They reported twenty-five people on the deck plus two at the cathead at the time of the collision. The captain was at the poop, and the second in command was on the bridge. It was not until three minutes before the collision and at less than a quarter mile that those aboard *Le Lyonnais* first perceived *Adriatic*. Luguiere saw no one on *Adriatic*'s deck save for the helmsman. *Adriatic*'s helm was located at the back of the ship, and although a helmsman on a sailing ship could see ahead, there would have been too many obstacles in the forward section of the ship for a helmsman alone to keep watch. Choupault and Cauvin said they were on deck and saw no one aboard *Adriatic* at the time of the collision. These statements were inconsistent with previous accounts in which both men said they awoke to the sound of the collision. Luguiere swore that Choupault rang the bell, and the captain sounded the whistle before the ships met.

Adriatic's crew said they saw *Le Lyonnais* twenty minutes before the collision. Thomas Warrer was at the helm and the others were on deck. It was customary for steamships to yield to sailing vessels because of the former's greater ability to maneuver. *Adriatic* maintained course and expected the steamer to adjust. Warrer made no move to alter course or speed and, safe in the knowledge he had the right-of-way, intended to pass *Le Lyonnais* at the bow.

Two to three minutes before the collision, the precise time those aboard *Le Lyonnais* say they first spotted *Adriatic*, Thombs, Warrer, and Koller said the steamer made an abrupt and unexpected turn. "If the steamer continued to steer as it did," said Thombs, "she would have passed astern of us."[2] Durham took the helm and ordered the men to adjust the sails to turn to starboard in response. The sails went dead, and *Adriatic* lost the ability to maneuver.

Those aboard *Le Lyonnais* said *Adriatic* came at full sail and showed no signs of slowing. Devaulx turned the ship to port to avoid the collision.[3] *Adriatic* continued toward *Le Lyonnais* at full speed. Each crew cried for the other ship to stop, but it was already too late. The combination of both ships making last-minute maneuvers caused the vessels to collide.

Dispute about which direction *Le Lyonnais* turned arose suddenly and entirely in Marseille. Durham's witnesses claimed she turned to starboard, while *Le Lyonnais*'s said she turned to port. Durham's first report, given at Belfast, made no reference to *Le Lyonnais* making a turn at all. None of his previous reports or interviews included the direction he claimed *Le Lyonnais* turned. All those aboard the steamer, both in their previous testimony and before the tribunal, swore that Devaulx attempted to turn the ship to port.

Custom is not the only law of the sea. It is every sailor's duty to avoid collision regardless of what custom or law demands. *Adriatic* and *Le Lyonnais* were so close by the time the steamer saw the barque that each side was compelled to do whatever good judgment demanded. As Choupault told the tribunal, "We could not make the maneuver to port until we saw *Adriatic*. It would have been easier for *Adriatic* that was coming to avoid *Le Lyonnais* rather than the other way around."[4] *Adriatic*'s witnesses testified that the opposite was true. Had *Le Lyonnais* seen *Adriatic* earlier, she might have been able to adjust. Had she continued her course, she would have passed *Adriatic* at the stern. The crux of the case was whether *Le Lyonnais* was responsible for a last-minute course adjustment or *Adriatic* was responsible for not making herself visible sooner.

The *Le Lyonnais* survivors consistently claimed that *Adriatic* bore no signal lights. The only mention of a light by a *Le Lyonnais* crewman was by Luguiere, who saw the faint glow of a compass binnacle after *Adriatic* struck and cleared away. Binnacle lights were used to allow the captain to read the compass at night and were not bright enough to serve as a substitute for signal lights.

Koller testified that there was a light at *Adriatic*'s stern, a reference to the one at the binnacle. He also claimed he hoisted a light on deck by hand a full fifteen minutes prior to the collision. He held it high enough to make it visible. Warrer said it was Thombs who hoisted the light, not by hand but by lifting it on the ship's mizzenmast. Thombs gave a third version: "*Adriatic* had a light on deck. It was a lantern held at fifteen feet above the deck."[5] Cauvin responded to their claims: "If the ship had any light, we would have seen it a long time before."[6]

The parties agreed that the steamship continued its course after the collision and showed no signs of slowing. "We supposed she did not have much damage," said Durham.[7] Those aboard *Adriatic* echoed the sentiments of their captain. They saw many people on the steamer's deck but heard no signs of alarm.

"The shock destroyed *Le Lyonnais*' machine," Choupault told the court in answer.[8] She was unable to stop until approximately ten minutes later, when the water choked out the last of the fires below. The steamer fired flares and raised two more lights at the end. On the basis of her speed and the extent of the damage, she could not have gotten farther than a mile from *Adriatic* before her engine seized.

The tribunal relied on both written and oral evidence and made procedural rulings about what evidence it would and would not accept. It barred Luguiere's New York report from consideration. French law required the highest-ranking officer of an injured vessel to make an official report containing the specific allegations of misconduct against the offending vessel within twenty-four hours of arrival in a place where such a report could be made. Luguiere passed the first two prongs of the test. The French consul in New York was French territory. Luguiere, who was the highest-ranking survivor, arrived there within twenty-four hours to give his statement. The tribunal took issue with the statement's content. It found that the statement both lacked specificity and failed to name *Adriatic*. The obvious argument, that Durham's delay in reporting prevented Luguiere from being able to name *Adriatic*, did not impress the tribunal. It opined that Luguiere could have rectified the matter by making a second report to the prosecutor in Le Havre upon arrival in France. His failure to do so rendered his New York statement inadmissible. The ruling prevented Franco-Américaine from pointing out the consistency between the two statements and required Luguiere to testify instead of relying on a report given when the events were fresh.

The tribunal, on the other hand, admitted the statement Durham made at Belfast. Aicard somehow convinced the court that American law required a captain to report a collision at sea only to his home port and not his port of arrival. They accepted the publication of his account in the Belfast newspaper, made more than nine days after the collision, as a report that complied with American law. There was, in fact, no specific requirement for how to report a collision at sea in the United States. Custom demanded a report be made quickly to facilitate rescue and minimize financial loss. Aicard introduced Durham's two statements and did not call him as a witness. This prevented him from being cross-examined about inconsistencies such as his failure to mention the course change, the extent of *Adriatic*'s damage, and why he never aided the steamer.

The tribunal issued six findings to resolve the factual disputes. The first related to the weather conditions and the states of both vessels when they first spotted one another. It found as fact that *Adriatic* caught sight of *Le Lyonnais* twenty minutes before the collision. The wind was blowing from the southwest. *Le Lyonnais* operated under full sail and steam. *Adriatic* steered close to the wind with topgallant sails furled and topsails double-reefed and stayed steady on her course.

Despite testimony to the contrary from *Le Lyonnais*'s crew, the tribunal concluded that both the captain and the watch were present on *Adriatic*'s deck, and reasoned that *Le Lyonnais*'s witnesses might not have been able to see them from their vantage points. Next, the tribunal ruled that Durham ordered his crew to hoist a lantern. It credited the second officer's testimony about him holding a lantern at an elevation of 3 to 4 yards above the top deck.

The court's third finding concerned the moments just before the collision. Three minutes before the ships met, Durham saw *Le Lyonnais* alter her course and maneuver to pass ahead of *Adriatic*. Durham ordered the helm to be put starboard and luffed his vessel, which caused *Adriatic* to slow her speed.[9]

The fourth finding concerned Devaulx. The tribunal determined that at the time of the collision, the captain, the watch, and the second officer were on deck, and two men stood at the cathead. Seaman Choupault was one of the two men at the cathead and yelled, "Vessel to starboard," and rang the bell.[10] Devaulx rushed to the helm in response and turned to port. He sounded the alarm whistle and continued course to pass *Adriatic*'s bow.

The tribunal's final two findings involved the condition of the two ships after the collision. *Le Lyonnais* appeared to have sustained no damage because she continued her course. *Adriatic*, by contrast, lost her figurehead and her fore works.

The tribunal weighed the findings of fact and, on April 2, 1857, sided with Durham. It resolved three arguments in *Adriatic*'s favor. First, the tribunal refused to hold *Adriatic* to French laws of the sea. French law required all ships to carry lights to make them visible to other ships at night or in bad weather. Such a light was to be affixed to the mizzenmast. There was no similar American regulation. The tribunal declined to apply the French law of signals to *Adriatic* and ruled that Durham went above and beyond what American law required by hoisting a light by hand the moment he spotted *Le Lyonnais*.

Second, the tribunal labeled the collision an accident. It accepted the worldwide custom that steamships must give way to sailing vessels. Because Durham made himself visible with the light, he was correct to continue his course and pass *Le Lyonnais* at the bow. The only recourse Durham had when the collision became inevitable was to attempt to slow down, as he did. *Adriatic* held her course northwest by west and maneuvered until collision with *Le Lyonnais* was imminent. The steamer perceived the barque three minutes before the collision for the first time and attempted to maneuver; thus, *Le Lyonnais* contributed to the collision.

Third, and perhaps most important to the court of public opinion, the tribunal forgave Durham's failure to render aid. Aicard argued that Durham had no reason to believe the steamer was in peril because she continued her course after the collision. Franco-Américaine's agent claimed *Adriatic*'s position was impossible because *Le Lyonnais* fired her cannons into the night. The tribunal reconciled the discrepancies in the testimony by assuming that *Adriatic* was too far away to hear *Le Lyonnais*'s sounds of distress. It also ignored Choupault's testimony about *Le Lyonnais*'s engine failure and faulted the steamer for not stopping to check on the barque. "It is proved that the steamer went on her way for some time, without inquiring what damage the barque had sustained, before it was discovered that she had received injury, and then the barque was too far away to perceive the signals."[11]

Durham could not be held liable because the collision was an accident.[12] The tribunal ordered the Gauthier brothers to pay Durham's attorneys' fees, but did not go so far as to award damages to the barque's captain, noting that *Le Lyonnais* was too far away to notice *Adriatic*'s condition. The court ordered authorities in La Ciotat to release *Adriatic* and threatened the Gauthier brothers with a fine of five hundred francs per day for every day of further detention.

Aicard noted his objection both to the court's jurisdiction and its failure to award damages. His purpose was to preserve Durham's right to appeal and to continue to accrue attorneys' fees if Franco-Américaine appealed.

American newspapers hailed the decision as a victory and a total exoneration of Durham. Some papers even went so far as to suggest that the barque's captain intentionally traveled to France to settle his dispute.[13] The tribunal's decision absolved the captain not just of liability for the accident but for the one thing he could never escape in his home country: the sin of leaving *Le Lyonnais* behind. The moral issue had been the final sticking point in debates about the collision. Now, Durham was free of it. One New York newspaper reflected, "The judicial investigation . . . resulted in exonerating the bark from the claim, and in relieving the captain from the reproach of having abandoned in haste the scene of the catastrophe, without seeking to render aid to its victims. It will be remembered that nearly 100 lives were lost by this calamity, and that among the sufferers, were several respectable citizens of New York. At the time of the occurrence, public opinion bore hard in condemnation upon the master of the *Adriatic*; but it would appear that, in the judgment of the French tribunal, the censure inflicted upon him was unjust."[14] The Belfast papers put it neatly. "Captain Durham, of the *Adriatic*, is not merely found innocent of causing the collision, but is fully exonerated from all and every accusation of inhumanity and not remaining by *Le Lyonnais* after the accident."[15]

CHAPTER 27
Notes en Réplique

FRANCO-AMÉRICAINE APPEALED TO THE IMPERIAL COURT of Aix en Provence, an appellate court that reviewed judgments entered below. Unlike the Tribunal du Commerce, Imperial Court judges had no specific background in business or intimate knowledge of the sea. They did their best to review the evidence admitted by the tribunal but soon realized they needed technical assistance in understanding maritime rules and customs.

They turned to a committee of experts. On May 12, the court appointed three experienced captains to investigate the collision. The committee was tasked to review the evidence gathered by the tribunal and to draft an expert report to aid the court. The parties and the court chose representatives for the committee. Durham chose a friend of his, American ship chandler John Stephen Martin. Franco-Américaine chose Captain Emile Vidal of the French marine. The court appointed E. de Tournadre, captain of the Port of Marseille. The court swore each of the commissioners to service and instructed them to "examine all the documents, and in view of all the facts related, and to be submitted, give their opinion on the causes of the collision and on the fact of fault and imprisonment to be imputed to one or the other of the captains of the two vessels."[1] The stakes were high. Not only would the committee decide who was responsible for the collision, but it had the power to recommend whether Durham, the only surviving captain, deserved a prison sentence.

The committee wasted no time getting to work and spent the latter part of May and the month of June 1857 reviewing documents and interviewing *Adriatic*'s and *Le Lyonnais*'s crew. Most of *Adriatic*'s crew had shipped for home or found work on other vessels by this time. Durham believed that this put him at a disadvantage during the investigation.

The experts met again on July 2, 1857, to conduct an experiment in Marseille Harbor. They put two buoys in the harbor spaced a third of a mile apart. They took a steamer the size of *Le Lyonnais* and, from that distance, turned the ship to port. They concluded from the experiment that *Le Lyonnais* would have avoided collision had Captain Devaulx done the same."[2]

The experts also inspected *Adriatic*, including her light. It was what the French described as a carcel lamp, a small household lamp with the strength of a single candle flame.

Adriatic languished in La Ciotat while the experts worked. Durham was confident of a favorable outcome, especially after his victory in the Tribunal du Commerce, but preferred not to take chances if he could avoid them. He had an idea. He asked Aicard to petition the court to move his ship to Marseille, and hoped he could sneak out of France before the case concluded. The court agreed to the transfer but refused to allow Durham access to his ship. Instead, four men appointed by Franco-Américaine and approved by the court towed the barque from La Ciotat to Marseille. Despite the missed opportunity to flee France, Durham was glad to have *Adriatic* close to him.

The experts finished their work in the summer and filed their report on September 9, 1857. The report was guidance for the court and had no independent legal authority, so it was not made public. The attorneys received copies to share with their clients and to incorporate into their legal arguments.

Durham devoured the report the moment Aicard put it in his hands. It was good news. He had prevailed once again. The experts declared *Le Lyonnais* at fault for attempting to pass the barque to port instead of starboard. It found Durham's last-minute decision to tack to avoid collision justified under the circumstances. The committee further determined that *Adriatic* satisfied the duty to signal by hoisting a light of sufficient size at least ten minutes prior to the collision.

French military officials and politicians received copies of the report and devoured it too. The conclusions in it incensed many of them, including Ferdinand-Alphonse Hamelin, minister of the French marine. Hamelin both controlled the French navy and oversaw French colonial territories. Ministers of the French navy typically concerned themselves with colonial politics, but Hamelin was more interested in matters of global expansion across the world's oceans.

Hamelin first went to sea at the age of ten as a cabin boy aboard *Venus*, a frigate commanded by his uncle, Rear Admiral Jacques Felix Emmanuel

Admiral Ferdinand-Alphonse Hamelin, minister of the French marine from 1855 to 1860. Photo ca. 1860.

Hamelin, during the Napoleonic Wars. The elder Hamelin commanded operations near Mauritius (then Isle de France), a French colonial territory in the Indian Ocean and a vital part of the French East India trading company. The island became a base from which Hamelin launched frigate squadrons both to protect French ships on trade routes and to disrupt trade from British India by raiding British merchant vessels. The raids continued until 1810, when the British unsuccessfully attempted to capture the island. In a war in which the British navy dominated at sea, the French navy's local victory stood out. The British eventually captured Mauritius, and at the age of eleven, young Ferdinand Hamelin was held prisoner of war by them for a short time.

The Mauritius campaign left Hamelin with a taste for battle and important lessons in naval tactics and strategies. He remained in the navy, rose through the ranks, and gained a reputation as a sailor who was both fierce in combat and astute in politics. He became vice admiral in 1848. In 1854, he led the Black Sea squadron in the Crimean War. He, along with British admiral James Whitney Dean Dundas, coordinated the bombardment at Sebastopol. It was rumored that he did not get along well with his British counterpart. Hamelin earned a promotion to admiral in late 1854, and Napoléon III appointed him minister of the French navy in 1855.

The Crimean War placed heavy operational demands on the French. Hamelin took charge of managing resources on multiple battlefronts. When the war ended, his principal tasks were to rebuild and modernize the French fleet. He ordered new ships constructed, including armored vessels. Rivalries between the French and British soon reemerged as both countries continued to colonize to establish international trade routes. Modernizing the French navy meant more than building ships, but also finding solutions to sharing a crowded ocean with vessels from all over the world. Hamelin became as adept at coordinating bureaucratic responses to problems as he was military ones.

The expert report infuriated him. He believed that respecting other vessels required shipowners to bear lights and take all proper precautions to avoid collisions at sea. He rebuked the report's conclusions in a formal response. "I invite you gentleman and captains who are paving the seas to consider the gravity of your responsibilities," he began.[3] Hamelin labeled the response a "bulletin," but it read like a manifesto about the responsibilities of captains to carry lights and to know the rules to avoid collisions at sea. He published the bulletin on October 30, 1857, a little more than a month after the experts finalized their report and while the Court of Aix was still deliberating on its verdict.

Durham shared the expert report with Captain Marks of the schooner *Python*, a fellow Mainer traveling through France. Both Durham and Marks wrote to convey the news back home. *Adriatic*'s captain felt optimistic for the first time in a long time. He had won at the tribunal and again before the committee. The court would no doubt rely on the experts, and it was only a matter of time before he could set sail and put the whole ordeal behind him.

Despite Hamelin's criticism, Consul Morgan shared Durham's cautious optimism. He had not intervened but had monitored the case for the American government. In October 1857, one month after the committee issued its report, George Schedel traveled to France and requested an audience, diplomat to diplomat, with Morgan. The two men met and discussed the collision and its aftermath. Schedel's disdain for Luguiere endured, and he was disappointed to see that the man he so despised had become the face of *Le Lyonnais* in the media and in court proceedings. Schedel told Morgan that a miscommunication between the captain and a deckhand caused the collision. Morgan passed the information on to Aicard and Durham but made no formal report. In an October 15 letter to Belfast, Durham claimed that Schedel told Morgan, "The officer having command of the deck at the time was a young man, a nephew of the captain; that even the men would not obey him unless they saw for themselves that they were right; when they saw the bark, he gave the wrong order. The captain heard the order and rushed upon deck, but before he could rectify the mistake it was too late."[4]

Morgan was suspicious of Schedel's claims. Schedel was in his cabin when the ships collided, and had no firsthand knowledge of what transpired on deck during the collision. He claimed he learned about it in the lifeboat, yet none of the other passengers ever mentioned such a conversation. Devaulx's nephew was a member of the ship's crew, but the survivors were unanimous that Devaulx was on the quarterdeck when the ships met. Schedel gave a detailed account of his time at sea to the *New York Times* in January 1857 and, even after reading his fellow survivors' accounts, never mentioned Devaulx's nephew. The conversation did not sit well with Morgan, and he never shared it further. Neither did Aicard. Schedel was neither called as a witness nor referenced in the Court of Aix's opinion.

The parties each presented arguments before the Court of Aix in written form. These arguments were referred to as "Notes en Réplique" or "Notes in Reply" because the parties replied to the tribunal's findings, the expert report, the witness statements, and the investigation in them. Aicard continued to represent Durham, along with an *avoué* named Tassy.[5] A lawyer named Avocat Thourel now represented Franco-Américaine along with his *avoué*, Marguery. This time, the court admitted Luguiere's statement at New York in addition to Durham's statements.

The parties focused on last-minute maneuvers made to avoid collision. Nautical custom required two ships heading toward one another each to move starboard, so they passed one another port to port. The rule was neither law nor absolute, particularly when two ships approached at angles. *Le Lyonnais* traveled east-northeast and *Adriatic* west-northwest. The ships did not come at one another directly but, rather, formed two lines of a triangle destined to meet at the apex.

Choupault insisted that the vessel was put to port to allow *Adriatic* to narrowly pass *Le Lyonnais* on the starboard side. *Adriatic*'s crew argued she turned the other way. A port turn made the most sense under the circumstances and, if taken too late, would have resulted in the T-shaped collision suffered by the steamer.

Aicard asked the court to ignore Choupault's testimony about the circumstances of the collision and the visibility of *Adriatic*'s light. He pointed to newspaper interviews in New York in which Choupault told reporters he was asleep when the ships met. Similarly, he asked the court to ignore Cauvin's testimony, because he was to take the midnight watch and had no reason to be on deck before then.[6] Thourel called American newspapers "novel sheets" and asked the court to disregard them in favor of sworn testimony.[7]

Thourel reinforced arguments about the signal light and pointed to an 1852 law that required French ships to maintain a signal light either at the bowsprit or the mizzen. There was no corresponding American law. Koller testified that he had sailed American ships for ten years, and none had such a light. Thourel countered, "Durham says emphatically that American law does not require captains to have lights during navigation on the high seas, and then makes the most useless efforts to prove that he lit one."[8]

None of *Adriatic*'s crew mentioned a light when they spoke with members of the Customs Exchange at Gloucester. Even if the court believed that *Adriatic* raised a light, Thourel argued it was too small, hoisted too late, and too far aft to be visible.

The light was Durham's first mistake, but according to Thourel, he made others. He faulted Durham for luffing the vessel when collision was imminent, and argued it would have been easier for Durham to steer with the wind rather than bracing his vessel abruptly against it. Aicard rebuffed this attack by citing nautical custom.

The parties also addressed Durham's failure to render aid. Thourel chastised Durham and alleged he was "blind in front of the distress rockets and deaf to *Le Lyonnais*' whistle, [took] care of himself, [took] the tailwind, and then [dared] to write that from the French side he was refused all assistance!"[9] Aicard claimed that Durham's vessel was in such dire straits that he could not have aided *Le Lyonnais*. He argued that Durham remedied the matter by making a "detailed" report to the Gloucester customhouse and the newsroom at Gloucester on November 5 and sending a copy of said report to *Adriatic*'s owners. It was the first time that Durham claimed he told reporters at Gloucester about the collision. It strained credibility because not a single story about the disaster appeared in any newspaper until the November 14 *Belfast Republican Journal* article. Aicard produced every document in support of his case except the Gloucester report, despite specific requests from the court and opposing counsel to view it. Aicard, in response, suggested that Durham had no reason to bring the report with him to France because the incident was "entirely the fault of the steamer."[10] He added that a guilty man would never have traveled to France. "Is this the conduct of a man who thinks he deserves the slightest reproach?"[11]

Aicard made one additional argument against Franco-Américaine. It was a practical one. Insurers had already indemnified them for the steamship's loss. There was no reason the court should further compensate them.

The Court of Aix announced its decision on December 24, 1857. It disregarded both the tribunal's findings and the experts' report and found in favor of *Le Lyonnais* and the Gauthiers. The court based its reasoning on the lights. *Adriatic* should have carried signal lights, not because French law compelled it, but because it was a prudent precaution to prevent collision in dark or foul weather. "Captain Durham sailed without displaying lights in a foggy night, which, even in the absence of American regulation, constitutes serious imprudence and fixes responsibility upon the captain, to whatever nation he belongs."[12]

Le Lyonnais, by contrast, showed her course with brilliant lights. It was only when imminent danger threatened *Adriatic* that her crew hoisted one. The court decided that the lantern was too small, in the wrong position, and too late; therefore, *Le Lyonnais* did not see it. Unlike the lower court, which found some fault on the part of both parties, the court attributed the entire loss to Durham. It was to the Americans "a disregard by the Appellate Court in France for anything but indemnity to the owner of *Le Lyonnais*."[13]

CHAPTER 28
The Marseille Predicament

"They have no right!" Durham paced the floor of Aicard's office. "They have no right to take her!" He ran his hands through his hair and balled it into fists. Tugging it against his scalp gave him the sensation of racking his brain. He would, from time to time, shout out a sentence or a fragment of one but never waited long enough for his lawyer to respond. "The decision is a sham—a deliberate mockery."[1] Aicard tried to speak, but Durham continued, "All they care about is French interests."

He was right. The court rejected the decision by the tribunal and the experts. It failed to address Aicard's arguments in any meaningful way. It attributed all damages to Durham and did not even try to offset them with money paid by insurers.

Durham protested to Aicard, but to no avail. There must be something he could do, some recourse to save his ship! "They ignored the experts," Durham complained. It was a fact with no legal significance. Aicard told him for the thousandth time that the experts' opinions were advice, not law. "The court can do with the experts what they will." Despite his protestations, Durham soon learned that there was no higher court, no opportunity to plead his case to more-sympathetic ears, and no alternative to sail his ship to friendlier shores. The only question that remained for the court to consider was an exact dollar figure to put on the loss sustained by the Gauthier brothers. After that, *Adriatic* would be theirs.

Aicard appealed the costs attributed to Durham. He, with the help of an appellate attorney named Henry Casey, argued that the Gauthier brothers were responsible for the costs of Durham's detention in Marseille and that the French unlawfully seized the freight bound for Sicily. The parties argued the issues before the Imperial Court of Aix on

December 15 and 21, 1858. This time, First Imperial Attorney General Landbournil argued Franco-Américaine's cause because the case involved governmental seizures of Durham's property. A small change in damages made little difference to Durham, but the appeal bought him some time.

Durham prevailed upon Morgan to do more, but the diplomat was in a difficult position. The US maintained delicate relations with Napoléon III, who had recently annexed Tourin and Nice and expanded his empire in parts of Asia, the Pacific, and Africa. The ruler set his sights on Central America in the mid-1850s, with the goal of creating a second French Empire with control over strategic international trade routes. The US opposed such ambitions. Napoléon recognized that civil war in America was inevitable, so he cultivated relationships with southern political leaders, who signaled they would tolerate his colonization in exchange for French support for what would within three years become the Confederacy.

Morgan considered the facts of the case and Durham's favorable outcomes before the tribunal and the committee of experts and concluded that the best course of action was to allow the French courts to resolve the matter. He now realized he had miscalculated. He boxed the US out of diplomatic options when he implicitly consented to French jurisdiction by allowing the case to play out. There was nothing more he could do without risking American political interests in France. He was honest with Durham: "There is nothing more I can or will do."

Christmas 1857 was grim. Durham remained helpless in the face of the court's decision. He received death threats from anonymous letter writers who held him responsible for those who lost their lives aboard *Le Lyonnais*. The captain tried to find solace in the friends he had made in Marseille, but it was no use. Any act of celebration felt like a funeral. The holiday reminded him only of his father waiting across an ocean to find out what he already knew; they were ruined.

He waited until the day after Christmas to send a letter home. "Since my last, I have received the decision of the Court of Aix. They have decided against us; the grounds they founded their decision on are these: That the light we carried was not large enough. In the commissioner's report, they *expressly* say 'that the light *was of sufficient size and* placed in a good position to be seen from the steamer; but the way *they* argue is, that the light could not have been large enough or they could have seen it, not stopping to inquire whether there was any lookout on the steamer or not. It is a rascally piece of business without even the shadow of justice in it."[2] He hoped the letter reached his father before word of the decision reached the local newspapers.

The year ended with another defeat. The court dismissed Durham's appeal on the court costs in a brutal December 30 decision. "What is it necessary to decide on the appeal of Capt. Durham? Is it necessary to decide that the collision had occurred through the fault of Capt. Durham and consequently to condemn him to the payment of all losses occasioned by this collision?" the court wrote. "As to the costs? Points sustained after argument on the punishment made at Aix."[3]

The ruling did not permit the French to take possession of *Adriatic* until the court put an exact dollar figure on *Le Lyonnais*'s loss and entered a final judgment, called a "verdict" in France. Regardless, the damages would be immense. Durham knew he would never be able to pay them without surrendering his ship.

His liberty was also at stake. *Le Lyonnais* was bigger than *Adriatic*. She was designed for transatlantic voyages with paying, cabin-class passengers. Her value, design, and earning potential surpassed that of *Adriatic*. *Adriatic* might offset the debt to the Gauthiers, but she could never repay it. Durham faced the possibility of being imprisoned or at least detained in France until *Adriatic*'s owners met the obligation in full.

There was no hope for reconsideration while *Adriatic* was captive in a foreign port. Morgan had made it plain; the Americans would not intervene while she remained in French custody. If he could just get back to America, he might be able to renegotiate. On American soil, he could seek the assistance of his government and the political influence of his father, Carter, and his family's friends in Maine, but Maine was a long way from Marseille.

Marseille was the most secure port in France. It was divided into multiple sections, including the Ancien Port (Old Port), Avant Port Sud (south), and Port de Joliette. The Old Port was a long and narrow rectangle. The longer sides ran north to south, and the shorter sides east to west. The city of Marseille surrounded the northern, southern, and eastern borders. The only opening to the sea was a bottleneck on the western end created by two masses of land that jutted into the harbor. At the tip of each land mass was a seventeenth-century fort, Fort Saint-Jean to the north, and Fort Saint-Nicolas to the south.

The mouth of Joliette Port was north and west of the Old Port. A barrier on the western side of Joliette prevented ships from going out to the open sea without passing a narrow opening with a guard station. If a ship wanted to leave the Old Port, it had to go through the opening to the western end, sail past the south port, and go through the checkpoint. The entire system was designed to funnel ships to sea through a series

CHAPTER 28 | *The Marseille Predicament*

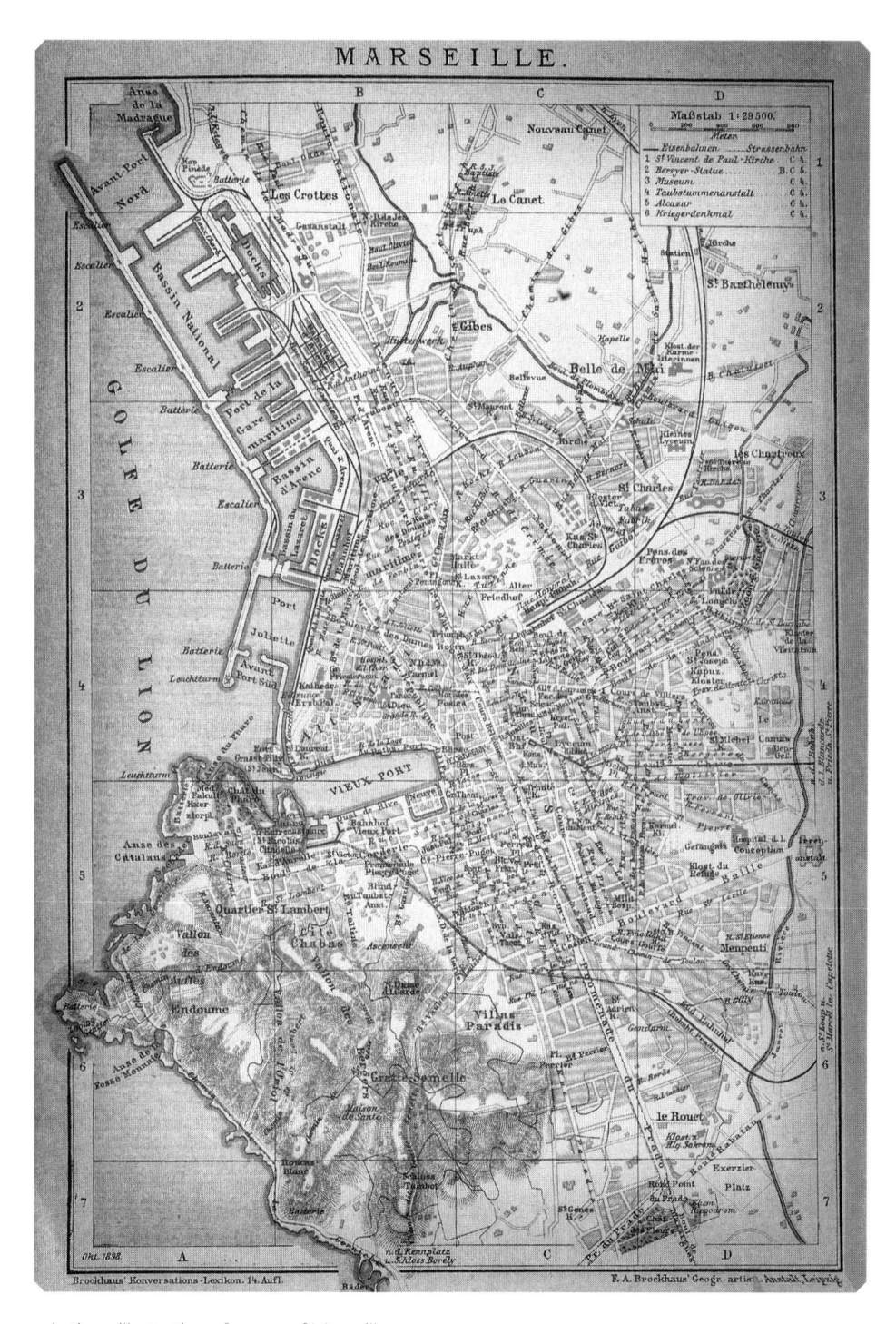

Antique illustration of a map of Marseille

of narrow openings under the watchful eye of French naval and customs authorities housed in the forts.

The French held *Adriatic* in the Old Port. Each day, Durham thought of nothing except how to move his ship from Marseille to home. His first problem was access. French officers guarded *Adriatic* around the clock. His second problem was that *Adriatic* was a prisoner at the dock. She was fastened to a line of other ships, part of a chain gang unable to move without towing her neighbors. The chains prevented a ship from leaving the harbor unnoticed. Durham would have to free *Adriatic* from the ships to which she was tethered if he wanted to put her to sea.

Durham looked at the masts of his ship and followed their lines to the sky. His next problem loomed above him. He had no sails. The French had removed every sail and piece of rigging from *Adriatic* in Marseille. Even if he could get ahold of some sails, without the ropes, cables, and chains necessary to support the masts, his crew would not be able to raise or adjust them. The inability to control the sails would leave her at the mercy of the wind and the waves and make a transatlantic journey impossible.

Durham was made aware of his last problem every time he looked to the beckoning sea. Ships leaving the Port of Marseille had to pass inspection at the guard station at the entrance to the port, an artificial boundary that separated the harbor and the open sea. The law required ships entering or leaving the harbor to show their papers—a port pass with the ship's name, purpose, and port of origin, as well as proof that the ship had clearance from the port captain to enter and exit the harbor. Durham's papers had been seized by the French and now bore a name that was on the lips of every sailor, lawyer, and dignitary in Marseille: *Adriatic*. He could not get out of Marseille with or without them.

He did not have much time. His lawyer told him it would take about a week for the court's assessors to calculate the amount that *Le Lyonnais*'s loss cost Franco-Américaine. Fate would play out in the narrow window between the court's pronouncement in favor of the Gauthier brothers and entry of the court's verdict.

Durham was not well. The magnitude of his predicament overwhelmed him, and he found it difficult to concentrate on anything else. He thought of his father, who put his life savings into *Adriatic* and was now heavily in debt. His family expected to use the earnings from *Adriatic*'s voyage to financially recover both from the construction of the ship and the new shipyard. Durham had long ago become accustomed to seeing pain on his father's face but could not bear the thought of being the cause of it.

He went out less. He drank more. He slept little, and his natural bravado and good humor waned. Durham's friends in Marseille watched

CHAPTER 28 | *The Marseille Predicament*

as he became more depressed by the day, and 1857 bled into 1858. The new year brought more bad news. The court informed Durham that the authorities would seize *Adriatic* if he did not settle his court costs within a week. The verdict would come a few days after that, at which time the total or the ship would come due.

John Stephen Martin, who had served as Durham's appointee to the Court of Aix's committee of experts, and an American captain named Ward L. Smith were among Durham's closest friends in Marseille. He met Martin shortly after his arrival in Marseille and Smith in August 1857, when Smith arrived in the city with financial troubles of his own. He confided in both about legal strategies, his concern for his father, and his desire to leave Marseille with his ship. It became less likely that Durham would make it out of France with each passing day. His persistent sadness concerned Martin and Smith. Durham became so despondent that his friends felt quite certain he would take his own life. Martin and Smith discussed their fears with one another and vowed to take turns watching him. They and some of the other sailors in Marseille worked in shifts to ensure that someone was always with Durham, especially at night.

Smith knew from experience what it was like to wait out uncertainty in Marseille. His ship, *Sarah E. Meaher*, had been sequestered because of a heavy debt she contracted in eastern Europe. *Meaher*'s debt was insurmountable, and it seemed Smith would not leave France anytime soon. Smith did not own *Meaher*, but he knew what it was like to be trapped in a foreign port on diplomatic whims. He took pity on his new friend and did his best to be there for him in his hours of need.

Martin rousted Smith from a sound sleep at around midnight on January 5. "It's Barney," he said. "He's missing." Durham had been drinking. He was nowhere to be found, and Martin feared the worst. He gathered Durham's friends together, and the men spread out around the city to look for him. "I'll take the waterfront," Smith told them. He searched the streets near Marseille Harbor. He wove in and out of the city's narrow passageways and onto the wider thoroughfares near the water's edge.

It was about two o'clock in the morning when he found his friend wandering the streets delirious with grief. He tried to convince him to go to bed, but he refused. "Walk with me," slurred Durham. He was drunk. Smith had no choice but to follow his friend as he stumbled along. He knew where they were headed. He could have stopped him but instead followed him down the street near the harbor, along the water's edge, and to the Old Port. It was not long before they stood in front of *Adriatic*.

Smith stood next to Durham, who got so close to the edge of the dock that Smith had to make sure he did not fall into the water. Durham stared at *Adriatic*. A French officer paced back and forth on her decks and leaned against her gunwale as he smoked a cigarette. He occasionally leaned over the rail to peer into the water or to look up at the stars. Durham remembered what it was like to stand on *Adriatic*'s deck and look past her long lines to the open ocean as men rushed about on his command. Now, he watched a stranger walk those decks.

Durham remained still. He was at the point of tears. Smith spoke for no reason other than to break the silence. He nudged Smith in the arm with his elbow. "I know what we should do," he said. "Let's jump on board, throw that man overboard, cut the ship out, and go home."[4] Durham remained quiet for a moment; then, he laughed. It was the first time in weeks. Smith could not help but laugh in response, and the two laughed just a little longer than necessary until their laughter faded back to calm. This time, it was Durham who broke the silence—with talk about a plan. He talked and talked and talked the way drunk men do, rambling in circles of nonsense punctuated by sudden bursts of coherence. He talked well into the night. Smith listened, not so much to the details but to the sound of his friend's voice. It was good to hear the lightness in it.

What Durham said was ridiculous, but it was so good to see the animation on his face that Smith could not help but nod vigorously in agreement. Durham talked. Smith nodded. Night gave way to day. Smith begged his friend to get some rest. "Promise me," mumbled Durham. "Promise me that you will help me." Smith let out a belly laugh. Durham said it again, "Promise!" This time his voice was as sharp as a dog's bark. Smith realized he would never get Durham to go home without making the pledge. He put his hand over his heart. "I swear it." He paused for a moment before he spoke again: "Now will you go home?" Durham nodded yes. Smith stumbled him out of the Old Port, past the water, through the harbor, and back to his boardinghouse and made sure he found his bed.

CHAPTER 29

Captain Ward L. Smith

WARD L. SMITH WAS A GIANT both in size and in character. He stood 6 foot, 3 inches tall, which was tall for any day but especially tall for a sailor in the mid-nineteenth century. He was as wide as he was high, with a strong back and broad shoulders. His head was a bit small for his body, which made his large frame seem even broader. He had small brown eyes set close together and capable of holding an intense gaze. His hair was spectacular. It was full and chestnut brown and puffed out in a wave both on the top and above each of his ears. The style might have looked elfish on a smaller man, but on Ward L. Smith it was just right. He had a full and neatly cropped beard that was the same color as his hair. It extended about 4 inches below his chin and covered so much of his face that it made his eyes even more penetrating. There was at once a strength and a kindness about him. One look at Ward Smith inspired confidence.

Ward L. Smith, ca. 1860. *Courtesy of Historic Mobile Preservation Society*

Smith was born in Geddes, New York, on August 19, 1825.[1] The town was named for James Geddes, a prominent settler who developed the salt industry there, and rests on Lake Onondaga. Smith was the eldest of four siblings, one brother and two sisters. His parents, Noah Hudson Smith Sr. and Cathalin Vrooman, worked in the salt industry. They gave up the business in 1840 and moved the family to a farm in nearby Lysander, New York. Geddes was hardly the big city, but Lysander was a far more rural and more agricultural setting. "Backwoods" is how Smith described it.[2]

Smith comes from a long line of family historians, who have chronicled his life and passed down stories about the man they all affectionately refer to as "Uncle Ward."[3] Myths about Uncle Ward have traveled across time and are as large and full of character as he was. One of the earliest is that he ran away from home at the age of twelve and joined a whaling ship. Like many family stories, it is not quite accurate, but Smith's grandniece, Sharon LaDuke, said it "sprouted from a kernel of truth."[4]

Smith was a dreamer. He always imagined leaving home to find his fortune. He was a fearless child. It was a fearlessness not born from knowledge, but from the lack of it—the easy fearlessness that comes from not knowing what life is like outside the shelter of a small town.

He did not run away at age twelve as family legend suggested. He did it at eighteen. Unlike many young boys with heads full of romantic dreams about traveling the world's oceans, Smith did not run straight to the sea. It was opportunity that called him. He left Lysander with the idea he would one day return home with a wealth amassed by his own gumption, and went in search of riches straight to "the Mecca of every boy's dreams of success and fortune," New York City.[5] He had no idea of how to find work or what he wanted to do for a living. All he knew was that he would never find what he was looking for in Lysander.

He traveled to Manhattan, a 300-mile journey that left him broke and hungry. He had no place to go and no place to sleep when he arrived, but it did not matter. He had no urge to sleep. He walked the city streets in astonishment. New York was like nothing he had ever seen.

Brick and stone buildings clustered in the city's downtown. One seemed taller than the next. Some were decorated with lavish columns, pillars, and carvings reminiscent of European chapels. Smith saw shops interspersed between the large buildings that sold everything from shoes to sweets to hats. Their large wooden advertisements competed for attention from passersby.

The city's wide thoroughfares teemed with life. Everyone moved with purpose. Carriages and hackney cabs transported wealthy New Yorkers about their daily business. Others walked the streets on foot. There was an elegance about them, as if the very act of walking down the street was part of a performance.

The women were nothing like the ladies in Lysander. They dressed in colorful costumes with large, hooped skirts and matching parasols and looked to Smith like spinning wooden tops. The men strutted in tailored pants, collared shirts, and waistcoats with short fronts and long pointed tails. They dressed as vibrantly as the women, with pants, vests, and coats covered in mixed patterns of tweeds and stripes. Smith wondered what his mother would think of them. The men wore their shirt collars turned down in a more casual fashion than she would have ever allowed. He looked down at his own drab clothing, reached up, touched his collar, and flattened it down just a smidge.

He continued. He walked what seemed like the length of the city looking for an idea of how to first feed his belly and then his fortune. It was early morning when he wandered toward the waterfront. New York broke into distinct neighborhoods here, but Irish enclaves dominated. The formation of the United Kingdom in 1801 had forced Irish Catholics to flee their homes to escape religious subordination. Many of these new immigrants were laborers familiar both with the sea and hard work. New York Harbor became a natural place to settle.

Rows of brick buildings made up the neighborhoods Smith passed on his approach to the East River. Each building looked to be attached to the one beside it. Some had multiple stories, but they were not as large and as ornate as those he had seen hours ago in the heart of the city. There were no columns or pillars or carved figurines here. Only some small shops broke up the monotony.

The streets narrowed as Smith inched closer to the waterfront. The straight lines of the brick buildings gave way to a tangle of passageways covered in cobblestone and littered with last night's trash. The scenery was darker here, the buildings lower to the ground. There were more taverns and rooming houses than permanent residences. The air smelled of stale beer and body odor with a tinge of food that had been left in the sun for too long. Some of the taverns were dug out underground and could be accessed only by stairs. Smith did not even try to imagine what went on in such places. He reached up, flattened his collar again, and walked just a little faster than necessary.

He saw glimpses of canvas and wood up ahead. Sails peaked out from above some of the buildings, and pointed bowsprits emerged from the cityscape as he approached the harbor. "Ships," he thought to himself. The sights comforted him. The air freshened with the ocean breeze, and the passageways opened to wider streets lined with office buildings. Smith reached Water Street. Water, as the name implies, ran along Manhattan's East River and served as home to shipyards and shipping companies.

It was still early. None of the merchants had opened for business. Smith made it to the water's edge and could go no farther. He had no idea where to go next. He looked up to get his bearings and saw a large sign hanging above the street, a painted canvas with a picture of a whale and some boats. Underneath it said, "Men and Boys Wanted for Whaling."[6] Smith sat down on the step beneath the sign and waited. He did not know what he was waiting for, but sitting under the sign gave him a sense of purpose.

Hours later, a neatly dressed gentleman arrived. He looked down at Smith, smiled warmly, and welcomed him inside his office. "I am the shipping agent for Swift & Allen," said the man as he turned the key and gestured for Smith to come inside. Smith did not know what a shipping agent was, but he nodded and followed him anyway. "We are looking for hardworking men like you to join a whaling adventure." The agent handed Smith the application. "After we get this out of the way, we will see to getting you some breakfast." Smith took the application, but heard only the word "breakfast." The application was nothing more than a formality. He got the job on the spot! Next, Smith signed something called "articles," a contract that laid out rules and regulations he would have to follow and what would be expected of him in his new position. Smith had a limited education and could not read the articles, so he just signed where the agent pointed. Besides, he had more-important business in the moment. It had been almost a week since he had eaten a proper meal. The first perk of his new job was a meal ticket for breakfast at a cheap boardinghouse. Smith rushed out of the agent's office and straight to the breakfast table, where he stuffed himself with eggs, sausage, bread, and everything else the boardinghouse had to offer. Years later he recalled, "On that breakfast, they lost money."[7]

It was only when his belly was full that Smith began to think about what he had done. He had signed a contract to board a ship he had never heard of, departing from a place he had never been, to spend the next four years of his life doing a job he did not know. He was not alone. Weeks sometimes passed between the time a new sailor signed articles with a shipping agent and the time the ship set to sea. Many young men had second thoughts about making such a long voyage. Shipping agents in the 1840s struggled not only to find strong boys capable of doing the work but to make sure they did not skip out on their obligations before a ship weighed anchor.

Four years. It seemed like an eternity at Smith's age, but there was money to be made. The voyage would bring him one step closer to returning to Lysander a self-made man. Practically speaking, staying the course meant he would no longer have to worry about room and board or how to fill his stomach or make ends meet. All he would have to do is work hard and, in the end, receive his just reward. The agent promised him a "lay" or share of the ship's profits—1/157 percent—in return for his efforts.[8] He did not know how much a whaling ship made, but the idea of his pay being bound to his hard work appealed to him. Besides, he had given his word, and a man did not go back on his word. Smith had no reason to think about the rest.

The agent told him to be ready for the five o'clock steamer to New Bedford. He arrived well before five and met a group of other boys, similar in age and aspiration, who had signed up to be whalers as well. The boys talked among themselves and traded stories about where they came from and how they got there. Some came from seafaring towns and had at least a vague idea of what they had gotten themselves into. Others, like Smith, did not. It was here that Smith first heard the word "greenhand," a term used by sailors to refer to crew members with little to no experience at sea.

The greenhands boarded the steamer at five and got underway at about six. The voyage north was a pleasant one. The ship ran close to the land, where the mainland to the west protected it from harsh winds. Smith and the others could not imagine why it was so difficult to get boys to go on whaling adventures, when the sea was so calm and greenhands received such royal treatment. The sailing was smooth. Meals were plentiful. Their accommodations had been good so far. Smith and the other boys concluded that all they needed to do was learn the ins and outs of how to work the sails, and the next four years would be a breeze. He later recalled, "We thought were whaling already and only had to learn to talk in sailor-like fashion to become able seamen."[9]

The New Bedford ship would not be ready for ten days. Swift & Allen sent the newly minted sailors to boarding homes until the ship was ready. They sent Smith to board with the widow of an old sea captain. Her home was not far from the water. He found the address and knocked on the door. The widow answered, welcomed him inside, and pointed him to his room. It was a small space with little more than a bed and a wooden table, but it suited Smith just fine. The boy carried few belongs with him from Lysander and did not need much space. Smith did not know what to do next, so he found the widow in the kitchen.

The first words the widow spoke to him left an indelible imprint on his life. They came in the form of a question she asked him with such intensity that it immediately piqued both his interest and his concentration. "Have you ever learned to use liquor or tobacco?" He answered, "No."[10] The widow beckoned him to sit down and poured him a cup of tea. She told him stories of sailors who had wasted their fortunes, and sometimes their lives, in pursuit of liquor and all the trouble to which it can lead. "Promise me," implored the widow. "Promise me, Ward, that you will never touch a drop of either liquor or tobacco as long as you live."[11] She was a good Christian woman with arguments so passionate and so compelling that Smith could not help but make the pledge.

Swift & Allen expected every man and boy on the whaling vessel to come prepared with everything he needed for a four-year voyage. "How are we going to get the money to pay for that?" the greenhands asked one another. They learned that the ship's owner, referred to as the "husband," provided an allowance. Smith received $152 in clothing and credit at local outfitting stores. The husband also gave each boy a donkey. The precursor to sailors' trunks, donkeys were small chests designed to contain all of a sailor's personal items at sea. The widow helped Smith choose clothing and supplies to fill his donkey. She saw to it that he had warm, sturdy clothes and enough yarn, needles, and dungaree cloth to repair his clothing in the likely event it was torn or became threadbare.

The widow asked Smith about his education and learned it was lacking. She told him to buy some reading books. "I can't," he responded. "I already spent all the money the husband gave me." The widow grabbed Smith by the hand and marched him down to the outfitter's store. She found the shopkeeper and demanded he provide Smith with spelling, grammar, and arithmetic books as well as writing paper at no additional charge. She was a difficult woman to refuse, and the shopkeeper obliged. The widow packed the books in Smith's donkey. She also purchased one additional book on his behalf, a Bible, and stored it in the donkey as well.

The widow had two sons, each of whom was at sea in the Pacific. She did not speak of them often. Smith wondered if the widow packed their donkeys with as much care as she did his, or maybe she was so insistent with him because she had not done so and now regretted it. Regardless, Smith never forgot the widow or the lessons she taught him about the importance of obtaining an education and leading a good Christian life. He thought of her often throughout the years and, owing the promise he made her, never touched a drop of alcohol or smoked tobacco as long as he lived.

On November 27, 1843, it was time. Smith made his way to the dock and got a look at his home for the foreseeable future, the whaling ship *Tuscaloosa* of New Bedford. She was 98 feet long and 25 feet wide, with depth of 12 feet. She had three masts, a square stern, and a billet head, a round piece of timber at the bow used for running harpoon lines. *Tuscaloosa* was built in 1825 and had been a whaling ship from the beginning. She was christened a sailing ship, but Swift & Allen reregistered her as a barque on November 26, just three days before Smith's voyage. The change in rigging cut down on the number of men needed to handle the sails, and allowed her to sail closer to the wind than a full-rigged ship.

The chaplain of the New Bedford Port Society recorded each crew member's name, hometown, and identifying features on a crew list kept for all whalers leaving from the port. Smith, like many of the greenhands, lied. He told the chaplain he was twenty-one. There was no minimum age requirement for being a whaler. Most vessels, including *Tuscaloosa*, employed boys much younger. Notwithstanding, it was so common for sailors to misrepresent their age on whaling crew lists that New Bedford historians treat the number as a rough approximation.

The wharf was crowded the day *Tuscaloosa* left. Families, friends, and young women who would soon be left behind came to say goodbye and wish the men safe journeys. Stoic wives feigned indifference in the face of yet another separation from their husbands. Mothers recited their prayers. There were only two boys who had no one to wave goodbye to them: Smith and Daniel "Dana" C. Hunt.[12] Both were on their own in New Bedford. Both were from landlocked towns and had never been to the sea. They were the only sailors aboard who declined their allowance for tobacco and liquor for religious reasons. The commonalities made them instant friends.

Smith boarded the barque and made his way to the deck. He wondered if he would ever see home again. He felt the parting more than those who had friends on the wharf to say goodbye. They had a place to call home. They had a return. He no longer did. His life was unwritten, but he no longer saw the limitlessness of that future through the eyes of a boy living in a small town. The crowd on the dock became smaller as the barque set to sea. Smith realized he was a man alone in the world. The reflection did not last long. Within an hour, the ship was really to sea.

The sea was rough the day *Tuscaloosa* left New Bedford. The barque pitched into a head sea, where the waves ran perpendicular to the course of the ship and caused the ship to rise and fall as large waves ran under them from bow to stern. *Tuscaloosa* suspended for a moment in the air when a wave took her bow, then crashed down in the gap left when the wave passed under the ship. The ship rose and fell, rose and fell, rose and fell over and over again for what seemed like an eternity. "Anyone who has never been seasick does not know what seasickness is," Smith later wrote. "The ship commenced to pitch into a head sea, and I commenced to part with all I ever ate. I sometimes would examine the soles of my boots to be sure I had not thrown them up. For twenty-four-hours I thought I had thrown up more than I had ever ate and felt sure I was going to die."[13]

The storm passed within a day, but for Smith and many of the other greenhands, the sickness did not. There was no place to escape seasickness. Greenhands and seasoned sailors alike slept in the forecastle, an enclosed bunk room that was part of the main deck. Each man had a bunk and a place to keep his donkey, but little room for anything else. Shipbuilders designed whaling vessels to maximize space for cleaning whales and storing oil and minimized space for anything else. There were no dining rooms or lounges. Men ate and drank and smoked in the forecastle. They kept clothes that stank of sweat and grease and whale guts there. They traded songs and stories and jokes there. It was their only living space.

John Ross Browne, *Etchings of a Whaling Cruise* (New York: Harper & Brothers, 1846), 214. Etching by A. A. von Schmidt and J. Halpin. *Library of Congress*

A bunk provided no reprieve from the smells and the sounds of a seasick sailor's comrades. "The forecastle was black and slimy with fifth, very small and hot as an oven," said one greenhand of his quarters on an 1840s whaling expedition. "It was filled with a compound of foul air, smoke, sea-chests, soap-kegs, greasy pans, and tainted meat." Men smoked, laughed, and cursed the greenhands in their seasickness. "There were groans on one side and yells, oaths, laughter and smoke on the other."[14]

Seasickness was no excuse to avoid work, and the captain required even the weakest among them to do their share. Smith attempted to combat his seasickness by borrowing tricks from more-experienced sailors, such as staring at the horizon and taking in fresh air, but it did little to help. The captain wrote about Smith and some of the others in a letter to Frederick Slocum Allen, *Tuscaloosa*'s agent in New Bedford. During the period from 1842 to 1860, some of the most prosperous years of American whaling, Swift & Allen served as industry agents, ship chandlers, and commission merchants. The company was founded in 1842 by Frederick Slocum Allen and his brother-in-law Jireh Swift. In addition to managing their own vessels, the firm acted as agents for twenty-four vessels from about 1844 to 1887 and handled accounts of crew members and masters and sales of whale oil and bone for each vessel. These vessels made a combined total of approximately eighty voyages.

Smith was one boy on one ship on one of these voyages. Allen and his associates saw so many boys at the New Bedford office that it was hard to keep track of their names. Boys who stood out got nicknames. Smith stuck out because of his extreme height. The merchants gave him an obvious but fitting nickname: 6'3". *Tuscaloosa*'s captain described the sight that Smith made during his bout of seasickness in a December 20, 1844, letter to Frederick Allen. He said that "6'3" was the longest coming to, and he was pretty sure he had a bad fever. I wish you could have seen him without hat, jacket or shoes for 4 days laying his length all over the deck, but when he did come [to] he came bright."[15]

Seasickness seemed endless to Smith. It took him more than a month to "come to" or, as Smith put it, come to "believe the seasickness would not kill [him]."[16] Smith also suffered from frostbite in the early days of the journey. The water in the North Atlantic was cold. Surface temperatures rarely reached more than 40 degrees Fahrenheit in the winter months. The air temperature was far colder. Whalers worked all day in preparation for the moment someone spotted a whale. They worked outside and remained wet from the cold water rushing over the sides of the ship. Smith's toes were so badly frostbitten he could hardly walk. He told the captain he had experienced frostbite before, during one of his long winters in upstate New York. Both of them feared he might now be prone to it, an affliction that could end a whaler's career before it began.

The officers and the merchants played a game of predicting which greenhands would make the best sailors. 6'3" made an impression on everyone, particularly the first mate, Mr. Almy, as a greenhand with great promise. Now the frostbite and the seasickness gave the captain and his mate reason to fear they might lose the young man's services. The captain composed a joking poem about it in one of his letters to Swift & Allen:

> Oh ever thus from childhood,
> I've seen my fondest hopes decay,
> I never shipped a great long man,
> but he was the first to limp away![17]

Smith did not limp away. He was an observer. He studied people even in his sickness. He watched veteran seamen. The wind and the weather and the constant pitching of the boat did not bother them at all. They moved as if on land. He wondered how long it took them to be able to move that way. He wondered if he ever would. He wondered about the places the men had been and the stories behind their weathered skin and rough hands. He watched them—the tools they used, the knots they tied, the way they prepared the boat for whales. Even when he was flat on his back and felt like he would die, he watched, so that in any moment required he could contribute to the prosperity of the vessel that he still believed would bring him his fortune. Above all, Smith kept his eyes on the captain. The captain noticed.

Tuscaloosa's captain was Albert G. Goodwin. He was a competent seaman, a good whaler, and a strict disciplinarian. He was also a devoted Christian. The same was true of the first mate, Mr. Almy, and the other officers.[18] It was not uncommon for whaling captains to combine the discipline of religion with that of vessel command. Regulation of alcohol helped keep order aboard a ship. Goodwin and Almy asked *Tuscaloosa*'s crew members to sign an abstinence pledge prior to their departure. All but three of the crew signed. Those who did threw overboard any private stock they had brought aboard the ship. Goodwin was skeptical about whether a desire to curry favor with him rather than genuine piety caused them to sign the pledge, but it did not matter, because both resulted in the discipline he required.

Once Smith's body adjusted to life at sea, he used his breaks from the business of whaling to study. He could barely read or write when he boarded *Tuscaloosa*. He remembered what the widow told him, and reviewed his books whenever he was not working. He sounded out the words in the reading books and copied words from his speller onto blank pages.

His studiousness got the attention of the cook, an African American man named Samuel Tillman. Tillman was twenty-eight, one of the older men aboard the ship. His white hair against dark skin added to his more mature appearance. Tillman was eager to learn to read. He offered to do Smith's laundry and give him extra food in exchange for lessons. Tillman was an excellent cook whose offer meant food beyond the salt beef, cracker-like bread the sailors called "hard tack," and coffee that made up a sailor's monotonous diet. Smith readily agreed. What Tillman did not know is that Smith could barely read himself. He studied even harder to stay ahead of his one and only pupil.

Smith kept his books in his donkey. He lifted them out when it was time to study, spread them on the deck, and moved from book to book as he worked through them. Goodwin walked by one day and saw him engaged in his studies. The industrious young greenhand impressed him. "Come every day and I will teach you how to navigate a vessel," Goodwin said.[19] That, and Tillman's extra food, was all the incentive Smith needed. He learned quickly, sounding out words until he could spell words with more than one syllable and read entire passages from his Bible.

"Long Island!" Goodwin shouted. It was a new nickname he had given Smith. The officers made sure that all greenhands learned the basics of navigation, but the captain paid particular attention to Smith. "Long Island, look to starboard and tell me when you see land," he might say, or "Long Island, tell me the ship's position." Smith soon learned how to navigate a sailing vessel and how to overcome the perils of the open ocean.

Men worked around the clock in two-hour shifts manning the vessel and watching for whales. The first thing a greenhand learned was how to differentiate a whale from other marine life. One greenhand, eager to be the first to spot a whale, caused a false alarm early in the voyage when he mistook a shark for a whale. He learned that such a mistake prompted endless taunts from the officers, veteran sailors, and even the captain.

Tuscaloosa sailed in search of right whales. Nineteenth-century whalers found this species the "right" whales to kill because of their plentiful oil and baleen. Right whales were also easier to hunt because they skimmed the surface, moved slowly, and floated after being killed. There were two primary whaling grounds for right whales in the mid-nineteenth century. One was in the North Atlantic, and the other in the South Pacific and parts of the South Atlantic. *Tuscaloosa* took the South Pacific route. The ship stopped in the Canary Islands to pick up fresh fruit, supplies, and four additional men to round out the crew. It was a brief stop, and only the officers went ashore. Goodwin set course for Cape Horn, the tip of South America, to the Falkland Islands. The crew stopped for supplies in the Falklands before they continued.

Five or six days later the men awoke at sea to sounds in the distance. The sound was one of great force, the combination of a geyser and the loud spit of a wet exhale. "There she blows!" called the watchman. Whales! It was too dark to see them, but the sound of air being forced through the blowhole was unmistakable even to Smith, who had never heard the sound before. "To the boats," ordered Goodwin. "Be ready at first light."[20] The entire ship came alive. Men jumped into their assigned boats, which were lowered to the water. They waited for the sun to crack the horizon with enough light to see. When it did, the boats raced one another to reach the whales first. Smith's boat took the lead:

> Our boat was leading and we tried to get ahead of the whale, and after getting where we thought the whales would come up, we rested with the order to keep a sharp lookout over the side and under the boats. Thus, we watched for perhaps ten minutes, when the mate whispered[,] "Here she comes," and sure enough she did come, for we had hardly time to look when a huge black object ran his head up and over the boat. I just took one look and surrendered. It seemed to me there was room for two or three meeting houses under that head and still have room on top; yet there was one man in the boats that was not frightened and that was Mr. Alm[y]. When he saw the whale coming up[,] he knew just what to do[,] and as the monster raised his immense head over the side of the boat, he took his hat off and commenced hitting the whale over his head and very coolly telling him, the whale, to go back. As this species of whale family is very particular about their heads, to our astonishment the whale settled back and left us untouched. This, my first experience with a whale, is still fresh in my memory and I think had a great effect in disarming my fear for the whole whale family. Our reasoning was that if a whale could be driven back by the blow of an old hat and thus lose his chance to defeat his pursuers[,] he was not to be feared, yet our experience with this same whale was not at all pleasant. As the whale settled back in the water[,] he turned part way around and proceeded to come up again to blow, and by doing so showed his side to us and gave us the opportunity to fasten to him, that is throw two harpoons into him.[21]

Illustration from an 1860 issue of *Harper's New Monthly Magazine* showing a whaling ship from New Bedford or Nantucket dispatching small open boats with harpooners prepared to kill a whale

CHAPTER 29 | *Captain Ward L. Smith*

Smith tried to keep up as the veterans lanced and followed the whale. Whales have sensitive hearing, so Almy delivered a stream of orders in a voice little more than a whisper. All of that changed when the whale came in close to the boat and showed the men his side:

> Mr. Alm[y] called out as loud as he could, "Get up—give him your first iron!," and "Give him the other iron!" Both orders were obeyed[,] and we were soon fast to the whale. In these few minutes incidents were happening so fast that it is difficult for one to know which came first. However, after getting fast to the whale and obeying the orders to "Stern all" (that is, back away), you can imagine our thoughts when we found we were backing right onto another whale, and at the same time a third one made his appearance, the three whales forming a triangle and our boat in the center.
>
> We had no time to make plans; we only saw the position but had hardly time to think when it was all changed, and not for the better. As the other whales showing themselves in the way they did made it impossible for us to back off, we had to take whatever our stuck whale would give us, which was not long in coming. As soon as he felt the harpoon of course he made an effort to clear himself from the attack and in doing so rolled nearly over, striking the bow of the boat with his fin and breaking off some four feet of the boat. As he turned down, the same fin went under the boat and again he caught the boat or what was left of it on his fin. Boat and crew were lifted fifteen or twenty feet in the air and dropped into the water together with oars and what was worse, some two or three thousand feet of lined with one end fastened to the whale.
>
> After striking the water and getting our heads out[,] the first thing we heard was the mate's order to "Get out of the way of the whale line." He was busy giving oars or anything he could find to each one of us that was too frightened to help ourselves. By this time the other two whales had become "galled" and disappeared, but the whale we had struck was still fighting, that is, rolling over and standing on his head and with his flukes thrashing the water all around him. However, he got so far away that we were out of his reach. . . . Each one of us had an oar or something to help float us but still everything was discipline as Mr. Alm[y] never got excited or lost control of himself or his crew. The only appearance of excitement I saw in him was when the whale would spout up big clots of blood as large as a water bucket. Then he would call out, "He is our whale," but all the time I thought we were Davy Jones's.[22]

Almy and Smith's boat was stoved in and now 4 to 5 miles away from the ship. The galled whales disappeared. The other boats hunted whales of their own. *Tuscaloosa*'s lookout saw them, but the wind was light. There was nothing to do but wait. It took the ship all day to reach them, and it was dark when they got on board.

The next morning, Goodwin found the dead whale. It took nearly the entire day to locate it, fasten chains to it, and attach it to the ship so the men could begin cutting in, the process of retrieving oil, blubber, and baleen. The weather was fine, and Goodwin decided to cut into the whale the next day.

The work began again at first light. The men attached chains to the whale's bonnet, the upper part of the head. After heaving up on the windlass and capstan for nearly an hour, they separated the bonnet from the body and hauled in on deck. The jaw measured about 30 feet and was over 20 feet high. Once they secured the head, the men removed the oil and bone and threw the remainder over the side of the ship.

Next came the process of cutting large chunks of blubber called blanket pieces. Each blanket piece was about 8 feet wide, 15 to 20 feet in length, and a foot thick. The crew hoisted them aboard by using blocks and tackles. Other members of the crew lit fires under three large kettles and began the process of turning the hunks of blubber into oil.

> In the first place the blanket pieces are cut up in what whalers call "horse pieces," that is in pieces about eight inches wide and ten feet long and as thick as the blubber, sometimes not more than four inches thick and sometimes as much as eighteen inches thick. From the blubber room the pieces are carried to the horse block[,] which is a long oak plank about eight inches wide and five or six feet long, one end lower than the other. At the higher end, a man stands with his "mincing knife," an article a good deal like an ordinary drawing knife, only one handle stood out straight. As these pieces are brought out[,] they are taken by the horse boy[,] whose business it is to put them on the horse block and feed them up as the mince man cuts them up in small thin slices.[23]

Whalers referred to the smaller pieces as Bible pieces because they were the size and shape of a small book. The officers reminded Smith and the other sailors to "remember your Bible and make them pieces of blubber look as like the leaves of the Book."[20] The men dropped the blubber into a big tub used to refill the kettle. Members of the crew moved the oil from the kettle to a large copper cooler until it was cool enough to put into casks and store.

Whaling was a different kind of education for Smith. The men took turns cutting blubber, manning the watch, and sleeping. They slept only four of twenty-four hours when there was cutting to be done. By the time they finished with the whale, it had been three days since they had caught it and five since they had first spotted it. It was only the first whale. The process of hunting, killing, and dismembering whales repeated itself over and over again. Smith got little sleep for the rest of the voyage. Whale oil perpetually coated his clothes and skin. He later said of the job, "No one who has never been on a whale ship with plenty of whales knows what work is."[24]

Tuscaloosa sailed to the South Pacific near Easter Island and the St. Paul Islands from the Falklands, but it was at the Cape of Good Hope in South Africa that they had their biggest success. Whales. Hundreds of them. Endless days of hunting and hauling and cutting in. The ship filled every crate with oil in just a few weeks' time. "Throw the flour overboard," cried Goodwin.[25] The crew devoted every usable space to storing whale oil.

The wind was in their favor. *Tuscaloosa* sailed to the Sandwich Islands and, finally, Honolulu. They found a ship heading back to New York and offloaded the oil and began the hunt for whales all over again.

Goodwin retraced his steps and sailed from Cape Horn back to the Atlantic. They traveled through the Falkland Islands, where they caught their first whale, and caught two more there. Next, they headed to Patagonia, at the tip of South America, where they caught two whales and calf, but it was in St. Joseph's Bay Patagonia, on October 5, 1845, that *Tuscaloosa*'s luck ran out.

"Pampero," whispered the sailors. A pampero, a winter storm with strong winds that appear during the passage of a cold front across South America's low-lying grasslands, headed their way. The storms were unique to the pampas of Brazil, Argentina, Uruguay, Paraguay, and Bolivia and brought with them devastating, hurricane-like weather. *Tuscaloosa* anchored close to shore in shallow water. Goodwin ordered all three anchors put down and sent all spars except the topmast down on deck. The temperature dropped. The wind picked up and soon it blew with hurricane force. The sea ran mountains high. The ship pitched in the storm and took hundreds of gallons of water on deck every time she did.

The men watched and waited while the wind howled through the rigging. It was cold. Snowy hail pelted their faces. The noise of the wind made it impossible to hear a voice 3 feet away and almost impossible to hear the captain, who spoke his orders through a trumpet. They all knew; if their anchors held, they would be safe. If they did not, there was no hope.

The first anchor chain broke at half past nine in the evening. The second broke behind it. There was only one left. Everyone knew what would follow. Goodwin called the men to the quarterdeck and gave his last order. He issued it in a tone of fatherly advice. "Strap in." The men lashed themselves down to something on the ship and remained ready to cut themselves free if the time came.

Smith was near the captain. "Long Island," he said, "put this rope around me and then give me the ends of it." He did as Goodwin commanded. "Now put the rope around yourself. Take the turn of the rope and tie it here."[26] The captain pointed to a small spar that used to be a studding-sail beam. Smith again obeyed. "Keep close to me, Long Island," he said now in a voice that was less like a captain's and more like a father's. Smith felt safer near the captain and made sure their ropes held fast to the same spar until there was nothing to do but wait until the end.

He was not afraid. He did not have time to be. Once the anchor chains broke, *Tuscaloosa* swung around the sea. Monstrous waves rolled over them. "It is only a matter of time," he thought to himself. He thought about the number of men who would go with *Tuscaloosa* to the bottom.

The suspense was dreadful. Every man knew the ship would sink, but not one of them knew when. Smith would have preferred the end to come as quickly as possible. Only twenty minutes passed from the time the chains parted to the time the ship struck bottom for the first time, but the wait seemed like hours. The wind spun the ship in circles. Men choked on the waves that crashed over them. The exertion required for Smith to keep his head above water was almost too much to bear.

The first time the ship struck the bottom, the rudder hit the ground 15 or 20 feet from the stern. Several casks of oil burst open in the crash and poured into the sea. It was only a few minutes later that another swell carried the vessel up, and she came down to the bottom with such force that all three masts went over the side and took several of the men overboard. It took only three or four swells for the barque to drive the ship toward the shore in a heavy surf. She hit the bottom and finally broke open. The captain and Smith cut themselves loose and swam the short distance to shore. The whole time, Smith feared he would be swept to sea.

He finally reached the place where the water met the sand and crawled hand over hand out of the surf and onto the beach. His body sank in the wet sand each time his hand or his knee touched down. He jogged forward in one final push and collapsed face first. It was only when he choked on dry sand that he knew he was out of harm's way. The captain kept his word. He stayed close to Smith and fell next to him on the beach.

They were drenched to the bone. The roaring wind felt freezing cold. The captain wasted no time in searching for his crew. The men started coming from all directions, and soon they were all there. They made a small fire, and after a rest, Goodwin ordered the men to gather as much cargo as possible. They waded in the surf and pulled barrels of oil to shore, but Goodwin was unable to fully assess the damage until sunup.

The ship was a loss. The men were able to retrieve most of the cargo from what remained on the ship and washed up onshore. The captain fitted two small boats and proceeded to the nearest town, Rio Negro, to obtain a new ship that could accommodate his crew and what was left of their cargo. All he found was an old schooner. He loaded it with water and returned to the crew. Shortly thereafter, the Dutch brig *Telfire* pulled into the bay and, for the sum of $2,500, agreed to take *Tuscaloosa*'s crew and the three hundred barrels of oil they had salvaged to Rio de Janeiro, where they could find a ship to transport them home. They arrived in Rio de Janeiro on December 21, 1845.[27]

Goodwin reported *Tuscaloosa*'s loss to the American consulate upon arrival. During the 1850s, all Americans who were shipwrecked were entitled to protection by the consul, who was required to send them home at the government's expense. The consul provided a stipend for food and lodging while the crew waited for vessels headed back to the northeast. American officials arranged passage for the more senior members of the crew on one ship and led Goodwin to believe that the remainder of his crew would soon follow.

The American consul at Rio de Janeiro, a man by the name of Mr. Crittendon, had other plans for the remainder of *Tuscaloosa*'s crew. His temperament and good nature changed the moment Goodwin and his senior officers set sail. Crittenden told the remaining *Tuscaloosa* sailors they would have to find work on another ship if they wanted to return to America. Smith and his friend, Dana Hunt, tried for weeks. They approached any ship bound for home, but not one needed crew.

Smith and Hunt reported back to the consulate and informed Crittenden of their efforts. "You are damned smart," he replied, "but I shall not send you home and, after tomorrow, I will not feed you. If you want to work, the frigate *Columbia* is here and needs men."[28]

USS *Columbia* was an American navy frigate. She served as the flagship of the Brazil Squadron, a fleet of ships charged with protecting American interests in South America, from 1845 to 1847. Unfortunately for Smith and Hunt, *Columbia* was stranded in Rio de Janeiro in the winter of 1846 because most of her crew had died of smallpox or been taken to the hospital. *Columbia* now sat in the harbor waiting for healthy men. Crittenden boomed, "If you want to ship in the Navy, I will send you off to the frigate in my boat."[29]

Smith and Hunt protested. They were whalers now and had no interest in joining the service. "Well, go home, but if you do not have a position by tomorrow, I will stop paying your board."[30] The boys stared at him in disbelief. "You may go," said Crittenden, who seemed intent on filling *Columbia*'s open spots. Had Goodwin been with them, it is unlikely that Crittenden would have succeeded, but he was gone. Smith and Hunt returned to the boardinghouse. The owner confirmed that Crittenden had cut off their allowance. He allowed the boys to stay a few extra days to try to find another solution.

Three days passed with no luck finding work on another ship. Smith and Hunt faced starvation or naval service. They chose the latter. Crittenden ferried the boys directly to the frigate in his boat, as promised.

Neither Smith nor Hunt knew anything about military discipline. They told the deck officer that they had never been aboard a warship. He called another officer, who gave each of them a hammock and showed them where to hang them. He handed each of them a pair of shoes and said, "You'll be on waste gang until you are assigned a regular place and a uniform." No one approached the boys the rest of the day, so they hung up their hammocks and went to sleep.

"All hands ahoy!" The boys awoke the next morning to the call. The men scattered. Smith and Hunt followed and learned that "All hands ahoy!" meant they must put away their hammocks and appear on deck in three minutes or less. With some help from a more experienced sailor, their hammocks passed inspection, and they reported to their assigned post.

Their morning consisted of washing down specific areas of the ship. An officer assigned Smith to clean an area around one of the ship's guns. He was beginning to learn that being in the navy meant an endless stream of orders followed by inspections. He looked to his left and looked to his right and satisfied himself that his cleaning skills were up to snuff. He also noticed that aside from his friend, Hunt, none of the other sailors were wearing their government-issued shoes. He removed his shoes, set them neatly on the bulwark, and continued to scrub the gun.

The officer on duty, Porter, came over. Porter was a man who inspired fear rather than respect. He pointed to Smith's shoes and said, "Take that trash to the lucky bag."[31] The lucky bag was a sack hung up near the mast. Anything found out of place was put inside it. "Those are my shoes, sir," said Smith. Porter stepped to Smith and looked him in the eye. He raised his fist in the air as though he was about to strike him. Instead, he unclenched his fist, pointed to the mast, and yelled, "Put those shoes in the lucky bag!"[32]

Smith had no tolerance for bullies. He ran to his shoes, scooped them up, and threw them overboard. He knew he should not have done it, but it was too late. He braced himself for whatever came next. Porter turned and left.

Smith breathed a sigh of relief and worked until it was time for breakfast. No one said another word about the shoes, and Smith forgot all about it. The boatswain entered the forecastle toward the end of breakfast and called, "All hands to witness punishment."[33] Smith had no idea who was about to be punished or what witnessing punishment meant. He followed the crowd of sailors from the mess and back out onto the deck. Porter was there again. This time the captain himself accompanied him. Porter's eyes searched the crowd of men. "Him!" Porter pointed at Smith. "Me?" Smith exclaimed. Before he finished his question, some sailors grabbed him and forced him to stand on a small platform next to the rigging, called a grating. They faced him toward the mast. Men on each side grabbed his hands, pulled them up over his head into a V, and tied them to the rigging. "Twelve lashes for insubordination," the captain announced.

The boatswain held a short piece of rope called a colt. The crew gathered around to watch. Smith felt their eyes on him, and he waited for the first lash to strike his skin. Until it did, he thought the anticipation was the worst part of the whole ordeal. The loud snap of the colt came with a biting sting that went through his skin and straight into his bones. He did not know how or why, but he did not cry out. "Eleven more," he told himself. Some of the blows brought blood, but Smith never made a sound. Tears welled in his eyes when the twelfth lash landed. He let his body go limp. Still tied to the rigging, he felt the wet sensation of blood seeping down his back and around his rib cage as gravity pulled the sticky liquid toward his center.

Porter walked up behind him. He leaned over the boy's shoulder and put his mouth close to Smith's ear. Smith's body tensed. Porter whispered, "The next time you get to the grating, I will make you yell."[34] Smith could not stand on his own when the men cut him down.

The captain sent him to the brig on the lower gun deck, a space between the two guns with an open porthole on each side. He spent a full day and night there. The next morning, the captain sent Hunt to bring him something to eat. Together, they made plans to escape what Smith described as "floating Hell." "It was agreed that Hunt should, by some means, come to me late in the night, and we would tie our clothes up in bundles, slip overboard[,] and try to swim to the shore. If we were successful[,] it would be all right, and if we should drown it would be better than trying to live in this way aboard this ship."[35]

Hunt came the next evening, and the two slipped overboard as planned. They swam away as quietly as possible. They saw the movement of sailors aboard *Columbia* soon after. Smith and Hunt heard the order "Call away the boats," and it was not long before they heard the boats launch into the water. "Head for the landing," the officers cried. "Keep lookout for a boat."[36] Smith and Hunt treaded water in relief as they watched the boats head toward shore. The boys quietly and carefully continued their swim. They hid in a shoal and made their way to shore about an hour after they escaped.

They remained close to shore the first day and headed for town the next day while staying sheltered by the bushes. On the third day, they saw the sails of the frigate *Columbia* leave the harbor and sail out of sight.

The boys reached Rio's downtown and found a boardinghouse that agreed to give them a place to stay until they could get work. They found it the next day on the barque *Brazillero*, a ship whose captain agreed to let them work for their passage. *Brazillero* was headed for Mobile, Alabama. Smith knew nothing about Mobile, but any place was better than Rio.

CHAPTER 30

Stranded

IT IS SAID THAT DURING HIS LIFETIME, Captain Timothy Meaher transported 1,700,000 bales of cotton up and down the Mobile River. Meaher was a wealthy landowner and shipbuilder who profited from Alabama's booming cotton business in the mid-1800s.[1] He was not a native of the South. Born in 1812 of Irish immigrants who settled in Lincoln County, Maine, Meaher moved to Alabama in 1835, attracted by stories of men who had made their fortunes there. He began his career as a deckhand and "rapidly worked his way up to mate by working on nine river steamers until he raised enough capital to build a sawmill and a shipyard north of the city on the Chickasabogue River."[2] Meaher wanted his family to share in his good fortune, so he asked his siblings to join him in Alabama.

Maine abolished slavery before Meaher was born, but the institution still thrived in the American South. Meaher's brothers joined his business, and with the money they earned came more land, more business, and the opportunity to cultivate both. The brothers owned human beings who worked their lands, labored in the sawmills, and built their ships. Enslaved people grew the cotton the boats transported and the food the crews ate. The Meaher family owned more than one hundred men, women, and children whose labor fueled every facet of their fast-growing family empire.

Meaher built his first steamboat, *William Bradstreet*, in 1847 at the yard he ran with his brother James. They built more of their own ships, including *Orline St. John* and *William G. Jones Jr.*, the first steamer built in Mobile. Meaher married Mary C. Waters in 1854, the niece of the late Edward Kavanaugh, who had served as governor of Maine.

This strengthened his resources, and he built more ships, including *William Hallett* and *Waverly*. The Meaher brothers built a schooner in 1854, *Sarah E. Meaher*, named for James's wife.

It was near the beginning of the Meahers' rise in the Mobile shipping business that *Brazillero* dropped Ward. L. Smith off in the city and in need of a job. Smith, like Meaher, was young, ambitious, and eager to make his way up the ranks. He wasted no time finding work, and, fortunately for him, experienced sailors were in high demand in 1840s Mobile to work both the riverboats and the ocean-bound ships that transported cotton around the world. Smith went to sea again from the southern port city, first as a sailor, then a boatswain, and then as a second and chief mate.

In the early 1850s, Smith worked with the New Orleans–based vessel *Abaellino*, which was under the command of Captain David Elliott.[3] *Abaellino* transported cotton from Mobile to ports in Boston, San Francisco, Marseille, and other parts of the world. Massachusetts shipbuilder J. T. Foster built the ship in 1848, and it was regarded as one of the fastest ships running out of the port of New Orleans. Elliott experimented with ways to increase profits by compressing cotton into tight bales to reduce space in the cargo hold by up to 20 percent. He did business with the Meahers and loaded the cotton in Mobile. By 1853, Elliott trusted Smith with readying the crew and preparing provisions for sail. Elliott, who spent a great deal of time in New Orleans, communicated orders via letter to Smith in Mobile, and Smith ensured that everything was satisfactory to sail upon the captain's arrival.

Meaher saw promise in the young sailor with a head for business. Smith became the superintendent of construction for his new ship, *Sarah E. Meaher*, in 1853 and took command of the vessel upon her launch in 1854. *Sarah E. Meaher*, or *S. E. Meaher*, was a three-masted, centerboard Gulf schooner built from oak and locust wood. Gulf schooners were usually small vessels designed for coastal trade. Average Gulf schooners of the day were less than 100 feet and registered at less than 100 tons. *S. E. Meaher* was 146 feet long and registered at 250 tons (gross tonnage of 400), making her an atypical example of her class. The Meahers built her as a "large[-]capacity ship capable of carrying 900 bales of cotton" and "constructed in the staunchest manner, of handsome model."[4] She was the largest Gulf schooner built in Mobile, and one of five with a tonnage capacity of more than 100 tons. Meaher built two of the five. The other was the two-masted vessel *Clotilda*, which was built by the brothers two years later, in 1855.[5]

Smith took all he learned about seamanship from Goodwin and all he learned about business from Elliott and put it to use as captain of the new ship. *S. E. Meaher*'s first voyage was from Mobile to Galveston, where she picked up a full freight bound to New York with Smith at the helm. She made it from Mobile to Galveston in "three days running time, having passed every vessel fallen in with."[6] Smith traveled the country aboard the schooner. On one voyage from Galveston to Boston, he rescued the captain and crew of the waterlogged brig *J. W. Elwell* off the coast of New York. They had been seven days without food or water, and two crew had been washed overboard by the time Smith reached them. Smith delivered them to Home's Hole, exchanged freight in Boston, and returned to Galveston with a load of merchandise.

Smith felt at home behind the helm of a schooner, but he never felt at home in Alabama. He was a staunch abolitionist, and his time in the South only solidified his position. Traveling helped, but although Smith was cordial and respectful to his employers, working for the Meahers never sat well with him.

The Meahers built *S. E. Meaher* specifically for deepwater and long-range trade, and Smith ached for the day he could take the ship across the Atlantic. He got the chance on a voyage to Wales. He returned from that country with the first cargo of iron rails to be used in construction of the Mobile and Ohio Railroad. He again crossed the Atlantic in 1855, when the French government hired *S. E. Meaher* as a transport vessel during the latter part of the Crimean War.

The Crimean War pitted an alliance of French, British, Sardinian, and Turkish troops against Russia. America was officially neutral, but American noncombatants played key roles on both sides. Businessmen seized the opportunity to supply arms, ships, and men to the highest bidder. The Black Sea was a strategic location during the war because of its access to Russia. The sea itself was encircled by land, with Russia to the north, the Ottoman Empire to the south, and Moldova, Wallachia, and Bulgaria to the west.[7]

Smith shuttled cargo to and from Algiers, Africa, and the Black Sea. The war ended on March 30, 1856, with the signing of the Treaty of Paris, and the Allies withdrew troops from the region. Smith brought a cargo of coal from Cardiff to Paris in 1856 and ferried troops from Algiers to the United Kingdom in the summer of 1856, but his service ended shortly thereafter. Several American crew members deserted when the lucrative war service ended, which forced Smith to hire foreign sailors to fill the balance of his crew.

He and his new crew accepted a charter to pick up a load of corn in Galatz to deliver to Cork, Ireland.[8] Getting to Galatz required him to travel the Danube River, which snaked through the heart of eastern

Europe. He left Constantinople for Moldova, where the river meets the Black Sea, on September 27, 1856. The Danube is the world's second-longest river. It flows through much of central and southwestern Europe and stretches from Germany's interior to the Black Sea. *S. E. Meaher* became the first American vessel to sail the Danube and the first to hoist the American flag in Moldova. Smith traveled to Galatz, where he stayed for about a month before loading the corn and returning to where his trip began.

The captain did not speak the language and found his stay in Galatz difficult. In 1849, Smith became a member of the Masons and found it useful to connect to local Masons in various ports when he traveled, so he thought he would do the same in eastern Europe. The British vice consul, Mr. Cunningham, happened to be a brother Mason and arranged for Smith to visit the only Masonic lodge in Moldova. There, he found a translator who accompanied him for the remainder of his journey.

Smith and his new friend encountered heavy weather upon their return to sea. Storms badly damaged *S. E. Meaher* along the way, and the schooner sprung a leak. Smith discharged a portion of the cargo of corn to repair the vessel. He returned to Constantinople and oversaw repairs to the ship that winter, from November until March, after which he accepted a charter to take a cargo of grain to Marseille. He had to go even farther up the river to Wallachia to get it.

He made his way through the Danube again in April 1857. *S. E. Meaher* sailed into strong winds on April 21, and Smith sought the assistance of a local pilot to navigate the unfamiliar waters. The pilot miscalculated the water depth, and the vessel grounded. Smith crashed into the opposite bank of the river and splintered the ship's stern while trying to get free. The crew dropped the anchor, but it did not hold. This time, her stern struck aground with such force that it carried away the rudder and damaged the sternpost. The schooner could not be moved without repair, but there was no suitable lumber in the small city of Sulina, where the vessel grounded. The next day, Smith traveled in a longboat down the river to Galatz, found a carpenter, and sent him back to the ship to make repairs. The carpenter tried but could not unhang the rudder. *S. E. Meaher* was stranded.

Strong winds, rain, and the state of the vessel made repairs almost impossible. Another ship came to Smith's aid on May 3. It hauled alongside and helped lighten the ship enough for the crew to inspect the rudder gudgeons, braces that mounted the rudder to the ship. Smith had no choice but to the remove the ship's cargo to lighten the ship and raise it higher above the waterline. He hired additional men to do the work and rented storage facilities for the grain. On May 12, the crew shifted the

CHAPTER 30 | *Stranded*

remainder of its cargo from aft into the forward compartments to try to lift the stern a bit higher out of the water. They managed to lift it another 3 feet. The crew removed the lower gudgeon, but Smith concluded that it was "impossible to heave down here or to lighten the vessel anymore, to shift up the front and put it in order to get to Marseille[,] the sternpost being badly split, and it is impossible to repair it here."[9] He instructed the carpenters to make a new rudder and employed blacksmiths to make the necessary fittings. Bills for storage, crew, lodging, repairs, porters, loading and unloading cargo, and advances on traveling expenses mounted. There was no American consul in Wallachia, so Vice Consul Cunningham vouched for the debt, which would become due upon Smith's arrival in Marseille.

By May 28, the ship was by no means repaired but able to sail, and Smith made way for Marseille. The Danube spat *S. E. Meaher* out at Constantinople, and Smith was glad to be rid of her. When he traded the Black Sea for the Aegean, the clear, open water comforted him. He rounded southern Greece and, by July 1, reached the island of Malta, south of Italy. He soon rounded Sicily, passed Sorrento on July 13, and arrived in Marseille on July 26, 1857.

S. E. Meaher remained in need of more-permanent repairs. Smith and his crew discharged the cargo of wheat and readied the ship for the voyage home. It took until August 14 to discharge the cargo to various buyers in the city, but it did not matter. The repairs would take longer to finish. Smith received letters from European merchants who sought to charter his vessel. Some referenced small loans or advances that had been provided, and inquired about using a subsequent charter to repay it. Smith owed money to suppliers, merchants, and laborers in the United Kingdom, France, Galatz, Constantinople, and Sulina.

He was overseeing repairs on the afternoon of August 24, 1857, when French gendarmerie, or police, boarded the vessel. "We are seizing your ship," one told him. Two days later, six police officers came aboard and took charge of *S. E. Meaher* and everything on the ship as payment for outstanding debt. The men left once they were certain the ship could not sail.

Five officers boarded the next day. This time, Smith protested. "We are here for the deck furniture," one replied. The men grabbed chests, tables, sideboards—anything that was not nailed down—and carried it off. Smith threw himself between a gendarme and a chair and flung his arms out wide in defiance. The gendarme answered, "I will shoot you and put you in irons if you try to stop me." Smith stepped to the side and gestured in the chair's direction, "Take the chair."

The next day, the captain of the harbor himself boarded the vessel and took inventory of everything aboard.

Smith's log entries for the days read:

> August 26. Light breeze and pleasant weather yet all 6 gendarmerie came on board and took charge of everything on board.
>
> August 27. The day commenced with light breeze and pleasant weather. Next 5 gendearms [*sic*] came on board and threatened to shoot me and put me in irons for refusing to let them take the cabin furniture from on deck.[10]

He sought the assistance of John Stephen Martin at the recommendation of the other American captains in port and waited for more than a month for some word about an end to the seizure, but it never came. He made daily notes in his logbook about repairs to the ship and the weather in Marseille, under the general heading "Marseille Harbor." Martin introduced Smith to Consul Morgan and to a friend of his, Captain Durham of the barque *Adriatic*. Like Durham, Smith was a prisoner and could not leave without clearance papers from French officials. He too had petitioned Morgan and awaited some sort of diplomatic resolution. Durham, who had already been in Marseille for more than six months, educated Smith about Marseille's complex legal, political, and diplomatic systems.

Smith continued to keep a ship's log, but his entries became shorter as time passed and his frustration grew. The last, a brief weather update, came on November 5, 1857. It was followed by Smith's drawing of his arrest and seizure by the gendarmerie. It depicted Smith attempting to escape the French officers, only to be captured and hanged, and portrayed both the hopelessness and the humor he found in his situation. There were no further entries.

S. E. Meaher's owners in Alabama were either unable or unwilling to assist. They did not lack the ability to do so. While *S. E. Meaher* languished in France, Meaher launched the steamboats *Roger B. Taney* and *Czar* in 1856 and 1857, two ships that would play prominent roles in the story of American slavery.[11] *Southern Republic*, the last boat that Meaher built and the largest steamboat to travel the Alabama River, would prove instrumental in the American Civil War. Smith, on the other hand, joined the ranks of a growing number of Americans stranded in Marseille.

CHAPTER 31

Escape from Marseille

THE MORNING AFTER HE JOKED WITH CAPTAIN DURHAM about killing a French officer, Captain Smith slept in. He opened his eyes and remembered he had promised to meet his friend for breakfast. He dressed and set out. Smith walked the street along Marseille Harbor, a stretch of waterfront dock lined on both sides with ships from far-flung ports. Most of them were sailing vessels, although a few possessed the telltale smokestacks of ships powered by steam. Smith admired the ships from the corner of his eye but thought about his friend and in what condition he would find him.

He stopped at one of the small cafés. It was not luxurious—the kind of place a sailor with a little extra money in his pocket might come to treat himself. He was surprised to find Durham already awake and seated at a table. He faced the door and looked up and waved. Smith walked toward him, removed his coat, and sat down. Durham did not take a moment's pause for Smith to settle. He launched back into the details of his plan to escape Marseille. It was as if he had not slept at all.

Smith cocked his head to one side, narrowed his small eyes, and studied Durham as he spoke. His friend was no longer drunk. He did not appear to be mad. Smith studied Durham until a thought finally occurred to him: "Maybe he actually believes his plan can work?" He smiled. The plan was so absurd that he could not help but be impressed by Durham's commitment to it.

Smith's grin did not phase Durham in the slightest. He rambled. Part of Smith was listening. The other part wondered if Durham had the guts to go through with it. Durham did not wait for a reaction. He stood up, grabbed his coat and hat, threw some coins on the table, and headed toward the door.

Smith looked over his shoulder and watched Durham walk out. "Good luck, Barney," he said, with a wide wave of his hand. His friend did not even notice.

Durham stepped onto the street. It was cold. The breeze that blew across the harbor made it feel even colder. He put his hat on his head, nestled it down to cover to his ears, and started to move. Marseille was a labyrinth of steep and narrow cobblestone streets. Its passageways once confused Durham, but now he strode about them briskly, with the ease of a person who had been in a place for too long. Tall office buildings and multistory sailors' rooming houses, packed together, lined the streets. Most were made from sand-colored limestone carved from the hills that surrounded the city. The buildings were so tall they blocked the sun's light and made Marseille's dark streets seem even darker and narrower. Durham shuddered. It was as if Marseille herself was closing in on him.

He shook his head and trained his thoughts on the task at hand, an unannounced visit to Olympe Besson, prefect of the prefecture des Bouches-du-Rhône. He rehearsed what he would say to Besson in his mind as he walked, turning the words over and over again until they were just right.

He reached Rue Montgrand and found the prefecture building, located at number 13. A limestone archway flanked by two large columns marked the entrance. It was banal by French architectural standards, but it was by far the prefecture's most impressive feature. The building was similarly unremarkable. It too was limestone, a three-story edifice with a series of long, rectangular windows that lined each floor. Durham stepped through the archway, crossed a small courtyard, and made his way to the door. He stopped. He looked up at the windows and wondered which one was the prefect's office. A smirk slowly crept across his face. He took a deep breath and did his best to twist it into an expression of concern.

The prefect supervised local government and police on behalf of Napoléon III's Ministry of the Interior. He was the emperor's representative in the region, and his word carried with it the legal authority of Napoléon III himself. Marseille was France's second-largest city and the Bouches-du-Rhône region's crown jewel. Roughly eighteen thousand ships and twenty million barrels of freight passed through the Port of Marseille every year in the mid-1850s, and those numbers were growing. Napoléon had sent Besson to modernize a city bursting at the seams of an industrial revolution, a task that required him to maintain relationships with local merchants and ensure that the city kept up with the infrastructure improvements their businesses needed to thrive.

Besson, however, was a bureaucrat's bureaucrat. The Ministry of the Interior had shuffled him from post to post not for his accomplishments but for the lack of them. Marseille was no exception. Besson's predecessor expanded the port in 1853 to accommodate both larger ships and greater numbers of ships. Companies eager to open businesses there flocked to the city from around the world, but Besson had done nothing to improve the city's infrastructure or to otherwise support its booming maritime economy. Local elections approached. Marseille's business elite, including the shipping merchants, pressured Napoléon III to replace him.

Besson's office building was a monument to his failure. It was far too small to hold the prefecture's growing number of police, civil servants, and officials, and far too plain to project political importance. Besson would soon be replaced by Charlemagne-Émile de Maupas, who, in 1860, would build an ornate prefecture in the center of town and turn Besson's office into the local girl's high school.

Durham was keenly aware of local politics when he stepped into the prefect's office, removed his hat, and lowered it to his chest in greeting. Besson gestured for him to sit, but the captain launched an impassioned plea. "It's about *Le Adriatic*." He spoke quickly and quietly. "I am gravely concerned about the condition of the ship." He told Besson that *Adriatic* had not been fully repaired in Gloucester and that the collision with *Le Lyonnais* and her subsequent voyage to France had left her in great peril. "She must be caulked immediately if she is to stay afloat," he told Besson. "She is so open she could sink right here in the harbor."[1]

Besson feared that the ship's loss would leave the brothers Gauthier without satisfaction. He agreed to let Durham caulk her. "At your expense," he added. Durham bowed his head and thanked Besson for his time and courtesy. He left the office and walked through the courtyard and out the archway through which he came. He got clear of the prefecture and all the way back to Rue Montgrand before he allowed the smirk to return to his face.

Caulking is the process of making the seams between the shell or deck planks of a wooden ship watertight. Sailors in the 1850s caulked by stuffing the open spaces between the planks with fibers, cord, or oakum.[2] Men opened any undersized seams with large iron wedges called ramming irons, forced the rope fibers into the seams with iron-tipped wooden mallets, and sealed the seams shut with a tar-like substance called hot pitch. Shipbuilders in a hurry to launch would sometimes leave the seams unsealed until the ship took a trip or two to clamp down on the fibers and compress them. The trip to France was *Adriatic*'s second voyage, so it would not have been out of the ordinary to caulk her before her next trip.

Most of Durham's original crew had found work on other ships and left France. Only Thombs remained with him. The only other people in

France he trusted were Smith, Smith's mate Baker, and a boy from the local sailor's boardinghouse who had proven a loyal admirer. Smith and Durham filled their friends in on the details of their plan. Durham told Prefect Besson that the six men would begin caulking right away and do the work themselves in the evenings. They planned to caulk the ship all the way around at about 5 feet above the waterline.

Caulking was noisy business. The men drove metal spikes into *Adriatic*'s hull with iron-tipped mallets from nine o'clock in the evening until midnight and sent a cacophony of pings and knocks and bangs from the ship into the air. The court's original order required a French officer to guard the ship around the clock, but not a single noise drew the guard's attention while the men worked. Smith and Durham enjoyed unfettered access to *Adriatic*, and by working at night, what transpired aboard the ship was hidden from inquiring eyes.

Durham procured the irons, ropes, and metal required to caulk the ship and brought it aboard. He procured supplies at the same time, enough to journey from France to Maine, and mixed them in with the other equipment. The French were still in possession of *Adriatic*'s sails and other rigging. The captains transferred rigging and cargo from *S. E. Meaher* to *Adriatic* under the cover of the caulking.

On January 7, 1858, Victor Fouriere, a court officer of the Imperial Court of Marseille, boarded *Adriatic*. The men froze. They had hidden the rigging and the cargo below deck but feared that the authorities might be on to them and search the ship. "Which one of you is Captain Durham?" the officer asked. Durham stepped forward. Fouriere handed him some papers. He did not say another word and left *Adriatic* as quickly as he had arrived. Durham opened the document to find an itemized list of court costs. They amounted to 2,496 francs and 49 cents. Durham did not have it. "One day."[3] The papers said he had one day to pay the court costs, or the court officers, police, and prosecutors would be back to take his ship. One day. An additional charge of twenty-three francs for the court officer's visit to his ship to serve the papers only added insult to injury. "We leave tomorrow," Durham told the others.

Smith went to town the next morning to make a final purchase. He bought three cannons, other arms, and some powder. The cannons were "nine-pounders," a measurement that refers to the weight of the cannonball. Nine-pounders were the lightest of all cannon ammunition and were fired from ships from portable deck cannons. Their size gave them longer range. It was not uncommon for merchant ships to keep cannons on deck to protect against pirates, but pirates were not the threat Smith had in mind. Smith smuggled the arms aboard the ship, and the men prepared to set the final stage of Durham's plot in motion.

CHAPTER 31 | *Escape from Marseille*

Durham, Smith, and Thombs met just before eleven o'clock the evening of January 8. They had rehearsed the plan a hundred times in conversation, but the moment to execute had arrived. If either of the captains had a reservation, he did not express it. Durham was too determined to turn back and Smith too curious not to move forward.

The first phase of the plan was the most dangerous. The men snuck aboard *Adriatic* to conquer their first obstacle: the French guard. It was Smith's joke about killing the guard and throwing him overboard that had started all of this, and now the guard was the only person who stood between Durham and command of *Adriatic*. Each man armed himself with a hatchet to slice any ropes, fastenings, or "other obstacles."[4]

They climbed aboard without making a sound. Durham and Thombs looked for the guard while Smith readied *Adriatic* for sail. They were not gone long when Durham returned and told Smith, "We're in luck. The officer went to shore."

Adriatic sat in the middle of the harbor, secured in place by two anchors ahead and a hawser astern. The men bent the topsails and the main topmast staysail where she lay. They unshackled the anchor and cut all the lines holding the vessel in place. *Adriatic*, now liberated from her chains, drifted free for the first time in almost a year.

The vessel next to *Adriatic* was held in place by the same chain, and when the men broke her free, they sent the other vessel into the harbor as well. "Damned Yankees!"[5] The captain of that vessel yelled when he awoke to find his own ship adrift: "Damned! Yankees!"

Durham had no time for apologies. It was just as well. Apologies were not in his nature. He had one purpose—to get clear of the drifting ship and race away from the sight of other vessels and anyone watching from shore.

Smith and Durham had conducted another errand prior to their departure. They visited a sailors' boardinghouse and recruited the boardinghouse keeper's helper, a boy, to supply them with ten sailors. They gave the boy money and instructions about what to do when and if *Adriatic* made it out of the dock. The boy now watched from shore and waited as *Adriatic* drifted toward the open sea.

The entrance of the dock was a little more than half a mile away from where *Adriatic* sat.

Raising the ship's sails would have drawn too much attention, so the captains drifted. Smith looked to the sky. "It would seem that providence is in our favor."[6] The wind blew across the dock, which made it easy to get out into the middle of it; however, a continued wind from that direction would make it impossible for the three men to haul the ship down to the entrance. Providence smiled yet again. No sooner did the men get into the clear than the wind changed and blew from the east and toward the mouth of the port. They reached the end of the dock with ease. Smith smiled. It was as if God himself was with them.

Durham neared the entrance to the Old Port and waited. It was somewhere between two and three o'clock in the morning when a small boat appeared with the boy from the boardinghouse at the helm. He pulled alongside the ship. Durham, Smith, and Thombs peered over the rail. Lying in the bottom of the boy's boat were ten drunk Black sailors. Some of them were unconscious. Others swayed back and forth and mumbled. Not one of them had any idea what was happening. Smith laughed at the sight of them, opened his arms out wide, and bellowed to his comrades, "Let's get our crew aboard!"

The captains had paid the boy to hire sailors at the local Negro boardinghouse and gave him more money to ply them with drinks. The sailors drank until they were so drunk that they no longer knew or cared where they were. The boy herded them aboard his small boat and rowed them out to the prearranged meeting point. Smith, Durham, and Thombs hoisted the sailors aboard one by one. They had no idea what vessel they were on, which was the point. Thombs dragged them to the forecastle and left them there to sleep it off.

It was four o'clock in the morning. *Adriatic* moved toward the mouth of the port, loaded with provisions, guns, and a crew of drunken sailors. Only one more obstacle stood in the fugitives' way—the guard station. Only 100 yards separated Fort Saint-Jean and Fort Saint-Nicolas, massive structures built in 1660 by Louis XIV and used by the French army as barracks throughout the nineteenth century. Guards patrolled the forts around the clock. An officer inspected papers and cleared every ship that approached for departure. *Adriatic*'s escape and the fate of the men on board now rested on passing through that narrow opening without papers in a now-infamous vessel.

The moon was bright and high in the sky. There was nothing strange about a ship leaving a port in the early-morning hours, especially under such fair weather and splendid moonlight. *Adriatic* approached the inspection station. Durham hoped to find the guardsman asleep at his post or, at the very least, uninterested in inspecting papers in the wee hours of morning. The officer instead waved his hand and hailed the ship. Durham summoned his courage and readied himself as the guard rowed his small boat from the fort and pulled alongside them.

Durham leaned over the side. "Are your papers all right?" the officer asked. "Oh, yes," replied the captain.[7] He pulled out a small, blank piece

CHAPTER 31 | *Escape from Marseille*

MARSEILLE.

Entrance to Marseille Port. Engraved by Rouargue Frères del & Sc. Provenance: *Histoire des Villes de France*, edited by M. Aristide Guilbert (Paris: Furne Perrotin Fournier). Original: antique steel-engraved print. *Author's collection*

of paper wrapped around two coins and rolled up to look like a permit. He pretended to toss the papers toward the guard's boat but was careful to come up just a little short and let the papers to fall into the sea. The guard lurched toward the water to catch them, but they sank to the bottom. The officer peered into the water for some time until he flicked his hand and declared the papers "perdus." Lost.

Adriatic's name was spelled out in bold letters high above the water on her stern. The captains had rearranged the letters under the cover of the caulking. They removed the letters that spelled "ADRIATIC of BELFAST," rearranged some, and cut others out of sheet lead to give the ship a new name, "RATTLER of CALLIE." The old letters were painted black and pressed against the ship's white hull. The name "ADRIATIC" was still visible in shadow where the missing letters now revealed the wood underneath. The captains put the new letters on top of the faded outline of the old. Smith later joked that they did such a terrible job removing, cutting, and rearranging the letters that it would have taken "a Greek scholar to make out the name of the ship."[8]

The captains tried to prevent the officer from rowing to their stern. They distracted him by engaging him in conversation, a strategy complicated by the fact that the officer spoke no English and the captains spoke little French.

"What is the name of your ship?" the officer inquired. Durham tried his French, "My ship is the Rattler of Callie."[9] The officer stared at him, put his oars in the water, and started to row toward *Adriatic*'s stern. Smith interrupted him by making small talk about the weather. He explained, in his best French, that they had waited for the moon to rise before departing Marseille. "La luna?" The officer reacted to the French word for "moon." Smith nodded. "Bien," said the officer as he gestured with his hand that they were free to pass. He understood the name of the ship to be *Luna*, an American ship that, unbeknownst to the captains and the guard, had cleared port the day before. *Luna* was built in Kennebunkport, Maine, in 1845 and, although larger than *Adriatic*, bore a similar appearance. The ship stayed in the port less than three weeks, enough time for the officer to know she was there but not enough time for him to recall what she looked like. With another flick of his hand, the guard cleared Durham to take his ship to sea.

The officer pointed his boat toward the fort, but as *Adriatic* moved forward, he wound up astern of the ship. A ship unfurling its sails under the light of the moon is always a beautiful sight, so the officer pulled his oars out of the water and waited there to watch. He looked up. The moon hit the vessel on the stern and flooded her with light.

The peace lasted but a few moments. The officer squinted. He did not speak English, but the words on the stern did not look to him like they spelled "*La Luna*." He studied them and sounded them out loud in broken English, muttering several combinations of the words and letters jumbled above him. After about two minutes, his eyes widened, he sat straight up, and his lips formed the words the captains had so desperately tried to keep hidden: "*L'Adriatic!*"

The officer yelled as loud as his voice would carry. "*L'Adriatic s'échappe!*"[10] He howled as he pulled the oars with all his might and made toward land. "*Les Américains s'enfuient!*" The Americans are getting away!

There was a sudden commotion in each of the forts. Lights came up from every direction. French military men poured from their barracks, scattered, and mobilized for a chase. An endless stream of soldiers filed out from the towers and took positions in what seemed like an endless supply of vessels. They even woke the band! Up rose the sounds of military musicians playing the fife and drums. The once-peaceful forts exploded with movement.

Durham, Smith, and Thombs got busy setting sail. The wind had freshened, and they managed to get their foretop sail set as a breeze sprang up. They left Marseille at a respectable 5 knots per hour, but that would be no match for French steamships. Providence smiled upon them again an hour later: a thick fog set in. The weather became so inky, the air so opaque, that they could not see more than 20 feet, and no one more than 20 feet away could see them. They heard the hum of steamboats turning their engines in the harbor. The puffing noises of those same ships getting closer and closer reached their ears soon after. *Adriatic* kept quiet and still.

She drifted for the next four hours. The captains and her crew held their breath as French steamships stalked them, and held it long after their noises began to dissipate. One by one the drunken sailors hoisted aboard the ship in the dead of night, awoke, and stumbled out of the forecastle to find themselves shrouded in fog and hunted by warships. No one had any idea where he was.

They waited until around eight o'clock in the morning, when the fog turned to mist and then haze and then slowly disappeared. Durham stood next to Smith on the deck, and both men looked out across the open water. It was quiet and still. Neither one of them could believe what they had accomplished. Durham broke the silence. "That was a pretty good night's work considering the circumstances."[11] Smith raised his eyebrows and nodded his head in agreement. The thirteen fugitives of *Adriatic* found themselves stone-cold sober, 12 miles from land and 3 miles outside French maritime territory.

CHAPTER 32
The Fog

ONCE THE FOG LIFTED, the Americans could see where they were. The French could see where they were too. *Adriatic*'s crew already had their foretop sail set and now worked to raise their main sail and get underway. A few moments passed before the skies darkened. This time, it was not a storm or a fog rolling in but a shadow that came over the ship. A vessel approached. It was a ship so large and so towering that for a moment it blocked out the sun. *Le Chacal*, "the Jackal," a French man-of-war, had arrived to drag *Adriatic* back to Marseille.

Men-of-war were designed for one thing: combat. These massive battleships were armed with cannons and propelled by a combination of sail and steam. They rose high out of the water and left three or more levels of lower decks exposed. The multiple decks were necessary to support the cannons' weight. Each deck was outfitted with a row of gun ports, openings in the ship covered by hinged wooden doors from which soldiers could fire cannons and other weapons. Men-of-war from opposing fleets pulled alongside one another in naval battles and exchanged gunfire through the gun ports at close range. The violence of these fights made the man-of-war the only exception to the English-language rule that ships be referred to in the feminine.

Chacal was a wooden paddle steamer built in Nantes in 1844. In addition to guns, *Chacal* carried two mortars capable of hurling projectiles at opposing vessels at close range. The ship sailed with a crew of seventy men, transported troops, and towed vessels seized in battle back to ports in and around Marseille. A man called Gazielle commanded her.

CHAPTER 32 | *The Fog*

All the warship's ports were open, and all its guns were out when it pulled alongside *Adriatic*. "You are under arrest," shouted Gazielle. "We are bringing you back to Marseille." He added, "Lower a boat and a line!" Durham froze, but while he faltered, Smith laughed. "Now this is an adventure!" he thought to himself. He remembered the purchases he made the day before in anticipation of a crisis he never thought would materialize. He stepped forward before Durham could respond, and puffed out his chest, which further accentuated his 6-foot, 3-inch frame. He stood next to the cannon, pointed his long arm in its direction, and answered, "If you want a line, come and get it!"[1] Durham's eyes widened. Smith paused for a second with arm still outstretched. "Anyone who boards this ship should prepare for a funeral."[2]

Smith locked eyes with Gazielle and remained frozen until everyone knew where they stood. Smith had already let the commander know that they were not afraid of him. Next, Durham let him know that they knew their rights. *Adriatic* was in international waters and more than 3 miles outside French territory. No one from *Chacal* could legally board *Adriatic* on the open ocean. Durham now made sure that the commander knew they knew the laws of the sea. He stayed behind Smith as he spoke: "We aren't in France anymore."

Gazielle knew he was right. *Chacal* responded by tracking *Adriatic*. The warship kept to the outside and used its weight and size to try to force *Adriatic* inside the 3-mile line, where she could be seized and her occupants arrested. For hours, they played a game of cat and mouse. French officers threatened the Americans. Smith stood by the cannon in response. *Chacal* sometimes pushed *Adriatic* closer to shore, but the sailing ship would gain or lose speed and move back out. Everyone grew tired of taunting one another after a few hours, and *Chacal*'s commander realized that the Americans were not stupid enough to get closer to land. He turned and steamed back in the direction of Marseille.

Chacal's departure was a weight lifted from captains and crew, but it was not the end of their plight. The men of *Adriatic* now found themselves alone and, for the first time since their adventure began, with an opportunity to contemplate their situation. They were a crew of thirteen with enough food for only two or three. Water was in short supply and already being rationed. Most of the crew were reluctant strangers. Their destination was America, but they had neither the provisions nor the equipment they needed to get there. The ship had no papers, so she could not pull into any port. They had been forced to cut both anchors in Marseille, so there was no way of stopping for someone to get to shore for provisions or papers. If they pulled into a port without papers, they could be seized. "Barney," Smith said to his friend, "we really [have] an elephant on our hands."³

The captains conferred. They decided to try Spezia, a port just south of Genoa in the kingdom of Sardinia.⁴ The United States had a navy supply station there, and the sailors hoped to find an American ship that might provide them with an anchor and the other items they needed to survive the long journey home.

CHAPTER 33

Spezia

"SINCE YESTERDAY THE WHOLE TOWN HAS BEEN TALKING of a strange affair, which it is thought may give rise to serious diplomatic complications."[1]

The Port of Marseille vibrated with gossip within hours of *Adriatic*'s escape. Prefect Besson was incensed. He told everyone who would listen that he ordered *Chacal* to find the ship and drag her back.

Durham's acts were no doubt illegal, but foreigners in Marseille, many of whom were bound to the port by the French, cheered him. His hometown paper reported that his actions were "highly commended by his many warm friends in this port, more particularly by the captains of the American vessels and others now lying [t]here."[2]

There were also tall tales of Durham's crew. Some said he left with thirty men. Others claimed it was a band of forty or more. Neither the gossips nor the papers were kind in their description of the sorts of fellows who accompanied the captain on his journey. French newspapers described them as "sailors ready for every emergency and recruited from the scum of the maritime population."[3]

Scum or saints, Durham and his new crew chose their next move carefully.

The most-logical options were Spain to the west or Sardinia to the east. Rumors about *Adriatic*'s whereabouts abounded. Some said Durham had been captured and placed in irons to await trial in a French dungeon. Sailors whispered that he evaded *Chacal* by sneaking into a creek along the Spanish coast. Some said he was hiding out in a Spanish port. Still others insisted that he sold his vessel and was destined for London overland. Some cheered him, and others delighted in tales of his capture. Said *Harper's Weekly*, which mistakenly reported that Durham had been captured by French warships, "It is satisfactory to know that the captain, who thus disgraced himself and his country, is in irons, and will probably suffer severely for his conduct."[4]

Most of the rumors proved to be untrue. By that time, Durham knew exactly where he was going—Spezia. The city was home to an American naval base and to an American consul whom Durham's friends in Marseille trusted.

The coastline connecting France to Sardinia formed a U shape, with Toulon at France's southernmost tip. Getting to Spezia required *Adriatic* to round Toulin and head north-northeast past Nice and Genoa. The journey required the vessel to hug the French coastline, which is why so many assumed that Durham had gone to Spain. It took Durham ten days to get there, a long time for such a short voyage. He and his crew either hid out somewhere along the way or took a more circuitous route before returning to the coast. *Adriatic* arrived in Spezia on January 18, 1858.

Durham knew that the Sardinian authorities would not permit *Adriatic* to land without papers. Smith fashioned a kedge, a light anchor attached to a long line that held the vessel in place by the weight of a heavy object dragging across the seafloor. He made his from a box filled with heavy stones fastened to the ship by 45 fathoms, or 270 feet, of chain. He and the crew improvised a second anchor by using a chain box with a hawser attached to it. The captains surmised that the weight of the boxes and the chain would hold *Adriatic* in place in calm seas. They did not plan to be in Spezia for too long. *Adriatic* spent the night grounded by the kedge, and her captains waited until morning to assess the situation.

Smith had always intended to return to Marseille. He and Durham discussed how he would get there from Spezia, and they concocted a story to cover up Smith's role in the whole affair and return him to France. The plan was to tell the French authorities that Smith had been accidentally left on board when Durham took *Adriatic*. If asked why he did not return sooner, Smith would tell them the fog was too thick to send him to shore, so *Adriatic* dropped him off as soon as was practicable. The next morning, January 19, Smith bid Thombs and the rest of the crew goodbye. He climbed into a small boat with Durham. The two men rowed toward shore, where Smith intended to take leave of the adventure and find a ship back to Marseille, armed with an elaborate story about how he had become an accidental fugitive.

CHAPTER 33 | *Spezia*

The men were about a half mile from shore when they saw people gathering at the pier. Shouts and the noises of excited talking rose in a great commotion. They got closer. The people gathering were soldiers, about one hundred of them. The soldiers waved their arms and shouted to one another. Their leader was dressed a uniform adorned with enough gold lace to instantly convey both his authority and the grandiosity of nineteenth-century Sardinian military fashion. Smith and Durham's small boat inched closer to shore. The men quieted, and the gold-laced officer placed his fists on his hips and turned toward the water.

His first words were part Italian, part French, and little English: "Were eeeet Captain Smith?" he asked. Smith, who was still in the boat, responded. "Here I am. What do you want?"[5] He could not understand how the officer knew his name. Durham barely stepped out of the boat when the officer pointed at him and cried, "You are arrest!" Soldiers grabbed each of the captains by the arms and held on to them.

"I demand to speak to the American consul," Durham blurted. The man in charge seemed to understand the word "consul," which sparked another commotion. Neither American captain spoke Italian. They watched as the soldiers debated among themselves and the officer in charge shouted orders back at them.

Much to their surprise, the American consul materialized. Durham was not sure whether the Sardinians called him or if he came on his own accord, but he did not much care. He introduced himself with a quick bow of his head: "R. H. Leese, at your service." The captains nodded back. They were glad to see him not only because he might be able to help but because he could translate.

Leese turned to the gold-laced officer, and the two spoke Italian so rapidly that neither Smith nor Durham could catch a word. "He's the general," Leese said over his shoulder, in an attempt both to speak to the officer and to update the Americans on the gist of the conversation. The conversation continued. Lesse turned his head toward them again. "He's come to take your ship."

Durham and Smith learned that the French had sent the Sardinian navy to seize *Adriatic* and her crew and to hold them under arrest. The gold-laced general was upset with Leese for getting in his way. He raised his voice and waved his arms. It seemed the more he moved his arms, the direr their predicament became.

Leese demanded to go to *Adriatic* with Durham. The general threw his arms out wide and shouted, "No!" He then returned his fists to his hips and pursed his lips like a pouting child. He warned Leese that if he attempted to aid the Americans or go to their ship, he would arrest them all and sink the vessel. "We'll see about that!"[6] Leese said as he folded his arms, turned around, and walked down the beach in a huff.

Smith and Durham thought Leese was leaving when they saw an old Black man walking down the beach in their direction. He carried a small American flag in his hands. "Pete," Leese waved his arms and called to the man, "get your boat out."[7] Pete continued down the beach with the stars and stripes in hand.

The gold-laced general raced toward Leese and Pete. Smith could not help but laugh as he ran in his dress uniform, complete with a long coat and tightly-fitted trousers, and lifted his feet high in the air to prevent his shiny leather shoes from filling with sand. Pete also spoke Italian, and the conversation between Leese and general soon enveloped him. Now it was Pete's appearance that caused the commotion. The general swung his arms and screamed at Leese, who responded calmly and this time, in English. "General, these are Americans and *Adriatic* is an American ship. They are in distress, and it is my duty to go aboard to assist them on this American vessel."[8] When he said the word "this," he took the flag from Pete's hands, twirled it in the air, and jumped into Pete's waiting rowboat. He sat on the thwart, grinned at the gold-laced general, and waited for Pete to row.

The general cried, "If you no get out boat, I fire on you!" Leese replied, "You do not fire on me. You fire on the American flag and, unless you kill me, I am going out to that ship."[9] He gave the flag another flick of wrist and yelled, "Pete! Row!"[10] The general could not stop the Americans. He ordered all his soldiers into small boats of their own. A hundred Sardinians scattered along the shoreline. They gesticulated to one another as they boarded every available vessel. Smith and Durham followed Pete's boat in theirs, not because they knew what was happening but because they saw no viable alternative.

All the small boats moved toward *Adriatic*. The gold-laced general pulled his between Pete's and Durham's. His arms were a windmill as he shouted to his men and to the Americans, but his orders fell on deaf ears.

Smith and Durham reached *Adriatic* and scrambled aboard. Another angry demonstration took place in the boats. The general threatened Leese. Leese ignored him. What seemed like hundreds of sailors now floated around in small boats, confused and waiting for orders. Durham feared that the entire Sardinian navy would board his ship, but they never did.

The consul pulled his boat alongside *Adriatic*. He had no intention of boarding. Durham leaned over the side and explained that they needed water, provisions, an anchor, and papers to get home. "Keep quiet," whispered Leese. "Say nothing. Do nothing. I will come again and let you know what I can do for you."[11] He flicked the American flag again, and Pete began to row. The Sardinians reluctantly followed. They were not as animated on the trip back to shore.

No sooner had the captains breathed a sigh of relief when they felt the shadow of a large vessel off their starboard quarter. Another ship had slipped into the waters off Spezia during the commotion. She anchored only about a cable's length, roughly 700 feet, away from *Adriatic*. It was, once again, *Chacal*. As usual, the ports were open and the guns out, but this time Commander Gazielle said nothing. Instead, he filled his boats with soldiers, lowered them into the water, and kept a constant eye on Durham, his ship, and his crew. "Barney," Smith sighed, "I miss the Sardinians already."

Prefect Besson was furious when he learned of the ship's escape. His trust in Durham had provided the small window the captains needed, and Besson was determined to get *Adriatic* back to Marseille by any means necessary. A network of telegraphs, merchants, and government offices connected the ports of Marseille, Toulin, Genoa, and Spezia. Besson furiously contacted every single one of them with orders to seize *Adriatic*. The French minister, Ferdinand Hamelin, was furious too. He republished his October 30, 1857, bulletin on January 19, 1858, and sent it to every port in Europe and every colony within French control.

Besson also telegraphed Sardinia's prime minister, Camillo Benso, Count of Cavour. Cavour was a friend of France and a close ally of Napoléon III. He believed in a united Piedmont, with its own separate constitution and governance. He argued for the cause as a newspaperman in the late 1840s, rose through the political ranks of Parliament, and became prime minister in 1852. He was bitter about Piedmont's loss of Milan to the Austrians during an 1848 uprising. Cavour cultivated ties with England and France during the Crimean War in the hopes his new allies would help Piedmont retake Milan. In 1856, he presented the issue before the Congress of Paris. He sought to further ingratiate himself to Napoléon III during 1857 and 1858. He was at the height of his campaign to make France an ally when *Adriatic* sailed into the Port of Spezia and created another opportunity for him to curry favor with the French emperor.

Cavour dispatched word of *Adriatic*'s arrival in Spezia to Marseille and Toulon. Prefect Besson, in turn, gave the news to Mr. Clappier, Franco-Américaine's agent, who petitioned the Court of Aix for an order to have the Sardinians seize *Adriatic* and hold her for twenty-four hours pursuant to a treaty between France and Piedmont inked in 1760, which required one country to hold a vessel at the other's request when a judgment had been entered against the vessel by the requesting country.

The Americans knew about the treaty as well. It required a final order entered by a court to be binding. A French final judgment was called a verdict. *Adriatic* left Marseille while French officials were still assessing the damages that Durham owed. No verdict had entered. As such, Durham had a tiny bit of legal leeway. What followed was a race between French authorities and American diplomats, the former working quickly to obtain a verdict against *Adriatic* and the latter working to supply *Adriatic* with the provisions she needed to be on her way.

Besson telegraphed a series of orders to Sardinia, all of which were communicated to Spezia and all of which contributed to the gold-laced general's confusion. The first came from Toulin: "Seize *Adriatic*."[12] In response, *Chacal* set its guns on *Adriatic*, with orders to fire if she moved from her place. The orders were soon modified to prohibit the French or the Sardinians from firing on *Adriatic* but warned that no man from *Adriatic* should be in communication with the shore and no assistance from the shore should be allowed to the ship. Providing *Adriatic* with anything, even a drop of fresh water, constituted grounds for seizure, which is the reason Leese never boarded.

The captains kept quiet until evening, when Leese returned. This time, he brought another man with him, Colonel William L. Long, the storekeeper of the US naval base at Spezia. Cavour had given the Americans the depot in exchange for the placement of a squadron in the city. It was nothing more than political theater designed to keep the Austrians at bay. The American "base" was a supply depot within a larger, Sardinian-run military complex.

Long told the captains he planned to inspect the government food stores in the morning. "Pull your vessel as close to the pier as you can, and wait with your block and tackle out," he said. Long told them he would "condemn" some of the food stores and several casks of water and throw them overboard. *Adriatic* could lift the barrels out of the water and onto their boat without ever having to touch Sardinian soil.

They got the vessel as close to shore as they dared during the evening and waited. *Chacal* was too large to follow into such shallow waters, so the warship had to be content with monitoring *Adriatic* from a distance.

The captains saw lights in the navy storehouse just before sunrise. Long was true to his word, and as soon as dawn broke, barrels came rolling down the wharf and into the water. Smith and Durham lowered their boat and hooked lines to the barrels, pulled them in, and hoisted them aboard. They continued to work until they had enough food and water to make it home.

CHAPTER 33 | *Spezia*

Two problems remained: the anchor and the papers. The most urgent of the two was the papers. *Chacal* was a warship. International law allowed warships to demand a ship's papers and seize her when she failed to present them. It was only a matter of time before the French invoked this law of the sea. Leese promised to provide *Adriatic* with a sea letter, a kind of emergency permit to travel. He instructed Durham to come to the head of the bay, where he had first attempted to land, to get the letter later that evening.

It was late in the afternoon by the time *Adriatic*'s crew finished hauling up the supplies. The men prepared their first proper meal since Marseille with delight. It began to rain. Soon the wind picked up. Durham knew that the boxes of stones and chains holding *Adriatic* in place would not hold if the winds increased much more, and so, without waiting for his dinner, he set off for town to find the consul and get his sea letter.

Winds blew toward shore as the storm developed. The rising gusts proved too strong for the makeshift anchors, and *Adriatic* started dragging closer to land, where she was in danger not only of being seized but of crashing into the fort at the edge of the bay or grounding in shallow water. The men worked to keep the shore at bay by raising and lowering the appropriate sails at Smith's command, but the storm soon became too much for them. *Adriatic* moved closer to land with each heavy gust. Everyone kept an eye out for Durham.

Smith had another elephant on his hands. If he did nothing, the winds would drag *Adriatic* to God knows where, but to cut the anchors and free himself from the drag, he needed to run a line ashore to keep the ship in place until her captain returned. Doing so meant the Sardinians could seize the ship.

It was close to eight o'clock in the evening. *Chacal*'s crew had already made their ship safe by firmly anchoring in the bay to withstand the wind and the waves. The warship was much farther out to sea. It was unlikely that *Chacal*'s lookouts could see them through the rain and dense fog. Even if they could, the weather was far too precarious for them to send boats to shore.

A sudden jolt rocked the ship. *Adriatic* lurched so close to the fort at the entrance of the bay that the men could have jumped to shore from the deck. Smith played the odds. He ran a line ashore and told the men to tie it on the first sturdy object they saw, which was a large cannon. They cut away one chain box to eliminate some of the drag. Smith thought the cannon would hold. He was wrong. *Adriatic* yanked against the cannon in the surf and began to drag it with them. It inched toward the edge of the fort as the ship jerked about in the waves.

Durham jumped aboard. He came out of nowhere, but the men were glad to see him. He had been searching for *Adriatic* all over the bay and had arrived just in time to find his ship amid a tug-of-war between an unstable anchor and a Sardinian cannon. The cannon pulled *Adriatic* so close to the rocks that she was within moments of crashing.

"I don't think I have time to explain," Smith said to Durham. The wind reached a gale. There was no time for thought, only action. "Cut the cannon! Cut the chain box!" Durham ordered his men to cut anything that tethered the ship to anything else. "Cut all the lines!" When the men cut the line to the cannon, it tumbled with a splash from the ledge of the fort into the water. *Adriatic* headed out to sea before the wind under top-reefed sails.

Smith and Durham put enough distance between themselves and Spezia to pause and apprise one another of what transpired during their time apart. Leese made good on his promise. Durham got his sea letter. Smith described the ordeal with the storm and the cannons and the chain boxes. "I do not grieve the loss of the king of Sardinia's cannon," he said to his friend, "but I am very sorry to lose your forty fathoms of hawser."[13] The men put to sea under the cover of darkness and hoped the storm would soon die out. They set sail for Gibraltar in the early-morning hours of January 21.

The sun rose. *Adriatic* was a speck of dust on the horizon by then. Said one captain in a letter to the *London Globe*, "It would appear that [the French] relied on the Genoese authorities for his safe custody; and the port captain on the French; but between them, amid the squalls and the darkness, the [*Adriatic*] crept out at night, and dashed off in smart and clever style."[14]

The Court of Aix was hard at work while the winds roared off Spezia. It reached a verdict on January 20 and sentenced Durham to reimburse the Gauthier brothers for the cost of *Le Lyonnais*, $1,500,000 francs, plus $40,000 francs in costs. Mr. Clappier arrived in Genoa the next morning and headed to Spezia overland with the verdict in hand, but by then Durham was gone. Clappier arrived just a few hours too late.

CHAPTER 34

Friends in High Places

MEN SUCH AS DURHAM AND SMITH WERE BUILT FOR THE SEA. Long days trapped in Marseille spent watching other captains sail in and out of the harbor had taken a toll on them. They passed the time by entertaining captains who came into port and providing them with good, old-fashioned American hospitality. Swapping their old stories for new ones was the only way to get back some of the adventure they craved.

Some of the captains they met were transient. Others were, like them, stuck. During their time in France, Smith and Durham forged friendships with a group of Americans who, either by choice or by chance, found themselves in Marseille. The men helped one another with business affairs and supported one another in their legal woes. Most of all, they kept one another company.

John Stephen Martin was in Marseille by choice. The son of Captain John Martin of Genoa, Italy, a merchant who dealt in overseas trade, John Stephen followed in his father's footsteps and dedicated his career to overseas commerce.[1] The elder Captain Martin settled in Philadelphia with his family, where John Stephen and his siblings were born, but John Stephen Martin lived abroad most of his life. He settled in Marseille, where he founded the firm of Martin and Blohorn & Cavagna: "Commission Merchants and Ship Chandlers."

Ship chandlers were central to the existence of the world's ports in the 1850s. Shipowners hired merchants both to recruit crew and supply ships for voyages. Chandlers provisioned ships. As both a merchant and a chandler, Martin could either manage the entire operation of a voyage for a ship or simply provide the ship with the tools, groceries, and other goods it needed. Items supplied by a chandlery included sailcloth, rosin, turpentine, tar, pitch, twine, rope and cordage, tools, mops, galley supplies, leather goods, and paper. Chandlers also supplied items to repair damage to ships, including sails, caulk, and anchors. Merchants kept accounts with the chandlers to supply crews with whatever they needed at a given port.

Martin became fast friends with both Durham and Smith, and Durham relied on him for counsel during his trial. Martin was sympathetic to *Adriatic*'s plight, not just because of his personal relationship with Durham but because he realized the impact the affair could have on his own business. It was Martin to whom Durham turned when it was time to choose his representative on the Court of Aix's committee of experts. Martin did all he could to secure a favorable report for Durham and to persuade the other experts, particularly the court's appointed captain, *Adriatic*'s way. The court ignored the report despite his efforts. When it came time to flee France, Martin was one of the few people Durham and Smith trusted with their plan.

The reception in Spezia by what seemed like an entire battalion of officers concerned Smith. Pursuit from France was to be expected, but it now seemed that all of Europe was on the lookout for *Adriatic*. More troubling, they were on the lookout for him. The gold-laced officer addressed him by name the moment *Adriatic*'s small boat neared shore. Smith needed to know why. Martin was the only man he trusted in Marseille.

Consul Leese, who made good on his word to supply *Adriatic* for her voyage home, had proven himself a reliable ally. As the American consul, Leese served as a point of contact beyond the city. Neither the French nor the Sardinian authorities could intercept correspondence going to or from his office. Smith took the opportunity to get a letter through Leese to Martin. He knew he had been implicated in *Adriatic*'s escape and wanted to know more as he contemplated his return. He wrote, "Is it safe for me to return to Marseille?"

Martin's reply was swift and his answer emphatic. "I haste to answer it to advise you not to come back here until you hear further from me. [Colonel] Morgan participates in my fear that the French laws will take hold of you for participating in the escape of the *Adriatic*."[2] Martin told Smith that someone saw him standing with Durham on *Adriatic*'s deck as the ship slipped past the guard at Joliette Port, and reported the observation to the authorities. This fact not only implicated him in Durham's plot but would contradict his story about being an innocent bystander swept away by the fleeing Durham. The French condemned Smith's conduct in the strongest language that maritime law allowed; they called it an act of piracy.

CHAPTER 34 | *Friends in High Places*

The English consul had also become involved in the matter. The shipping master, from whom *Adriatic* enlisted unwitting sailors, lodged a formal complaint. A man called MacGregor, who worked for the "Negro shipping master," and Baker, Smith's mate, were implicated in the plot to ship the crew. MacGregor testified before the English consul. He acknowledged that he and Baker shipped the crew for *Adriatic* the same as they would any other vessel and had no knowledge of any restrictions that prevented the vessel from leaving port. "It is not my duty to question captains about their affairs," he testified. "I did the same as I would for any other captain."[3] The British government concluded that the men had no obligation to question the captain's representative, and the matter ended there.

Baker did not testify for the counsel. He could not. He disappeared the day *Adriatic* left. He was not the only one who decided it was time to leave Marseille. American ships left port in rapid succession in the days after *Adriatic*'s escape. The authorities questioned anyone who might have information, especially foreigners. American captains feared reprisals for knowing too much or too little.

Two of Smith's and Durham's friends had already left. Another, Captain Wells of *Zone*, was the only American still in port and was scheduled to leave the following day. Martin assured Smith that new American ships would arrive in the days to come, but his friends would be long gone by the time he returned.

Smith told Martin in his letter that *Adriatic* cut its anchors in Marseille and could not make an ocean crossing without a replacement. Martin offered no assistance in response, only a wish that "*Adriatic* not long ride her chainbox."[4] Martin's business was supplying ships with the equipment they needed. He had the connections to get an anchor for his friends in Spezia but could not risk a business that relied on cooperation with the French government to help famous fugitives, even if he called those fugitives friends. Martin provided information and advice and gave some assistance in getting Durham the papers he needed to leave Spezia. He already suspected that because of his assistance, he would be called to testify before the French about being an accomplice for his complicity in a "piratical act." The prospect of it amused Martin, who wrote, "I am expecting the fools will even summon me for being an accomplice . . . it would be a good joke for me, but I fear Mrs. [Martin] would feel it rather seriously."[5]

Martin extended best wishes from the other American captains and asked Smith to write him as soon as possible without committing himself to too much on paper. Toward the end of his letter, he included a warning for Durham. "I wish Captain Durham would properly gallant and leave direct for home—his receipt for his papers from the consul will show any collector at once, where they are, and at all events[,] it is better to be stopped at home than abroad."[6]

Smith did not receive the letter before he left Spezia. Martin wrote it on January 23, 1858, three days after *Adriatic* fled the city and escaped capture by the gold-laced general and *Chacal*. He never received his friend's final warning, "[Do] not come back here until you have heard from me."[7]

CHAPTER 35

Piracy

SMITH KNEW THAT HE WOULD NEVER SEE *Adriatic*'s adventure to its conclusion. He had to get back to Marseille. He did not own the ship he left behind, and he owed a duty to the Meaher family to bring her home. After a long conference with his cocaptain and without the benefit of Martin's warning, they decided to wait for the weather to moderate and, when it did, get as close to shore as possible, lower a boat, and send Smith to shore. They had hoped to be only three or four days away from Marseille, to give Smith enough time to get back before anyone other than his American friends began to suspect he was a willing accomplice.

The storm raged on, and it was all they could do to keep the vessel before the wind. By the time the weather eased, they were 300 miles from Marseille, near Barcelona, off the eastern coast of Spain.

On January 26, 1858, the weather was good enough for them to run in close to the coast. *Adriatic* hailed a nearby fishing vessel and Smith spoke to the captain.[1] He was an elderly man who worked the boat with his son. Neither of them could speak English, and Smith spoke no Spanish, but he managed to communicate some portion of his plight. The old fisherman was reluctant to help but found it difficult to resist the handsome sum of twenty-five dollars Smith offered in exchange.[2] The man and his son agreed to land Smith in a town called Tarragona, an ancient port city just south of Barcelona, and hide him until dark. Smith promised he would stay out of sight and follow the fisherman's instructions. Smith bid Durham goodbye once again. "I don't know what sort of scrape I shall have next," said Durham, "but I shall miss you."[3] Smith bid Durham farewell at four o'clock in the afternoon and started for the shore with his newly hired friends.

He decided to be overcautious when heading in. His main concern was not *Adriatic* but the laws of quarantine in Spain, which required anyone traveling to and from the country to have a passport. His was in Marseille. The possibilities of punishment for being caught traveling without a passport could be prison or worse. Any punishment would also extend to the old man and his son and could include seizure of their vessel or even death.

Smith climbed aboard the fishing boat, which was so small and so open that it prompted him to ask the old man, "How am I to keep out of sight?" He pointed to the fishing nets in the bottom of the boat. The man pointed again to the boat's bottom when they got close to the entrance of the port. Smith lay down. The boy lifted the nets and covered him. He heaped net after net into a pile atop Smith. They were wet and heavy and covered in a jellylike slime of algae and mud. Smith nestled beneath them as the boat moved closer to the shore. Louder and louder grew the sounds of the busy port. Fisherman called out to their brethren. Birds circled and cawed. "We must be close," Smith thought. He lay still and tried not to inhale the salty stench of the nets. The boat stopped, but no one removed the nets from on top of him. He waited and hoped that his new friends did not forget about him or, worse, report him to the authorities.

Smith waited in the boat all night. The boy returned early the next morning and led him to a nearby hotel. Smith feared what would happen if he tried to book a room without a passport, so he went in search of the American consul.

The consul did not keep the same hours as local fishermen. Smith arrived early in the morning, sat on the ground, and waited several hours. It reminded him of that day many years ago when he sat beneath the sign "Men and Boys Wanted for Whaling" in New York. "What an adventure it has been so far," he said to himself. He was not as patient as he was all those years ago. He rose and paced outside the office until he saw some movement inside. He knocked on the door, and a man opened it and gestured for him to come in.

Smith launched into the story of how he had accidentally gotten swept out to sea at the hands of the intrepid Captain Durham. It turned out that the person to whom he was speaking was the American vice consul. He interrupted him: "So you are the captain of the ship *Meaher* that ran away with the *Adriatic*."[4] Smith persisted in his story that his involvement was all a misunderstanding. The vice consul did not buy it, and Smith finally stopped denying it. "Stay right here," said the vice consul, "while I see what I can do for you."

CHAPTER 35 | *Piracy*

The vice consul invited the captain to join him for breakfast. Smith relaxed and regaled him with the full story of how he and Durham escaped Marseille. He told him how they slipped through Joliet Port under the name *La Luna*, about the gold-laced general who would not stop waving his arms, and about the fisherman who covered him with nets and delivered him to Spain. The story kept the vice consul entertained for the entire morning. They had a good laugh imagining the astonishment of Marseille officials when they discovered that *Adriatic* was missing.

The vice consul told Smith he would help him get to Barcelona to obtain passage on a ship bound for Marseille. "But I don't have my passport," Smith replied. The vice consul rummaged through his desk and pulled out a folded piece of paper. "This will do." He handed the paper to Smith. Smith unfolded it. It was an old passport from Tarragona to Marseille for one Dr. Mann and a servant, which, for some unknown reason, had been left in his office. "All I have to do is change my name to Dr. Mann and get a seat on a stagecoach to Barcelona," said the captain to the vice consul. "That's easy."[5] He thanked him for the passport and the breakfast and went on his way.

Smith arrived in Barcelona on January 28 and searched for a ship. He learned that the steamship *Tarragona* departed for Marseille within the next forty-eight hours, and booked a ticket. Several people inspected his passport in Barcelona. The port officer told him he would need to have his passport signed by the American consul to board the ship. He found the consulate and waited for an official to assist him.

The consul was deep in conversation with a man with a British accent and seemed not to care that someone was waiting for him. When their conversation ended, the American consul snapped at Smith, "What do you want?" Smith handed him the passport. The consul looked up at Smith and then the passport and then up at Smith again. "You are not Dr. Mann! You have no right to this passport, so I shall keep it." He pulled the passport close to his chest. "And further, who are you?"[6]

Smith hesitated. He did not like the consul's tone and paused to think about what to say next, but he was an American citizen entitled to any protection that the consul could give, whether the man liked him or not, so he decided to tell him the story of his accidental voyage on *Adriatic*. "I am the captain of the ship *S. E. Meaher* now in Marseille." The consul interrupted, "You are the thief that helped to steal the *Adriatic*! I will have you arrested and punished."[7] Smith started to speak, but words escaped him. He spun and ran as fast as he could into the street.

He did not get far before a man with a British accent stopped him: "I think I can get you off all right." He recognized him as the man who had

The Adriatic Affair

just left the American consul's office. He followed him and soon found himself just a few doors down at the British consulate.

Spanish police swarmed the American consulate to arrest Smith, but they were unable to do so while he was in English custody. Smith explained his predicament one more time. The British consul was sympathetic and agreed to fix him a passport. He prepared the necessary documents and escorted Smith from his office and onto a stagecoach. Smith stayed close to his escort and avoided eye contact with American officials and Spanish police as he walked out of the British consulate. The consul refused to leave Smith's side until Smith arrived at the waterfront and boarded *Tarragona*. He even waited for the ship to weigh anchor and depart.

The voyage to Marseille lasted two unremarkable days. The ordeal in Spain confirmed what Smith already knew; he would be arrested in Marseille. He thought about making his own grand escape, but his honor got the better of him. *Tarragona* arrived. Smith mixed in with the other passengers and avoided French officials as he disembarked. It was February 4, 1858, almost one month since he left Marseille.

Ward L. Smith's handwritten log of the escape from Marseille. *Courtesy of Historic Mobile Preservation Society*

He first checked on *S. E. Meaher*, and then he found his friends. They were relieved to see him and to learn that Durham was safe. He told them about their exploits in Spezia and Spain. They described the excitement and embarrassment that *Adriatic*'s escape had caused in Marseille. He learned that in response, heads had rolled. The French government relieved nearly all the port officers of their duties and appointed new ones.

Smith enjoyed the revelry of his homecoming, but he knew it would be short lived. The next morning, he put on a bold face and stepped outside. He knew he would not get far. He heard them as soon as he stepped out onto the street—the gendarme. "There he is! There is the captain that ran away with *Adriatic*! Arrest him."[8] Smith did not reply; this time, he did not run. He said nothing as officers seized him.

Smith went to court and to trial. French prosecutors paraded former port officers and guards as witnesses. They testified in vivid detail about *Adriatic*'s flight from Marseille, but none of them implicated Smith directly in the plot. There was, however, one officer whose absence was noticeable. The guard posted aboard *Adriatic*, the one whom Smith threatened to throw overboard, never appeared to testify. Durham and Thombs always swore to Smith that the guard left his post. Smith now wondered whether this was a fortunate coincidence or a lie. The French sought to question the guard both after *Adriatic* disappeared and now at Smith's trial, but he vanished without a trace. The evidence of Durham's guilt was overwhelming, but no other witness could prove that Smith was a willing accomplice. The French government had no choice but to dismiss the charges.

A few days later, to his delight and surprise, Smith accepted a dinner invitation from a French sea captain, who thought that the authorities in Marseille were corrupt, and approved of the Americans who got the better of them. After that, Smith took up his old position of waiting for the courts to reach a decision on the fate of his own vessel. He entertained his friends with stories of *Adriatic*'s escape on more than one occasion and, often at the prompting of those who had heard the tale before, retold the story when new captains arrived in port. He thought of Durham often and remained grateful for an adventure that broke up the monotony that was waiting for justice in Marseille.

CHAPTER 36
The Adriatic Affair

THERE WERE NO AMERICAN OR INTERNATIONAL LAWS that governed accidents at sea in 1856. The collision between *Le Lyonnais* and *Adriatic* and the debacle that ensued became a perfect justification for the creation of such standards. "The *Adriatic* affair," as it became known in political circles, launched discussions in public meetinghouses and private boardrooms across the country. Debates extended beyond the establishment of rules for when two ships met on the open ocean, but also contemplated limitations on insurance liability, requirements for carrying lights, and the adoption of signal systems to allow ships to communicate with one another prior to meeting. Every resolution pointed to the *Adriatic* affair as the example of what happened absent such rules.

The New York Chamber of Commerce ("Chamber") found in the *Adriatic* affair an opportunity to move Congress to establish firm guidelines. Commerce was synonymous with shipping in the 1850s. The Chamber regularly took positions on maritime controversies. The American railroad boom would not begin in earnest until the 1860s. New York's location both as a strategic port and as an epicenter of business and society made it a prime location for shipping merchants. The Chamber comprised not only shipowners but the bankers, insurers, and other business owners who thrived on maritime commerce.

Adriatic's seizure and trial in France struck fear into the hearts of them all. Any one of their ships could be next. Insurance contracts meant nothing if foreign courts could demand payment even after an insurer made the aggrieved party whole.

News of Durham's escape both fueled their hope and furthered their anxiety. Their negotiating position depended on his successful return.

His recapture, on the other hand, would cause irreparable harm to American relations with France and further threaten business interests throughout Europe. The shippers of New York concluded that the US government should do something to help Durham.

The *New York Times*, a newspaper critical of the Chamber for what it described as its penchant to engage in "political and sanitary hobbies," cautioned that maritime rules could never obviate the need for prudence.[1] The paper pulled no punches when it referred to the deaths of those aboard *Le Lyonnais* as "lives sacrificed to the stubbornness of the captain of the barque *Adriatic*, who, expecting the steamship to keep out of his way, ran blindly down upon her before the wind, and struck her in a death blow amidship" and urged the Chamber to set aside political and business interests and to consider the matter from a more objective point of view.[2] The editors pointed to models such as the Boston Board of Trade, which had a standing committee to investigate and track statistics of collisions at sea involving Boston-flagged vessels, and to the British Board of Trade, an organization with similar tracking methods. "Every dictate of justice requires that [shipwrecks] be investigated by a legal tribunal, and every dictate of humanity demands that something be speedily done to stop this wholesale slaughter on the sea."[3]

The Chamber had no intention of taking an objective approach. The stakes were too high. They met on February 19, 1858, to adopt resolutions regarding liability for maritime collisions. At the time, Durham had escaped French custody but had not been heard from for almost three weeks. They saw an opportunity to act within the window that the uncertainty about his absence created.

They debated two resolutions. The first was whether to support a rule that required American ships to use Roger's Maritime Signals. Roger's system involved the use of ten numbered Union Jack flags that could be hoisted alone or in combination to communicate information to other vessels. The Chamber voted in favor of moving to the signal system in January 1855, but some of the members developed reservations because a bill introduced in Congress during the 1858 term recommended the imposition of taxes and penalties for ships that failed to comply. The Chamber called the resolution "a needless tax and burden on commerce" and opposed it.[4] One month later, on April 1, 1858, the Chamber voted to support the bill after Congress struck the provision that required shipowners to participate.

The second resolution involved direct intervention in the *Adriatic* affair. John Henry Brower, a powerful shipping merchant with interests that stretched from New York to California, argued for the Chamber to take swift action to assist Durham and to read a statement of support into the record. He spoke at length about the impropriety of the case being heard in a French court and the fear of the precedent it might set for future cases. He railed against the French for awarding full damages for *Le Lyonnais*'s loss to Franco-Américaine.

Some members of the body were not familiar with the facts of the case. Brower stressed that the laws of the sea required a sailing vessel free of the wind to yield to a vessel that is jammed or close-hauled on the wind, and extended the logic to situations in which a steamer met a sailing vessel. The Chamber, without a firm grasp of the facts, relied on the proposition to conclude that Durham could not be liable because he had the legal right-of-way.

The Chamber erupted in discussion following Brower's remarks. Several members expressed sympathy for Durham. Brower spoke again, this time to caution them. He reminded his colleagues that French authorities described Durham's conduct as an act of piracy, and urged them to proceed with that in mind. His comments were based less on righteous indignation and more on political astuteness about how it might look for the Chamber to take a position without hearing any testimony or reports about circumstances of the collision. His caution caused swift reflection among the group.

Pelatiah Perit listened to the discussion. The son of a ship captain, he became a prominent New York banker who served as president of the Seamen's Savings Bank and had most recently retired from his post as New York City's commissioner of police to become Chamber chair. He was responsible for moving the group's discussion into action. Public attention to the case concerned him, as did the uncertainty of Durham's fate. "This matter is a delicate one," he said. "Perhaps it would be best to handle it outside the Chamber."[5]

Moses H. Grinnell nodded in response. He was a banker, businessman, and politician in several industries; however, his real fortune came from shipping. Grinnell, Minturn & Company, a firm he built with his brother, was one of the leading transatlantic shipping companies in the mid-nineteenth century, with a fleet that included almost fifty clippers and steamships. Grinnell packet steamers from the Red Swallowtail and Blue Swallowtail Lines carried passengers to and from New York and Liverpool, and his clippers were employed in the California gold rush. The company was best known for being the owner and operator of *Flying Cloud*, the ship that set the world record for the fastest passage between New York to San Francisco and held it for more than 130 years. When Grinnell died, Henry Collins Brown, director of the

CHAPTER 36 | *The Adriatic Affair*

Museum of the City of New York, wrote in a tribute to him, "Practically all of the great fortunes prior to the Civil War were made in shipping. Grinnell, Minturn & Company [was] the largest."[6]

Grinnell told the Chamber it was their duty to intervene on Durham's behalf. "I feel great sympathy for the poor fellow. He has been very harshly treated[,] and I wish someone would put the matter into a form of a resolution so that it might come . . . before the Chamber."[7]

The men discussed the issue further. Grinnell stood to address the Chamber again and waited for Perit to recognize him. "There [is] strong sympathy for Captain Durham, which will no doubt find . . ." He paused for a moment in search of the perfect words: "the right expression."[8] Several of the men grunted their approvals.

The "expression" that Grinnell and Perit had in mind was the formation of a committee composed of members who supported Durham and would work in secrecy. Members included Brower and Grinnell, Captain Ezra Nye, Abiel Albert Low, Captain Charles Marshall, Thomas Tileston, Theodore Dehon, and A. B. Neilson.

Brower, whose remarks inspired the committee, was first to be named. He began his career in the grocery business but worked his way up to a cargo transport business that involved more than fifteen vessels, including both a New York and Texas line of packet ships. He is most remembered for his two famous clipper ships, *Andrew Jackson* and *Harvey Birch*, designed to carry cargo for sale to participants in the California gold rush. The ships, built in 1854 and 1855, respectively, were built for J. H. Brower & Company by Irons & Grinnell, a shipbuilding concern owned by fellow Chamber and committee member Moses H. Grinnell.

Massachusetts-born Captain Ezra Nye made his living sailing packet steamers from New York to Europe. He was a tough and short-tempered man who hailed from a long tradition of New Bedford whalers. He earned his reputation by running fast passages on *Independence*, a packet steamer owned and operated by Grinnell, Minturn & Company. When the Swallowtail line launched *Henry Clay*, the largest packet on the Atlantic, Nye earned the command. When Edward Knight Collins sought to find captains for his new line of luxury steamers, competition among the New York captains was fierce, but Collins chose Nye to command the steamship *Pacific* on voyages between Liverpool and New York.

Abiel Abbott Low made his fortune in Asia. He worked his way up from clerk to partner in the mercantile house of Russell and Company, the largest American firm in China. The company formally specialized in importing silk and tea from China and Japan but was reputed to be the country's leading American opium trading and smuggling enterprise in the 1840s. Low returned to New York and in 1850 erected the A. A. Low Building on South Street.[9] He launched a fleet of clipper ships that became known for their speed carrying goods between New York and the Far East.

Charles H. Marshall owned and operated the Black Ball Line of sailing ships, the line that transformed transatlantic travel by leaving New York on a fixed schedule. Paul N. Spofford and Thomas Tileston owned the largest investment and mercantile houses on the East Coast, Spofford, Tileston & Company of New York. Tileston amassed an impressive fleet composed of everything from schooners to packet ships. A. B. Neilson served as president of Sun Mutual Fire and Marine Insurance Company of New York. The firm specialized in marine insurance with no liability beyond the premium. Theodore Dehon was a businessman and stockholder in the Pacific Mail Steamship Company, a joint stock company formed by a group of New York City merchants and established to carry US mail on the Pacific leg of the transcontinental route via Panama.

Every member of what became the New York Chamber of Commerce Committee on Maritime Collisions had a vested interest in the outcome of the *Adriatic* affair. They also had the ears of Washington politicians and the national press. The interests of New York shipping concerns in 1858 were the interests of the nation, and the Chamber's report would carry great sway with members of Congress and even the president of the United States. The uncertainty of Durham's fate ensured that those in power would both listen and act.

Durham had no way of knowing about the fervor his escape had caused among some of the wealthiest and most powerful men in the world. He had not entered a foreign port since his escape from Marseille. He set course for Madeira, a small island off the western coast of Portugal. The crew enjoyed beautiful weather on the journey and the ease that came with the increased distance between *Adriatic* and France. He passed Cape Palos, on the eastern coast of Spain, on January 28.

Durham left Spain with neither an anchor nor enough provisions to make a transcontinental voyage. He hailed and boarded an American ship, *Elizabeth Dennison*, at sea on January 30, 1858. She was a passenger ship that regularly traveled to and from New York and Le Havre. Her captain, Captain Williams, listened to Durham's tale and provided him with an anchor and the provisions he needed to make the long voyage home. On February 6, people near Cartagena, Spain, spotted an "American Bark, name unknown, painted black, with a white rail, having a white signal flag with a blue border, and a black letter M in the centre, passed the Rock [of Gibraltar.]"[10] The "M" flag was the private signal of the schooner *S. E. Meaher*.

CHAPTER 36 | *The Adriatic Affair*

The anchor enabled *Adriatic* to stop in Madeira and at a few other ports to drop off those among the crew who had no desire to continue to America. Most of his sailors, Black men who had been tricked into service aboard the ship, refused to go to a country where slavery still thrived, and chose instead to find work in Europe.

The voyage from Madeira to the United States was "tedious."[11] The weather alternated back and forth between calms and headwinds. The calm stopped *Adriatic* in her tracks for days at a time. Headwinds beat her back when the winds did come, and made progress both slow and punishing. Except for a small quantity of beef, the skeleton crew exhausted all the *Elizabeth Dennison* provisions. Only a handful of sailors remained. The men worked around the clock to maneuver the sails, man the lookouts, and steer the ship. They were exhausted and eager for the solace of dry land.

Durham's father was beside himself. He had heard nothing from his son for almost a month. Newspapers and businessmen and politicians debated the implications the *Adriatic* affair might have on their livelihoods, but Jonathan Sr. feared for his son's life. The family first received word that Durham had escaped and then that *Adriatic* had been confiscated again. It was difficult to know which of the many rumors to believe.

Accounts of Durham's exploits had been widely publicized, and Jonathan Sr. knew that his son traveled with a less-than-willing crew and borrowed rigging. He also believed that his son traveled without an anchor, which meant he would not be able to stop for any reason or weather a storm.[12] Jonathan Durham Sr. could not shake the thought that he would lose a fifth son to the sea.

He was also concerned about his son's future. He knew that French law recognized imprisonment as punishment for the inability to pay a debt, and it was easy to imagine prosecutors imposing such a sentence against a captain who had embarrassed some of the highest-ranking politicians and military figures in Europe. The *New York Daily Herald* reported, "It may be assumed that our countryman, Captain Durham[,] will see the inside of a French jail."[13]

Jonathan Sr. shared his concerns with his friends and partners, which prompted the Belfast, Maine, business community to organize a public meeting. They gathered on the evening of February 27 at the local alderman's office. Unlike the Chamber's effort, which used the urgency of the *Adriatic* affair to further the organization's goals of establishing rules for collisions at sea, the Belfast committee's primary purpose was to bring Durham home. The alderman's office was crowded with lawyers, politicians, captains, merchants, and citizens on the day of the meeting, all of whom gathered to figure out a way to force the US government to intervene on the Durham family's behalf. People expressed their condolences and proposed possible solutions.

Belfast attorney Horatio H. Johnson suggested they form a committee to mull the suggestions over and distill them into a plan of action. The group concurred and made Johnson committee chair. George Moore, owner and editor of the *Belfast Republican Journal*, agreed to serve as secretary.[14] Some of Maine's most prominent businessmen became members, including Jonathan Durham Sr.'s partner, Columbia Perkins Carter.

The room quieted when attorney Andrew Thatcher Palmer rose to speak. Palmer was a well-respected member of the Penobscot bar, known for his willingness to come to the aid of community members in need and his ability to identify and find creative approaches to legal dilemmas. "This case is about more than Captain Durham," he said. "It is about commercial marine interests generally, and that is how we capture the government's attention."[15] He recommended that the committee lay out the facts of the case in writing and submit a report with recommendations to the State Department.

Captain Charles H. Wording agreed and spoke about the dangers of the French court's action becoming precedent in future disputes. He had recently been hired to set sail for ports across Europe as captain of the ship *Western Chief*. Others joined Wording in the belief that they needed to act now, while Durham was at large, in the event the French recaptured him. They also considered what would happen if he made it home. They concluded that the US government would still be required to seek reimbursement from the French for the loss of *Adriatic*'s freight. None of the members seemed to be concerned that the only facts they would be able to gather until Durham arrived were from his letters and newspaper reports.

On January 29, while still one day's sail from Gibraltar, *Adriatic* flagged down a ship off Cape Palos. Durham told the other ship's captain that he and his crew were headed for New York. He anticipated that the captain of the Cape Palos ship would spread the word when he arrived in port. He did just that. The information was a ruse. *Adriatic* had no intention of going to *Le Lyonnais*'s home port of New York. Instead, Durham rounded Gibraltar and made way for Savannah, Georgia. The captain later insisted that he changed the destination because his provisions were running low, but he knew he was bound for Savannah, where he had social and political connections, all along.

CHAPTER 37

Rules of the Road

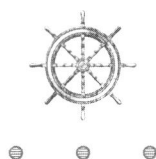

AMERICAN MERCHANTS FEARED what would happen if Durham was recaptured. American politicians feared what would happen if he was not. The Gauthier brothers' rights and liability remained unclear with Durham at large. The French government would look to the Americans for redress the moment Durham set foot on American soil. "If the *Chacal* does not succeed in seizing the *Adriatic* and its bold commander, it seems impossible to us that a formal claim should not be made on the American government to ensure respect of our laws and of our courts," wrote the *Courier de Havre*. "We don't know if ever a similar circumstance has occurred in the judiciary annals or in international relations; but we know well that, in one way or another, such defiance thrown in the face of justice—the only institution which is yet unanimously respected in France—cannot remain without an answer."[1]

Word of Durham's misadventures spread. American politicians realized that his success could result in a full-blown international incident. Legislators from around the county felt pressure from the New York Chamber of Commerce ("Chamber"), the Belfast committee, and other business organizations to intervene.

On Monday, March 8, 1858, Miles Taylor, Democratic member of the United States House of Representatives from Louisiana, introduced House Resolution 13 relative to the seizure of *Adriatic* by French authorities. He took the facts that formed the basis for the resolution from the discussion that had taken place just two weeks before at the Chamber. Durham's whereabouts were still unknown. The last report was that he had escaped the French in Spezia and was making his way west.

Taylor claimed that the Gauthier brothers libeled Durham in France by alleging he was at fault for the accident so they could hold him responsible for *Le Lyonnais*'s loss. He further argued that the Court of Appeals overstepped its bounds when it applied French law to an American vessel about a collision that occurred on the open sea. Unlike French law, which required sailing vessels to display lights after dark, there was no equivalent American or international law that required sailing vessels to carry lights in the nighttime or to signal the course they were steering. The thrust of the preamble was that French laws are obligatory only to her own people and that the court's decision represented, among other things, "a wrong done to the owners of the said American vessel in their capacity as American citizens and also an invasion of the sovereignty of the United States, and an infringement of her rights as a member of the great family of nations."[2]

Two resolutions followed. Each entreated President James Buchanan to act. The first asked the president to inquire of the French government about the basis for the court's findings, to clarify the exact French laws requiring sailing ships to carry lights, and to ask the French government to provide official confirmation that the court's decision was based solely on a French law. Assuming they confirmed that this was the case, the second resolution directed the president to seek redress from the French government for the owners of *Adriatic* and to prevent similar wrongs in the future.

The leap to a conclusion before an investigation did not go unnoticed by some of Taylor's colleagues, who asked him to clarify the procedural posture of his resolution. Congressman Humphrey Marshall, a political moderate from Kentucky, asked if Durham had made any representations to the government on the subject, and suggested that the executive branch investigate the facts before Congress acted. Others objected because the preamble asserted facts not yet known to members of the legislature. Congressman John Millson, a Democrat from Virginia, said, "some of the statements in the preamble involve not very clear principles of international law," and he suggested removing it.[3] The legislature had neither the French court's decision nor an official statement from Durham. All of Taylor's information was based on newspaper accounts and the February 19 meeting at the Chamber, which was based on newspaper accounts. Several members asked that the issue be referred to the Committee on Foreign Affairs for a factual investigation before a vote.

Taylor rose again to speak. His first speech was long, and the congressmen in the crowd shouted, "No!"[4] Taylor persisted. He rebuked the legislature for spending the current session of Congress on "matters which are of little importance," and called the situation surrounding *Adriatic* "one of great public moments connected with the great interests of this nation."[5] He addressed the House again to underscore the importance of his resolution.

He spoke at length about the perils of steam navigation. When navigation was confined to sailing vessels, he claimed, two ships traveling in opposite directions rarely collided. This was because sailing ships, which were beholden to the wind, would not always pursue the same route. There is no source for this statement. One of the *New York Times*' criticisms of the Chamber report on which Taylor relied was the absence of reference to any professional board that kept statistics on maritime collisions. The Boston Board of Trade kept such statistics and reported that in 1855 there were 351 vessels sunk, forty-seven of them by collision. That number referred only to ships owned and registered in Boston.

Collisions among vessels were on the rise. Steam navigation allowed ships to take the shortest possible routes, regardless of the wind. Taylor theorized that this created more opportunities for sailing ships traveling in the opposite direction of a steamship to come into a collision. Poor record keeping made it difficult to know if Taylor was correct or if the increased accidents were caused by record volumes of traffic on the high seas.

A single problem rested at the heart both of Taylor's arguments and the *New York Times*' criticism. It was the same one identified by the Chamber as early as 1855, which was how to ensure that ships signaled to one another with lights, bells, or other signal systems to avoid collision.

France and England had already enacted legislation regarding lights at sea. English law required a sailing vessel to show a light when approaching a steamship. France followed suit. Failure to follow these laws deprived the sailing ship of the right to recover damages from a steamship in those countries. International maritime law did not mandate lights but considered the absence of a light when determining fault in the event of a collision.

England and France instituted their laws in the early 1850s, but the US Congress had yet to act. The only American requirement that sailing ships carry lights applied to travel on the Great Lakes.

There were, however, advocates for such measures. Affixing a light to the bow was common practice by prudent shipowners. As one critic noted, "If [Captain Durham] had made his ship visible by a brilliant light in the bow, the steamer would have known exactly where he was and how he was standing.... But if he had paid as much regard to the value of human life as he did to his own legal rights in the case, that dreadful disaster would never have occurred."[6]

Silas Burroughs, a Republican representative from New York, interrupted Taylor's speech to ask an obvious question: "I would inquire of the gentlemen from Louisiana whether it is his intention to encourage sailing vessels to navigate the high seas in the nighttime without carrying lights?"[7] Taylor assured Congress that he was in favor of lights at sea and would vote for such a law if offered. He clarified that his argument about *Adriatic* was restricted to the impropriety of subjecting an American to French laws, which would "destroy the equality of the United States with the other nations of the world."[8] He refocused the argument on the French government's intrusion on American sovereignty.

Following Taylor's speech, Representatives Henry Phillips of Pennsylvania (D) and Thomas Clingman of North Carolina (D) pointed to a deficiency of facts. Clingman again suggested they turn the matter over to the Committee on Foreign Affairs to investigate. "Facts are assumed in the preamble of which we know nothing,"[9] said Phillips. Taylor relented, and Congress voted to send the matter to the committee for action. Ten days later, Captain Durham arrived in Savannah.

CHAPTER 38

Celebrity

• • •

THE CITY OF SAVANNAH WAS ABUZZ with news of Durham's arrival. It seemed everyone had heard the story of the intrepid captain who escaped Marseille. Now they would get to see him in the flesh.

Savannah in the 1850s was the largest exporter of cotton in the world. Its population exploded in the early part of the nineteenth century and consisted of white landowners and laborers, enslaved people, and free Black people. Four- and five-story cotton warehouses lined River Street, a long thoroughfare that hugged the Savannah River waterfront. A bluff, known as Bay Street, overlooked and ran parallel to the river below. Ships pulled into Savannah's ports nonstop. They arrived full of ballast, which they exchanged for cotton bound for destinations worldwide. The Bay Street bluff and River Street connected through a series of iron-and-concrete walkways and cobblestone ramps built from ballast tossed into the streets by the many ships that visited the city.

Adriatic's watchman spotted the Tybee Island Light in the distance, a lighthouse that marked the entrance to the Savannah River to ships coming in from the ocean. "Land ahead," he shouted. Durham had seen the light so many times before, but the sight of it on the day he reached home from France brought with it a wave of emotion that almost brought him to his knees.

Adriatic approached the mouth of the Savannah. Fort Pulaski, built in the nineteenth century to control the passage of ships and defend Savannah against would-be attackers, greeted them. Major Samuel Babcock and his assistant, a recent US Naval Academy graduate named Robert E. Lee, supervised construction of the fort on Cockspur Island in

The Adriatic Affair

Illustrated engraving of the mouth of the Savannah River, Savannah, Georgia. American Victorian engraving, 1872.

1829. Cockspur was the first in a string of barrier islands that separated the Savannah River into two channels. *Adriatic* passed the fort and then the island and navigated through the shoals upriver to the city. Durham arrived in Savannah Harbor on March 18, 1858, a little more than two months after he escaped Marseille.

Word of his arrival spread as he moved upriver. The men who worked in the cotton warehouses and merchant buildings were the first to hear it. It was not long before people came out of their buildings on Bay Street, walked down the ramps, and stepped onto the waterfront to catch a glimpse of the famous vessel and her infamous captain.

Durham knew that people expected three things when he stepped off *Adriatic* and touched American soil for the first time in almost two years: answers about what happened during the collision, the details of his escape from France, and a captain who lived up to the image conjured by such exploits. What the captain lacked in the former two, he made up for in the latter.

The young captain was personable. He was pleasant. He was spirited. His wit and charm solidified his celebrity status. He embraced his newfound fame and discovered in it a way not only to further endear himself to his supporters but to mollify those who doubted him. People liked him. Those who did not like what he had done liked him so much they found themselves willing to overlook it.

CHAPTER 38 | *Celebrity*

The safe arrival of the bark *Adriatic* furnishes food for comment in the newspapers. Captain Durham, her commander, has shown so much pluck and dexterity that no very heavy censure will be bestowed upon him. Nobody but a born Yankee would have escaped from the crowded port of Marseilles, and again from the surveillance of a French fleet in the Gulf of Spezia. There is such a dashing, fly-away, privateer sort of éclat in the recent history of the bark *Adriatic*, that the American character, with its strong love of adventure, will lose sight of Captain Durham's original error in admiration for his boldness and seamanship.[1]

The next day, he gave an interview to the *Savannah Morning News*. He remained scant on details of the crash and focused on the court's judgment against him and his escape. He told the paper that he shipped the crew under the name of another vessel but did not mention how he scrounged up and tricked the sailors from the boardinghouse. He claimed he bought supplies in Spezia so as not to implicate Colonel Long, who provided him with food and water at great risk. He claimed he left Spezia "unmolested" and never mentioned his flight from *Chacal* in the storm. He told the reporter he had assistance from others, but he did not name them.

Durham could not resist telling a tale that centered on his own cunning and daring. There were, in his statement at Savannah and those made after it, attempts to minimize both the audacity of his escape and the illegality of his conduct. He did so not only to protect his friends but because he still feared retribution from the French government and could not afford to engender their ire unnecessarily. It was also good for his public image.

He sent word to his brother in a private letter and described the lengths to which Smith and Martin went to help him escape France. Charles, who also was careful not to commit too much to writing, wrote to Smith to express his gratitude for the "sympathy and kindness shown Captain Durham from his friends in Marseilles," and to inform him of *Adriatic*'s arrival at Savannah. He wrote, "If it had been the great *Leviathan* that should have arrived it should not have caused a greater sensation."[2]

Durham's hometown newspaper hailed him a hero and similarly compared *Adriatic* to *Leviathan*. "Thus, the *Adriatic* has become one of the five famous vessels of the world—the *Ark*, the *Argonaut*, the *Flying Dutchman*, the *Leviathan*, and the *Adriatic*, and Captain Durham will hardly escape being lionized."[3]

The diplomatic debate about France's intervention in American maritime affairs had continued in Durham's absence. He had the sympathy of statesman, merchants, and sailors, but, according to Charles, the political situation was nevertheless "complicated."[4] The government began to intervene on Durham's behalf. Within a week of his arrival, the American government agreed to register *Adriatic* and insisted that Consul Morgan retrieve and send Durham's papers home.

Business leaders encouraged the United States to act. Most supported Durham, but others expressed concern for the way in which his conduct might impair their interests aboard. "We fear that the [*Boston*] *Courier* will prove right in predicting that the consequence of the escape will be that every American captain who may hereafter come within the 'clutches' of a French tribunal will be treated with peculiar rigor and severity; and will be dealt with as a man with whom no faith can be kept, and thus the interests of American commerce will be made to suffer heavily for the fault of one."[5] The pleas reached the highest levels of government, including the president himself, who summoned Durham to Washington to provide the details of his ordeal in France.

Durham arrived in the nation's capital on April 6, 1858, less than three weeks after his return from France. He stayed with a friend and relative from Bangor, Dr. Charles A. Jordan.[6] The next morning, he met with the president. Buchanan sought to learn more about the exact circumstances of his seizure and escape from France. Durham asked Buchanan to help him recoup his cargo losses. The young captain must have been reassured by whatever he learned in the meeting, because, days later, he relisted his boat for charter in the Savannah newspapers.

CHAPTER 38 | *Celebrity*

On April 12, Durham received notice from the US Congress about a hearing scheduled for April 19. The House Committee on Foreign Relations ("Committee") requested Durham to appear. He agreed and submitted the following statement on April 14, 1858:

> I left Belfast, Maine, on October 31, 1856, with the bark *Adriatic*, loaded with lime and hay, bound to Savannah, Georgia. On the night of second November, at half-past ten o'clock, being under double[-]reefed topsails and steering by the wind blowing fresh from the southwest, the watch on lookout made a light about three points on the weather bow. I then caused a good and sufficient signal light to be hoisted in a proper position to be seen by the approaching vessel, which came steadily towards us. It was visible to my crew and myself on deck that the approaching steamer must clear us if she continued the course she was then steering; but when within about one-third of a mile her course was suddenly changed, bearing down upon us. Fearing a collision would take place I put the helm down. The bark came into the wind, so that her sails were all shaking, and her headway nearly stopped. It was the only remedy I had to prevent the steamer from running over me. Had I not put the helm down the steamer would have struck me midships and buried the bark and the crew in the ocean.
>
> The steamer struck the bark forward, carrying away jibboom, bowsprit, cutwater, and starting all the starboard bow from the deck frame, leaving me a perfect wreck.
>
> The steamer pursued her course without stopping, until she was lost in the distance. I shaped my course for the nearest port to repair damages; arrived at Gloucester, Mass.; reported the facts as to the collision, and repaired at a cost of $2000. From thence I proceeded to Savannah, Georgia, discharged, and loaded with a cargo of timber for France. Arrived at La Ciotat [on] February 10, 1857; on the 20th finished discharging, paid my customs dues, and cleared for Sicily. The following day an officer from the customs reported to me there was a mistake in my clearance at the customs house, requesting me to go to the customs and have the matter rectified, which I did. After a few minutes, they gave me to understand that they would keep my papers and refused to settle the freight, which amounted to about $5000. There being no American consul at La Ciotat, I went to Marseilles, a distance of twenty-five miles, where I made my complaint before the American consul.
>
> During my absence from the vessel the civil authorities ordered my mate to unhang the rudder, and unbend the sails, threatening in case of refusal to put him in prison, together with all hands.

The Adriatic Affair

My attorney pled the case of jurisdiction on the 17th of March following. It was decided by article 14, code Napoléon, that the Courts of France had jurisdiction in cases of this kind.

The case was tried before the tribunal of commerce and decided in my favor on the 3d of April, acquitting me of all blame and awarding the bark 500 francs per day for every day detained by the prosecutors. About the 8th of the same month the case was taken to the court of Aix, where it was argued. The judges, being unable to give their decision, it was referred to the Commission of three shipmasters. They went on board bark and examined the signal light used at the time of the collision and reported that the light was of sufficient size and in a proper position and was set ten minutes before the accident occurred; and they also reported that the steamer violated a well-known regulation by putting her wheel to starboard and endeavoring to pass the bark to the left instead of the right.

After this report the case was again brought before the imperial court of Aix. Notwithstanding the report of experts chosen by themselves, they decided against the *Adriatic*, on the ground that if the light had been really set, it was either too small, or placed in no position to be seen by the *La Lyonnais* [sic], or, finally, set too late.

The decision was rendered against me on the 24th of December 1857, after a detention of ten months.

After confiscating my vessel, freight, and 2000 francs of my own private property, feeling my case was a hard one, and that I had been deeply wronged, I deemed it just to myself and to the owners of the *Adriatic*, knowing not at what moment I might be arrested and placed in prison for nonpayment of the value of the *Lyonnais* (1,500,000 francs), to attempt an escape. Accordingly, I left the port of Marseilles, with the *Adriatic* (without asking leave), and arrived at the port of Savannah in the United States on the 18th of March 1858, after an absence of thirteen months, and a pecuniary loss of much more than the value of my vessel.

Restfully submitted,
J. B. Durham
Master of the bark *Adriatic*
Washington, April 14, 1858[7]

No alternative testimony was requested or offered. The formal declaration of facts was all the committee needed to move forward. The chair appointed Massachusetts congressman Anson Burlingame, a man known for his diplomacy, to report a resolution and request that the president inquire of France into the facts concerning *Adriatic*'s seizure, request an explanation of the grounds for the seizure, and demand redress.

Durham did not remain in Washington to watch the politics play out. He had received several applications from shipowners in New York and Boston to take charge of their vessels and was eager to set sail once again. His exploits made him a marketable captain. The *Savannah Georgian*, which advertised *Adriatic*'s availability for charters, quipped, "He is every inch a sailor, and one who would not be likely to 'give up the ship.'"[8]

CHAPTER 39

Collisions at Sea

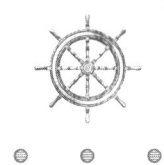

DURHAM'S SUCCESSFUL ARRIVAL IN SAVANNAH provided the New York Chamber of Commerce Committee on Maritime Collisions ("Chamber") with the information it needed to try to codify favorable regulations into law. The Chamber relied on Durham's statement to Congress and issued its report, "In Relation to Collisions at Sea," on May 6, 1858. The report introduced a new approach to insurance liability for shipowners.

Court decisions to date held that the insurer was responsible to the owner for damages only to his own ship but not to damage caused to another ship in a collision when an accident occurred at sea. When both parties were at fault, each divided the losses equally. For example, if one ship incurred $10,000 in damage and another $250,000, both ships would be responsible for $130,000. Each party bore his own loss when no one was at fault.

The obvious difficulty with the approach was that one ship may wind up paying an exorbitant sum. Congress sought to alleviate this burden in an 1851 statute that created an exception for surrender, which allowed any vessel to surrender itself to the opposing party prior to judgment by a court. Take, for example, a ship worth $100,000 that sustained $10,000 worth of damage in a collision with a $1,000,000 ship that sustained $250,000 in damage in which both parties were at fault. The small ship's liability would be $130,000, $30,000 more than her worth. Surrender gave the smaller vessel the opportunity to transfer ownership to the owners of the larger one and limit the liability to the worth of the ship, in this case $90,000, or $100,000 minus the $10,000 in damages. One of the difficulties with the statute was that it required the vessels to decide whether to transfer ownership prior to any judgment of fault or damages. It also posed a greater financial risk to small vessels.

CHAPTER 39 | *Collisions at Sea*

Other nations treated the problems of collisions at sea differently. Some divided damages equally, with no option to transfer. Others allowed for division not only of damage but of cargo and freight. Some apportioned damage according to the level of fault. The differing approaches created problems when two ships from different nations met at sea.

Although shipowners could be held responsible to one another for damages, the rule did not extend to insurance carriers. Court decisions in both the US and England limited the insurer's liability to the policy. The insurer was bound to cover damages for the policyholder but not for claims made by the other ship against the policyholder. Shipowners were forced to constantly calculate damage to the other ship and reimbursement for their own damages, and to navigate the issue of whether it was in their best interest to cut their losses by transferring ownership.

The Chamber aimed to simplify the rules. It proposed that each ship bear responsibility for his own damages in cases involving "accident, misfortune, or, at most, misjudgment."[1] Intentional conduct, such as robbery or other forms of piracy, would be treated under a different set of rules. The word "misjudgment" caused the most debate. The Chamber defined "misjudgment" as negligence such as failure to signal, runaway vessels, and other errors of seamanship. The report referred at length both to the *Le Lyonnais* and *Arctic* disasters. It compared them to the steamers *Columbia*, *Franklin*, and *Humboldt*, all of which became lost in fog and ran aground. The difference between the former and the latter was that *Le Lyonnais* and *Arctic* sank by collision. *Columbia*, *Franklin*, and *Humboldt* ran aground on unseen rocks or shallows in dense fog. These instances were attributable to bad weather, not another party. The Chamber report, however, treated these situations equally because they all involved negligence as opposed to intentional conduct.

It was a purposeful analogy. Both the *Le Lyonnais* and *Arctic* incidents involved high-profile situations in which small vessels were forced to pay large sums to much-larger ships. *Vesta* and *Arctic* met head on in a fog. *Vesta* was much smaller than *Adriatic*. The ships were in equal fault, yet *Vesta*'s liability was $750,000 because the damages were equally divided.

Many of the Chamber members owned fleets of merchant ships employed in transcontinental trade. Recent events taught them some hard lessons. One was that small ships were capable of surviving collisions that crippled larger vessels. A system of equal fault would almost always require the smaller ship to pay a huge sum to the larger one.

There was also the issue of insurance. Even those ships that made their primary income carrying passengers rented space to businesses for shipping cargo. Many, such as *Adriatic*, made their living on shipping goods alone. The cost of uninsured cargo was divided equally among shipowners under the current system. This only compounded the losses and further burdened the smaller vessel.

Last, there was the matter of seamanship. All shipowners relied on hired sailors. Large maritime concerns employed hundreds of sailors—from captains to boatswains—to man their ships. "In doing so, [the shipowner] is thrown upon the market for mariners, of whose character and capacity he cannot know more than the shipper of the cargo or the underwriter upon—nor can he have any better security than they for the fidelity of the master or the wakefulness at night of the watch upon deck."[2]

The *Arctic* mutiny, during which sailors allowed women and children to drown to save themselves, and the questionable conduct of the watch aboard *Adriatic* served as ever-present reminders that shipowners were always at the mercy of the hired help. This truth had an equal impact on steamship giants such as the Collins Line, which owned *Arctic*, and small partnerships such as Patterson & Carter.

The Chamber proposed a system whereby fault would not be determined, a system in which "each vessel by itself, be settled without recourse to the other."[3] It was, essentially, a proposal for no-fault insurance. Each ship would be responsible for its own losses. The contemplated rule extended from accidents to what the Chamber referred to as "misdirected judgment."[4] If a man was so deranged as to "cause willful collision with a neighboring ship," the Chamber argued, "the laws of nations should . . . punish the perpetrators as pirates."[5] The Chamber envisioned a new class of laws to punish gross negligence and intentional acts that caused a collision at sea.

The body resolved to send its report to Congress, President Buchanan, and boards of trade in principal commercial cities in the United States and authorized five hundred copies to be made and distributed among its members. The Chamber sent the report to major port cities in Europe and asked for foreign cooperation in the effort. Further consideration of the report was postponed to a special meeting on May 13, 1858, to give members and the public one week for review and comment.

Some of the most vocal criticism of the Chamber's conclusions came from Boston. On May 12, 1858, the *Boston Daily Courier* articulated its concerns in a swift and devastating response. The newspaper echoed the sentiments of many who were aghast at the notion that mariners would not be responsible for their own conduct, and picked the Chamber's efforts apart line by line without mercy. It called the report "one of the most extraordinary documents of the times" and summarized it as follows: "The object of the report is to introduce and recommend a new law, to be established by all commercial nations, to the effect that in cases of collision, no person, owner, master or mariner shall be liable for any damage caused by collision, however carelessly or negligently occasioned, unless the offending party is deemed a pirate."[6]

The core of the *Courier*'s opposition was that the Chamber's proposal left no incentive for responsible navigation at sea. The newspaper also called new criminal penalties unnecessary because the crime of piracy already punished intentional misconduct.

While the Chamber focused on issues of liability, the Congressional Committee on Foreign Affairs ("Committee") prepared its recommendation to President Buchanan. It reported back on June 1, 1858, without amendment, the joint resolution Taylor offered in March, accompanied by a report.

The committee decided that the *Adriatic* affair called for intervention of the US government but refused to opine on the appropriateness of Durham's escape from France. It pivoted from Durham's specific conduct to broader concerns. "However obligatory may be the duty of the government of the United States to demand reparation for a grievous wrong committed by a foreign government against one of its citizens, that duty is insignificant compared with its obligation to assist the establishment of principles which may impose fetters upon all American Commerce."[7]

The committee did not mention the Chamber by name but referenced discussions in "commercial districts" about the need for uniform maritime laws that governed collisions and liability for accidents at sea.[8] Committee members unanimously approved the resolution and ordered the report be printed and referred to the full House of Representatives.

Durham's European critics were not amused:

As an exemplification of what may be expected from Jonathan [Durham], in any attempt to elicit a just and equitable settlement of any disputed or debatable claims, whether about foreign enlistment, filibustering, imprisonment of black seaman, or prostitution of the star-spangled banner to piracy and slave-dealing, the denouement of a grand melodramatic nautical farce, beginning most tragically by the loss of lives run down by Captain Durham of the clipper *Adriatic*; his escape from the legal consequences of his criminal and disastrous neglect; his second breaking out of limbo and shooting the moon; his final refuge across the Atlantic at Savannah; his summons to Washington on complaint of France; and, to wind up the whole, a demand of indemnity for this injured Yankee from the merchants of Marseilles, whose steamer . . . he sent to the bottom, and whose brothers and relatives, in the dead of night, he whelmed into destruction! Such is the cool report of Mr. Burlingame, Massachusetts, addressed to the president.[9]

It took more than six months, until December 1858, for the Chamber to respond to its own critics and issue its final report. It defended against the Boston critique but made no substantive changes to the recommendations outlined in the May 1858 version. Chairman John H. Brower read the Chamber's proposed response into the record at a January 9, 1859, meeting, and the full Chamber voted to append it to the original report and recirculate it.

This time, the Chamber acknowledged the modernity of its ideas about liability. "Although the suggestion to relieve shipowners from liability may be new, it is entirely just that they should be released, in the very nature of the case, to accord with the commercial circumstances of the age."[10]

The recirculation of the report provoked more responses from at home and abroad. The Commercial Law Committee of the Liverpool Chamber of Commerce issued a report on "Collisions at Sea" in June 1859. It echoed the Boston critic and rejected the Chamber's suggestions "to exonerate shipowners, or any other class of employers, from all pecuniary liability for negligence to their servants, whatever its degree, would be, as your Committee conceive, to weaken, unduly, the motive to vigilance in the choice of servants so trusted."[11] The Liverpool Chamber agreed with the New York Chamber's proposal to attach criminal penalties to anyone who caused a collision at sea through willful negligence or malice, and agreed such prosecutions should apply only to flagrant conduct.

The Liverpool Chamber submitted a copy of its comments to the New York Chamber in September 1859. It centered its analysis on the recent collision between the American ship *Tuscarora* and the British ship *Andrew Foster*. *Andrew Foster* foundered and sank after colliding with *Tuscarora* off the coast of Wexford on April 28, 1857. The British Merchant Shipping Act of 1854 limited shipowner liability to loss or damage to life or property, without fault, to the value of the vessel and her freight. The court deemed *Tuscarora* at fault for the collision, and attorneys for the American shipowner sought to limit liability under the act. The court rejected the argument and concluded that the act applied only to British vessels. American vessels were responsible to British shipowners to an unlimited extent. This left American ships at great risk of bearing responsibility for the entire loss resulting from collision with a British-flagged ship, which is exactly what happened in *Tuscarora*'s case.

The Baltimore Board of Trade voiced concerns about the *Tuscarora* case. Although it did not take a position on the New York Chamber's proposal, it pointed out in an 1861 publication the dangers posed to American shipowners by the British court's decision, and quoted the Chamber's warning: "No prudent man would be willing to be engaged in commerce at such risks, especially when no vigilance of foresight on the part of the owners can guard against the danger of collision—a peril of the seas which constant increase of navigation by steam as well as sails continually augments."[12]

On October 1, 1859, the Chamber president, Perit, submitted the full report to President James Buchanan as the body's final word "In Relation to Collisions at Sea." The memorial read as follows:

> Sir, the Chamber of Commerce of New York begs leave to call the attention of the president of the United States to the accompanying document, relative to collisions at sea and the multi-form liability to which ships and their owners are subject by the judicial practice of our own as well as of other important commercial countries; and also, to the great injustice of the continuance of such liabilities, which, although they may have been appropriate to the early days of maritime commerce, are plainly inconsistent with the character of that commerce at the present day, and will, naturally, become increasingly inconsistent in its future progress.
>
> It cannot be doubted that seamen must be entrusted with very large discretions in a great variety of cases. Whatever may be the ultimate legal consequences, the rule which governs them, in times of peril, is that which, according to their best judgment and skill, shall most conduce to the protection of life and property; and we consider that each interest in peril should, legally, be subject to the chances and results.
>
> The risks involving such liabilities as it is sought to release ships and their owners from, are insurable, and it is believed, are generally insured against. This fact indicates that ships and owner should not be bound, directly or collaterally, for what are treated, in commercial practice, as a risk for which there is legitimate cover, independent of the "carrier," who receives no compensation as insurer, and therefore should be released from common-law liabilities in reference to insurable risks.
>
> The documents herewith treat the general subject somewhat at length, and it is hoped that the facts therein set forth, with the reasoning naturally flowing from them, may lead to a conviction of the propriety and necessity of the changes sought.

It is essential to any changes which may be made, that they should become treaty engagements between all commercial nations, by which the laws of the ocean shall be the same, wherever maritime cases may be adjudicated. This object can be affected by treaty only, because the mere statute of one country can have no binding influence on another. In the absence of such treaty engagements, common-law penalties have been inflicted to ruinous amounts, and in the present condition of things, it would seem that the shipowner, with his whole fortune, may be at the mercy of a single casualty at sea, and under circumstances entirely without his privity and control.

The Chamber of Commerce of New York invokes the executive influence upon the subject. With great respect, your obedient servant, P. Perit, President Chamber of Commerce.[13]

Eighteen months had passed between Durham's arrival at Savannah and submission of the Chamber's final product. The fervor over *Adriatic* had died down on both sides of the Atlantic during that time, and the Gauthier brothers were no longer in any position to revive the dispute.

A lucrative contract that Franco-Américaine won with the Spanish government to deliver mail expired in late 1857 and was set to be renewed. Spanish authorities were, at the time, already under public scrutiny for awarding mail contracts to foreign shipping lines and refused to renew Franco-Américaine's most profitable route, mail service from Le Havre to Cádiz.

Passengers complained about the poor maintenance of Franco-Américaine's ships and frequent delays. The Spanish government fined the company in February 1858 because *Barcelone* failed to leave from Cádiz to Havana on time. *Cadix* experienced mechanical failures in Puerto Rico around the same time and was unable to deliver mail to Havana. The Spanish government used one of its warships to bring the mail the rest of the way.

The death knell for Franco-Américaine came in early 1858. Prosecutors arrested one of the Gauthier brothers for stock fraud. They sent him to a Lyon prison to await trial and charged him with manipulating Franco-Américaine's business records to inflate earnings to entice investors. The company declared bankruptcy. Durham and his advocates breathed a sigh of relief. The arrest made it far less likely the French government would further intervene in the *Adriatic* affair.

The French declared *Le Lyonnais*'s captain, Pierre Stanislas Devaulx, dead on February 19, 1858, more than a year after the collision.

His wife, who was left behind with three children, applied for a pension from Franco-Américaine, but she was too late. The company was already bankrupt. She appealed to the French government for assistance. They offered her son, Stenio, a scholarship to the Marine College in Dieppe. She received nothing more in compensation for her husband's death.

Franco-Américaine's fleet was broken up and sold. Inman Line purchased *Vigo* and used her as a replacement for its ship *City of Manchester*, which had gone into transport service during the Indian Mutiny, an uprising against the British East India Company's colonial rule. *Vigo* participated in the uprising herself before being put into service between Liverpool and New York. The company sold her to the American government in 1861, which scrapped her ten years later.

Peninsular & Oriental Steam Navigating Company (P&O) bought the remaining ships on November 26, 1858. *Habana* became *China* and sailed in and around India and Australia. P&O sold her to W. Hartman in 1882. Hartman intended to remove her engines and use her as a sailing ship, but the renovations were unsuccessful. Hartman scrapped her in 1883. *Barcelone* became *Behar* and, after a refit, sailed the seas of northeast India. She was sold to ship-breakers in Kobe, Japan, in 1897.

Cadix became *Ellora*. P&O refit her and put her into service in the Mediterranean Sea. P&O sold her to Australian owners, John Blyth & Company, in 1872, and they rerigged her as a barque. Blyth sold her back to her original builder, Laird & Company of Liverpool, in 1889. She

China ca. 1859. Courtesy of © P&O Heritage Collection, www.poheritage.com

was sold two more times in quick succession before being scrapped in Panama in 1899.

Franc Comtois had the longest life of the sisters. Renamed *Orissa*, she sailed in the Far East for P&O through 1872, when the company sold her to John C. Irving in Shanghai. Irving rerigged her as a sailing vessel. She was the only ship to see the turn of the century. *Orissa* sailed for thirty-four more years before being sold to ship-breakers in 1906.

Ellora as a barque in Sydney Harbor, Australia, 1875. Allan C. Green Collection. *State Library of Victoria*

By as early as April 1858, the French felt no need to advocate on behalf of shipowners who were now bankrupt and confined to prison. One British reporter quipped, "Napoléon will no more trouble himself about Captain Durham than he would about an American student who on returning home forgets to pay his Paris tailor."[14]

President Buchanan never acted on the Chamber's recommendations. Taylor's House Resolution 13 died and was revived again during the next term as House Resolution 27. After a procedural argument on May 25, 1860,

CHAPTER 39 | *Collisions at Sea*

Smauel Walters' painting of one of *Le Lyonnais*' six sister ships, likely *Vigo*, in 1858. It is the closest to understanding what *Le Lyonnais* looked like in 1856.
Courtesy of Wirral Archives Service

it was again referred from the Foreign Affairs Committee to the full House, where it languished until the congressional term expired.

Congress resumed in 1860, two months before President Lincoln's election. The Gauthier brothers were ruined. Durham knew to avoid French ports. There had been no more requests for compensation to or from the French or American governments, and no more discussion between the two countries on the *Adriatic* affair. It appeared that the United States, now confronted by more-pressing matters such as impending civil war, preferred to let sleeping dogs lie.

CHAPTER 40

Fate

ADRIATIC ADVERTISED FOR CHARTER as early as March 22, 1858, just days after Durham reached Savannah. "The *Adriatic* is a superior vessel... and has been tested, both as to her strength and speed. If any are in doubt on the above points, we refer them to the French!"[1]

Merchants Carleton & Parsons chartered the vessel to carry a cargo of lumber to Cork, Ireland. *Adriatic* awaited delivery as early as March 27. Durham postponed the voyage to visit Washington, DC, but returned to his ship as soon as the politicians were finished with him. He cleared for Cork on April 19, 1858, and departed on April 20. The *Savannah Republican* wished, "Better luck to Capt. Durham this time!"[2] He and his crew traveled from Cork to Queenstown, England, and to Savannah again without incident.

The sea was Durham's only real home, so his brother Charles's residence became his official address following his return from Marseille. Charles and his family had moved from Belfast to Chelsea, Massachusetts, during Durham's time in France. His lumber company, C. Durham & Company, took over *Adriatic*'s management in the summer of 1858 and changed her home port to Charlestown, a city located at the junction of the Mystic River and Boston Harbor waterways. The company metaled the ship in August 1858, a process by which the wooden frame was sheathed below the waterline with sheet copper fastened with copper nails. Metaling a ship deterred shipworms, which would eat away at the ship's timbers much like termites in a house, and prevented barnacle and weed growth, which would slow a ship down.

Durham captained *Adriatic* for the next two years and carried cargoes of lumber to and from ports in the US, Europe, and South America. She was not the only ship he commanded. His services were in demand following his escape from France, particularly from Belfast- and Boston-based merchants. He served as captain on two of his old ships from 1858 to 1860, including *Siam* in 1858 and 1859 and *Malabar* in 1859, but he never gave up his ownership interest in *Adriatic* and preferred to go to sea with her whenever he could.

Durham married on December 10, 1858. His bride, Elizabeth Parrot Pearce, was born in 1833 in Gloucester, Massachusetts. She had been married once before to Samuel Alexander, who died in 1854. She was twenty-seven when she married Durham, who was then thirty-three. The newlyweds moved in with Charles and his family.

Ward L. Smith did not have to wait much longer after Durham's arrival in Savannah to leave Marseille. *S. E. Meaher* went on the market for sale on May 25, 1858. A Havre-based businessman paid the value of the ship to Smith on bottomry, a type of loan for which the ship is used as collateral. Consul Morgan issued a sea letter for *S. E. Meaher* to travel. The document asked civil and military authorities to let him leave "freely and safely" and pledged that the US government would do all in its power to assist the captain.[3] It was a change of heart that resulted not just from Smith's financial circumstances but from the change in the Gauthier brothers' positions. Smith sailed for home and reached Mobile in July 1858.

He had not seen his family since he left Lysander to go whaling in 1844. He proceeded from Mobile to New York and arrived there in August. He was still enamored with the South and spent the next two years traveling back and forth between his relatives in Oswego County, New York, and his beloved Mobile, Alabama. Smith's brother, William Wallace, died in New York on January 10, 1859. He traveled home for the funeral and spent extended time with his relatives. He met and courted a woman named Anna Williams and married her in January 1860. Anna was perfect for Smith. She graduated from Falley Seminary School in 1857. She was a smart, god-fearing woman who enjoyed theology and literature.

John Stephen Martin wrote to Smith from Marseille to congratulate him on "the prospect of an early marriage with the lady of [his] heart." He advised, "The first year is always the hardest[;] there are so many little things that occur that touch a sensitive person during that period. . . .The first year over without cause of complaint on either side, there is great chance of happiness all the rest of your life—Bear and forebear is the secret of married life."[4]

Smith enjoyed New York, but he missed the South. He bought land and built a home on the Sabine River, the Gulf border between Texas and Louisiana. He and Anna moved there in 1860. Smith was still in possession of *S. E. Meaher*, and Anna, who was not afraid of an adventure, joined Smith on two oceangoing voyages.

Joseph Thombs achieved the rank of captain after the escape from Marseille and served as *Adriatic*'s commander when Durham was engaged in other work. *Adriatic* made frequent voyages to South America, and Thombs captained the ship on some of them. He was the only other person whom Durham trusted with her. He had been with Durham from the beginning, and *Adriatic* meant as much to Thombs as she did to him. It was Thombs, not Durham, who was at *Adriatic*'s helm when she finally met her end.

Thombs sailed *Adriatic* to Buenos Aires in the summer of 1860. The ship was in the harbor when a storm approached. It was a pampero, the same type of storm that destroyed the whaling ship *Tuscaloosa* in 1845. Thombs ordered the crew to drop two of the ship's three anchors to secure *Adriatic* in the harbor in preparation. The winds picked up, and Thombs watched as the squalls closed in. They looked harmless enough from afar, like swirls of smoke in the air, until they struck and brought with them furious bursts of wind and rocks of icy hail.

The storm thundered. *Adriatic* held on. One of the gusts sent a brig, an Argentinian man-o-war, adrift. It struck *Adriatic* across the bow but did not wound her. The sea tossed the brig about in the harbor, and it threatened to collide with the barque a second time. "Give out chain!" Thombs shouted to the men over the storm. They let out anchor chain to free *Adriatic* from her position. "Faster!" Thombs screamed as the chain tumbled through the crewmen's hands and over the side of the ship. *Adriatic* moved and dragged her second anchor along the bottom. The men dumped 90 fathoms, or 540 feet, of chain until it all gave out. *Adriatic*, which now rode a single anchor, swung around and struck a Norwegian brig with a thump. Thombs dropped a third anchor to steady *Adriatic*, but a loud cracking sound stopped him. *Adriatic*'s fore works tumbled into the water before she could get clear of the brig. She lost her rigging, rail, bulwarks, cathead, forecastle, bowsprit, jibboom, cutwater, and headsails. Thombs could not help but remember that he had been here before. It had been four years since *Adriatic* lost her fore works to *Le Lyonnais* and survived.

She would not be so lucky again. It was low tide. Enormous swells lifted *Adriatic* out of the water and, when they passed, smashed her against the bottom. The barque took on water. Thombs and his crew tossed cargo overboard and bailed as much water as possible, but they could barely keep her afloat. The men and what remained of the ship held on.

The pampero rolled through them and out to sea. The temperature dropped as the cold winds it brought with it passed through. Thombs assessed the damage. The repair costs would be substantial. He advertised for cash on bottomry. A handful of merchants came to see what remained of *Adriatic* in the harbor, but not one took the gamble that she could survive another ocean crossing. The ship was condemned on August 25, 1860, and sold for scrap to the highest bidder. A massive hurricane devastated Buenos Aires a few days later and destroyed most of the ships in the harbor.

Durham was in Belfast working with Patterson & Carter, the venture his family formed in 1856 to build *Adriatic*, when he learned of *Adriatic*'s loss. He took command of *Laura Russ*, a barque built by the company for James A. Russ in 1856, the same year Patterson & Carter built *Adriatic*. Durham's time with *Laura Russ* was brief. He soon set sail for England to command the ship *Gibraltar*. The law required the captain of a British-flagged vessel to obtain a Master Mariners certificate from the Lords of the Committee of Privy Council for Trade. Durham obtained his certificate March 1862 and spent the next seven years as *Gibraltar*'s captain. His wife lived in Chelsea, Massachusetts, with her family while he navigated *Gibraltar* around the globe.

Thombs returned to Belfast after *Adriatic* sank. His wife gave birth to a son, Charles E. Thombs, in April 1862. The baby died eighteen months later, on December 18, 1863. Thombs was drafted into the Union navy five months after his son's death. He served as acting ensign from May 3, 1864, to July 9, 1865, aboard USS *Flambeau*. It was the first and only time he ever crewed a steamship. The ship joined squadrons in Georgia and Florida and took the schooners *Betty Kratzer* and *John Gilpin* as prizes for the Union in 1864. Thombs participated in the blockade squadrons at Georgetown and Port Royal, South Carolina, for the remainder of the war.

Smith remained in possession of *S. E. Meaher*. John Stephen Martin attempted to untangle his complicated history of debt in France but was unable to do so because Smith could not produce the necessary paperwork from the vessel's owner, Timothy Meaher. Meaher had problems much larger than a wayward schooner with unpaid bills. They stemmed from a voyage made by *S. E. Meaher*'s Gulf schooner sister, *Clotilda*, one that ended with Meaher's federal indictment.

The international slave trade had been abolished in 1808, making the transportation of slaves from foreign ports to America an act of piracy. In 1859, one of Meaher's friends bet him $100 he could not bring slaves from

Africa to Alabama without getting caught. Meaher upped the bet to $1,000 and declared that inside two years he would bring a cargo of human beings from Africa to Mobile Bay. He employed his most trusted captain, William Foster, and his ship *Clotilda* to do it. The vessel arrived months later with 110 enslaved people whom Foster bought in West Africa.

Rumors about the wager alerted federal authorities. Foster, Meaher, and their accomplices transferred the slaves to *Czar* and scuttled *Clotilda* in Mobile Bay. The US government brought federal criminal charges against Meaher and the men who funded the *Clotilda* expedition. Meaher had meticulously documented his travel aboard *Roger B. Taney* during *Clotilda*'s absence, including trips that coincided with the dates *Clotilda* reached Mobile. The government did not have sufficient evidence to link him to the crime and was forced to dismiss the case on the eve of trial. Some historians have posited that the dismissal of this case was the final straw in a series of controversies between federal and local authorities that ignited the Civil War. *Clotilda* lives in infamy as the last American slave ship.[5]

Smith bought *S. E. Meaher*. He distanced himself from the Meaher family and their politics and sought peace in his new marriage, his vessel, and his land on the Sabine River. He sailed for New Orleans in early 1861. Louisiana succeeded from the Union on January 26, 1861, while he was on his way. Confederate officers threatened to imprison any captain who entered the Gulf flying the Union flag.

Smith had sailed under the flag since he took his first voyage from New York to New Bedford. It served as "his pride and comfort on many distant seas."[6] He arrived in New Orleans ignorant of Louisiana's formal declaration of secession and entered the port flying Old Glory high. He did not get far before Confederate forces surrounded his ship and commanded him to lower it. "I will not," Smith answered. "I have sailed under this flag for many years, and it has protected me. I will not do violence to its sanctity."[7] The soldiers explained the situation, but Smith was unmoved. A Confederate sailor boarded the vessel and lowered the flag from its position. Smith did not cooperate, but he knew better than to interfere. The frustrated sailor ripped the flag from the mast and threw it into the water, but it did not sink. It drifted on the surface in silent mockery. This only further incensed the soldiers, who confiscated *S. E. Meaher* and sent Smith for a few days of "reflection" in the local jail.[8]

Smith's act defied not only Louisianan rebels, but *S. E. Meaher*'s former owners. Soldiers burned his home and his business and put his wife, Anna, on a steamboat up the Mississippi River. They ordered him to leave Louisiana. "The Civil War broke out. Half hour later he and Anna were on a boat up the Mississippi. He took only a few clothes and silverware. As they [fled] up the Mississippi by boat, Smith [was] taken prisoner by Confederate forces. Anna continued upriver to Cairo. After a short period of imprisonment, Smith [was] released and [joined] his wife."[9] Smith's rebellion in the Port of New Orleans is the last public mention of the schooner *S. E. Meaher*.

The Smiths arrived in Cairo penniless and had little choice but to settle there. Smith's experience building ships for the Meahers and as a captain who sailed the ocean, the waters of the American South, and the Mobile River made him a marketable employee. He found work as a master mechanic building ironclad ships designed for the US Navy by Samuel L. Pook. The gunboats were intended for service on the Mississippi River and meant to battle Confederate ironclads. Locals dubbed the gunboats "Pook's Turtles" because of their sloped sides and squat appearances. Others referred to the ships as Eads's gunboats for shipyard owner James Buchanan Eads, who risked his fortune to support the Union. Eads built seven gunboats at the Carondelet Marine Ways and Mound City Marine Railway & Shipyard during the time Smith worked there: USS *Cairo*, *Carondelet*, *Cincinnati*, *Louisville*, *Mound City*, *Pittsburg*, and *St. Louis*. Smith registered for the draft in 1863 and worked as a carpenter.

His father died in December 1861, shortly after his arrival in Cairo. He had just lost his home and his ship and could not afford to make the journey to New York. He traveled home again less than two years later to fetch his widowed mother. His niece Ellen Smith Slade, who had been working at a teacher in Geddes, New York, returned to Illinois with them. Smith continued in service as a carpenter until the war ended, after which he started a successful sawmill in Cairo, Smith & Stewart Lumber Dealers. He acquired land in Illinois and in Missouri.

On February 10, 1865, Ellen left Cairo with little warning. She told Smith and Anna that her sister had fallen ill. The truth was that she was having an affair with a married man, Lieutenant Joseph Mitchell. Mitchell came to Cairo, and the two ran away together. Two years later, the Smith family was thrust into the local spotlight when called to testify in *Mitchell v. Mitchell*, Mitchell's divorce proceedings. Lawyers deposed Smith and Anna, who testified to the suspicious circumstances of Mitchell's appearances in Cairo and Ellen's sudden departure. During this time, Smith and his wife adopted a child, William Wallace Smith, named for Smith's late brother. The boy was six years old at the time. Family historians suspect that William was Joseph Mitchell and Ellen Slade's child.

The Civil War ended in April 1865. Thombs was honorably discharged and returned to Belfast. Just eight months later, on December 30, 1865, his wife, Ella, died of quick consumption. They had been separated by the *Adriatic* affair, the sea, and war for more than half their marriage. Thombs resumed work as a merchant seaman. He purchased an ownership interest in the Belfast-built brig *Ocean Wave* and became her captain in 1867.

He sailed *Ocean Wave* from the Satilla River in Georgia on a return voyage to Boston on December 28, 1867. The crew experienced a heavy northeast gale at sea two days later and took on water. Thombs ordered the men to throw the cargo overboard to lighten the ship, but the water overwhelmed them. The men kept two pumps running but could not clear the ship. The waves soon swept everything away, including spars, water casks, and even the galley stove. The gales lasted two weeks, and for two weeks the crew held on. Sudden squalls split their sails on January 16, and *Ocean Wave* took on more water. The crew bailed and worked the pumps around the clock for the next three days, but it was of no use. Thombs knew it was only a matter of time before the vessel sank. He hailed the ship *John Sidney*, and she came to their aid. The exhausted crew abandoned *Ocean Wave*. Many suffered from severe exposure to the elements. By the time they reached the deck of *John Sidney*, the water had reached *Ocean Wave*'s cabin floor, and the brig was a total loss. She was uninsured, and Thombs lost his investment. The following year, he took command of *General Marshall*, a brig once captained by Durham.

Durham's father, Jonathan Sr., died on November 3, 1865, at the age of seventy-five, while Barney was working in England. The family buried him at Grove Cemetery next to his four sons. His tombstone is so close it almost touches the marker he erected eleven years earlier for the three sons he lost at sea.

Durham's stint as a British captain was a lucrative one. His household income increased by 60 percent in the years he sailed *Gibraltar*.[10] He returned home briefly before leaving again for Wales in 1871 in command of *Majestic*. He arrived in Cardiff, Wales, on March 25, 1871, and cleared for departure on April 3.

Thombs remained in Belfast and began work as the captain of the brig *James Miller* in 1871. He married again, on June 17, 1873, to Alice Irene Matthews. Alice gave birth to a daughter, Josie, in 1874 and a son, Joseph Emery, on June 19, 1876. A year later, the couple bought a house on Belmont Street in Belfast. One of Alice's sons from a previous marriage, J. C. Perry, moved in with them. Thombs became captain of the brig *Ned White* and sailed her between New York to ports in the American South and Cuba from 1875 to 1882.

Durham's career slowed as his former mate's flourished. He returned home from England aboard *Atlas* as a passenger in 1873. He and his

CHAPTER 40 | *Fate*

wife continued to reside in Chelsea at the 87 Tudor Street address. He served as the captain of vessels out of England in the mid-1870s. He and his wife spent a year during this time in Mendocino, California, where they bought a parcel of land, but they soon returned home. By the early 1880s, Durham commanded American vessels on coastal routes out of Massachusetts ports.

Durham's mother, Eunice, moved to Chelsea to live with Charles and his family after her husband's death. Durham and his wife lived there too, but after visiting his native Belfast for a summer or two in the mid-1870s, he bought a house on Church Street. Eunice was in her late eighties at the time and traveled between Chelsea and Belfast. A caretaker hired by Charles in Massachusetts, Clara Burrill, traveled with her, which was a great comfort to the family. Eunice died in Massachusetts on April 23, 1887, at the age of ninety-seven. Durham and his brother sailed her body to Belfast, where she was buried alongside her husband and her four sons.

Thombs took a job as the captain of the Belfast-built ship *Cora* from 1883 to 1884. *Cora* left Liverpool on October 26, 1883, bound for Louisiana. She encountered a hurricane rounding Cape Horn on January 14, 1884, and was thrown off her beam ends. She jettisoned more than 400 tons of cargo to right herself and stay afloat. *Cora* arrived in Montevideo on April 12, 1884, leaking badly, and was forced back to Belfast for repairs. The mishap ended Thombs's adventures at sea. He moved to Minneapolis in 1884 and, throughout the late 1880s and most of the 1890s, tried his hand first at real estate and then at mining.

Unlike Thombs and Durham, Smith had long ago given up the sea for the land. He and his family relocated to Oran, Missouri, in 1869, where he expanded his sawmill and acquired 1,000 acres of timber. His business thrived. He donated money and land to his local church, became involved in community affairs, and remained an active member of the Masons. His wife, Anna, died in 1887. He took pen in hand to write his relatives back in New York to inform them of the news. "My home is desolate. What can I say? I wait for the time when, as unworthy as I am, I may be permitted to associate with her in the world beyond the grave. I have lost the one true friend; all that I am I owed her. Oh, how patiently she aided in every living word and work."[11]

Smith could not bear the loneliness of an empty house. He took in a boarder, Louisiana Clemson, and her two children the following year. Their presence renewed his spirit. Smith found love again with "Lou" and married her on September 2, 1889. He cherished her children, Mabel and Georgianna, as his own.

Life at sea was a distant memory, but he thought about the old days from time to time. Smith reached out to his former employer, Timothy Meaher, in 1891. He told him of his marriage and his new business. Meaher was seventy-nine at the time. His son Augustine responded, "Father is much pleased to hear from you but is somewhat surprised to hear that you have become a land lubber."[12]

Durham stopped sailing in the mid-1880s. He and his wife returned to Massachusetts by 1892 and bought a home in Malden, a city north of Boston. His sister Sarah E. Durham Wilson died in 1878, while he was living in Belfast. His other sister, Mary Anna Durham, died in 1892. Charles died in 1898.

Thombs returned to Belfast in August 1899 and moved into a house on the corner of Grove and Church Streets. He was in poor health but still able to work and found a job as a night watchman at a shoe factory. He suffered a heart attack and died in his home on November 29, 1899. He was sixty-five years old.

Thombs family gravesite at Grove Cemetery, Belfast, Maine. *Photo by author*

Smith's eclectic career continued in later life. He became the postmaster of Bleda, Missouri, in 1894. In 1895, he was invited to speak at an exposition on commerce in Oran, where he regaled the audience with the story of the whaling adventure that began his career at sea. His penchant for storytelling ushered in a new occupation as newspaper editor. He was seventy-two years old. "Ward L. Smith is now the editor of the *Madison County Democrat*," another newspaper wrote in response. "The old man is a kicker!"[13] Smith, who taught himself to read and write aboard a whaling schooner, became the editor and co-owner of the paper.

Smith also wrote a column for the *Meridian Star*, where his son-in-law was an editor. His first story, "A Whaling Adventure," appeared in 1900. He later published stories about his tour through eastern Europe during the Crimean War, a ghost story about haunted ships, and one about his escape from Marseille with Captain Durham of the barque *Adriatic*.

Durham never read what Smith wrote about their adventures, but he did see the turn of the century. He lived his later years in Malden with his wife and a live-in nurse. He died of a cerebral embolism on September 3, 1900. He was seventy-three. He left behind no children. His wife lived to be ninety-four and was buried in a family grave next to her husband in Malden's Woodlawn Cemetery.

Ward L. Smith, May 4, 1890.
Courtesy of Historic Mobile Preservation Society

Durham was lifetime member of the Boston Marine Society and the Masons. His obituary noted, "He was well known in marine circles and during the 35 years he followed the sea he commanded some of the best ships from Boston to New York."[14] The *Belfast Republican Journal* devoted one of the ten paragraphs in his obituary to his accomplishments, and nine to the *Adriatic* affair.

Ward L. Smith outlived them all. He experienced a setback in April 1900, when he suffered excruciating pain in one of his eyes. Doctors removed the eye in August 1900, which eased his suffering, and he bounced back. He visited the St. Louis World's Fair with Lou in 1904 and, in 1905, traveled to New York to visit relatives. It was the last time he went home.

Smith lived his remaining years in Fredericktown, Missouri, surrounded by Lou, her daughters, and a network of friends. He fell ill in July 1907 and never recovered. He died on August 27, 1907, at the age of eighty-two. His obituary called him

> one of the most remarkable men of his generation—a rare combination of mental, moral, and physical strength expressed in a long life of struggle and achievement, illuminated by a sturdy integrity, a fine moral sense and a wonderful serenity of temper and disposition.... He died loved by his neighbors, honored by acquaintances, and universally trusted. His end was one eminently benefiting from the life he lived, achieving that love and honor that was the just reward of an unconscious endeavor.[15]

Captain Smith and Captain Durham saw one another only once after they escaped France and parted company off the coast of Tarragona, Spain. It was in late August 1858. *Adriatic* set sail for Providence, Rhode Island, from New Haven, England, with a load of coal. Before Durham left Europe, he sent Smith an invitation to join him there for "a good long chat."[16]

Providence in the 1850s was home to some of the largest manufacturing plants in the country. Multistory factories with stacks that pumped out columns of black smoke lined the city's interior. Ships awaiting goods churned out by those factories lined the waterfront.

The scenery did not impress Smith. It was nothing like his beloved South or even picturesque Marseille. The view was a little better by the water, where swaths of greenish sand separated the colorless city streets from the Providence River. "It's always better by the water," Smith thought to himself. It was a warm day, and people strolled about the riverbank. Men wore large-brimmed hats and women raised their parasols to protect themselves from the blazing sun. Smith passed them as he made his way. His gait was more purposeful than theirs as he searched the waterfront for his friend's ship.

He spotted *Adriatic* immediately. She had new rigging and sails, but her clipper-like shape was unmistakable. "Barney!" Smith hollered. Durham disembarked from the ship with the same spring in his step that Smith had always admired. Durham threw out his arms, embraced his old friend, and motioned for him to come aboard. It felt to Smith like being home again.

The men spent several days aboard *Adriatic*. It had been little more than six months since their escape from France, but so much had happened to each of them since. They exchanged stories and gossip. Durham began with the most important question. He asked, using his best impression of a French accent, "What did the Frenchmen have to say about the *grand voleur* American?"[17] Smith let out an enormous laugh before he launched into the story with characteristic wit and detail.

Durham was eager to hear about his friends in Marseille. He inquired about Martin, Aicard, and even Morgan. He asked about Baker and McGregor, the men whom Smith enlisted to ship *Adriatic*'s crew. He entertained Smith with stories about his arrival at Savannah, his summons to Washington, and his recent travels.

Smith told Durham about his time under the Spanish fisherman's nets, his narrow escape from Barcelona, and the British diplomat who came to his aid. He talked about the dinner with the French captains who sided with Durham. He asked about Thombs. He spoke about the piracy

CHAPTER 40 | Fate

> North Shields June 20 1858
>
> Dear Smith I received your letter on the 1st and I do not think that I am so much to blame for not writing as you think I am for I have not received but one letter from you and that was sent to me at Savannah and was written only a few days after your arrival at Marseille so you see that I did not know whether you was in Marseille or not I am all ready for sea and shall sail tomorrow bound to Providence and if this should reach you before you leave write me there give me the name of the ship if you go in a sail vessel and if you come to Boston or New York I will come on and see you or you must come and see me for I want to have a good long chat with you about all my friends in Marseille and hear what the Frenchmen say about the grand voleur american do you plague Baker as much as you used to when you was on board the Adriatic remember to Mr Baker and tell him I am in hopes that we may again under different circumstances as I write

Letter from Durham to Smith, June 20, 1858. *Courtesy of Historic Mobile Preservation Society*

309

> before if there is any thing that I can do for you don't be bashful about asking, for I will do it with pleasure give my respects to Mr Martin and tell him his old bark the Garland is here loading for Buenos Ayers there is a Dutchman in her now I have nothing further to write at present direct your letters to the care of my Brother at Chelsea
>
> Your Truly J B Durham

trial and the absence of key witnesses. If any secrets about the escape were exchanged at Providence, the men took them to their graves.

Talk soon turned to their plans. Smith was headed south and then to New York to spend time with the family he had not seen in almost fifteen years. Durham prepared to set to sea with *Adriatic* to rebuild what Marseille had cost him, and to start his family business anew. Time stopped for both men during the visit, but soon it was time to move on.

Smith disembarked from *Adriatic* and stepped out onto the dock below. He turned and looked up at his old friend. "I hope I will see you again soon," yelled Durham with a wave of his hand and the same broad smile Smith had seen him flash to so many people so many times before. Smith waved back in response. He hoped he might see Durham again one day, but he doubted it. He paused and smiled back at him before he turned and walked away.

Smith walked along the water's edge and past ships coming from and going to all parts of the world. "It's a funny thing," he thought to himself. Just six months ago, his life and Durham's were intertwined. They calculated every move together. Their mission was focused, their purpose singular. They were brothers united in a common objective, but all that was over now. Smith stopped walking as the thought sank in—how soon men return to who they once were.

CHAPTER 40 | *Fate*

He looked over his shoulder and took one last look at *Adriatic*. She hung there silhouetted against the morning sun as if already transforming into a distant memory. He turned around and started to move forward again. He did not look back a second time. He lost all knowledge of Durham after Providence in the summer of 1858 and never saw or heard from him again.

Durham enjoyed seeing his old friend but did not dwell on the visit. He had things to do. He discharged his cargo of coal at the Providence docks. He soon accepted a charter of lumber bound for Buenos Aires and was gone again in a week's time.

Epilogue

Everything Is Possible:
The 2024 Le Lyonnais Discovery

KURT MINTELL SHOOK ME AWAKE, the signal that it was my turn for the night's watch. "2:30 a.m. already?" I thought as I rolled out of my bunk, pulled on a flannel shirt, and met him at the helm for a briefing. "Anything happening?" I asked. The answer was the same as the one he had received from the crewman before him and the crewman before him had received before that: "Nothing." He shook his head. "I haven't seen another boat all night."

Kurt shuffled to his bunk, and I undertook my watch ritual. It started by confirming the absence of other ships and noting the wind and weather—15 knots out of the southwest. Then came the music. I popped one headphone into my left ear and kept the right ear open to listen out for the radio or other alarms.

It was early in the morning on September 6, 2023. The night was an uncomfortable one. Hurricane Idalia, which had recently ravaged the Florida coast, now churned as a low-pressure system to our east. The storm no longer posed much of a threat but still kicked up swells large enough to rock the boat from side to side over and over and over again. The wind now blew a steady 18 knots, with gusts of 20 or more thrown in for good measure. It was what our captain, Joe Mazraani, refers to as "a bump." "Bump" is a charitable way of saying that the weather is going to be miserable during certain points of the trip but not quite miserable enough to stop the team from getting the job done.

I steadied myself and stepped out onto the deck under a pitch-black sky. We were far from land, farther than our dive vessel *Tenacious* had ever been before. Ambient light from the cities and towns that brightened the night skies of the East Coast of the United States could not reach us where we were. Frankly, not much could reach us where we were.

The night clamped down in all directions, and the water was as black as the sky. A seamless circle of darkness engulfed the boat and set the stage for the planets and the stars. The current working against the anchor held us parallel to the luminous band of the Milky Way. I looked up and saw the galaxy's white threads, formed from stars so numerous they could not be discerned by the naked eye. They cascaded overhead and stretched beyond our stern to an invisible horizon where the sky melted into water.

The Milky Way's lights were the brightest I had ever seen them. Gas clouds and radiant white stars with hints of pale blue and copper spun on the horizon.

I followed the galaxy's arc with my eyes. It danced overhead and dissolved far off the point of our bow into the black ocean.

It takes tens of thousands of years for the light from these stars to reach the earth; tens of thousands of years for it to cross the galaxy; tens of thousands of years for the light to reveal itself to a woman standing on the deck of a small boat at anchor in the vast North Atlantic. Staring at the Milky Way is staring into the past.

Shipwreck hunting is staring into the past too. It may not have been tens of thousands of years, but, in this case, it was a couple of hundred. *Le Lyonnais*'s story began in a Birkenhead shipyard in the mid-1850s. The story of what happened on August 23, 2024, when we knew we had found her again after a 167-year absence, began decades ago.

Captain Eric Takakjian and his dog Violet in his Fairhaven, Massachusetts office on April 24, 2022, during a meeting to plan the search for *Le Lyonnais*. Photo by author

Epilogue

Captain Eric Takakjian has spent much of his life hunting shipwrecks off the Massachusetts coast. A professional master captain of oceangoing tugs and barges engaged in the coastwise petroleum transportation trade, Eric is also an historian, storyteller, author, shipbuilder, craftsman, and walking maritime encyclopedia. He stands 5 feet, 7 inches tall. His unassuming stature matches his quiet disposition, but not a single detail gets by him. He is credited with the discovery of more than seventy shipwrecks.

In the 1990s, Eric discovered and located the remains of four of five vessels that were sunk by German submarine *U-53* off the coast of Nantucket in 1916. *U-53*'s commander, Hans Rose, made an unannounced visit to the United States Second Naval District in Newport Harbor on October 7, 1916. After the visit, during which Rose gave the American navy and members of the public tours of his U-boat, he set to sea. He sank five ships south of Nantucket the next day. America had not yet entered World War I. Powerless to retaliate, the American military could only watch as Hans Rose sent ally-flagged ships SS *Strathdene*, *West Point*, *Christian Knudsen*, *Bloomersdijk*, and *Stephano* to the bottom. It was in the early 1990s, while doing research about the *U-53* wrecks, that Eric came across a reference to the ill-fated *Le Lyonnais*.

Eric met Joe Mazraani in the mid-2000s. Joe was an up-and-coming New Jersey–based diver, a lawyer who spent some of his weekends captaining Gene Holmes's New Jersey–based dive boat, *Home Wrecker*. Joe was young and eager, and Eric was doing what he had always dreamed of—finding new wrecks and pushing the boundaries of distance and depth to reach them. Mutual friend and veteran diver Steve Gatto orchestrated an introduction, and Joe soon began making dive expeditions with Eric on his boat R/V *Quest*. Joe, Steve, and diver Tom Packer, another North Atlantic wreck-diving pioneer, regularly made the drive from New Jersey to Fairhaven, Massachusetts, to join Eric on searches for new shipwrecks during the 1990s and first decade of the 2000s.

Shipwreck hunting is a combination of painstaking research, ever-changing technology, data analysis, and a fair amount of luck. At its core, it involves finding and examining anomalies on the seabed. This can be done with either sonar equipment or a bottom sounder, a simpler but effective way of determining the height of objects below the boat on the ocean floor.

Eric combined regular dive trips with wreck hunting. Sometimes he dedicated entire trips to a search, but, more often, he would take a few detours on the way home from a dive expedition and run his bottom sounder over areas of interest. *Le Lyonnais* was one of the targets on his mind in the late first decade of the 2000s, and it was from Eric that Joe first heard about the wreck. From 2006 to 2010, Eric examined various locations around the Nantucket Shoals. He dedicated a 2009 search trip to looking for *Le Lyonnais* but had no luck. With him on that trip were Steve Gatto, Tom Packer, Pat Rooney, Paul Whittaker, and a young Joe Mazraani.

Sometimes a project catches fire and becomes an obsession for a member of the team. Other times it does not and becomes more of a back-burner project, something that remains on the list until another piece of the puzzle comes along. *Le Lyonnais* never caught fire with a team that already had so much to do, and so, after 2010, Eric shelved *Le Lyonnais*.

Although that project languished, others proceeded. Eric brought Joe with him when he located and identified the wreckage of SS *Newcastle City*, SS *Sagaland*, and other Nantucket shipwrecks. Joe soaked it all in—not just the experience, but how Eric ran a boat, how he conducted research, and how he systematically combed the ocean for sunken vessels. He learned everything he could from Eric, who was generous with his knowledge and time. Eric became Joe's mentor. It is not an understatement to say that much of what Joe knows about running a dive boat and leading a crew comes from Eric.

When Joe was not with Eric, he took turns as *Home Wrecker*'s captain, exploring New Jersey's numerous shipwrecks and salvaging artifacts from them. The New Jersey coast is littered with shipwrecks, many of them World War I and World War II casualties. Diving these wrecks is not for the faint of heart. Water conditions, poor visibility, and depth make the dives challenging but also provide a training ground for divers who want to advance. Wrecks closer to shore, especially the deeper ones, lie in an area that divers and fisherman refer to as "the Mud Hole," a Hudson River outflow notorious for its muddy bottom and poor visibility. The water is cold and dark. Visibility rarely exceeds 10 feet and can often be less than 5.

One day in 2007, Joe announced that he was going to salvage the massive 6.5-foot-diameter auxiliary stern helm from a local favorite, SS *Ayuruoca*. *Ayuruoca*, originally named *Roland*, was a cargo ship built in 1912 by Akt Ges Wessner in Bremen, Germany. On June 6, 1945, she was bound for Rio de Janeiro when she collided with the Norwegian vessel SS *General Fleisher*. *Ayuruoca* rests in the Mud Hole at a depth of approximately 170 feet.

The problem was that the helm was firmly affixed in place. It had a large diameter and an oversized shaft because it was built to turn the rudder under muscle power in the event of a steering failure. The helm was contained on three sides by doghouses and under a steel shroud, which covered the shaft and bearing. A gun tub placed aboard the vessel during World War II loomed overhead. The team came together and strategized a way to free the helm, but they needed a boat to conduct the systematic work the project demanded. Joe bought one as the final piece of the project.

It took problem-solving, blood, sweat, and even some tears to get the job done, but the team accomplished its goal and raised *Ayuruoca*'s helm aboard Joe's new boat on November 15, 2010. Diver Harold Moyers later wrote, "The big helm was one of the most well-known, most sought-after artifacts in the Hole. [Other] helms disappeared quickly. This helm resisted all efforts for over forty years. The team was proud to be there, and Captain Joe 'Tenacious' Mazraani earned our respect, as well as his new nickname."

Joe christened his new 45-foot NOVI-built dive vessel *Tenacious*. She had previously worked as a fishing boat out of Maryland, but Joe remodeled her into a multiday offshore vessel with a dive platform and equipment for locating, exploring, and salvaging shipwrecks.

Raising the helm was only the beginning. Joe soon began exploring wrecks that charter dive boats in the area rarely frequented. These expeditions were preparation for another project he had in mind, the search for a wreck that had consumed Eric and many other divers and historians throughout the years: *U-550*, a submarine then touted as the last German U-boat known to rest in diveable North Atlantic waters. *U-550* sank far off the coast of Nantucket, and hunting her would take coordinated expeditions far from the safety of shore. This U-boat was elusive. Well-known wreck hunters had searched for her, some for more than two decades, without success. The competition to find her heightened in the late first decade of the 2000s, when Joe and other teams of divers reignited their searches.

Joe poured himself into the project and worked with a team that included Eric, Steve, Tom, diver/photographer Brad Sheard, Harold, diver Anthony Tedeschi, and others. When the team knew they were close, they enlisted the assistance of friend and world-renowned sonar operator Garry Kozak. Kozak joined the crew on sonar searches for *U-550* in July 2011 and July 2012. Joe took *Tenacious* farther from home than she had ever been during those voyages. On July 23, 2012, less than two years after Joe bought his boat, the team located *U-550* and the stern remains of her last victim, SS *Pan Pennsylvania*. It was *Tenacious*'s first big conquest.

I met Joe two years later, in 2014. Both of us are criminal defense lawyers by profession, and we met in court. We became fast friends and eventually fell in love and embarked on a life together. Loving a diver is not easy. Loving a wreck-hunting diver and boat captain asks the impossible. The pursuit and exploration of sunken shipwrecks is more than a hobby; it is a way of life that consumes endless hours of effort and attention. Boat maintenance, gear, and research devour energy, passion, and spare time at a rate most relationships cannot endure. I did not realize it then, but I waded into Joe's life at the time when he and *Tenacious* were making their mark in a universe I did not yet understand.

I knew nothing of shipwrecks or boats or diving when I met Joe, but the universe intrigued me. It was one of sunken ships, buried treasure, and adventure. Joe's friends were captains and explorers. What struck me most about them was how fully they lived their lives. None of them wasted a second. They embraced every opportunity to explore places no one else had ever been, and pushed their minds and their bodies to, quite literally, cross new horizons.

And then there was the other woman, *Tenacious*. She had been a part of Joe's life for more than four years before me, and Joe had transformed her into exactly what he wanted her to be. Their relationship was perfect. It did not take long for me to realize that *Tenacious* was Joe's first love, and loving him meant doing more than accepting her but making peace with knowing I could share him but never compete. I began going on dive trips with Joe and the team not so much because I was interested in diving but as a way of understanding and being a part of his world.

What I came to learn is that Joe loves *Tenacious*. He also loves me. He loves us both wholly and completely, not unlike the way a man's heart expands enough to love both their partner and their child. Committing to Joe meant sharing him with an obsession no relationship could replace. The acceptance brought us closer and paved the way for an obsession of my own. It was not the diving that got me hooked; it was the stories. I soon came to be as fascinated with the history of the shipwrecks that *Tenacious* visited and the stories of those who lived and died aboard them. I started helping Joe and the team tell those stories at museum talks and conferences.

One day in early 2016, I asked Joe if I could help research an undiscovered shipwreck. "Yeah. Find out what you can about a ship called *Le Lyonnais*," he answered. He did not give it much thought. It was just the first back-burnered ship that popped into his head. By the end of the weekend, I had amassed a stack of articles and documents, some of which those who had looked for *Le Lyonnais* before had never seen. "Send these to Eric," Joe said, "and keep going." I did. The research was not nearly enough to find the ship, but my excitement moved *Le Lyonnais* closer to the front burner.

Epilogue

So did my naiveté. I had absolutely no idea what I was doing when we started. Joe arranged an email introduction to Eric, and he and I exchanged messages about *Le Lyonnais*. We did not meet in person until 2017 at a Boston Sea Rovers dive conference. Joe introduced me to him in an aisle on the busy exposition floor and then disappeared. There, between a booth selling brightly colored dive socks and one offering vacations to Cozumel, Eric and I had our first real conversation about *Le Lyonnais*. I was terrified. I was so afraid of saying something stupid that I barely remember the words that passed between us. *Le Lyonnais* research had consumed me for more than a year, but I had little experience at sea and no experience hunting shipwrecks. I feared that a professional captain who had discovered so many sunken vessels would not take me seriously. I could not have been more wrong. Eric was kind and encouraging and welcomed me with open arms into a project he had begun decades ago. Although we did not say it, in that meeting we silently committed to finding this lost ship. We dubbed the endeavor "Project Mayonnaise," an obvious nod to the ship's name.

I scoured documents and embarked on several more years of research. Project Mayonnaise emails flew back and forth regularly. There were trips to archives, museums, and historical societies. I traveled to Mobile, Alabama, in search of information about Captain Ward Smith. Bob Peck of the Historic Mobile Preservation Society opened the closed museum for me on Mardis Gras, and we spent the day sorting through a bag of documents one of Smith's relatives had dropped off years ago. I paged through Smith's logbook and held in my hand the letter that Captain Durham sent to Captain Smith after their escape from Marseille. Martin Cleaver, at the Wirral Archives in Birkenhead, helped me reconstruct what *Le Lyonnais* looked like. We worked via an email exchange that began in 2018 and lasted well into 2024. Researchers from around the world contributed pieces to a puzzle that spanned more than 150 years.

Clues to *Le Lyonnais*'s whereabouts were few and far between. I more often bent Joe's and Eric's ears about the lives of those who traveled aboard her. "That's not going to help find it," Joe would say, but I could not let the stories go. I began to separate information I uncovered into two categories: clues to location and backstory.

Each year that followed, Joe and I made a trip to Eric's house in Fairhaven, Massachusetts, and spent a day or two discussing clues amassed the preceding year. The meetings took place in "the bunker," my nickname for Eric's office. A detached structure decorated with artifacts from some of Massachusetts's most famous shipwrecks, the bunker is an archive of books, charts, photographs, and other documents that

Eric has collected over the years, set on shelves he made by hand in his woodworking studio. Once a year, usually in December or January, we huddled around Eric's charting table and watched as he plotted new information by hand on enormous charts of the Atlantic Ocean. I thought our first Project Mayonnaise bunker meeting was successful until Eric pronounced that we had narrowed our search area down to 100 square miles. "A needle in a haystack," Joe replied.

A needle in a haystack. If I had a dollar for every time Joe called *Le Lyonnais* a "needle in a haystack," I would be a wealthy woman. He used the phrase to temper my excitement before I understood just how difficult it is to find a shipwreck. The ocean is vast and constantly moving. Ships rarely sink in their last reported position, so finding any wreck is a significant accomplishment. Modern ships can be easier to find because there is more information about where they sank. For example, when searching for a World War II wreck, there are often US military records, radio transmission, firsthand accounts, German U-boat records, American navy and coast guard reports, approximate coordinates, and even living survivors.

More-modern ships are also likely to be larger and less broken down. All ships fall victim to North Atlantic storms and shifting sands. Fishermen dragging nets and dredges can and often do rip shipwrecks apart. The longer a ship sits on the ocean floor, the more camouflaged and damaged it becomes.

Le Lyonnais sank in 1856, a time when captains used stars for navigation and measured their speed by using a chip of wood and a line of knotted rope. They did not report their positions in coordinates, but rather estimates of how far they were from a mark on land or at sea. The ship was made of wood covered by iron plating and sank in an area frequented by draggers and dredge fishermen. She was not just a needle in a haystack. She was a shot in the dark.

Newspapers reported that *Le Lyonnais* sank anywhere between 40 and 60 miles from Nantucket's South Shoal. Eric and his R/V *Quest* team operated on those reports in the late first decade of the 2000s. In 2019, I uncovered a document that put the collision site farther east. The problem was that it did not correspond with other information provided by survivors. We turned to the backstory. We went beyond the reported facts and examined the motive of each person who told the story of the collision and when. We took a calculated risk and changed our search area on the basis of what we believed was deceptive testimony provided to French courts. The small change made the other clues make sense.

Epilogue

We plotted the new information in the winter of 2019–20, and the circle Eric had previously drawn around the search area drew tight enough for us to start planning a search trip. I was elated. We could finally move from the bunker to the open sea!

Joe waited until we got into our car to break the news. The expression on his face was grim and his voice firm when he spoke the words "She's too far." The new information put *Le Lyonnais* much farther than *Tenacious* could safely reach. My heart sank. "Is she off the shelf?" I asked, referring to the continental shelf, where depths in the Atlantic Ocean drop abruptly from a diveable 400 feet to undiveable 1,000s. "I don't think so," he responded. We both sat in silent realization that diveable and doable were not always the same. It was several miles before either of us spoke again.

Eric and Joe determined that the ship's final resting place was on the eastern edges of Georges Bank, a large, elevated area of the seafloor that lies between Cape Cod, Massachusetts, and Cape Sable Island, Nova Scotia. Georges Bank is considered part of the continental shelf and separates the Gulf of Maine from the Atlantic Ocean. It is 200 miles from New Bedford, our summer launch point for Nantucket Shoals trips. A distance of 200 miles is far for a vessel *Tenacious*'s size. It 2020, it might as well have been a million miles away.

Hollow. That is the best way to describe the way I felt after the 2020 meeting. I had spent much of 2018 and 2019 digging into the lives of those who had perished aboard *Le Lyonnais*, and I felt I owed it to them not only to tell their story but to find the place where they spent their final moments. The thought of one day finding the shipwreck kept me going. Between 2016 and 2020, I learned to dive, started spending more time aboard the boat, and earned my captain's license—anything to help contribute more to the project. The thought of it all ending without a search was devastating. I decided to finish the book. If we could not find the ship's final resting place, the least I could do was tell the story that had long been the source of my inspiration. It was cold comfort, but I kept the depth of my disappointment from Eric and Joe.

Le Lyonnais was not the only project on their minds. They had long wanted to find the last of the *U-53* wrecks. Eric and his team found and dived four of the five wrecks in the mid-1990s, but the locations far offshore and dive technology at the time made thorough exploration and documentation difficult. During the 2017 and 2018 dive seasons, we revisited the *U-53* wrecks aboard *Tenacious* to determine which wreck was still missing.

Andrew Donn splashing on *Le Lyonnais* in a rebreather with two bailout bottles. *Photo by author*

Epilogue

Diving has changed a lot since the 1990s. Today, our divers use closed-circuit rebreathers, technology that greatly increases the time and safety of deep dives. We often dive to depths between 200 and 400 feet. Unlike open circuit diving, in which the diver is limited by the amount of gas in the tanks they carry, rebreathers "recycle" harmful carbon dioxide and make gas expelled by the diver breathable again. This allows the diver longer bottom times—time at the depth of the wreck. The scrubbers that remove carbon dioxide from expelled gas last anywhere from four to eight hours, so rebreather divers are not limited as much by how much gas they carry but by the amount of decompression they are willing to endure and the amount of emergency backup gas, or bailout, required. The *U-53* wrecks lie at depths between 160 and 270 feet. Strong currents plague the shallower ones. Rebreathers allowed our 2017 and 2018 team to spend more time exploring the ships than was possible decades earlier. The team positively identified the remains of *Strathdene*, *Christian Knudsen*, *Bloomersdijk*, and *Stephano* and concluded that *West Point* remained undiscovered. Joe, working in collaboration with Eric, embarked on a mission to find her.

We bought a side-scan sonar system in the summer of 2020 and modified the boat to accommodate it. Sonar uses multiple physical sensors, called a transducer array, to send and receive acoustic pulses to detect objects on the seafloor. The integration of the sonar system prepared us to scan large swaths of ocean for the missing wreck. We put it to the test and mounted our first search for *West Point* in August 2020.

Once again, we took the boat farther than she had been, approximately 130 miles from our launch at Montauk Point, Long Island. We did not find what we were looking for, but we got a feel for the new equipment and tested our fuel capacity for longer expeditions that incorporated both diving and sonar operations.

We planned a second expedition in September 2020, with two objectives. The first was to search for *West Point*. The second was to scan and dive what members of the team believed to be the bow wreckage of MS *Stockholm*, the vessel that collided with and sank the Italian ocean liner SS *Andrea Doria* in 1956. *Stockholm* lost her bow in the collision but limped to shore carrying survivors. Steve Gatto, Tom Packer, and John Moyer, *Andrea Doria*'s salvors in possession, believed that a portion of *Stockholm*'s bow sheared off and sank in a large chunk.

It was a successful mission. We dived and identified *Stockholm*'s bow remains on September 8, 2020. One day later, we located SS *West Point* using side-scan sonar and dived her to confirm the identification.

Joe is driven but measured, a man who never lets emotions dictate decisions, especially when it comes to *Tenacious*. It is one of the many qualities that make him a trustworthy captain, but the *West Point* project was different. Scanning trips require not only fuel capacity and speed to reach the site but fuel to power the boat, sometimes for days at a time, while scanning the ocean floor. The second trip required more fuel and more days at sea. *West Point* was at the fringes of our range for this type of work, but Joe was uncharacteristically passionate about making it happen.

In the days leading up to the search, he spoke often about Eric and the time, effort, and research he had put into the *U-53* wrecks and about all Eric had taught him. It was as though the mission of finding Hans Rose's last victim had been entrusted to him. It became clear to me that the search for SS *West Point* was about more than finding a missing World War I casualty—it was about the student completing the work of his mentor.

Finding SS *West Point* was bittersweet for me. When I watched the sonar record of the broken freighter crawl across our computer screen, I was elated for the team. Closing the *U-53* chapter was exciting, but the expedition pushed us to our limits. We estimated that *Le Lyonnais* was much farther east. Finding *West Point* was a sobering reminder that the French liner remained too far out of reach.

Anyone who knows Joe knows that modifying any challenge with the word "too" is not in his vocabulary. *Ayuruoca*'s helm was not "too difficult" to remove. *U-550* was not "too elusive" to find. *West Point* was not "too difficult" a search. If Joe Mazraani has a defining characteristic, it is turning the impossible into the ordinary. It is just who he is. It took him only a few weeks to decide that "too far" was just another in a series of surmountable obstacles.

Tenacious needed to go much farther than 130 miles offshore to reach *Le Lyonnais*. This meant better fuel efficiency to operate hundreds of miles offshore and tools that made it easier for the crew to work together to scan large swaths of ocean. Joe confided a plan to me about a month later. It involved repowering the boat to push her beyond where she had ever gone for longer than she had ever been to sea.

We got to work in the winter of 2021–22. Joe and a team of professionals too numerous to count repowered the boat to increase her capabilities and cover greater distances. He spent every waking hour refitting the boat for a goal he shared with only those closest to him: to reach *Le Lyonnais*.

Just the idea of it was madness. *Andrea Doria* is less than half the distance to *Le Lyonnais*, and most consider it a dangerous operation for a vessel of *Tenacious*'s size. We planned to go the distance alone in a 45-foot boat with a single engine. Not only did we plan to go there, but to stay offshore for a week at a time, combing the ocean floor for the wreck while turning the propeller and burning fuel. Success meant conducting dive operations in deep, current-laden water in a location so remote that there are no tide tables or even anecdotal information about dive conditions, and so far away from land that there would be no meaningful chance of rescue if something went wrong.

Transforming *Tenacious* was a massive undertaking. For six straight months, Joe went to the boat around three o'clock in the morning, came home and prepared for work at his law office, went to work, went back to the boat, and came home well after ten o'clock in the evening. It was all I could do to hold down our home and my job and continue doing everything else both of our lives required. The impossible goal slowly moved into reach, but reaching it tested our strength. We made it through and put the new and improved *Tenacious* to sea in July 2022.

If you ask most people how they know their partner loves them, they will answer with the obvious—simple words and deeds that show care, concern, and compassion. How do I know Joe Mazraani loves me? The answer is a brand-new single D11-725 Volvo Penta engine, an upgrade to a 700-gallon fuel capacity, and the balls to take a 45-foot Novi 200 miles from New Bedford to the edge of Georges Bank.

"You can't run a boat by yourself. You can't salvage artifacts by yourself. You can't hunt wrecks by yourself." I have heard Joe say that a thousand times, but I never knew what it meant until we went through this project. Although only a handful of people embarked on the searches for *Le Lyonnais*, so many people made it possible—researchers from around the world, mechanics and laborers who converted the boat, historians who poured over data, friends who lent Joe a hand with rebuilding the boat, and even fishermen who provided us with critical pieces of the puzzle.

Fishermen are the unsung heroes of wreck hunting. Their business requires them to drag nets and dredges across the ocean floor. Sometimes that equipment crashes into or catches onto an anomaly that costs them precious time and expensive gear. They record the locations to avoid losing another piece of gear in the future, and those recordings provide clues to the locations of sunken ships. Eric collected "hang logs" from fishermen throughout the years. Joe added new data he collected from contacts of his own. The result is a database that contains more than 150,000 locations where East Coast fishermen have gotten hung up on the ocean floor, all of which are potential wrecks. The secret to wreck hunting is matching the historical data to those hangs. Matching a wreck to one of those hundreds of thousands of points is finding the needle in the haystack. We readied ourselves to do so in search of *Le Lyonnais*.

We assembled a team. I had participated in other search expeditions, but this is the first time I helped lead one. Choosing the right team was important. Wreck hunters, especially those of us who operate in water where the salvage of shipwreck artifacts is legal, are an interesting lot. We often joke about being modern-day pirates, but the comparison is not far off. Pirates are known to work together until working alone better suits them. For some divers, the pursuit of artifacts is more important than understanding and documenting the historical importance of a shipwreck. I had come to feel responsible for those who lived and died aboard *Le Lyonnais*. If we were to find her, I wanted to share that experience with people who would appreciate her story and, when the time came, prioritize the team's objectives over their own. Rick Simon, Andrew Donn, and Joe St. Amand, divers who fit that description, rounded out a 2022 team that already included Joe, Eric, and me. We headed east together in September 2022.

When most people think of hunting for shipwrecks, they think of pirates racing to exotic locations and leather maps marked with the letter "X." Real shipwreck hunting is boring and more arduous. It consists of towing sonar equipment, referred to as "a fish" or "towfish," behind a boat on an armored cable for hours at slow speeds—between 3 and 5 knots—for hours on end. "Mowing the lawn," they call it. The helmsman drives the boat back and forth over predetermined search areas while everyone else stares at a computer screen at an endless stream of acoustic "images" of the ocean floor. Sonar operators refer to what appear as images as "records" because they comprise sound waves rather than pictures. Rust- and yellow-colored lines and dots and the occasional shadow roll continuously from the top of the screen to the bottom. "The Sand and Rock channel," is what Rick Simon dubbed it. Drink coffee. Watch Sand and Rock channel. Eat. Sleep. Repeat.

Our search grids contained multiple lines, like yard lines on a football field. The time it took to complete each grid depended on the number and length of those lines. It also depended on the turns. The sonar cable extended far behind the boat, sometimes 600 feet or more, and made the turning radius wider. It often took as long to complete the turns as it did to complete a line.

We had flat calm conditions in 2022, which made operating the boat and the sonar much easier than it would have been in normal North Atlantic weather. We searched several grids and found one promising new shipwreck. It was obvious to us that it was not *Le Lyonnais*, but it was an accomplishment. We also learned some things. Our data and search grids were not well organized, our sonar had limitations, and we were still missing critical details about *Le Lyonnais*.

Epilogue

We went back to the drawing board and, in the winter of 2023, transitioned to an EdgeTech 4205 tri-frequency sonar. Its software made it much easier to operate the system in difficult seas, and the tri-frequency capability produced better, clearer images. Longtime friend and sonar operator Garry Kozak, who was with the team on the search for *U-550*, spent hours teaching Joe and me how to use the new system and how to interpret data, create better search grids, and make the best possible records.

Joe reorganized the hang logs into a more efficient database and added thousands of marks to it. I focused on research, which included going through historical documents, newspaper accounts, and court documents to pull from them anything we might have previously overlooked. We knew that *Le Lyonnais* drifted before she sank, so I focused on looking for any indications of wind and weather in survivor reports. Joe and I spent too many Sunday mornings going over the data. I sat behind my computer and read him dates, times, and weather references, while he sat at a different computer and manipulated the information into new search grids. We shared the data with Eric, who added his experience and insight.

Seafolk are superstitious people, and Joe and I had our share of signs along the way. We visited Captain Durham's grave in Everett, Massachusetts, shortly after we returned from the 2022 search. His final resting place is Woodlawn Cemetery, a garden-like expanse built in the 1850s and known for its beautiful landscaping, its Richardsonian Romanesque architecture, and the historical figures interred there. The cemetery is surrounded by the bustling town of Everett, an urban atmosphere that disappears beyond the cemetery's ornate gate. Durham's grave, located in Woodlawn's older section, was immaculate. We wondered if someone had recently cleaned it—maybe a family member who could provide another clue—but later learned that the groundskeepers pay extra attention to maintaining historic headstones.

D/V *Tenacious*'s long-time project manager, Joel Garcia, lining up the new engine for installation. *Photo by and courtesy of Joe Mazraani*

Joe Mazraani in front of Captain Jonathan Barnet Durham's grave in October 2022. *Photo by author*

We approached the marker and greeted the captain. There was nothing specific on my mind as I stood before his grave. Durham remained a stranger about whom I had so many unanswered questions. After I photographed his headstone, Joe approached. He did not speak, but he was concentrating. He pronounced that he was finished, and we went on our way. "What was that all about? I asked. Joe replied, "I asked Durham how to find the wreck." "And?" I laughed. "He said it's farther south." I shrugged. Later, on those mornings Joe and I spent going over weather data and plotting, one of us would say to the other, "But Durham said it was farther south," as if it were a fact rather than a projection of what Joe's gut was telling him about *Le Lyonnais*'s final resting place.

I was never one to believe in signs, but my father, Rudolph Sellitti, always did. He served in the Navy during the Korean War. He had orders to serve aboard USS *Midway*, but they were changed at the last minute, and he spent his five years of wartime service as a clerk in a Virginia supply depot. He loved the sea and military history and always regretted not serving aboard a ship. He was ninety-two in 2022 but followed *Tenacious* and all her adventures. Every time I got a new clue about *Le Lyonnais*, we discussed it. He was sharp as a tack, especially for a man of his age, and full of advice on how to research the ship and tell her story. I called him after our trip to Durham's grave and joked about the voice Joe thought he heard in his head, the one that told him the wreck was farther south. My father stopped me. "Believe in the signs, Jenny," he said in the tone he reserved for serious things. "Everything is possible."

We held another bunker conference at Eric's in early 2023, shortly after the visit to Durham's grave and, once again, huddled around the table as Eric plotted. We had finally done it. The search area was narrow and well-defined. This time there was no hesitation, and, with the boat repowered and remodeled, there was nothing to get in our way. Eric and Joe hatched and blessed a plan.

Durham was still a villain to me when I stood before his grave in 2022, and even as I left the bunker with a plan to follow him to the east and just a little farther to the south. He had been the one at fault for leaving those aboard *Le Lyonnais* to their fate, but I never bothered to understand why he might have done it. He had been one-dimensional, but there was something about our experience in Everett and my father's advice to follow the signs that led me to dig deeper. In the winter of 2022, just a few months after our visit to Durham's grave, I discovered new information about him and his brothers' deaths at sea. It came in small references to Durham's mental health hidden in documents I had reviewed a thousand times before and in newly discovered documents. Durham began to take shape as a flawed human being whose life had been marked by loss and grief and fear. Anger dissolved into empathy. I sought to learn more about who he was, not as a captain but as a person, so, in March 2023, I went to his hometown, Belfast, Maine.

To walk through Belfast is to step back in time. The city backs up against a gently sloping waterfront dotted with large warehouses, which today serve as home to restaurants, maritime supply companies, and marinas. It is easy to imagine the time when this same space along the Passagassawaukeag River was occupied by shipyards, sail lofts, and ship chandlers. Shops and local art galleries make up Belfast's town center, which meets at the intersections of Main, Church, and Beaver Streets. Early-nineteenth-century buildings such as the Belfast National Bank, the Belfast Free Library, and the First Church punctuate the area and serve as a reminder that some things never change.

Homes once occupied by captains, ship owners, and merchants line the city's interior. Some bear small black plaques with the home's historic name written in gold lettering. Rows of small homes painted in historic greens, blues, and mustard colors seem to go on and on without end on lines of streets that run parallel to the riverbank. The area contains one of Maine's largest single concentrations of residential architecture from the first half of the nineteenth century. Homes once owned by the most-prominent families are closer to the water, and those once occupied by sailors and their families line streets farther up the hill. Belfast has always revolved around the sea, and the contributions of families like Durham's now exist as scattered remnants throughout the town.

I imagined Durham as a boy running down streets lined with trees so tall that they dwarfed the houses below them. I pictured him as a young sailor walking down Front Street to C. P. Carter's offices in search of work and as a seasoned captain passing the Carter buildings to get to the Upper Steamboat Wharf shipyard where *Adriatic* was built. I saw him as an older man sitting with his wife and elderly mother in the drawing room of their stately Church Street home. He was everywhere.

My visit ended in the cemetery where Captain Durham's parents are buried and where the monument to his lost brothers still stands. I went alone and late in the afternoon. March was ending. There were large patches of snow on the ground, but the air felt warmer than it should have been.

Grove Cemetery is located at the intersection of Belfast's historic and more modern section of town. The grounds have expanded several times since the cemetery was first built in 1830 and now comprise almost 50 acres. Nine thousand people are interred there, many of them ship captains or sailors descendent from Belfast's founding families. Most of them are buried in the "old" section, which is organized by ranges and lots.

The cemetery was closed when I arrived. I had the plot, range, and lot number for the Durham grave but saw no map or numbers anywhere. It was not difficult to find the old section. Tombstones weathered by time and lined up close to one another abounded. Names such as Sergeant and Sanborn and Carter etched on granite and marble stones stretched for what seemed like miles. I later learned that there are more than thirty-two separate ranges in the old section. I followed stones through range after range and hoped I would find some clue to point me in the right direction. I walked the main path but also among the markers. Patches of thick brown leaves encircled by remnants of winter ice and snow served as a guide of where to put my feet as I navigated a maze of monuments to lives lived more than one hundred years ago, and searched for signs of the Durham family gravesite.

Epilogue

After an hour of wandering, I saw a person—a tall woman wearing a camel-colored corduroy jacket, hiking pants, and tartan scarf. Eager for help, I greeted her and asked if she could direct me. She told me she walked the cemetery on a regular basis but never bothered to learn the plot numbers. Before I could thank her and excuse myself, she said, "Want to see a different headstone?" I nodded yes, not because I wanted to but because it seemed rude to refuse. She walked me quite a distance across the cemetery. Her legs were so long and her stride so giant that it was difficult for a short person like me to keep pace. We eventually found ourselves standing over the grave of an entire family who had died tragically in the 1800s. The woman in corduroy and tartan did not know them, nor was she related to them, but she said she visited their grave each time she walked the cemetery because "someone should. They deserve that much." We talked for a while before we parted ways. She left me alone and lost but grateful for the lesson.

The sun had turned from yellow to an intense orange during the excursion and now backlit the endless rows of stones. I gave up and headed toward my car. I returned to the cemetery's main path, stretched my arms out wide and yelled, "Thank you, Durhams, wherever you are!" Small gray pebbles crunched loudly beneath my feet. The graveyard was quiet except for my voice's echo, followed by the pebbles' crunch crunch. I stopped. I do not know why; I just did. Not more than a second later, my entire body turned. It felt like someone came up behind me, grabbed me by both arms, and turned me 90 degrees to the left. I whipped my head over my shoulder, expecting to see the woman in corduroy and tartan, but there was no one there. My heart pounded. Something in the center of my chest told me to walk forward. I found the Durham family gravesite about ten paces ahead and to my right.

The name "Capt. Geo. A. Durham" appeared first. The letters were carved deeply into a slab of plain granite and stood at the start of a row of four white stones spaced closely together. My eyes went to the far right: "Eunice Sergeant Durham," the mother who had endured so much heartache. The graves of her husband, Captain John Durham, and the monument to the three Durham brothers lost at sea rested between them. The markers of all four sons predated their parents'.

I reached out and touched the lost brothers' stone. My fingertips rested on top of it until my palm fell downward and touched the words inscribed on it: "Their bodies rest beneath the waves. Their spirits with their God." An emotion overwhelmed me. It was not sadness but a tremendous sense of peace. "It was you," I whispered as I slid my hand from the top of the stone to the base, bending my knees as I traced the words to the bottom and came to sit between the sons' and their father's graves.

An hour passed. I was so enveloped by the peace that I barely noticed the sun had set and the sky had turned from orange to navy blue. The fog of my thoughts cleared, and I soon realized I was alone and sitting in an old cemetery after dark. I bid the Durham family goodbye and left with the feeling that I finally understood—that I had permission to tell their story. "Someone should. They deserve that much." The words gifted to me by the woman in corduroy and tartan rang in my ears as I walked to my car.

The *Tenacious* team relied on more than the ghosts of dead captains to prepare for our 2023 search. We spoke to living captains too. Van Strickler, a legendary fishing-boat captain who has worked out of New Bedford and other ports around the country, provided us with hang logs and vital information about our search plan and the conditions we could expect to encounter.

During one conversation, Captain Strickler described what it is like on Georges Bank. "I can't really explain it. Everything is just . . ." He paused and grasped for the right words. "Everything is just wilder there." The thought of it intrigued me, not just the thought of a "wilder" ocean but that captains such as Strickler noticed the differences in the way the waves moved in different parts of the ocean, and recognized the differences from place to place. It is knowledge born from both experience and a deep respect for a dynamic environment.

Spring turned into the summer of 2023. We had everything we needed to search for *Le Lyonnais* in earnest. We chose August 31 through September 10 as our weather window and moved the boat to New Bedford, Massachusetts, in mid-July as we usually do, to accommodate expeditions to wrecks such as SS *Andrea Doria*, SS *West Point*, and other Nantucket Shoals shipwrecks. Our last trip from New Bedford was to be the search for *Le Lyonnais*.

My father died on June 25, 2023. If my universe had a center, my father was mine. He went into the hospital in early June 2023. By mid-June, we knew he was dying. He knew it too. His body could no longer keep both his heart and his kidneys working simultaneously. He made the decision to enter hospice care, and we decided he would come home, where the family could administer that care until the end.

You never know when you will be able to speak to someone for the last time. Before he started hospice care, we had so many conversations. We talked about important things. We also talked about unimportant things such as the boat and our plans to pursue *Le Lyonnais*. My father was as determined as we were to find her. During one of our last conversations he said, "Hey, maybe I'll track down that French sailor in heaven and tell you where to find your ship." We both laughed at the idea of him orchestrating the search from above. "How hard can it be to find a few old sea captains in heaven?" he smiled. It was only a few days later that he came home to die.

My childhood home has a large room behind the house, an addition my parents built when I was in the sixth grade. It was a family room in every sense of the word, a place we all gathered. There are no solid walls. The room is enclosed entirely in glass with skylights above. I grew up in suburban-bordering-on-rural New Jersey in a community carved out of the woods. Bear, foxes, and deer were frequent visitors to our backyard and often stared through the glass at us and us at them. Being in the family room was like looking out into a forest from a fishbowl. Through the panes of glass, I saw the yard where I played as a child. My father's bocce ball court, where he used to host family tournaments, was now overgrown with patches of weeds. It was in this backyard that he used to set up a telescope and, through it, show me the planets and the stars. He was no astronomer. He knew only a few of the constellations and planets, but when I was a young child, his ability to name objects in the sky was pure magic.

It was in that room, surrounded by glass and all those memories, that we set up his hospital bed. They started morphine in the hospital, and my father could barely speak when the paramedics brought him home. He looked through the skylight above his head and said the word "home" before he drifted off to sleep. He went in and out of consciousness for three days before he died in that room, surrounded by family.

I felt an aching need to go to sea after his death. It was not running away. Going to sea was running toward something—a place where I did not have to be anything for anyone. Our next voyage was a two-day trip to a local wreck, USS *Murphy*, followed by a weeklong expedition to SS *Andrea Doria*. The *Doria* expedition was special. We took a group of three Italian divers, one the descendent of an *Andrea Doria* survivor, to dive the wreck in commemoration of the sixty-seventh anniversary of the sinking.

My father, who was a first-generation son of Italian immigrants, knew about the trip and would often say, "The Italians are coming!" I felt him everywhere on that trip. July 25, exactly one month after his death, was the anniversary of the *Andrea Doria–Stockholm* collision. That morning, Italian diver David D'Anna dived the wreck in the memory of his grandfather, who survived the *Doria* sinking. David was in tears as he described how it felt to touch the ship on such a special day. When the sun set that evening, I was overwhelmed by emotions of my own but had nowhere to let them out. There is nowhere to hide on a 45-foot boat shared by seven crew. I went to the only place I could be alone—the roof.

The ocean was flat as a lake and the sky a deep, royal blue. The moon was round and bright and half covered in clouds and projected a spotlight onto the water off our port side. I cried. I cried for the first time since my father's death. I cried so hard I could not stop. It felt impossible to catch my breath, and that just made me cry even more. The clouds parted and the circle of moonlight grew until it flooded over the boat and me. At first it felt like an intrusion, as though the light had exposed me, but then it calmed me. The clouds came again and darkened the circle once more. I collected myself and joined the others, who were now huddled in front of a television screen watching a documentary about early *Doria* expeditions. They were so wrapped up in the film that they had not noticed the light or the sky or even that I had been gone, but being there in that small space with them comforted me. It reminded me that the people who share these experiences are more than just friends. They are family.

The weather turned soon after the Italian expedition. Storms came up from the south and turned to hurricanes offshore. Hurricane season begins in late August, when water temperatures rise above 79 degrees Fahrenheit and meet cold winds that come from the north. The storms used to churn up the coast in September, but rising ocean temperatures have made them more common earlier in the season.

Storm after storm forced us to cancel operations for the next three weeks. Eric and Joe immersed themselves in weather data. The Project Mayonnaise search trip was in jeopardy. We were about to cancel when they saw a narrow window of tolerable weather. We held our breath and prayed it held. It was touch and go until the moment we slipped the ropes and motored east on September 3, 2023.

This time, our team consisted of Eric, Joe, Rick, Andrew, me, and newcomers François Merle and Kurt Mintell. François, who was born and raised in France, helped translate documents for the search and took on the role of expedition videographer. We took turns doing all the work the mission required. Andrew and I operated the computer while Eric and Joe took turns mowing the lawn in 8-to-10-foot, long-period swells. Rick monitored the Sand and Rock channel alongside us. François and Kurt manned the winch, cables, and other deck equipment. Together, we scanned the ocean floor almost eighteen hours each day for three straight days.

When you spend enough time at sea, you feel changes in the ocean. It is not just the rhythm and the pattern of the waves. It is the feeling that comes once you get far from shore. Call it a feeling of no return. Call it crossing over. Call it a loss of control. The feeling of crossing over came, for me, when we passed through Little Georges and headed to Georges near the Canadian maritime border and the continental shelf. I could not help but think of Captain Strickler's comment, which now seemed both an observation and a warning: "It's wilder there."

We kept mowing the lawn. Records rolled across the screen. Some of them were deceiving. What appears on the screen can depend on the angle at which you approach an anomaly, how close it is, and what the bottom geology looks like. Shipwrecks on the Sand and Rock channel can hide in plain sight. Distinguishing wreckage from sea junk takes years of experience we did not have, so we marked anything and everything that came close to looking like the remains of a lost ship.

We scanned from 6:08 a.m. on September 4 and did not haul the fish back on deck until 10:27 that evening. We marked a few targets during the day, including one that appeared to us to be either a barge or a low-lying sailing vessel. Barges are floating cargo platforms, which are sometimes made from converted ships, and often appear on a sonar record to be more interesting than they are. The only way to tell is to dive the target. September 4 came and went with some targets acquired but no real cause for celebration.

September 5 passed the same as the day before. Fish in the water by 7:00 a.m. Watch the Sand and Rock channel. Eat. Sleep. Repeat. Haul the fish in at 10:00 p.m.

Early on the morning of September 6, I did my 2:30–3:30 a.m. watch, woke the next watchman, and caught another hour's sleep before getting up to make breakfast. We began what we labeled "Survey Grid #10" at 7:09 a.m. Joe was at the helm. At around 10:30, we reached line 4. I had been at the monitor for four hours. The weather was rough and starting to get the better of me. I was about to hand it to Andrew, when a shipwreck rolled across the screen. We all knew it was a wreck. She was approximately 280 feet long and buried, but we needed a better record to determine if it was a good candidate for *Le Lyonnais*. We finished the grid and returned to do a few more passes. Eric and Andrew relieved Joe and me, and together they gathered additional data.

On the afternoon of September 6, Eric stood at the helm. His stance was wide to counteract the movement of a bumpy ocean. We were all exhausted. We had been scanning all day, each taking turns at our various stations. Eric stretched his arms straight out in front of him and gripped the wheel at 10 and 2 like a teenage driver and grinned from ear to ear. "Where does he get the energy?" I thought. He glanced at me over his left shoulder and did his best impression of an overzealous airline pilot: "Ladies and gentlemen, we are now 200 miles from New Bedford." I laughed, but in that moment, I felt the significance of what we were doing.

Three years ago, *Le Lyonnais* was a needle in a haystack too far to reach, and now, we were here.

We examined the sonar record. It did not look like *Le Lyonnais* to me, but as we dug into the images, it added up. *Le Lyonnais* measured 260 by 36 feet. The target measured 40 feet wide and roughly 280 feet long, which is consistent with a ship that has endured more than 150 years on the seabed. The wreck was significantly buried, a sign of age. Old shipwrecks frequently appear as vague, ship-shaped outlines marked by an engine, boilers, and a propeller shaft. The engine typically casts a shadow, and we measure the shadow to determine height. The record revealed all the telltale signs, but records can tell us only so much. What we saw did not give us nearly enough to make an identification.

We had capable divers aboard and one more day on Georges Bank before the weather promised to turn. That afternoon, Joe and I talked about putting divers into the water. The wreck is deep, approximately 300 feet. Diving conditions were suboptimal. The long-period swells persisted, and the current looked ferocious. We were too far for rescue if something went wrong, and we did not have a dive plan in place for what we needed divers to do in the water. The conversation was not a difficult one. We agreed to wait, which meant returning to dive the wreck the following year.

Shipwreck hunting requires discipline. Putting divers in the water would have satisfied our curiosity and allowed us to claim the wreck as "found," but the risk was too great. My stomach sank. The idea of waiting an entire year to confirm what we thought we knew was daunting, but I cared far more about our crew than I did about any shipwreck. The team's collective reaction was a mixture of disappointment and relief.

The data were promising but seemed too good to be true. I had heard Eric's stories about searching for wrecks for years and knew plenty of people driven to obsession by such hunts. I had prepared myself to search for this wreck for years or decades or the rest of my life. I had prepared for an obvious record of her to roll across the screen and for us to erupt in celebration as happened with *West Point* and the *Stockholm* bow. What I had not prepared for is a team of seven people cocking their heads, staring at a computer screen, and saying to one another, "This *might* be it." Everything looked correct, but we could not know for sure until divers came face to face with her.

Our celebration was lackluster. Andrew broke out a bottle of Lagavulin 16 and said with genuine confusion, "Is this a party?" Joe said, "I think it might be." I said, "I don't think so." Eric shrugged. We drank anyway. "We should take some pictures of the group tomorrow,"

I mumbled, "just in case we just found it." We lifted our glasses, forced smiles, and toasted to something to which shipwreck hunters grow accustomed—the unknown.

Tenacious reached land on September 8, 2023, and we spent the next several months reviewing the sonar records, including what we now referred to as the *Le Lyonnais* target. One of the challenges was the records themselves. Sonar operates best in calm seas. The swells we experienced caused the fish to heave as it moved through the water, which disrupted image continuity and corrupted our records with long black lines. Heave was unavoidable in the conditions but made it more difficult to interpret the data.

We focused on the portions of the ship that we knew would survive on the seafloor—the machinery. We remeasured the record and compared every detail to historical documents about *Le Lyonnais* and her sister ship, *Cadix*. It added up. The *Le Lyonnais* target had a single engine. She was the correct length and width. She was upright but showed damage on her starboard side, which is consistent with *Le Lyonnais*'s lurch to starboard in her final moments. The location matched numerous data points we had gathered.

The 2023–24 winter was a long one. Not a single day passed without the thought of returning to Georges Bank to put divers on this ship. Joe developed some secondary targets during that time, including the "something interesting or a barge" target we scanned on September 4. We set July 7–21, 2024, as our window to return and dive as many targets as possible.

Shortly after setting the schedule, François informed us he would not be able to rejoin the expedition for personal reasons. It was difficult to replace someone with as much passion for the project and team spirit as François, but we ultimately decided on Tim Whitehead, a young diver who started diving with us locally in 2022. He is a solid diver with a thirst for adventure. More importantly, he is a team player—one who understood that the team's priority was not recovering artifacts or individual glory but the pursuit of a historic shipwreck.

We needed at least five good-weather days in a row to make the trip worthwhile. June brought a heat wave and miserable offshore weather. The trend continued through July. Our three-week weather window came and went with no chance of departure and forced us to reschedule the expedition to August 15–30.

Being weather dependent requires unwavering commitment. We agreed that when the weather came, we would drop everything else in our lives—work, social engagements, family, friends—to jump on a boat and head east. Hurricane Ernesto passed our way the weekend of August 15, and headed east faster than we thought. A stretch of good weather tracked behind it, and we set a departure date for August 21.

Later that week, torrential rains caused floods that hit Connecticut particularly hard. Rick Simon, who had been with us on the first two search trips, owns a commercial dive business that contracts with the state to haul sunken vessels from local marinas. On August 19, the Monday after the storm, he sent us a photograph of a pile of boats at the bottom of a Connecticut marina—boats he was contractually obligated to salvage. There are times you can drop the rest of your life to go wreck hunting, and times you cannot. For Rick, this was one time he could not. We understood, but the prospect of doing this without Rick, a dear friend who had been so supportive during the entire journey, felt like a bad omen.

Enter Tom Packer. Tom was one of the few individuals involved in Eric's original searches for *Le Lyonnais*. He knew both *Le Lyonnais*'s story and the history of our search efforts well. Most important to me, Tom had quietly encouraged me to embark on this journey, to write the book, and to pursue this obsession in the earliest days of it. Life prevented Tom from joining us in 2022 and 2023—no matter how hard Joe and I begged him—but, when Rick dropped out, he rose to the occasion.

D/V *Tenacious* leaving New Bedford on August 21, 2024. *Photo by and courtesy of Paul Whittaker*

Epilogue

Our newly assembled team departed Fleet Marina in New Bedford on August 21, 2024, and set out for Georges Bank. We headed straight for our most promising target. It took a full day of motoring to get there, and we spent most of the evening of August 21 fine-tuning dive plans and sharing *Le Lyonnais*'s story with our newest team member, Tim.

Georges Bank is remote and uncharted dive territory. The technical dive community on the East Coast is small, and, to our knowledge, no one has dived shipwrecks there. There are no tide tables—no way to determine when the current might slack enough to put divers into the water. The *Le Lyonnais* target is in approximately 300 feet of water. The toll that diving that deep takes on the body, combined with the risks inherent in operating so far from shore, limited the divers to one dive per day. Each diver planned for twenty-five minutes of bottom time, followed by two hours of decompression, a process by which divers slowly ascend to rid their bodies of excess nitrogen that accumulates at depth. Those twenty-five minutes had to count.

Eric, Joe, Andrew, and I had met the month prior and agreed that the team should concentrate on the engine during the first dive. *Le Lyonnais* had a horizontal engine, which looked much different from triple-expansion or compound engines used by later steamships. It promised to be the easiest way to identify her.

Eric explained horizontal engines in detail as we motored east. Unlike triple-expansion or compound engines, which were tall because they are vertical, horizontal engines are squat and low. He warned the divers not to expect the machinery to stand high like the engines they were accustomed to seeing on more-modern shipwrecks. As Joe listened, he realized something: what we identified as the engine from our sonar record was tall—possibly too tall to be what Eric described.

Sometimes things do not click until you get down to the wire. There are no reference photographs for *Le Lyonnais*'s engine. We had been over the record a thousand times, but the foreign shape of the horizontal engine did not register with Joe until we were underway and prepping the dive team. He had missed it.

Joe started to doubt that the morning dive would bring good news. He stayed up all night measuring the length of the shadow cast by the engine on the sonar record; it did not add up. He tried to shake it off—to convince himself it was just last-minute jitters—but did not sleep much that night. He kept the creeping doubt to himself.

We arrived on-site the next morning. The current was already slacking. We did not know how long it would last, so we immediately set up to put divers into the water. Eric and Kurt headed to the ship's bow and waited for Joe's signal to "throw the hook," a method by which we throw an anchor into the water and hope to catch it on the wreck. "Fishing for a shipwreck," Joe sometimes calls it. It did not take long before the rope went tight, a sign we firmly caught the wreck. The first divers into the water would "set the hook" by lashing it into the wreckage with a secondary line.

Being the first to splash on a new shipwreck is considered an honor for any wreck diver. This is both because the first diver is the first person to see a ship since she sank but also because it gives them the opportunity to claim unique artifacts strewn on the ocean floor. It is not uncommon for prized items such as bells, helms, and telegraphs to be resting in the sand. Before the trip, Joe and I discussed who would dive the target first. We decided on Tim. If there is anything that people like Tom and Eric have taught us, it is that wreck diving and wreck hunting are generational, traditions passed down from veteran explorers to newer ones. We chose divers for this project who respected tradition and what it meant to dive in a sacred place. Eric is fond of saying that he "passed the torch" to Joe with SS *West Point* and to me with *Le Lyonnais*. It seemed only fitting for us to pass it to the youngest member of our team.

We planned for Andrew to pair with Tim for that first dive. Andrew is a veteran wreck diver who has been a part of numerous discoveries. He was part of the team that raised the gun turret of the Civil War ironclad USS *Monitor* in the early 2000s. An aerospace engineer by day, he is meticulous with his observations of machinery. He is also an underwater photographer, and we wanted to get him in the water before other divers disturbed the visibility. He and Tim would splash, followed by Joe and Tom. Kurt, who was recovering from an ear injury, stayed topside to help Eric and me on surface support.

Plans often change at sea, but when Joe gave the go for the first dive, I was surprised to find Tom and him suiting up before Tim and Andrew. It was not the plan, but I assumed they had their reasons.

Joe was quiet, but the mood among the rest of the team was positively giddy. Divers smiled and chattered as they donned their dry suits, checked their rebreathers, and clipped on equipment. It did not take long before Joe and Tom made their way to the dive platform, stepped off, and slipped beneath the surface. Tim and Andrew followed.

The water was dark but clear. The visibility was a rare 100 feet. Tom's eyes adjusted themselves to the darkness when an extraordinary sight materialized beneath him: a massive, vertical steam engine. Despite the ravages of age and time, it was standing upright like a robot frozen on an alien planet. Tom has been diving for nearly fifty years, but he described the descent as one of the most beautiful he can recall. He hooted and hollered and waved his flashlight until a thought momentarily pierced his joy: "This is not our wreck." He tried to restrain himself but could not. Although this was not *Le Lyonnais*, a spectacular, unidentified shipwreck loomed out of the darkness below him.

Joe did not share Tom's joy. He was angry. A spectacular, unidentified shipwreck with a massive vertical engine was not the goal. Joe soon came face to face with the culprit that had kept him up all night, the one that cast such a long shadow on our sonar record. The machinery stood some 30 feet high. The other divers met Joe and Tom at the engine. Together, they swarmed and photographed it.

Eric, Kurt, and I waited on deck for one of the divers to emerge and tell us what they had seen below. Tom surfaced first and walked to the bench. It took what seemed like forever for him to remove his rebreather from his mouth, take off his mask, and pull off both of his two hoods. He looked me straight in the eye and said, "It's not your wreck." He paused for a second before launching into an animated story of his unexpected dive.

I wish I could say it was a gut punch, but it was not. I was prepared for this. For a year, I prepared myself to be wrong. What I did not expect was for it to be easier than I thought. Veterans always say that wreck hunting is not about what you find but about the process of finding it. It sounds good, but I never really believed it. The moment I locked eyes with Tom and took in what he said, I realized it was true. The discovery of a steamship that, on the basis of our limited exploration, dates between the 1880s and the 1920s eclipsed my disappointment about *Le Lyonnais*. "At least we found something awesome," I replied.

Joe climbed out of the water twenty minutes later. He always looks angry when he surfaces, so it was difficult to read his mood. He walked up the ladder, side-stomped to the bench, and spit the rebreather loop from his mouth. He and Tom exchanged observations, but Joe's eyes kept moving to me. I nodded to let him know I was okay. Eventually, I said, "She's still out there. We'll find her." Then, in typical Joe fashion, he responded, "I'm hungry. When can we eat?"

The team exchanged dive details over lunch. We reviewed video footage and discussed the data already collected and the data we would need to identify what we now referred to as the "Big Engine Steamer." We also decided to leave. Although the Big Engine Steamer was a promising mystery, she was not the mission. The wind grew stronger and brought swells with it. Our anchor dislodged from the wreck, a convenient break because it meant that no one would need to waste a dive on releasing us the next morning. We were free to leave. We motored closer to our next target, the "something interesting or barge" wreck, and anchored nearby for the evening.

We expected a weather bump on the evening of August 22, and Mother Nature delivered. The winds strengthened throughout the afternoon and, by evening, blew a steady 15 to 20 knots. After the rest of the team hunkered down in their bunks, Joe and I talked. It was the first time we had been alone since the revelation that the Big Engine Steamer was not our wreck. We talked about what to do during the remainder of the trip and about picking up the search next year, but the most-important things were left unsaid. We did not need to say them. We knew. *Le Lyonnais* was a needle in a haystack. We did not find her this time. One day we would, but we were here. We were here and we were together, and we were searching for her. "I love you," I said as I headed to my bunk and left Joe to take the first watch. The current took the boat's keel, and the waves rocked us on the beam all night.

I slept like I had not slept in a year. I may have been the only person who slept. The rocking of the boat continued throughout the morning and left most of the crew somewhere between under the weather and downright seasick. We hooked the wreck, but the current was running too strong to put divers into the water. We watched and waited for slack.

Just three days before, on August 19, there was an event called a blue supermoon, a phenomenon that occurs when the moon is closest to the earth's orbit. Tides are most pronounced when the moon is full and closer to the earth, and the supermoon did not do us any favors. The next target was in shallower waters, approximately 250 feet. Under ordinary circumstances, the shallower depth would allow two dives per day, but with a supermoon and unpredictable currents, we could not count on two slacks. The divers agreed that Joe would dive last and decide whether to release us from the wreck by pulling the hook. Simply put, if he liked what he saw, we would stay and wait for a second dive even if it meant spending the night there.

We put equipment lines into the water. These long ropes with weights on the end allow divers to offload gear they no longer need as they ascend, but they also serve as indicators of current strength. They quickly came up to the surface and extended straight behind the boat, which meant the current was too strong to dive.

While we were waiting on the current, Joe called me up to the bow. It is one of the few places to talk out of earshot of others, and the place he calls me to discuss things he wants only the two of us to know. "Listen," he said, "this is a viable target." I was almost annoyed because

Epilogue

I had come to terms with the fact that the search for *Le Lyonnais* would have to continue the following year. "The barge? Why?" The "something interesting or barge" wreck had all the hallmarks of a barge masquerading as a shipwreck except for one thing: a bulge amidships. Joe remembered something Garry Kozak once told him about machinery on older shipwrecks appearing on sonar records as bulges with everything else around them flattened out. I looked at him. "I'm serious," he said. "I didn't realize just how flat these horizontal engines were. The bulge matches Eric's description." Rennie & Sons made *Le Lyonnais*'s engine. During the night, Joe studied diagrams of Rennie & Sons machinery I had previously found in a British magazine from the 1850s. We had dismissed these diagrams because they did not depict the same type of engine as the one *Le Lyonnais* used. "But they're the same size and shape," Joe argued. "I measured. The length and width of the anomaly makes sense." He was rarely this enthusiastic, but I could not tell if the enthusiasm came from a genuine belief in the target or from a desire to turn things around. His hope lifted my spirits but not my expectations.

Five hours later, the equipment lines reached a 45-degree angle. Slack was imminent. Joe asked Andrew and Tim to splash first. Joe and Tom followed. Eric, Kurt, and I waited on deck.

Tom reappeared two hours later. We helped him to his seat and waited for him to remove his rebreather from his mouth, take off his mask, and pull off both of his two hoods. He just stared at us. "Well?" I asked. "Well," he paused. "When I got down there, the first thing I saw was Tim carrying portholes to the anchor line like a golden retriever." We laughed. I did not think much of it. It was not uncommon to find portholes resting in the sand near a virgin shipwreck, but at least it was not a barge. It was what Tom said next that got Eric's and my attention: "There were iron plates all over the place. They looked almost stringy like they had some age."

Tim emerged next. It was the first time he had found a porthole on a shipwreck. He was elated. "When I first got down there, all I saw were hull plates. They were everywhere," Tim said. "The next thing I saw was Andrew carrying portholes to the line."

Andrew surfaced next and described what appeared to be an engine and machinery. "The wreck is old and low lying–definitely not a barge," he reported. "We're staying," he added. There was something definitive about the tone of Andrew's voice. We were onto something.

Joe surfaced shortly after Andrew, but, to me, it seemed like an eternity. He climbed up the ladder as angrily as he always does and marched to his seat on the bench. He spit the rebreather loop out of his mouth and said, "I found the engine cylinder." He spread his arms out long on each side of his body: "It's big." Joe looked at me. "And it is parallel to the sand." He was right about the bulge being squat and low machinery, and this was an old wreck with an iron hull, but it was the big cylinder that first gave me hope.

Cylinder diameters are precise. In the 1850s, Lloyd's Register of Ships, a maritime classification and certification service, recorded construction details such as cylinder size. *Le Lyonnais* launched in January 1856 and sank in November 1856. She does not appear in the Lloyd's register for that year. Her identical twin with an identical engine, *Cadix*, does. Her cylinders were big. They measured 57 inches with a 30-inch stroke.

The team discussed other observations: iron plates, low-lying engine machinery, a vertical sternpost, and one engine cylinder sticking out of the sand and the other buried beneath. Much of the wreck was buried, a sign of age and time. We reviewed video footage taken by Joe and Tim, and raw photos taken by Andrew. Eric pointed out the engine cylinder in Joe's video and instructed the team on what to do on the next dive. "Measure from lip to lip just inside the cylinder casing," Eric told Joe. "It will give us a precise measurement."

The question was when. It was Friday. Saturday was to be our last dive day, and since the current had not slacked again, it meant there was only one dive left. There was a pile of portholes at the anchor line. Someone needed to float them to the surface, a task that would consume one diver's entire dive. We discussed how to make the most of the dive each diver had left.

"I'll go again today," said Tim. I walked to the back of the boat and looked at the equipment lines, which were straight behind the boat, and then looked back at Tim with raised eyebrows. "I'll do a fifteen-minute dive and shoot the portholes. That way, we don't have to do it tomorrow, and we can all work together on other things." Everyone paused to think it over. Tim is young but not reckless. He is disciplined. If he thought he could make the dive, we knew he could. Joe finally spoke: "It's up you, man." We all agreed to support whatever choice he made. The decision was easy for Tim. After a decent surface interval, he suited up.

The team strategized. Tim would go down the anchor line, string the portholes together, and connect them to a lift bag, a device that looks and acts like a triangularly shaped balloon. Using a spare tank of air, Tim would fill the balloon with enough gas to float the portholes to the surface, where we would wait for them and lift them aboard. The current was running, but Tim did not plan to leave the safety of the anchor line and carried with him a diver propulsion vehicle, or scooter, to fight against it.

Tim splashed. The remaining six of us became surface support. Andrew and Joe got into the chase boat and waited for Tim to send the portholes. Eric and Kurt stood on the bow of the boat to watch for bubbles and point the chase boat to the right location. Tom and I manned the deck to keep track of the time and to make sure that neither Tim nor the lift bag swept past the boat with the current.

"Fifteen minutes," I yelled to the others. Fifteen minutes had passed with no sign of the bag. "Eighteen!" Still nothing. "Twenty!" Nothing. "Twenty-three minutes!" At just over twenty-three minutes, Kurt spotted bubbles, the sign that Tim was filling the bag. The loud woosh of the bag hitting the surface followed. Andrew and Joe lassoed and delivered it to Tom and me at the back of the boat. Tim was on his way up, but at twenty-five minutes on the bottom, his second decompression promised to be longer than the first.

We inspected the portholes. There were five of them. The divers reported seeing many more strewn about the wreckage. The presence of so many portholes was itself an indicator that the ship was a passenger liner. The portholes were old. "They look just like the *Newcastle City* portholes," said Tom. Like *Le Lyonnais*, SS *Newcastle City* was a transitional steamship with an engine and sails. She was built in England in 1882. Eric noticed that the glass in the portholes was either broken or intact, but there were no signs of burning. There was another steamship similar in age and size to *Le Lyonnais* that burned and sank off the coast of Nantucket. When a ship burns, the glass in portholes heats to such high temperatures that they shatter when they hit cold water. Brass portholes can get so hot they melt. None of the glass in the portholes Tim recovered was shattered, and none of the divers saw any signs of melted brass or burnt wood. We were later able to rule out the burning ship completely, on the basis of her engine type, but at the time, the condition of the portholes gave us some relief. Tim surfaced about two hours later to the sound of applause. He smiled from ear to ear when he saw the pile of portholes resting safely on deck.

The weather calmed as the day wore on, and it promised to be a peaceful night. We grilled cheeseburgers on the aft deck for dinner. The mood had changed. The crew was lively once more. No one spoke it, but we all suspected that this was our lost ship. We reviewed footage taken during the day and planned for the next. Engine cylinder measurement was the top priority. We needed to make the day count, which meant doing two dives instead of one. Tim's dive proved that the current was not bad enough to prevent a diver from doing a short dive to release the hook.

The weather turned blissfully calm by nightfall, but now I was the one who did not sleep. The iron and the engine and the portholes were not enough to make an identification, but given the location and condition of the wreck, this was a viable target. I laughed. If ten years ago anyone had told me I would be some 200 miles from land on a boat and pinning my hopes on the measurement of a nineteenth-century engine cylinder, I would have said they were mad. More realistically, I would have asked, "What's an engine cylinder?"

I was still awake at 2:00 a.m. when Tom woke me for my watch. I popped my music into one ear and stepped out onto deck to gaze at the stars. I could not help but think about how far I had come since Joe and I met all those years ago, about how far we all had come.

The supermoon shined so brightly it blotted out most of the stars, but I could still pick out planets. Jupiter, Mars, and Mercury were in conjunction with the moon and sat together in the night sky. My father was the one who taught me how to find them and how to distinguish them from stars. "Planets don't twinkle, Jenny," he used to say. "Only stars do." I felt him there with me. It was almost as though I could feel him smiling.

In moments like these, we often pray for the things we want. I would be lying if I said my first thought was not to ask my father for help—to pray to wake up the next morning and know I had found the thing that had consumed me for the past eight years, but there was something holding me back.

I am not a religious person, at least not in the traditional sense, but my father was. One day in the hospital, I pulled my father's priest, Father Stephen, into the hallway and asked him a question. "I want to say a prayer with my father," I told him. "But I don't know any. Can you teach me one?" Father Stephen looked at me with kindness and said, "The greatest prayer ever written has only two words, Jenny. Those words are 'thank you.'"

My mind drifted back to my conversation with Father Stephen as I stared at the sky. A feeling of gratitude overwhelmed me until tears rolled down my cheeks. *Le Lyonnais* did not matter. What mattered was the pursuit of her—one that brought me closer to Joe and to Eric and to so many people I call family. "Thank you," I said out loud to my father, to the stars, to the planets, and to the big, blue supermoon.

An hour had already passed. It was time to wake Kurt for the next watch. I wiped the tears from my eyes, shook him awake, and briefed him. Before I returned to my bunk, I said, "Come outside." He followed. "That's Jupiter," I pointed. "And that's Mercury and that's Mars." Kurt looked at me strangely and replied, "Okay. Thanks?" The next morning, Kurt told me that he pointed out the planets to Tim when he passed the watch to him. That made me smile.

D/V *Tenacious*'s bunks where the crew sleeps during dive expeditions.
Photo courtesy of Joe Mazraani

Less than three hours later, we all awoke to the sound of Joe's voice. "Pool's open," he called. "Let's go, everybody!" It was not even 6:00 a.m., but the current was slack. One by one, we crawled from our bunks and rallied on deck. Eric, Kurt, and I scrambled to get everyone ready. Divers suited up and hit the water. Tim and Andrew splashed. Joe, armed with a tape measure and accompanied by Tom, followed.

Tom returned first. We helped him to the bench and waited for him to remove his rebreather from his mouth, take off his mask, and pull off both of his two hoods. He stared at me blankly. "Well?" I asked, "how big is the cylinder?" "I don't know," he said. "Joe wouldn't show me the other end of the tape measure." I knew Tom knew the measurement. I also knew he wanted Joe to be the one to tell me either way.

Joe surfaced twenty minutes behind Tom. He looked as angry as ever as he climbed the ladder and shuffled to his spot, but I could tell the answer by the way his eyes darted around to everyone else but me. He spit the rebreather loop from his mouth and said, "57 inches!" Eric was next to me. I threw my arms around him and squeezed. "We did it!" There were hugs all around. Tim and Andrew surfaced later, and Joe delivered the news to them. In addition, Joe saw the ship's donkey engine, an auxiliary engine used to work the ship's winches. It matched one specified in the contract between Laird & Sons and Franco-Américaine for *Le Lyonnais*. We finally celebrated.

One problem still plagued us. The team had observed machinery consistent with historical documents but, so far, had found no evidence of sails. *Le Lyonnais* was a sail-and-steam hybrid. Such ships are rare. Absent finding something with the ship's name on it, we needed proof our wreck was also rigged as a sailing vessel to solidify an already convincing identification.

The divers were back on the boat by 10:30 a.m. It had been more than four hours since the slack, but the current did not pick up again. We ate an early lunch of roasted eggplant and mozzarella sandwiches and found the ropes still slack when we finished. The supermoon had finally given us a break. When the appropriate surface intervals passed, the divers suited up again for one last dive.

Andrew and Tim went in first, so Joe and Tom could pull the hook when everyone was back to the anchor line. Joe reached the bottom before Tom. An object out in the sand on the starboard side caught his eye. He swam over to it while he waited for Tom to reach the wreck and get his bearings. The first object turned out to be nothing, but he saw something interesting as he turned left toward the machinery. It was not the object itself but the barnacles attached to it that drew Joe's attention. Barnacles

Epilogue

do not grow on sand. They attach themselves to metal and wood. The tiny outcrop caught Joe's eye. He went over and fanned some of the sand away to reveal a hard object underneath. He kept fanning and digging until a round shape appeared. More fanning, and then the sand slipped through two holes. His heart pounded fast now. He immediately recognized the familiar object. He yelled and waved his flashlight until Andrew arrived to photograph his find.

Eric, Kurt, and I waited above. Tom came out of the water smiling. He took his rebreather out of his mouth, removed his mask, and pulled off both of his hoods. "What?" I asked. "Joe found something that is going to make you very happy." He would not say what it was. "Do you want a hint?" I nodded yes. "You're not getting one!"

What Joe found was a deadeye. Deadeyes are wooden blocks used on older sailing ships, particularly in the rigging. They are circular, flat pieces of wood with holes in them, used in conjunction with lanyards to secure the rigging and maintain the tension of a ship's shrouds and stays. Our ship had both a unique horizontal engine and sails. The deadeyes, location, age, material, engine, engine cylinder measurement, and portholes, as well as the presence of other machinery consistent with historical records, convinced us that we had found *Le Lyonnais*'s final resting place.

The team spent most of their dives focused on machinery amidships and at the stern. During his final dive, Tim swam forward toward the bow. As he strayed farther and farther, he came across an enormous pile of anchor chain. The links were large, the iron stringy and marred by time. He hovered there, alone in the darkness, and stared at the chain with wonder until a thought occurred to him, "I am the first person to see this chain in more than 167 years." The last people to see that chain were likely the fifteen French sailors who decided to go down with the ship, the ones the water forced forward until *Le Lyonnais*'s stern grew so heavy that the ocean finally claimed her.

There is much more work to do on *Le Lyonnais*. The team will return next summer and continue diving and documenting the wreck. She is significantly buried and broken up by years of shifting sands, strong currents, and powerful storms. Other damage is man-made. Three scallop dredges have already plowed into her and come to rest at the site. They ripped her iron plates and dragged parts of her across the seafloor in the process. Fishing nets strangle portions of the wreckage. The team's mission will be to find and raise artifacts to help share *Le Lyonnais* and her story with the public and to preserve more of her from being forever washed away by time.

Le Lyonnais is more than a twisted pile of metal and wood on the ocean floor; she is a revenant. She connects us to a bygone era and to unresolved mysteries. More than a mere ghost, what remains of her has a story to tell. It is up to us to give that story voice.

We packed up and set course for New Bedford. On the way home, we toasted a successful expedition, exchanged stories of underwater observations, and talked about what finding such a historic shipwreck means. For me, finding *Le Lyonnais* was the fulfillment of a promise—one I made silently to those who lived and died aboard her more than 167 years ago.

Tenacious reached land on August 25, 2024, and announced the news of our discovery on September 4. People have asked me the same question every day since: "What was it like to find a shipwreck for which you have been searching for almost a decade?" My answer is polite and somewhat dishonest. I describe the joy of seeing a shipwreck roll across a computer screen, the thrill of sending divers into the water, and the relief and sense of accomplishment that come with making an identification. I also use it as an opportunity to educate people about the importance of maritime history.

None of that is really the truth. Yes, shipwreck hunters are genuinely glad to be able to contribute to history and underwater exploration, but it is not what really moves us. It is not what drives us to risk our lives to seek shipwrecks farther and farther from shore. What moves us is the hunt. The truth is that we are addicts—addicted to the pursuit, addicted to the rush, addicted to the feeling we get when we find the thing for which we have been searching. The problem is how quickly the moment fades. The only way to get it back is to find something else. The search never ends. Old obsessions just morph into new ones. The truth is that we are consumed not by discovery but by the search and satisfied not by finding something but by the freedom that finding something gives us to decide what to find next. We had barely left *Le Lyonnais* when Eric, Joe, and I started to discuss the next undiscovered wreck on our list.

That is why if I had to pick one moment in this journey that means the most to me, it is that moment in the early-morning hours on September 6, 2023, when I stood alone on *Tenacious*'s deck in the middle of the night and stared at the Milky Way, with no idea we had already run over *Le Lyonnais* and made the first-ever sonar record of her. I had no idea that a few hours later we would discover the Big Engine Steamer, and no idea it would take us almost a year to untangle the two. In that moment, Joe and so many people I hold dear slept fast in their bunks 200 miles from where we started. The untamed ocean that Captain Strickler promised me spread

Epilogue

out before me and moved beneath my feet. A band of brilliant stars created a highway of light in the night sky. They were the same stars that guided Captain Durham when he left home in command of his own vessel and his own destiny, the same stars Choupault followed when he set a small lifeboat's course for land, and the same stars my father pointed out to me as a child through the lens of a backyard telescope. In that moment, the past, the present, and the future existed all at once. We were in the thick of the search. In that moment, everything was possible.

Members of the 2024 expedition team celebrate after confirming the target's identity as *Le Lyonnais*. *Left to right:* Tom Packer, Andrew Donn, Eric Takakjian, Joe Mazraani, Jennifer Sellitti, Tim Whitehead, and Kurt Mintell. *Photo courtesy of Atlantic Wreck Salvage*

Endnotes

Chapter 1: A Wreck in Sight
1. "The Lost *Lyonnais* and Her Boat," *Brooklyn Evening Star*, December 16, 1856.
2. Ibid.

Chapter 2: All Ashore!
1. "Terrible Disaster at Sea—Loss of the French Steamer *Le Lyonnais*," *Morning Chronicle* (London), December 2, 1856.
2. "The Ocean Steamer: Crossing the Atlantic in Early Steamships," *Harper's New Monthly Magazine* 243, no. 41 (July 1870): 188.
3. The breakdown of first- and second-class passengers is unknown.
4. There are numerous spellings of Captain Devaulx's name and the names of other crew members in historical records. Names herein are spelled according to official French documents. For example, Devaulx's name is spelled in accordance with French military records.

Chapter 3: Crossing the Atlantic
1. "New Line of Packets Between Liverpool and New York," *The Guardian* (London), November 26, 1836.
2. "Compliment to Captain Russell," *New York Evening Post*, April 1, 1837.
3. Douglas Burgess Jr., *Engines of Empire: Steamships of the Victorian Empire* (Stanford, CA: Stanford University Press, 2016), 1. Burgess explores the psychology of Victorian steamship travel in his book and devotes a chapter to the concept of annihilating space. The Webster quote comes from "On the Beginning of Transatlantic Steamship Service," *Bulletin of the Business Historical Society* 12, no. 3 (June 1938) 40–43.
4. John Randolph Spears, *The Story of the American Merchant Marine* (New York: Macmillan, 1910), 265.
5. "Arrival of the First Boston and Liverpool Steamship," *Hartford Courant*, June 5, 1840.
6. John Protasio, *The Day the World Was Shocked: The Lusitania Disaster and Its Influence on the Course of World War I* (Haverford, PA: Casemate, 2011).
7. "Celebrating Cunard's 175 Years of Ocean Travel in Numbers," *Mirror* (London), May 16, 2015.
8. The bridge linked the two paddles and became the place that a captain would stand and give the crew their orders. Although paddle wheelers are no longer in use, the room or platform from which the captain commands is still called the bridge today.
9. Brothers John and George Rennie owned and operated two companies. J. and G. Rennie manufactured railway engines, and George Rennie and Sons manufactured steamship engines.

10. The earliest propellers were two blades. The number of blades and the number of propellers grew as engineers experimented with different designs.
11. Ericsson moved to the United States to continue his work and built the famous ironclad military ship USS *Monitor* during the American Civil War.
12. Steamships used the prefix designations of "PS" for paddle steamer or "SS" for screw steamer. As paddle steamers became less common, "SS" assumed the definition "steam ship."

Chapter 4: Franco-Américaine

1. The company was later renamed Cammel Laird.
2. Birkenhead is in the borough of Wirral, Merseyside, England. Liverpool is on eastern side of the river, and Birkenhead on the western side.
3. "Extraordinary Dispatch," *The Guardian* (London), March 6, 1830.
4. *Robert F. Stockton* used sail to make her journey. After delivery, she was renamed *New Jersey* and used as a tugboat on the Delaware River.
5. David Charles Cumming, *A Historical Survey of the Boiler Makers and Iron and Steel Shipbuilder's Society from August 1834 to August 1904* (Newcastle on Tyne, UK: R. Robinson, 1905), 171.
6. Nos. 117 and 118 were sisters in the traditional sense, meaning they were the same size and build. The remaining four ships were also true sisters. All six ships ultimately became part of the same line.
7. "The Spanish Transatlantic Mail Steam Packet Company Now Run Their Magnificent Steamers," *Glasgow Herald* (Glasgow, Scotland), October 12, 1855. *Vigo* launched on June 2, 1855. "Launch of a Screw Steamer," *Liverpool Mercury*, June 5, 1855. *Cádiz* launched on August 30, 1855, and *Barcelona* on September 1, 1855. "Launches of New Steamers at Liverpool," *The Guardian* (London), August 30, 1855. The *Guardian* reported that *Habana*'s October 25, 1855, trip from Liverpool to Cuba would be its second crossing. "Steam to Havana—Spanish Steamers from Liverpool to Havana," *The Guardian* (London), October 10, 1855.
8. "Spanish Steamers from Liverpool to Havana," *Manchester Weekly Times and Examiner* (Manchester, UK), October 13, 1855.
9. Ibid.
10. Approximately 3,750 pounds today.
11. New York & Havre's *Arago*, built by Westervelt & Sons in New York, and Franco-Américaine's *François Arago* are different ships. Both were named after French physicist François Arago.
12. Cammel Laird records list the ship's name as "*Lyonnais*" or "*Le Lyonnais*." Nineteenth-century French records are often inconsistent when it comes to the use of articles such as "le" before a ship's name. Official documentation lists hull numbers 134 and 136 as *Le Franc-Comtois* and *Le Lyonnais*, as they were named after specific regions of France, while vessel 117 (ex-*Habana*) was renamed *L'Alma*, after the then-recent Crimean War battle. Le Lyonnais is the name for the region around the city of Lyon. Le Franc-Comtois is the area around Besançon, sandwiched between Burgundy and the Swiss border. *The London Times*, the newspaper of record during the relevant period, dutifully stuck to *Le Lyonnais* in all its contemporary reports of the collision even if it meant writing "the *Le Lyonnais*." In the late nineteenth century, the French transatlantic steamship line Compagnie Générale Transatlantique had several ships named after the regions of France, such as *La Lorraine*, *La Savoie*, *La Bourgogne*, *La Champagne*, and *La Normandie*, and in each case the definite article was officially part of the vessel's

name. It was not until the twentieth century that French lines dropped articles to be more consistent with English names. For these reasons, the ship's formal name, *Le Lyonnais*, which includes the article "Le," is used herein.
13. "Gatherings from Our Exchanges," *Triweekly Washington Sentinel* (Washington, DC), March 27, 1856.
14. Portions of chapters 4, 5, and 6 pertaining to *Le Lyonnais*'s construction and early operation were written in collaboration with Martin Cleaver, archives & records officer, Wirral Archives, Birkenhead, UK.

Chapter 5: Iron and Steam

1. Cammell Laird, "Contract to Build Hull Numbers 133–136," Wirral Archives Service, Birkenhead, UK, 1855, 143–44.
2. Ibid., 144.
3. Sir Edward James Reed, *Shipbuilding in Iron and Steel: A Practical Treatise, Giving Full details of Construction, Processes of Manufacture, and Building Arrangements* (London: Murray, 1869), 213.
4. Cammel Laird, "Contract," 148.
5. Ibid. Box-type boilers, which were common at the time, performed at approximately 10 pounds per square inch, but *Le Lyonnais*'s tubular boilers were capable of bearing a working pressure of 20 pounds per square inch and were tested at twice that amount. Each boiler had 240 square feet of fire bar surface and 6,300 square feet of heating surface.
6. "A Bill Regulating the Carriage of Passengers in Merchant Vessels," *Parliamentary Papers*, vol. 4 (March 12, 1849), 7.
7. There are no reports that indicate the specific net tonnage of *Le Lyonnais*. P&O reported that *Ellora*, formerly *Cadix*'s and *Le Lyonnais*'s sister, was 1,070 after modifications. P&O Heritage, P&O Ship Fact Sheet: *Ellora*, P&O Heritage Collection, November 2008.
8. "Communication with France Loss of the *Normandy*," *Hansard Parliamentary Debates*, 3rd ser., vol. 200 (March 21, 1870), 324.
9. "Saving Life at Sea—Report of the Select Committee of the House of Commons, 1887," *Nautical Magazine* 56, no. 7 (July 1887): 717.
10. Laws passed in the 1880s began to regulate the size of lifeboats, but the number of boats required continued to depend on gross tonnage alone. *Titanic*, with a gross tonnage of 46,000 tons, carried twenty lifeboats. Although this was beyond what the standards at the time mandated, the boats accommodated only 1,200 of the 3,300 on board when the ship struck ice in 1912. It was only after this widely publicized disaster that regulations changed to ensure that there was space for every passenger and crew member on a lifeboat in the event of an emergency.

Chapter 6: 132 Souls

1. Burgess, *Engines of Empire*, 12; and Rodrigo Andres, "The Bellepotent as Heterotopia, Total Institution and Colony: Billy Budd and Other Spaces in Melville's Mediterranean," *Leviathan*, 13, No. 3 (October 2011).
2. Ibid.
3. Henry Wadsworth Longfellow, *The Letters of Henry Wadsworth Longfellow*, Longfellow Trust (Cambridge, MA: Belknap Press of Harvard University Press, 1983), 537.
4. Charles went on to establish the Gibson House, a now-famous architectural site in Boston's Back Bay.

5. "Frightful Collision at Sea. Loss of the French Steamer *Lyonnais*—over One Hundred Persons Lost," *New York Tribune*, November 17, 1856.
6. The common abbreviation for forecastle is fo'c'sle, which mimics the phonetic pronunciation of the word.
7. She had on board her captain, five executive officers, three civil officers, five engineers, six warrant officers, fourteen petty officers, thirty-two European seamen, and ninety-three non-European seamen.
8. William B. Silber, *A History of St. James' Methodist Episcopal Church at Harlem, New York City, 1830–1880: With Some Facts Relating to the Settlement of Harlem* (New York: Phillips & Hunt, 1882), 67.
9. Ibid.
10. "Tout ce qui se rattache au naufrage du *Lyonnais*," *Le Propagateur: Journal d'ypres et de l'arrondissement* (Ypres, Belgium), December 10, 1856.
11. *The Foreign Office List and Diplomatic and Consular Year Book*, vol. 10 (London: Harrison and Sons, 1857), 75. Schedel's name is sometimes misspelled "Schedell." Consular documents list him as "Schedel."
12. Michele Anders Kinney, "Doubly Foreign: British Consuls in the Antebellum South, 1830–1860," partial fulfillment of the requirements for the degree of doctor of philosophy, University of Texas at Arlington, August 2010, 59.
13. Dr. Howe married Crawford's sister, Julia Ward. Crawford had just returned to New York from Rome to deliver plans for his famous statue *Freedom* when he visited with Sumner. Senator Charles Sumner commissioned the artist to build the statue to decorate Congress, where it can still be seen today.
14. Florence Howe Hall, *Memories Grave and Gay* (New York and London: Harper & Brothers 1918), 116.0
15. "Musical," *New York Times*, May 13, 1854.
16. Ibid.

Chapter 7: Sailors, Watchmen, Firemen, Passengers

1. "Loss of the *Lyonnais*: Sailing of the Marion in Search of Survivors of the Wreck," *New York Daily Herald*, November 17, 1856.
2. Ibid.
3. Ibid.
4. Ibid.
5. "Barque" is a French word that was adopted by American shipbuilders. It is sometimes spelled "bark" in the United States. Barque is used herein unless a direct quote uses the alternate spelling.
6. "Loss of the *Lyonnais*."
7. "The *Lyonnais*—Interesting Details," *Augusta Chronicle* (Augusta, GA), November 20, 1856.
8. "Loss of the *Lyonnais*."
9. Ibid.
10. "Wreck of the *Lyonnais*: Statement of a Female Passenger," *Hudson Daily Star*, November 18, 1856.
11. Ibid.
12. "Loss of the *Lyonnais*."
13. Ibid.
14. Ibid.

Chapter 8: Abandon Ship

1. "The Wrecked Steamer *Lyonnais*—Rescue of the Captain and Fifteen of the Passengers and Crew," *Charleston Daily Courier* (Charleston, SC), December 29, 1856.
2. "The Loss of the *Lyonnais*: Statement of One of the Survivors—the Rescue of the Third Mate's Party," *New York Times*, February 7, 1857.
3. Ibid.
4. Ibid.
5. Ibid.
6. Ibid.
7. Ibid.
8. Ibid.
9. Ibid.
10. Ibid.
11. "Terrible Disaster at Sea—Loss of the French Steamer *Le Lyonnais*," *Morning Chronicle* (London), December 2, 1856; and "Further Particulars: Loss of the French Steamer *Le Lyonnais*," *Daily Pennsylvanian* (Philadelphia), November 17, 1856.

Chapter 9: The Dragon

1. "Junk," *New World Encyclopedia*, 2023, https://www.newworldencyclopedia.org/entry/Junk_(ship).
2. America produced 435 clippers during this period. William L. Crothers, *The American-Built Clipper Ship, 1850–1856: Characteristics, Construction, and Details*, reprint ed. (Brattleboro, VT: Echo Point Books & Media, 2017), XI.
3. Penobscot Marine Museum, "Ships and Shipbuilding," Education, 2012, https://www.penobscotmarinemuseum.org/pbho-1/ships-shipbuilding/ships-shipbuilding-introduction.
4. March E. Honey, "Carter & Perkins: A Ship Building Dynasty, Part II," *Before the Mast* 3, no. 22 (March 24, 2000): 1.
5. A board foot is a piece of unmilled wood 1 foot by 1 foot by 1 inch; 12 board feet equals 1 cubic foot. Penobscot Marine Museum, "Ships and Shipbuilding."
6. "Generalities: The Barque *Adriatic*," *Belfast Republican Journal* (Belfast, ME), October 17, 1856.
7. Ibid.

Chapter 10: Adrift

1. "The Loss of the *Lyonnais*: Statement of One of the Survivors—the Rescue of the Third Mate's Party," *New York Times*, February 7, 1857.
2. Ibid.
3. Ibid.
4. Some conflicting accounts suggest the boat was not equipped with oars, but survivor accounts frequently mention oars and rowing.
5. Thourel, "Notes en réplique pour MM. Gauthier frères contre le Captaine Durham," (Aix, France: Frederic Vitalis, 1857), 22.

Chapter 11: Perils of the Sea

1. Samuel Taylor Coleridge, *Rime of the Ancient Mariner* (Cambridge, MA: Harvard University Educational, 1906), 30–31.

2. The brain and heart are composed of 73 percent water; the lungs, 83 percent water; the skin, 64 percent water; the muscles and kidneys, 79 percent water; and the bones, 31 percent water. H. H. Mitchell, T. S. Hamilton, F. R. Steggerda, and H. W. Bean, "The Chemical Composition of the Adult Human Body and Its Bearing on the Biochemistry of Growth," *Journal of Biological Chemistry* 158, no. 3 (1945): 628.
3. William H. Allen, "Thirst: Can Shipwrecked Men Survive If They Drink Seawater?," *Natural History Magazine*, December 1956, 1.
4. Ibid.
5. "Shocking Loss of an American Steamship," *Bury and Norwich Post* (Bury, UK), November 6, 1866.
6. Ibid.
7. "Shipwrecks and Loss of Life and Awful Sufferings among Icebergs," *Hull Packet and East Riding Times* (East Yorkshire, UK), April 11, 1856.
8. "Survivors of the Missouri, Distressing Tales of Their Suffering at Sea," *Chicago Tribune*, November 4, 1872.
9. Ibid.

Chapter 12: Forged in a Storm

1. "The Loss of the *Lyonnais*: Statement of One of the Survivors—the Rescue of the Third Mate's Party," *New York Times*, February 7, 1857.
2. Ibid.
3. "The Disaster to the *Lyonnaise*: Further Particulars," *Baltimore Sun*, November 18, 1856.

Chapter 13: Purgatory

1. "The Lost *Lyonnais*," *Poughkeepsie Journal* (Poughkeepsie, NY), March 7, 1857.
2. Ibid.
3. "Interesting Account of the Loss of the Steamer *Lyonnais*," *Louisville Courier* (Louisville, KY), March 11, 1857.
4. Ibid.
5. "The Lost *Lyonnais*."

Chapter 14: 1856

1. "The Screw Steam-Ship *City of Glasgow*," *The Standard* (London), August 31, 1854.
2. "Weekly Summary: Foreign," *Manchester Weekly Times and Examiner* (Manchester, UK), September 20, 1854.
3. "The Missing Steamer *Pacific*," *Liverpool Mercury*, July 26, 1861.
4. Antelope, "A Letter from Antelope," *Times Picayune* (New Orleans), January 4, 1857.
5. "Late Gale: Packet-Ship *St. Denis* Foundering at Sea," *New York Daily Herald*, January 17, 1856.
6. Ibid.
7. "Dreadful Shipwreck," *Buffalo Evening Post* (Buffalo, NY), May 9, 1856.
8. "The Late Severe Weather and Its Consequences—Frustrated Absence of a Large Fleet of Vessels," *New York Daily Herald*, March 29, 1857.

Chapter 15: Goodbye

1. The *Van Capellan* survivors also resorted to eating the dead. "Horrible Death and Suffering of a Ship's Crew," *Glasgow Herald* (Glasgow, Scotland), July 25, 1865. Drinking blood has a similar effect as drinking salt water and urine.
2. "Total Loss of the Ship *Van Cappellan*," *The Standard* (London), July 22, 1865.
3. "Loss of the *Lyonnais*: Sailing of the *Marion* in Search of Survivors of the Wreck," *New York Daily Herald*, November 17, 1856.
4. "Awful Calamity at Sea," *Charlotte Democrat* (Charlotte, NC), November 25, 1856.
5. "Shipwreck of Frightful Sufferings," *Cambridge Chronicle and University Journal* (Cambridge, UK), April 12, 1856.

Chapter 16: Laughter

1. "The Loss of the *Lyonnais*: Statement of One of the Survivors—the Rescue of the Third Mate's Party," *New York Times*, February 7, 1857.
2. "Central America. San Jose, in Costa Rica, Central America, Tuesday, October 25, 1853," *Washington Sentinel* (Washington, DC), November 27, 1853.
3. Ibid.
4. Ibid.
5. Ibid.
6. Ibid.

Chapter 17: Ship!

1. "Terrible Disaster at Sea," *New York Daily Herald*, November 17, 1856.
2. Ibid.
3. "The Loss of the *Lyonnais*: Statement of One of the Survivors—the Rescue of the Third Mate's Party," *New York Times*, February 7, 1857.
4. Ibid.
5. Ibid.
6. "Loss of the *Lyonnais*: Sailing of the *Marion* in Search of Survivors of the Wreck," *New York Daily Herald*, November 17, 1856.
7. "The Loss of the *Lyonnais*: Statement of One of the Survivors."

Chapter 18: On a Barrel

1. "Additional Respecting the French Steamer *Lyonnais*," *Brooklyn Daily Eagle*, February 19, 1857.

Chapter 19: Two Ships *Elise*

1. "The Loss of *Le Lyonnais*," *New York Daily Herald*, November 17, 1856.
2. "The Loss of the *Lyonnais*: Statement of One of the Survivors—the Rescue of the Third Mate's Party," *New York Times*, February 7, 1857.
3. The Bremen-bound *Elise* was built by Johann Lange, Vegesak/Grohn, and launched on May 10, 1835, for the Bremen firm of Albers & Koncke. In 1850, she belonged half to the firm of J. D. Koncke Hermanns Sohn and half to Ferdinand Henschen. The New York–bound *Elise*'s home port was Hamburg. Originally called *Norden*, she was built at Nyborg, Denmark, in 1842. On January 14, 1850, the Hamburg firm of C. Robcke & Woellmer purchased her and renamed her *Elise*. "*Elise* (1835)," Palmer List of Merchant Vessels, December 9, 1997, https://www.oocities.org/mppraetorius/com-el.htm.

Chapter 20: Gloucester

1. "The Loss of *Le Lyonnais*," *New York Daily Herald*, November 17, 1856.
2. "Disasters," *Belfast Republican Journal* (Belfast, ME), November 14, 1856.
3. Ibid.
4. "The Wreck of the Steamship *Le Lyonnais*," *New York Daily Herald*, November 18, 1856.
5. "The Latest News Received by Magnetic Telegraph," *New York Tribune*, November 18, 1856.
6. "Wreck of the Steamship *Le Lyonnais*," *Green Mountain Freeman* (Montpelier, VT), November 27, 1856.
7. The comment later caused some to believe that *Le Lyonnais* was a paddle steamer.
8. Joseph Williamson, *History of the City of Belfast in the State of Maine: From Its First Settlement in 1770 to 1885*, vol. 1 (Portland, ME: Loring, Short, and Harmon, 1887), 345.
9. "Disasters—Barque *Adriatic*," *Belfast Republican Journal* (Belfast, ME), November 14, 1856.
10. "The Collision with *Le Lyonnais*—Safety of the Vessel with Which She Was in Contact," *Boston Traveler*, November 17, 1856.
11. "Calamity at Sea," *Belfast Republican Journal*, November 21, 1856.
12. "The Late Marine Disaster: Conduct of Officers at Sea," *New York Daily Herald*, November 19, 1856. Lieutenant Matthew Fontaine Maury suggested the development of international standards to make ships take different inbound and outbound routes to avoid collision. Maury is often referred to as the father of modern-day oceanography for studying weather data from thousands of shipping logs to help shorten the shipping routes.
13. "To the Editor of the Herald: Foresheet," *New York Daily Herald*, November 19, 1856.
14. "The Disaster to the *Lyonnais*," *Belfast Republican Journal* (Belfast, ME), December 5, 1856.
15. "The Wreck of the *Lyonnais*—Statement of Captain Durham," *Baltimore Sun*, November 20, 1856.
16. "The Disaster to the *Lyonnais*: Gloucester, Nov. 14th, 1856, to the Editor of the *Boston Journal*."
17. "To Correspondents," *New York Tribune*, November 18, 1856.
18. "Loss of *Le Lyonnais*: Further Developments," *Buffalo Daily Republic* (Buffalo, NY), November 21, 1856.
19. "The Disaster to the *Lyonnais*: Gloucester, Nov. 14th, 1856, to the Editor of the *Boston Journal*," *Belfast Republican Journal* (Belfast, ME), December 5, 1856.
20. Ibid.
21. "Disaster to a French Steamer—130 Lives," *Eastern Mail* (Waterville, ME), November 20, 1856.
22. "The Loss of the *Lyonnais*," *Belfast Republican Journal* (Belfast, ME), November 28, 1856.
23. "The *Lyonnais* Disaster," *Buffalo Morning Express and Illustrated Buffalo Express*, November 20, 1856.
24. "The Loss of *Le Lyonnais*," *New York Morning Courier*, November 18, 1856.
25. "Loss of the French Steamer *Lyonnais*: Further Explanations Necessary," *New York Daily Herald*, November 18, 1856.
26. "A Dispatch from Havre," *Belfast Republican Journal* (Belfast, ME), December 19, 1856.

Endnotes

27. "United States: From Our Correspondents," *The Guardian* (London), December 2, 1856.
28. Ibid.

Chapter 21: The Phantom Ship

1. Sumner's friend Dr. Samuel Gridley Howe replaced Cleveland in the club after his untimely death in 1843.
2. Samuel Longfellow, ed., *The Life of Henry Wadsworth Longfellow, with Extracts from His Journals and Correspondence*, vol. 2 (Boston: Ticknor, 1886), 281.
3. Ibid., 289.
4. Ibid.
5. Katie Shinabeck, "History Repeats Itself," *Gibson House Museum Blog*, Gibson House Museum, January 1, 2015, https://thegibsonhousemuseum.blogspot.com/2015/01/history-repeats-itself.html.
6. The *New York Times* published a retraction at the insistence of the Bassford family. "Condition of the *Lyonnais* Sufferers: The Bark *Adriatic* That Ran the Steamer Down," *New York Times*, November 18, 1856.
7. "The Lost Steamer *Lyonnais*," *Baltimore Sun*, December 15, 1856.
8. The boat also contained a white shirt, a white skirt, and a fine chambric handkerchief with the monogram F.E., L.E., T.E., or F.C., depending on the source. There is no one with the initials F.E. or L.E. on the cabin passenger list. It is possible it belonged to a member of the crew. "Halifax, December 31," *Alton Weekly Telegraph* (Alton, IL), January 8, 1857.
9. The equivalent of $30,000,000 today.
10. Hall, *Memories Grave and Gay*, 117.
11. Ann Laurens Dawes, *Makers of America: Charles Sumner* (New York: Dodd, Mead, 1892), 127.
12. An article about the lawsuit describes Solomon as an attendant to Ms. Bassford. To reporters in New York, she described herself as Ms. Dummer's "lady in waiting." The Bassfords' passport applications list a servant, but the Dummers' do not. It is possible that *The New York Times* misinterpreted Solomon's statement and that she worked for the Bassfords. "Law Intelligencer," *New York Daily Tribune*, April 2, 1857; and "Condition of the *Lyonnais* Sufferers: The Bark *Adriatic* That Ran the Steamer Down." *New York Times*, November 18, 1856.

Chapter 22: Survivors

1. Du Montholon became ambassador to France during American president Andrew Jackson's administration.
2. "Frightful Collision at Sea," *Gazette & Courier* (Greenfield, MA), November 24, 1856.
3. "Terrible Disaster at Sea—Loss of the French Steamer *Le Lyonnais*," *Morning Chronicle* (London), December 2, 1856.
4. Ibid.
5. "The Officers of the *Lyonnais*," *Morning Chronicle* (London), December 2, 1856.
6. "The Loss of *Le Lyonnais*," *New York Daily Herald*, November 17, 1856.
7. "The Loss of the *Lyonnais*: Statement of One of the Survivors—the Rescue of the Third Mate's Party," *New York Times*, February 7, 1857.

Chapter 23: Command
1. This is not the same *Essex* that picked up *Le Lyonnais* survivors years later.
2. Honey, "Carter & Perkins: A Ship Building Dynasty, Part II."

Chapter 24: La Ciotat
1. "Alleged Seizure of the Barque *Adriatic*," *Belfast Republican Journal* (Belfast, ME), July 16, 1858.
2. Ibid.
3. Ibid.
4. Ibid.
5. Ibid.
6. The modern spelling is Marseille. The city name was spelled Marseilles in the 1850s.
7. "The Barque *Adriatic*," *Washington Union* (Washington, DC), April 8, 1857.
8. "The Barque *Adriatic*," *Washington Union* (Washington, DC), March 28, 1857.
9. "Bark *Adriatic* and the *Lyonnais*," *New York Times*, May 1, 1857.
10. "The Case of the Steamer *Lyonnais*, Collision between the *Lyonnais* and the *Adriatic*—Claim of Damage—Question of Competency," *New York Daily Herald*, April 27, 1857.
11. "The Bark *Adriatic*," *Bangor Daily Whig and Courier* (Bangor, ME), March 20, 1857.

Chapter 25: Mourning
1. New York Chamber of Commerce, *In Relation to Collisions at Sea* (New York: John W. Amerman, 1858), 18.
2. "No. 5681—Decret Imperial." *Bulletin des lois de la Republique Francaise*, vol. 11 (Paris: Impr. Nationale des Lois, 1857), 126.
3. Jules Gemming presided over the *Adriatic* case with businessmen Emile Martin and Bruno Pechier. Capt. John H. Bell, "Rules of the Road at Sea," *California Nautical Magazine*, 1868, 164.
4. French documents misspelled some of the sailors' names. It is possible that William Koller is a misspelling of William Kelly, a sailor who served with Durham.
5. George Durham's death certificate contains no cause of death. Although he was a captain, there is nothing to indicate that he died at sea, and his absence from his siblings' tombstone suggests a different cause of death.

Chapter 26: Exoneration
1. "Parisian Gossip," *Buffalo Commercial* (Buffalo, NY), April 21, 1857.
2. Thourel, "Notes en réplique pour MM. Gauthier frères contre le Captaine Durham."
3. *Le Lyonnais* had a reverse-acting helm. When the helm was turned in one direction, the rudder pivoted in the opposite direction. If the captain put the helm to port, the ship would turn starboard and vice versa. For simplification, the direction the ship turned, and not the direction to which Devaulx put the helm, are used to describe what occurred.
4. Thourel, "Notes en réplique pour MM. Gauthier frères contre le Captaine Durham," 27–28.
5. Ibid., 29.
6. Ibid., 27.

7. "The Wreck of the *Lyonnais*—Statement of Captain Durham," *Baltimore Sun*, November 20, 1856.
8. Thourel, "Notes en réplique pour MM. Gauthier frères contre le Captaine Durham," 26.
9. Luffing is when a sailing vessel is steered far enough toward the direction of the wind that airflow over the surfaces of the sail is disrupted, and the sail begins to "flap" or "luff."
10. Le Tribunal de Commerce de Marseille, "Jugement," (France), April 2, 1857, 3.
11. Albert Aicard, "Notes in réplique pour le Cap Durham de *l'Adriatic*, contre MM Gauthier frères, gérants de la Compagne Franco-Américaine, armateurs du *Lyonnais* (Marseille, France: Arnaud et Comp, 1857), 18; and "The Bark *Adriatic* and the *Lyonnais*," *Bangor Daily Whig and Courier* (Bangor, ME), April 27, 1857.
12. The tribunal cited Article 407 of the commission code.
13. "Decision of Court in France," *Baton Rouge Tri-Weekly Gazette and Comment* (Baton Rouge, LA), May 11, 1857.
14. The Shipwreck of the *Lyonnais*," *Buffalo Courier* (Buffalo, NY), April 24, 1857.
15. "Decision of the French Court in the Case of the Barque *Adriatic*," *Eastern Argus* (Portland, ME), May 11, 1857.

Chapter 27: Notes en Réplique

1. Bell, "Rules of the Road at Sea," 164.
2. "The American Barque *Adriatic*: Can American Vessels Be Confiscated in France, for Collisions in Americans Waters, When Their Captains Sail Them Strictly according to Our Laws?" *Belfast Republican Journal* (Belfast, ME), February 26, 1858.
3. Ferdinand-Alphonse Hamelin, "Circulaire Ministérielle—Abrodage—Eclairage des navires—Responsabilité—Notification d'un Arret de la Cour Imperial d'Aix," *Bulletin Officiel de La Martinique*, serie 7: 1–12 (Paris: Bureau de l'imprimerie du gouvernement, 1858), 109.
4. "The American Barque *Adriatic*: Can American Vessels Be Confiscated in France, for Collisions in Americans Waters, When Their Captains Sail Them Strictly according to Our Laws?"
5. An *avoué* is a French lawyer who does not argue in court but prepares paperwork and documents related to court cases. French courts did not eliminate the distinction between *avoué* and *avocat* until 2012.
6. Cauvin told reporters in New York that he was asleep at the time of the collision, but this fact somehow escaped Aicard's review of the evidence.
7. Thourel, "Notes en réplique pour MM. Gauthier frères contre le Captaine Durham," 10.
8. Ibid., 14.
9. Ibid., 13.
10. Ibid., 24.
11. Aicard. "Notes en réplique pour le Cap Durham de *l'Adriatic*, contre MM Gauthier frères, gérants de la Compagne Franco-Américaine, armateurs du *Lyonnais*," 22.
12. "The French Steamship *Lyonnais* and the Barque *Adriatic*," *New York Daily Herald*, January 21, 1858.
13. Bell, "Rules of the Road at Sea," 164.

Chapter 28: The Marseille Predicament

1. "The American Barque *Adriatic*: Can American Vessels Be Confiscated in France, for Collisions in Americans Waters, When Their Captains Sail Them Strictly according to Our Laws?"
2. Ibid.
3. "The Bark *Adriatic*," *Savannah Republican* (Savannah, GA), March 22, 1858.
4. Ward L. Smith, "Escape of the *Adriatic*: From the Harbor of Marseilles, France, in 1858," undated, Historic Mobile Preservation Society.

Chapter 29: Captain Ward L. Smith

1. Family historians believe that the "L" stands for Lawrence, but there are no official documents to verify it.
2. Ward L. Smith, "A Whaling Adventure: Life on a Whale Ship Fifty-Five Years Ago," New Bedford Whaling Museum, Pam +176, 1900.
3. Sharon Davey LaDuke, Ward Smith's grandniece, has collected stories about Uncle Ward passed down through the family. The Smith family has been an invaluable resource.
4. Author's correspondence with Sharon Davey LaDuke.
5. Smith, "A Whaling Adventure: Life on a Whale Ship Fifty-Five Years Ago."
6. Ibid.
7. Ibid.
8. The captain received the largest share, $\frac{1}{14}$ of the vessel's profits. Whaleman's Shipping Paper, District Port of New Bedford, New Bedford Whaling Museum, Swift & Allen Papers, Mss 78, S-g3, series Y, S-s 1, folder 1.
9. Smith, "A Whaling Adventure: Life on a Whale Ship Fifty-Five Years Ago."
10. Ibid.
11. Ibid.
12. The crew list for *Tuscaloosa* lists a man by the name of Daniel C. Hunt. Ward Smith refers to him as Dana C. Hunt, a nickname, in his memoir about *Tuscaloosa*. "*Tuscaloosa* of N. Bedford at Ind. & Pa. Oceans," New Bedford Whaling Museum, *Tuscaloosa* Crew List, no. 129, Smith & Allen Papers, November 27, 1844.
13. Smith, "A Whaling Adventure: Life on a Whale Ship Fifty-Five Years Ago."
14. John Ross Browne, *Etchings of a Whaling Cruise with Notes of a Sojourn on the Island of Zanzibar to Which Is Appended a Brief History of the Whale Fishery, Its Past and Present Condition* (New York: Harper & Brothers, 1846), 24.
15. Albert Goodwin, "1844 Letter from Captain Goodwin," New Bedford Whaling Museum, Swift & Allen Papers, S-g, series F, S-s 1, folder 3, box 41.
16. Smith, "A Whaling Adventure: Life on a Whale Ship Fifty-Five Years Ago."
17. Goodwin, "1844 Letter from Captain Goodwin."
18. The first mate's name is misspelled "Alma" in some records.
19. Smith, "A Whaling Adventure: Life on a Whale Ship Fifty-Five Years Ago."
20. Ibid.
21. Ibid.
22. Ibid.
23. Ibid.
24. Ibid.
25. Ibid.
26. Ibid.

27. Smith's story goes on to say that he and his crew were captured by Patagonian natives and lived with them for a time until the captain returned for them. Goodwin's reports to his employers and financial records of the *Tuscaloosa* voyage suggest otherwise. It is possible that Smith fictionalized the latter portion of the story when he wrote it for a newspaper later in life. Smith, "A Whaling Adventure: Life on a Whale Ship Fifty-Five Years Ago."
28. Ibid.
29. Ibid.
30. Ibid.
31. Ibid.
32. Ibid.
33. Ibid.
34. Ibid.
35. Ibid.
36. Ibid.

Chapter 30: Stranded

1. The family's original name, Maher, was modified first to Meagher and then to Meaher. The surnames Meagher and Meaher are used interchangeably in historical records.
2. James Delgado, *Archaeological Investigations of 1Ba704, a Nineteenth-Century Shipwreck Site in the Mobile River, Baldwin and Mobile Counties, Alabama: Final Report*, report prepared for the Alabama Historical Commission, the People of Africatown, the National Geographic Society, and the Slave Wrecks Project, May 2019, 20.
3. Documents are unclear as to whether Durham was in Elliott's employ or working for the Meaher family on contracts with *Abaellino*.
4. Delgado, *Archaeological Investigations of 1Ba704, a Nineteenth-Century Shipwreck Site in the Mobile River, Baldwin and Mobile Counties, Alabama: Final Report*, 22.
5. The remaining three were built by Florida shipbuilders.
6. "Schooner *S. E. Meaher*," *Jones Valley Times* (Birmingham, AL), August 4, 1854.
7. The modern names for these countries are Ukraine to the north, Turkey to the south, and Moldova, Romania, and Bulgaria to the west.
8. Galatz or Galati is a city on the Danube River in modern-day Romania.
9. Ward L. Smith, Logbook of *Sarah E. Meaher*, 1855–1857, Historic Mobile Preservation Society.
10. Ibid.
11. Roger B. Taney was named for the Supreme Court chief justice who penned the Dred Scott decision, which held that enslaved people were not US citizens and, therefore, could not sue in federal court.

Chapter 31: Escape from Marseille

1. "Escape of the *Adriatic*," *Belfast Republican Journal* (Belfast, ME), April 2, 1858.
2. Oakum is loose fiber created by untwisting old ropes by hand.
3. "The Bark *Adriatic*," *Savannah Republican* (Savannah, GA), March 22, 1858.
4. Smith, "Escape of the *Adriatic*: From the Harbor of Marseilles, France, in 1858."
5. "Escape of the *Adriatic*," *Belfast Republican Journal* (Belfast, ME), April 2, 1858.

6. Smith, "Escape of the *Adriatic*: From the Harbor of Marseilles, France, in 1858."
7. "Escape of the American Bark *Adriatic* from Marseilles," *Belfast Republican Journal* (Belfast, ME), February 5, 1858.
8. Smith, "Escape of the *Adriatic*: From the Harbor of Marseilles, France, in 1858."
9. Ibid.
10. Ibid.
11. "Escape of Captain Durham," *Harper's Weekly, The Year 1858* 2 (March 6, 1858).

Chapter 32: The Fog

1. Smith, "Escape of the *Adriatic*: From the Harbor of Marseilles, France, in 1858."
2. Ibid.
3. Ibid.
4. Prior to the unification of Italy, the section of the country from Genoa to Sardinia belonged to the Kingdom of Sardinia under the rule of King Victor Emmanuel.

Chapter 33: Spezia

1. "The American Barque *Adriatic*: Can American Vessels Be Confiscated in France, for Collisions in Americans Waters, When Their Captains Sail Them Strictly according to Our Laws?," *Belfast Republican Journal* (Belfast, ME), February 26, 1858.
2. Ibid.
3. "French Justice and a Yankee Captain [Translated from the *Courrier du Havre* of Jan 13, for the *New York Herald*]," *New York Daily Herald*, February 1, 1858.
4. "Second Escape of the Bark *Adriatic*," *Harper's Weekly Magazine*, February 27, 1858, 135.
5. Smith, "Escape of the *Adriatic*: From the Harbor of Marseilles, France, in 1858."
6. Ibid.
7. Ibid.
8. Ibid.
9. Ibid.
10. Ibid.
11. Ibid.
12. "Escape of the *Adriatic*," *Belfast Republican Journal* (Belfast, ME), April 2, 1858.
13. Smith, "Escape of the *Adriatic*: From the Harbor of Marseilles, France, in 1858."
14. "The American Barque *Adriatic*: Can American Vessels Be Confiscated in France, for Collisions in Americans Waters, When Their Captains Sail Them Strictly according to Our Laws?"

Chapter 34: Friends in High Places

1. He changed his name from Giovanni Martini to John Martin when he married an American woman, Maria Biby. Ruth Charlton, Martin, Campbell, Furlong Family Papers, MC 90, Philadelphia Archdiocesan Historical Research Center, October 17, 2012.
2. Jonathan Stephen Martin, Letter to Ward L. Smith, January 23, 1858, Historic Mobile Preservation Society.
3. Ibid.
4. Ibid.
5. Ibid.

6. Ibid.
7. Ibid.

Chapter 35: Piracy

1. Captain Smith's story says the date was on or about January 21, 1858, but his log entries indicate the date was January 26, 1858. Ward L. Smith, "Slip of paper with dates of *Adriatic*'s escape written on it," 1858, Historic Mobile Preservation Society.
2. Twenty-five dollars is $625 today.
3. "Escape of Captain Durham," *Harper's Weekly Magazine*, March 6, 1858.
4. Smith, "Escape of the *Adriatic*: From the Harbor of Marseilles, France, in 1858."
5. Ibid.
6. Ibid.
7. Ibid.
8. Ibid.

Chapter 36: The *Adriatic* Affair

1. "Collisions at Sea," *Essex County Standard* (Colchester, UK), January 2, 1857, quoting the *New York Times*, January 6, 1857.
2. Ibid.
3. Ibid.
4. "Chamber of Commerce: Rogers' Marine Signals—the Case of the Bark *Adriatic*—Laws with Regard to Collisions at Sea—Custom House Forms," *New York Daily Herald*, February 20, 1858.
5. Ibid.
6. Henry Collins Brown, *Fifth Avenue Old and New: 1824–1924* (New York: Henry Collins Brown), 1924, 32.
7. "Chamber of Commerce: Rogers' Marine Signals—the Case of the Bark *Adriatic*—Laws with Regard to Collisions at Sea—Custom House Forms."
8. Ibid.
9. The building is now part of the South Street Seaport Museum.
10. "Later from the Bark *Adriatic*," *Daily Exchange* (Baltimore), March 11, 1858. February 4 is the date the story was posted, but it is unclear when the *Daily Exchange*'s correspondent made the observations. It is possible that Durham took a longer route from Cape Palos to Gibraltar, but more likely that the newspaper reports were published some days after the observations were made.
11. "Arrival of the Runaway Barque *Adriatic* at Savannah," *Washington Union* (Washington, DC), March 23, 1858.
12. News that Durham received an anchor from *Elizabeth Dennison* was not reported until March 18, 1858. "Escape of the *Adriatic*—Her Safe Arrival at Savannah!" *Daily Constitutionalist and Republic* (Augusta, GA), March 20, 1858.
13. "The Case of the American Bark *Adriatic*," *New York Daily Herald*, February 22, 1858.
14. Moore was the owner of the journal from 1849 to May 1858, when he sold the paper to William H. Simpson. He remained editor until 1861. Joseph Williamson, *History of the City of Belfast in the State of Maine: From Its First Settlement in 1770 to 1885*, vol. 1, 354.15; and "Public Meeting," *Belfast Republican Journal* (Belfast, ME), March 5, 1858.

Chapter 37: Rules of the Road

1. "French Justice and a Yankee Captain [Translated from the *Courrier du Havre* of Jan 13, for the *New York Daily Herald*]," *New York Daily Herald*, February 1, 1858.
2. *Congressional Globe*, House of Representatives, 35th Congress, 1st Session, March 8, 1858, 991.
3. Ibid.
4. Ibid.
5. Ibid.
6. Lord William Pitt Lennox, "Chapter V," in *Pictures of Sporting Life and Character*, vol. 2 (London: Hurst and Blackett, 1860), 127.
7. *Congressional Globe*, House of Representatives, 35th Congress, 1st Session, March 8, 1858, 991.
8. Ibid.
9. Ibid., 992.

Chapter 38: Celebrity

1. "The Bark *Adriatic*," *Buffalo Commercial* (Buffalo, NY), March 22, 1858.
2. Charles Durham, Letter to Ward L. Smith, March 24, 1858, Historic Mobile Preservation Society.
3. "The *Adriatic* Arrived," *Belfast Republican Journal* (Belfast, ME), March 26, 1858.
4. Durham, Letter to Ward L. Smith.
5. "The Barque *Adriatic*," *Richmond Dispatch*, May 3, 1858.
6. Jordan had recently been appointed clerk to the United States Court of Appeals in the Third Circuit. "In the Third Circuit," *Evening Star* (Washington, DC), April 21, 1857.
7. "The Case of the *Adriatic*," *Brooklyn Evening Star*, April 17, 1858.
8. "Captain Durham," *Savannah Georgian*, April 12, 1856.

Chapter 39: Collisions at Sea

1. New York Chamber of Commerce, *In Relation to Collisions at Sea*, 9.
2. Ibid., 13.
3. Ibid., 14.
4. Ibid.
5. Ibid., 15.
6. Ibid., 13.
7. "Alleged Seizure of the American Barque *Adriatic* [to Accompany Joint Resolution H.R. No. 13]," Reports on Committees, 16th Congress, 1st Session—49th Congress, 1st Session, vol. 5 (June 1, 1858), 4.
8. Ibid.
9. "Moderation of Jonathan," *Morning Chronicle* (London), June 14, 1858.
10. New York Chamber of Commerce, *In Relation to Collisions at Sea*, 49.
11. Liverpool Chamber of Commerce, *Report of the Commercial Law Committee on the Successive Judgments in the Case of Cope v. Doherty, the "Tuscarora," and the Existing State of the Law Applicable to Collisions at Sea, as Regards Limitation of the Liability of Shipowners* (Liverpool, UK: Benson & Mallett, June 1859), 24.
12. Baltimore Board of Trade, "Tenth Annual Report of the Board of Trade of Baltimore: Being for the Year 1859," vol. 10 (Baltimore: J. B. Rose, 1860), 12.

13. New York Chamber of Commerce, *Annual Report of the Chamber of Commerce of the State of New York: For the Year 1859–'60* (New York: John W. Amerman, 1860), 84–85.
14. "The Barque *Adriatic*," *Liverpool Mercury*, April 6, 1858.

Chapter 40: Fate

1. "The *Adriatic*," *Savannah Republican* (Savannah, GA), March 22, 1858.
2. "The *Adriatic*," *Savannah Republican* (Savannah, GA), April 20, 1858.
3. George W. Morgan, "Sea Letter Issued to Ward L. Smith," United States Consulate at Marseille, June 26, 1858, Historic Mobile Preservation Society.
4. Jonathan Stephen Martin, Letter to Ward L. Smith, October 7, 1859, Historic Mobile Preservation Society.
5. The discovery of *Clotilda*'s remains was announced by a team of divers and historians in 2019. The report produced in connection with the discovery suggests that the wreck was discovered at least one year earlier. Allison Keyes, "The '*Clotilda*,' the Last Known Slaveship to Arrive in the US, Is Found by Researchers," *Smithsonian Magazine*, May 22, 2019.
6. "A Remarkable Career," *Meridian Evening Star* (Meridian, MS), September 3, 1907.
7. Ibid.
8. Ibid.
9. Author correspondence with Sharon LaDuke.
10. Census records report Durham's income as $3,000 annually in 1860 and $4,800 in 1870.
11. "A Worthy Record," *Manford's Monthly Magazine* 31 (1887): 647.
12. Augustine Meaher, Letter to Ward L. Smith, January 22, 1891, Historic Mobile Preservation Society.
13. "Ward L. Smith . . . ," *Cape Girardeau Democrat* (Cape Girardeau, MO), December 18, 1897.
14. "Obituary," *Belfast Republican Journal* (Belfast, ME), September 13, 1900.
15. "A Remarkable Career," *Meridian Evening Star* (Meridian, MS), September 3, 1907.
16. Jonathan Barnet Durham, Letter to Ward L. Smith, June 20, 1858, Historic Mobile Preservation Society.
17. Ibid.

Bibliography

Primary Sources

"A Bill Regulating the Carriage of Passengers in Merchant Vessels." *Parliamentary Papers*, vol. 4 (March 12, 1849).

Aicard, Albert. "Notes en réplique pour le Cap Durham de *l'Adriatic*, contre MM Gauthier frères, gérants de la Compagne Franco-Américaine, armateurs du *Lyonnais*." Marseille, France: Arnaud et Comp, 1857.

"Alleged Seizure of the American Barque *Adriatic* [to Accompany Joint Resolution H.R. No. 13]." Reports on Committees, 16th Congress, 1st Session—49th Congress, 1st Session, vol. 5 (June 1, 1858).

American Lloyds' Registry of American and Foreign Ships. New York: E. & E. G. Blunt, 1859.

American Lloyds' Registry of American and Foreign Ships. New York: E. & E. G. Blunt, 1861.

American Lloyds' Registry of American and Foreign Ships. New York: E. & E. G. Blunt, 1862.

Ancestry.com. "Durham." Year: 1868. US City Directories, 1822–1995.

Ancestry.com. "Durham." Year: 1872. US City Directories, 1822–1995.

Ancestry.com. "Durham." Year: 1874. US City Directories, 1822–1995.

Ancestry.com. "Durham." Year: 1876. US City Directories, 1822–1995.

Ancestry.com. "Durham." Year: 1892. US City Directories, 1822–1995.

Ancestry.com. "Jonathan Barnet Durham." Massachusetts, Mason Membership Cards, 1773–1900. Provo, UT: Ancestry.com, 2013.

Baltimore Board of Trade. "Tenth Annual Report of the Board of Trade of Baltimore: Being for the Year 1859." Vol. 10. Baltimore: J. B. Rose, 1860.

Berzolese, Michele. "Charter Party for *S. E. Meaher*." July 1857. Historic Mobile Preservation Society.

California Superior Court. "In the Mater of the Estate of Jonathan B. Durham, Deceased." Mendocino County Probate Case Files, 1854–1917, no. 1308. California County, District and Probate Courts.

Cammel Laird. Laird Contract to Build Hull Numbers 133–136. Wirral Archives Service, Birkenhead, UK, 1855.

Charlton, Ruth. Martin, Campbell, Furlong Family Papers. MC 90, Philadelphia Archdiocesan Historical Research Center, October 17, 2012.

Civil War Pension Index: General Index to Pension Files, 1861–1934. NAI no. T288. Record group title: Records of the Department of Veterans Affairs, 1773–2007. Record group no. 15. Series title: US, Civil War Pension Index: General Index to Pension Files, 1861–1934. Series no. T288. Roll 470.

"Communication with France Loss of the *Normandy*." *Hansard Parliamentary Debates*, 3rd ser., vol. 200 (March 21, 1870).

Compiled Marriages for Belfast, Hallowel and Pittsdon, 1748–1875. "Joseph S. Thombs." Belfast, ME.

Cunningham, Charles. Account of *S. E. Meaher* repairs at Galatz. May 21, 1857. Historic Mobile Preservation Society.

Delgado, James. *Archaeological Investigations of 1Ba704, a Nineteenth-Century Shipwreck Site in the Mobile River, Baldwin and Mobile Counties, Alabama: Final Report*. Report prepared for the Alabama Historical Commission, the People of Africatown, the National Geographic Society, and the Slave Wrecks Project, May 2019.

Dumas. Private letter of protection for Ward L. Smith. June 4, 1857.

Durham, Charles. Letter to Ward L. Smith. March 24, 1858. Historic Mobile Preservation Society.

Durham, Jonathan Barnet. Letter to Ward L. Smith, June 20, 1858. Historic Mobile Preservation Society.

Elliot, David. Letter to Ward L. Smith. January 4, 1853. Historic Mobile Preservation Society.

Elliot, David. Letter to Ward L. Smith. January 12, 1853. Historic Mobile Preservation Society.

Elliot, David. Letter to Ward L. Smith. January 14, 1853. Historic Mobile Preservation Society.

Elliot, David. Letter to Ward L. Smith. January 23, 1853. Historic Mobile Preservation Society.

Empire of France. "Certificate of Health" issued to Ward L. Smith at the Port of Algiers. September 1856. Historic Mobile Preservation Society.

Empire of France. Customs document issued to Ward L. Smith. May 22, 1856. Historic Mobile Preservation Society.

Empire of France. Visa issued to Ward L. Smith to enter Cherbourg. March 3, 1856. Historic Mobile Preservation Society.

Flint, James. "Jonathan B. Durham." Middlesex County, Massachusetts, Probate Index, 1871–1909 (Part A–K).

Flint, James. "Jonathan B. Durham." Waldo County, Maine, Births, Belfast.

Flint, James, comp. *Waldo County, Maine Deaths, 1743–1892: Belfast* (online database). Provo, UT: Ancestry.com, 2000.

The Foreign Office List and Diplomatic and Consular Year Book. Vol. 10. London: Harrison and Sons, 1857.

Golart, Eusebio. *Memoria sobre la adjutoccacion del servicio transatlantico provisional a la compañía francesa de Gauthier hermanos de Paris*. Barcelona: Narciso Ramirez, 1857.

Goodwin, Albert. "1844 Letter from Captain Goodwin." New Bedford Whaling Museum, Swift & Allen Papers, S-g, series F, S-s 1, folder 3, box 41.

Goodwin, Albert G. December 20, 1844, letter to Federick Allen. New Bedford Whaling Museum, "Swift & Allen Papers." Mss 5, S-g 3, series F, S-s 1, folder 3, box 41.

Hamelin, Ferdinand-Alphonse. "Circulaire Ministérielle—Abrodage—Eclairage des navires—Responsabilité—Notification d'un Arret de la Cour Imperial d'Aix." *Bulletin Officiel de La Martinique*, serie 7: 1–12. Paris: Bureau de l'imprimerie du gouvernement, 1858.

J. Gary Nichols Cemetery Collection, ca. 1780–1999. "Maine." Salt Lake City, UT: FamilySearch, 2016.

Letter to Ward L. Smith c/o J. O. Baker, New York [signature of sender is illegible]. July 14, 1858. Historic Mobile Preservation Society.

Letter to Ward L. Smith promising work [signature of sender is illegible]. August 25–26, 1857. Historic Mobile Preservation Society.

Le Tribunal de Commerce de Marseille. "Jugement." France, April 2, 1857.

Liverpool Chamber of Commerce. *Report of the Commercial Law Committee on the Successive Judgments in the Case of Cope v. Doherty, the "Tuscarora," and the Existing State of the Law Applicable to Collisions at Sea, as Regards Limitation of the Liability of Shipowners.* Liverpool, UK: Benson & Mallett, June 1859.

"Log Book of the *Savannah*." In *Report of the U.S. National Museum during the Year Ending June 30, 1890.* Washington, DC: Government Printing Office, 1891.

Lowell, John. "Monthly Law Reporter." Vol. X. Boston: Crosby Nichols, 1858.

Martin, Jonathan Stephen. Letter to Ward L. Smith. January 23, 1858. Historic Mobile Preservation Society.

Martin, Jonathan Stephen. Letter to Ward L. Smith. October 7, 1859. Historic Mobile Preservation Society.

Marziou v. Pioche, 10 Cal. 545 (Cal. 1858).

Massachusetts Death Records, 1841–1911. "Jonathan B. Durham." Massachusetts Vital Records, 1840–1911. New England Historic Genealogical Society, Boston, MA.

Massachusetts Marriage Records, 1840–1915. "Jonathan B. Durham." Massachusetts Vital Records, 1840–1911. New England Historic Genealogical Society, Boston, MA.

Massachusetts Passenger and Crew Lists, 1820–1963. *"Atlas."* Passenger Lists of Vessels Arriving at Boston, Massachusetts, 1820–1891. Records of the US Customs Service, Record Group 36, series M277. National Archives & Records Administration.

Meaher, Augustine. Letter to Ward L. Smith. January 2, 1891. Historic Mobile Preservation Society.

Methodist Episcopal Church Missionary Society. *Annual Report of the Missionary Society.* Vol. 38, part 1857. New York: Methodist Episcopal Church, 1857.

Miscellaneous Financial Records, Receipts, and Contract Documents Issued to Ward L. Smith from 1855–1858. Historic Mobile Preservation Society.

Missouri Probate Court (Madison County). "Last Will and Testament of Ward L. Smith." Wills and Probate Records, 1821–1948. Record of Wills. Vols. A and 2–3, 1822–1923. Index, 1821–1886. Madison, MO.

"*Mitchell v. Mitchell* Divorce Papers: Summary and Deposition." St. Louis, Missouri, Circuit Court, Case Files—Civil, no. 3724, box 147, folder 29, December 1866.

Morgan, George W. "Sea Letter Issued to Ward L. Smith." United States Consulate at Marseille, June 26, 1858. Historic Mobile Preservation Society.

New York Chamber of Commerce. *Annual Report of the Chamber of Commerce of the State of New York: For the Year 1859–'60.* New York: John W. Amerman, 1860.

New York Chamber of Commerce. *In Relation to Collisions at Sea.* New York: John W. Amerman, 1858.

New York Marine Register: A Standard Classification of American Vessels, and Such Other Vessels as Visit American Ports. New York: R. C. Root, Anthony, 1858.

New York, Passenger and Crew Lists (including Castle Garden and Ellis Island), 1820–1957. "Quaker City." Arrival, New York, New York, 1856. Microfilm serial M237, 1820–1897, microfilm roll 168, line 4, list number 1131.

"No. 5681–Decret Imperial." *Bulletin des lois de la Republique Francaise.* Vol. 11. Paris: Impr. Nationale des Lois.

Officers of the Continental and US Navy and Marine Corps. "Joseph S. Thombs." US Navy Officers, 1798–1900.

Ogden, Charles. "Certificate of Inability Procuring American Seaman." July 2, 1856. Historic Mobile Preservation Society.

P&O Heritage. P&O Ship Fact Sheet: *Behar* (1855). P&O Heritage Collection, November 2008.

P&O Heritage. P&O Ship Fact Sheet: *China* (1856). P&O Heritage Collection, November 2008.

P&O Heritage. P&O Ship Fact Sheet: *Ellora* (1855). P&O Heritage Collection, November 2008.

P&O Heritage. P&O Ship Fact Sheet: *Orissa* (1856). P&O Heritage Collection, November 2008.

Parks, Alex. Transfer of debt owed by Ward L. Smith. June 1857. Historic Mobile Preservation Society.

Passenger Lists of Vessels Arriving at New York, New York, 1820–1897. "Black Warrior." Microfilm publication M237, 675 rolls. NAI: 6256867. Records of the US Customs Service. Record Group 36. National Archives & Records Administration, Washington, DC.

Reports of Committees: 16th Congress, 1st Session—49th Congress, 1st Session. Vol. 5. Washington, DC: n.p., 1858.

Rives, John Cook, et al. *The Congressional Globe*. Washington, DC: Blair & Rives, 1858.

Rogers, Henry J. *Rogers and Black's American Semaphoric Signal Book: For the Use of Vessels Employed in the United States Naval, Revenue and Merchant Service*. Baltimore: F. Lucas, 1847.

Seventh Census of the United States, 1850. Microfilm M432, 1009 rolls. Record Group 29. Records of the Bureau of the Census. National Archives, Washington, DC.

Smith, Ward L. "A Sailor's Adventure: Masonic Experience in the Wilds of Bulgaria during the Latter Part of the Crimean War by an American Sea Captain." Historic Mobile Preservation Society.

Smith, Ward L. "A Whaling Adventure: Life on a Whale Ship Fifty-Five Years Ago." New Bedford Whaling Museum, Pam +176, 1900.

Smith, Ward L. "Escape of the Adriatic: From the Harbor of Marseilles, France, in 1858." Undated. Historic Mobile Preservation Society.

Smith, Ward L. Handwritten draft of "A Sailor's Adventure: Masonic Experience in the Wilds of Bulgaria during the Latter Part of the Crimean War by an American Sea Captain." Undated. Historic Mobile Preservation Society.

Smith, Ward L. Letter from Ward Smith to Edwin Smith. September 18, 1881. Family collection of Sharon Davey LaDuke.

Smith, Ward L. Logbook of *Sarah E. Meaher*. 1855–1857. Historic Mobile Preservation Society.

Smith, Ward L. Slip of paper with dates of *Adriatic*'s escape written on it. 1858. Historic Mobile Preservation Society.

Smith, Ward L. Summary of repairs at Galatz signed by Consul Morgan. September 1, 1857. Historic Mobile Preservation Society.

State Archives, Augusta, Maine. "Thombs." Maine Veterans Cemetery Records, 1676–1918.

The Survey of Federal Archives Division of Professional and Service Project Work Projects Administrations. "*Tuscaloosa* Ship." Ship Registers of New Bedford, Massachusetts. Vol. 1, 1796–1850. National Archives Project 1940. Boston: New Bedford Whaling Museum.

Thourel. "Notes en réplique pour MM. Gauthier frères contre le Captaine Durham." Aix, France: Frederic Vitalis, 1857.

"*Tuscaloosa* of N. Bedford at Ind. & Pa. Oceans." New Bedford Whaling Museum, *Tuscaloosa* Crew List, Smith & Allen Papers.

United Kingdom and Ireland, Masters and Mates Certificates. Greenwich, London, UK: National Maritime Museum.

United States Census Collection, 1825–1865. "Smith." Illinois State Census, 1865. Illinois State Archives, Springfield, Illinois. Archive collection no. 103.010, roll no. 2171, line 18.

United States Federal Census, 1850. Durham, Belfast, Waldo, Maine. Roll no. M432_270, p. 127A.

United States Federal Census, 1850. "Thombs." Castine, Maine.

United States Federal Census, 1860. Durham, Chelsea, Suffolk, Massachusetts. Roll no. M653_526, p. 823. Family History Library Film: 803526.

United States Federal Census, 1860. "Thombs." National Archives & Records Administration. Record group: Records of the Bureau of the Census, record group no. 29. Series no. M653. Belfast, Waldo, Maine. Roll no. M653_453, p. 69. Family History Library film 803453.

United States Federal Census 1870. Durham, Chelsea, Suffolk, Massachusetts. Roll no. M593_650, p. 141B. Family History Library film 552149.

United States Federal Census, 1870. "Smith." Moreland, Scott, Missouri. Roll no. M593_805, p. 579A.

United States Federal Census, 1880. Durham, Belfast, Waldo, Maine. Enumeration District 074. Roll no. 488, p. 229A.

United States Federal Census, 1880. "Smith." Sylvania, Scott, Missouri. Enumeration District: 148. Roll no. 737, p. 304C.

United States Federal Census, 1880. "Thombs." Belfast, Waldo, Maine. Enumeration District 074. Roll no. 488, p. 229B.

United States Federal Census, 1900. Durham, Malden, Ward 5, Middlesex, Massachusetts. Enumeration District 0844. FHL Microfilm 120662, p. 5.

United States House of Representatives. House Documents, vol. 32. Washington, DC: US Government Printing Office, 1860.

United States of America. Sea Letter Issued to Ward L. Smith to travel to Cherbourg and "one or two more foreign ports." Undated. Historic Mobile Preservation Society.

United States of America. Seamen's Protection Certificate Issued to Ward L. Smith. Undated. Historic Mobile Preservation Society.

United States Passport Applications, 1795–1925. National Archives & Records Administration. Washington, DC. Roll no. 58, August 25, 1856–November 5, 1856.

United States Passport Applications, 1795–1925. National Archives & Records Administration. Washington, DC. Roll no. 57, June 27, 1856–August 23, 1856.

Wales Census, 1871. "*Majestic of Boston.*" RG10, piece 5370, folio 43. GSU roll 849474, April 2, 1871.

Whaleman's Shipping Paper, District Port of New Bedford. New Bedford Whaling Museum. Swift & Allen Papers. Mss 78, S-g3, series Y, S-s 1, folder 1.

Secondary Sources

Books

Appleton, William Sumner. *Record of the Descendants of William Sumner, of Dorchester, Mass., 1636*. Boston: D. Clapp & Son, 1879.

Bibliography

Avery, Clara A. *The Averell-Averill-Avery Family: A Record of the Descendants of William and Abigail Averell of Ipswich, Mass.* Cleveland, OH: Press of Evangelical Publishing House, 1906.

Bayley, William, and Oliver O. Jones. *History of the Marine Society of Newburyport, Massachusetts, from Its Incorporation in 1772 to the Year 1906: Together with a Complete Roster and Narrative of Important Events in the Lives of Its Members.* Newburyport, MA: Press of the Daily News, 1906.

Bliss, Perry. *Life and Letters of Henry Lee Higginson.* Boston: Atlantic Monthly Press, 1921.

Brown, Henry Collins. *Fifth Avenue Old and New: 1824–1924.* New York: Henry Collins Brown, 1924.

Browne, John Ross. *Etchings of a Whaling Cruise with Notes of a Sojourn on the Island of Zanzibar to Which Is Appended a Brief History of the Whale Fishery, Its Past and Present Condition.* New York: Harper & Brothers, 1846.

Burgess, Douglas, Jr. *Engines of Empire: Steamships of the Victorian Empire.* Stanford, CA: Stanford University Press, 2016.

Burke, Edmund, ed. *The Annual Register or a View of the History and Politics of the Year 1856.* London: Woodfall and Kinder, 1857.

Busk, Hans. *The Navies of the World: Their Present State, and Future Capabilities.* London: Routledge, Warnes, and Routledge, 1859.

Carhart, Lucy Ann Morris. *Genealogy of the Morris Family: Descendants of Thomas Morris of Connecticut.* New York: A. S. Barnes, 1911.

Coleridge, Samuel Taylor. *Rime of the Ancient Mariner.* Cambridge, MA: Harvard University Educational, 1906.

Creighton, Margaret S. *Rites and Passages: The Experience of American Whaling, 1830–1870.* Cambridge, UK: Cambridge University Press, 1995.

Crothers, William L. *The American-Built Clipper Ship, 1850–1856: Characteristics, Construction, and Details.* Reprint ed. Brattleboro, VT: Echo Point Books & Media, 2017.

Cumming, David Charles. *A Historical Survey of the Boiler Makers and Iron and Steel Shipbuilder's Society from August 1834 to August 1904.* Newcastle on Tyne, UK: R. Robinson, 1905.

Dawes, Ann Laurens. *Makers of America: Charles Sumner.* New York: Dodd, Mead, 1892.

Dickens, Charles. *American Notes for General Circulation.* London: Chapman and Hall, 1842.

Diouf, Sylviane A. *Dreams of Africa in Alabama: The Slave Ship Clotilda and the Story of the Last Africans Brought to America.* New York: Oxford University Press, 2007.

Fowler, William M., Jr. *Steam Titans: Cunard, Collins, and the Epic Battle for Commerce on the North Atlantic.* New York: Bloomsbury, 2017.

Fox, Stephen. *Ocean Railway: Isambard Kingdom Brunel, Samuel Cunard, and the Revolutionary World of the Great Atlantic Steamships.* London: Harper Collins, 2003.

Friedman, Norman. *British Cruisers of the Victorian Era.* Barnsley, UK: Seaforth, 2012.

Hall, Florence Howe. *Memories Grave and Gay.* New York and London: Harper & Brothers, 1918.

History of Southeast Missouri: Embracing an Historical Account of the Counties of St. Genevieve, St. Francois, Perry, Cape Girardeau, Bollinger, Madison, New Madrid, Pemiscot, Dunklin, Scott, Mississippi, Stoddard, Butler, Wayne, and Iron. Chicago: Goodspeed, 1888.

Longfellow, Henry Wadsworth. *The Letters of Henry Wadsworth Longfellow.* Longfellow Trust. Cambridge, MA: Belknap Press of Harvard University Press, 1983.

Longfellow, Samuel, ed. *The Life of Henry Wadsworth Longfellow, with Extracts from His Journals and Correspondence*. Vol. 2. Boston: Ticknor, 1886.

Murphy, Brian. *Adrift: A True Story of Tragedy on the Icy Atlantic and the One Who Lived to Tell about It*. New York: Da Capo, 2018.

O'Meagher, Joseph Casimir. *Some Historical Notices of the O'Meaghers of Ikerrin*. New York: n.p., 1890.

Paasch, Heinrich. *Illustrated Marine Encyclopedia*. Antwerp: H. Paasch, 1890.

Pinnete, Megan. *Belfast*. Images of America. Charleston, SC: Arcadia, 2020.

Pond, Edgar LeRoy. *Junius Smith: A Biography of the Father of the Atlantic Liner*. New York: F. H. Hitchcock, 1927.

Protasio, John. *The Day the World Was Shocked: The Lusitania Disaster and Its Influence on the Course of World War I*. Havertown, PA: Casemate, 2011.

Reed, Sir Edward James. *Shipbuilding in Iron and Steel: A Practical Treatise, Giving Full Details of Construction, Processes of Manufacture, and Building Arrangements*. London: Murray, 1869.

Roberts, Lee. *Commerce and Culture: Nineteenth-Century Business Elites*. Farnham, UK: Ashgate, 2011.

Sewell, William Hamilton, Jr. *Structure and Mobility: The Men and Women of Marseille, 1820–1870*. Cambridge, UK: Cambridge University Press, 1985.

Shaw, David W. *The Sea Shall Embrace Them: The Tragic Story of the Steamship Arctic*. New York: Free Press, 2003.

Shulman, Peter. *Coal & Empire: The Birth of Energy Security in Industrial America*. Baltimore: Johns Hopkins University Press, 2015.

Silber, William B. *A History of St. James' Methodist Episcopal Church at Harlem, New York City, 1830–1880: With Some Facts Relating to the Settlement of Harlem*. New York: Phillips & Hunt, 1882.

Smith, Crosbie. *Coal, Steam and Ships: Engineering, Enterprise and Empire on the Nineteenth-Century Seas*. Cambridge, MA: Cambridge University Press, 2018.

Spears, John Randolph. *The Story of the American Merchant Marine*. New York: Macmillan, 1910.

von Scherzer, Karl Ritter. *Travels in the Free States of Central America: Nicaragua, Honduras, and San Salvador*. London: Longman, Brown, Green, Longmans, & Roberts, 1857.

Williamson, Joseph. *History of the City of Belfast in the State of Maine*. Vol. 1, *From Its First Settlement in 1770 to 1885*. Portland, ME: Loring, Short, and Harmon, 1887.

Wilson, Mehitable Calef Coppenhagen. *John Gibson of Cambridge and His Descendants, 1634–1899*. Washington, DC: McGill & Wallace, 1900.

Articles

"A Dispatch from Havre." *Belfast Republican Journal* (Belfast, ME), December 19, 1856.

"A Message from the Sea." *The Age* (Melbourne, Australia), October 7, 1861.

"A Remarkable Career." *Meridian Evening Star* (Meridian, MS), September 3, 1907.

"A Worthy Record." *Manford's Monthly Magazine* 31 (1887): 647.

"Additional Foreign News by the *Canada*." *Washington Evening Star* (Washington, DC), January 29, 1858.

"Additional Respecting the French Steamer *Lyonnais*." *Brooklyn Daily Eagle*, February 19, 1857.

Bibliography

"The *Adriatic*." *Savannah Republican* (Savannah, GA), March 22, 1858.

"The *Adriatic*." *Savannah Republican* (Savannah, GA), April 20, 1858.

"The *Adriatic* Arrived." *Belfast Republican Journal* (Belfast, ME), March 26, 1858.

"*Adriatic* and *Lyonnaise*, a Sad Chapter." *Evening Star* (Washington, DC), January 27, 1858.

"Advises from Buenos Ayres." *Alexandria Gazette* (Alexandria, VA), October 25, 1860.

"The Affair of the Barque *Adriatic*." *Belfast Republican Journal* (Belfast, ME), March 12, 1858.

"Alleged Seizure of Bark *Adriatic*." *Belfast Republican Journal* (Belfast, ME), July 1, 1858.

"Alleged Seizure of the Barque *Adriatic*." *Belfast Republican Journal* (Belfast, ME), July 16, 1858.

Allen, William H. "Thirst: Can Shipwrecked Men Survive If They Drink Seawater?" *Natural History Magazine*, December 1956.

Ament, Wim, and Gijsbertus J. Verkerke. "Exercise and Fatigue." *Sports Medicine* 39 (2009): 389–422. https://doi.org/10.2165/00007256-200939050-00005.

"The American Barque *Adriatic*: Can American Vessels Be Confiscated in France, for Collisions in Americans Waters, When Their Captains Sail Them Strictly according to Our Laws?" *Belfast Republican Journal* (Belfast, ME), February 26, 1858.

"American Passengers on the French Steamer." *Baltimore Sun*, November 18, 1856.

Andres, Rodrigo. "The Bellepotent as Heterotopia, Total Institution and Colony: Billy Budd and Other Spaces in Melville's Mediterranean." *Leviathan* 13, no. 3 (October 2011).

"Another Awful Calamity: Terrible Disaster at Sea." *New York Herald*, November 15, 1856.

"Another Report in Regard to the Steamer." *Boston Evening Transcript*, January 2, 1857.

Antelope. "A Letter from Antelope." *Times Picayune* (New Orleans), January 4, 1857.

"Arrival of the First Boston and Liverpool Steamship." *Hartford Courant*, June 5, 1840.

"Arrival of the French Steamer." *Brooklyn Daily Eagle*, July 9, 1847.

"Arrival of the Runaway Barque *Adriatic* at Savannah." *Washington Union* (Washington, DC), March 23, 1858.

"Arrival of the Steamship *Union*." *New York Daily Herald*, July 9, 1847.

"Arrivals and Clearances—Foreign Ports." *Boston Evening Transcript*, April 1, 1857.

"Arrived." *Belfast Republican Journal* (Belfast, ME), September 4, 1884.

"Arrived." *Savannah Georgian*, March 19, 1858.

"At Buenos Ayres." *Eastern Argus* (Portland, ME), October 25, 1860.

"Awful Calamity at Sea." *Charlotte Democrat* (Charlotte, NC), November 25, 1856.

"The Bark *Adriatic*." *Bangor Whig and Courier* (Bangor, ME), March 20, 1857.

"The Bark *Adriatic*." *Buffalo Commercial* (Buffalo, NY), March 22, 1858.

"The Bark *Adriatic*." *Pittsfield Sun* (Pittsfield, MA), April 9, 1857.

"The Bark *Adriatic*." *Richmond Dispatch*, April 12, 1858.

"The Bark *Adriatic*." *Savannah Republican* (Savannah, GA), March 22, 1858.

"The Bark *Adriatic*." *Times-Picayune* (New Orleans), April 2, 1857.

"The Bark *Adriatic* . . ." *Brooklyn Daily Eagle*, March 9, 1858.

"The Bark *Adriatic* Again Escaped." *Detroit Free Press*, February 20, 1858.

"Bark *Adriatic* and the *Lyonnais*." *New York Times*, May 1, 1857.

"The Bark *Adriatic* and the *Lyonnais*." *Bangor Daily Whig and Courier* (Bangor, ME), April 27, 1857.

"The Bark *Adriatic* at Savannah—Interesting Narrative of the Voyage across the Atlantic." *Richmond Dispatch*, March 23, 1858.

"The Bark *Adriatic* Ordered to Be Released." *Bangor Daily Whig and Courier* (Bangor, ME), April 24, 1857.

"The Bark *Adriatic*: Another Escape." *Belfast Republican Journal* (Belfast, ME), February 26, 1858.

"The Bark *Adriatic*—Her Escape from the French." *Daily Morning News* (Savannah, GA), March 19, 1858.

"Bark *Tuscaloosa*." *New York Daily Herald*, February 7, 1846.

"The Barque *Adriatic*—Her Escape from the French." *Cooper Clarksburg Register* (Clarksburg, WV), April 23, 1858.

"The Barque *Adriatic*." *Liverpool Mercury*, April 6, 1858.

"The Barque *Adriatic*." *Richmond Dispatch*, May 3, 1858.

"The Barque *Adriatic*." *Washington Union* (Washington, DC), April 8, 1857.

"The Barque *Adriatic*." *Washington Union* (Washington, DC), March 28, 1857.

Bell, John H., Capt. "Rules of the Road at Sea." *California Nautical Magazine*, 1868, 164.

"Body Washed Ashore on Nantucket—Possibly One of the Lost of the *Lyonnais*." *New York Times*, November 21, 1856.

Boebert, Earl. "The Model Sailing Yachts of Franklyn Bassford." *Model Yacht* 4, no. 1 (2000).

"*Boston Courier* on Captain Durham." *Belfast Republican Journal* (Belfast, ME), April 30, 1858.

"Brazil Squadron." *US Nautical Magazine* 3, no. 1 (March 1846).

Brindeau, Louis. *Les premiers Bateaux a vapeur au Havre*. Le Havre, France: Impr. du Journal du Havre, 1901.

"Calamity at Sea." *Belfast Republican Journal* (Belfast, ME), November 21, 1856.

"Captain Durham." *Savannah Georgian*, April 12, 1856.

"Captain Durham of the Bark *Adriatic*." *Belfast Republican Journal* (Belfast, ME), April 16, 1858.

"Capt. Joseph S. Thombs." *Belfast Republican Journal* (Belfast, ME), November 29, 1899.

"Case of the *Adriatic*." *Belfast Republican Journal* (Belfast, ME), March 19, 1858.

"The Case of the *Adriatic*." *Brooklyn Daily Eagle*, April 17, 1858.

"The Case of the American Bark *Adriatic*." *New York Daily Herald*, February 22, 1858.

"The Case of Captain Durham." *Buffalo Morning Express and Illustrated Buffalo Express* (Buffalo, NY), April 15, 1858.

"The Case of the Steamer *Lyonnais*." *New York Daily Herald*, April 17, 1857.

"The Case of the Steamer *Lyonnais*." *New York Daily Herald*, April 22, 1857.

"The Case of the Steamer *Lyonnais*, Collision between the *Lyonnais* and the *Adriatic*—Claim of Damage—Question of Competency." *New York Daily Herald*, April 27, 1857.

"Celebrating Cunard's 175 Years of Ocean Travel in Numbers." *Mirror* (London), May 16, 2015.

"Central America. San Jose, in Costa Rica, Central America, Tuesday, October 25, 1853." *Washington Sentinel* (Washington, DC), November 27, 1853.

"Chamber of Commerce: Rogers' Marine Signals—the Case of the Bark *Adriatic*—Laws with Regard to Collisions at Sea—Custom House Forms." *New York Daily Herald*, February 20, 1858.

"City Hall: Paul Julien." *Hartford Courant* (Hartford, CT), September 6, 1855.

Bibliography

"Cleared." *Savannah Republican* (Savannah, GA), December 31, 1856.

"Cleared This Day." *Boston Evening Transcript*, September 21, 1854.

"Collisions at Sea." *Essex County Standard* (Colchester, UK), January 2, 1857, quoting the *New York Times*, January 6, 1857.

"The Collision with *Le Lyonnais*—Safety of the Vessel with Which She Was in Contact." *Boston Traveler*, November 17, 1856.

"Compania Franco-Americano de paquetes a vapor." *Jornal do Commercial* (Rio de Janeiro, Brazil), August 6, 1856.

"Compania Franco-Americano de paquetes a vapor." *Jornal do Commercial* (Rio de Janeiro, Brazil), May 7, 1856.

"Compania Franco-Americano de paquetes a vapor." *Jornal do Commercial* (Rio de Janeiro, Brazil), May 12, 1856.

"Compliment to Captain Russell." *New York Evening Post*, April 1, 1837.

"Condition of *Le Lyonnais* Sufferers." *New York Times*, November 18, 1856.

"Condition of the *Lyonnais* Sufferers: The Bark *Adriatic* That Ran the Steamer Down." *New York Times*, November 18, 1856.

"Cunard's Line of Steamers." *Pilot and Transcript* (Baltimore), June 15, 1840.

"Death of a Former Resident." *Belfast Republican Journal* (Belfast, ME), April 28, 1887.

"Death of a New York Merchant." *New York Times*, February 9, 1864.

"Decision of Court in France." *Baton Rouge Tri-Weekly Gazette and Comment* (Baton Rouge, LA), May 11, 1857.

"Decision of the French Court in the Case of the Barque *Adriatic*." *Eastern Argus* (Portland, ME), May 11, 1857.

"Departure of the French Ocean Steamers." *New York Daily Herald*, October 26, 1847.

"Disaster to a French Steamer—130 Lives." *Eastern Mail* (Waterville, ME), November 20, 1856.

"Disasters—Barque *Adriatic*." *Belfast Republican Journal* (Belfast, ME), November 14, 1856.

"Disasters." *Belfast Republican Journal* (Belfast, ME), November 14, 1856.

"The Disaster to the *Lyonnais*." *Belfast Republican Journal* (Belfast, ME), December 5, 1856.

"The Disaster to the *Lyonnais*: Gloucester, Nov. 14th, 1856, to the Editor of the *Boston Journal*." *Belfast Republican Journal* (Belfast, ME), December 5, 1856.

"The Disaster to the *Lyonnaise*: Further Particulars." *Baltimore Sun*, November 18, 1856.

"A Dispatch from Havre." *Belfast Republican Journal* (Belfast, ME), December 19, 1856.

"Domestic Ports." *Charleston Daily Courier* (Charleston, SC), September 9, 1857.

"Dreadful Shipwreck." *Buffalo Evening Post* (Buffalo, NY), May 9, 1856.

"Eastern Ports." *New York Daily Herald*, November 8, 1845.

"Escape of the *Adriatic*." *Baltimore Sun*, February 22, 1858.

"Escape of the *Adriatic*." *Belfast Republican Journal* (Belfast, ME), April 2, 1858.

"Escape of the *Adriatic*." *Buffalo Daily Journal* (Buffalo, NY), March 25, 1858.

"Escape of the *Adriatic*—Her Safe Arrival at Savannah!" *Daily Constitutionalist and Republic* (Augusta, GA), March 20, 1858.

"Escape of the American Bark *Adriatic* from Marseilles." *Belfast Republican Journal* (Belfast, ME), February 5, 1858.

"Escape of the American Bark *Adriatic* from Marseilles." *Buffalo Commercial* (Buffalo, NY), February 1, 1858.

"Escape of the American Bark *Adriatic* from Marseilles: Captain Durham Raising His Anchor and Replying to French Officers." *New York Daily Herald*, January 31, 1858.

"Escape of Captain Durham." *Harper's Weekly: The Year 1858* 2 (March 6, 1858).

"Express from Paris." *The Times* (London), February 6, 1855.

"Extraordinary Dispatch." *The Guardian* (London), March 6, 1830.

"The Famous Captain Durham." *Evening Star* (Washington, DC), April 7, 1858.

"Fearful Sufferings of a Shipwrecked Crew." *Leeds Mercury News* (Leeds, UK), February 6, 1869.

"For Sale, Freight, or Charter." *Savannah Georgian* (Savannah, GA), April 16, 1856.

"For San Francisco." *Times Picayune* (New Orleans), May 9, 1850.

"Foreign Ports." *Belfast Republican Journal* (Belfast, ME), December 3, 1858.

"Foreign Ports." *Belfast Republican Journal* (Belfast, ME), February 17, 1860.

"Foreign Ports." *Belfast Republican Journal* (Belfast, ME), July 15, 1859.

"Foreign Ports." *Belfast Republican Journal* (Belfast, ME), June 10, 1859.

"Foreign Ports." *Belfast Republican Journal* (Belfast, ME), June 11, 1858.

"Foreign Ports." *Belfast Republican Journal* (Belfast, ME), June 11, 1858.

"Foreign Ports." *Belfast Republican Journal* (Belfast, ME), June 28, 1859.

"Foreign Ports." *Belfast Republican Journal* (Belfast, ME), October 14, 1859.

"Foreign Ports." *New York Daily Herald*, July 6, 1846.

"Foreign Ports." *New York Herald*, January 7, 1858.

"Foreign Ports." *Portland Daily Press* (Portland, ME), July 10, 1884.

"France and the French." *The Era* (London), June 1, 1856.

"Freights." *New York Daily Eagle*, August 27, 1858.

"French Justice and a Yankee Captain [Translated from the *Courrier du Havre* of Jan 13, for the *New York Herald*]." *New York Daily Herald*, February 1, 1858.

"The French Screw Steamer *Barcelone*." *New York Daily Herald*, March 15, 1856.

"The French Steamship *Lyonnais* and the Barque *Adriatic*." *New York Daily Herald*, January 21, 1858.

"French Transatlantic Steamship Company." *National Daily Whig* (Washington, DC), December 4, 1847.

"Frightful Collision at Sea." *Gazette & Courier* (Greenfield, MA), November 24, 1856.

"Frightful Collision at Sea. Loss of the French Steamer *Lyonnais*—over One Hundred Persons Lost." *New York Tribune*, November 17, 1856.

"From Commerce." *Scott County Kicker* (Benton, MO), July 20, 1907.

"From Merchant's Exchange." *Portland Daily Press* (Portland, ME), September 2, 1884.

"From Oran." *Newsboy* (Benton, MO), June 15, 1895.

"From Rio Janeiro." *Weekly National Intelligencer* (Washington, DC), March 7, 1846.

"From This Port." *Charleston Mercury News* (Charleston, SC), May 8, 1845.

"From This Port." *Charleston Mercury News* (Charleston, SC), May 12, 1845.

"From Washington." *Oswego Times* (Oswego, NY), May 21, 1858.

"Further Particulars: Loss of the French Steamer *Le Lyonnais*." *Daily Pennsylvanian* (Philadelphia), November 17, 1856.

Garcia, Olga Vega. "A Regal Music Album Produced in Cuba." Jose Marti National Library, September 10, 2020.

"Gatherings from Our Exchanges." *Triweekly Washington Sentinel* (Washington, DC), March 27, 1856.

Bibliography

"Generalities." *Belfast Republican Journal* (Belfast, ME), August 20, 1858.

"Generalities: The Barque *Adriatic*." *Belfast Republican Journal* (Belfast, ME), October 17, 1856.

"George W. Morgan." *Evening Review* (East Liverpool, OH), August 16, 1900.

"Grand Soiree Complementary to Louise Payne and Little Ada: Only Four Years Old." *Brooklyn Daily Eagle*, April 21, 1856.

"Halifax, December 31." *Alton Weekly Telegraph* (Alton, IL), January 8, 1857.

"Home Ports." *New York Daily Herald*, July 25, 1845.

"Home Ports." *New York Daily Herald*, June 1, 1845

"Home Ports." *New York Daily Herald*, May 29, 1845.

Honey, March E. "Carter & Perkins: A Ship Building Dynasty, Part II." *Before the Mast* 3, no. 22 (March 24, 2000).

"Horrible Death and Suffering of a Ship's Crew." *Glasgow Herald* (Glasgow, Scotland), July 25, 1865.

"House of Commons: Wednesday." *Bristol Mercury and Daily Post* (Bristol, UK), August 2, 1832.

"Interesting Account of the Loss of the Steamer *Lyonnais*." *Louisville Courier* (Louisville, KY), March 11, 1857.

"In the Third Circuit." *Evening Star* (Washington, DC), April 21, 1857.

"Joseph S. Thombs." *Lewiston Daily Sun* (Lewiston, ME), November 30, 1899.

Keyes, Allison. "The '*Clotilda*,' the Last Known Slaveship to Arrive in the US, Is Found by Researchers." *Smithsonian Magazine*, May 22, 2019.

Khouri, Yamil H. "Los vapores de la Compañía Franco-Americana (Gauthier frères) in Cuba." *Cuban Philatelist* 8, no. 22 (October 1996).

Kinney, Michele Anders. "Doubly Foreign: British Consuls in the Antebellum South, 1830–1860." Partial fulfillment of the requirements for the degree of doctor of philosophy, University of Texas at Arlington, August 2010.

"Late Gale: Packet-Ship *St. Denis* Foundering at Sea." *New York Herald*, January 17, 1856.

"The Late Marine Disaster: Conduct of Officers at Sea." *New York Herald*, November 19, 1856.

"Later from the Bark *Adriatic*." *Daily Exchange* (Baltimore), March 11, 1858.

"The Late Severe Weather and Its Consequences—Frustrated Absence of a Large Fleet of Vessels." *New York Herald*, March 29, 1857.

"The Latest News Received by Magnetic Telegraph." *New York Tribune*, November 18, 1856.

"The Late Terrible Disaster at Sea." *New York Daily Herald*, November 16, 1856.

"The Late Terrible Disaster at Sea." *New York Herald*, November 22, 1856.

"The Late Terrible Shipwrecks." *New York Times*, November 18, 1856.

"Launched." *Belfast Republican Journal* (Belfast, ME), December 26, 1856.

"Launches of New Steamers at Liverpool." *The Guardian* (London), August 30, 1855.

"Launches of Two Iron Screw Steamers." *Liverpool Mercury*, January 12, 1856.

"Launch of a Screw Steamer." *Liverpool Mercury*, June 5, 1855.

"The Launch of a Steamship." *Daily Union* (Washington, DC), January 26, 1855.

"Law Intelligencer." *New York Daily Tribune*, April 2, 1857.

"Law Intelligencer." *New York Tribune*, April 2, 1857.

Lennox, Lord William Pitt. "Chapter V." In *Pictures of Sporting Life and Character*. Vol. 2. London: Hurst and Blackett, 1860.

"Letters from France." *Weekly National Intelligencer* (Washington, DC), March 21, 1857.

"Letters from Marseilles." *Bangor Daily Whig & Courier* (Bangor, ME), April 9, 1857.

"Letters from Marseilles." *The South-Western* (Shreveport, LA), April 15, 1857.

"List of Vessels in Port." *Savannah Republican* (Savannah, GA), March 27, 1858.

"Local Items." *Fredericktown Democrat News* (Fredericktown, MO), August 4, 1900.

"Loss of an Atlantic Steamer." *Glasgow Herald* (Glasgow, Scotland), December 3, 1856.

"Loss of Brig *Ocean Wave* of Belfast." *Bangor Daily Whig and Courier* (Bangor, ME), February 8, 1867.

"Loss of French Steamer *Le Lyonnais*: Over 100 Lives Probably Lost." *Brooklyn Daily Eagle*, November 15, 1856.

"Loss of the French Steamer *Le Lyonnais*—with One Hundred Lives." *Nautical Magazine and Naval Chronicle: A Journal of Papers on Subjects Connected with Maritime Affairs*. London: Simpkin, Marshall, 1857.

"Loss of the French Steamer *Le Lyonnais* with 100 Lives." *The Standard* (London), December 1, 1856.

"Loss of the French Steamer *Lyonnais*: Further Explanations Necessary." *New York Herald*, November 18, 1856.

"Loss of the French Steamer *Lyonnais*—over 100 Lives Probably Lost." *Brooklyn Daily Eagle*, November 15, 1856.

"The Loss of *Le Lyonnais*." *New York Daily Herald*, November 17, 1856.

"The Loss of *Le Lyonnais*." *New York Morning Courier*, November 18, 1856.

"Loss of *Le Lyonnais*: Further Developments." *Buffalo Daily Republic* (Buffalo, NY), November 21, 1856.

"The Loss of the *Lyonnais*." *The Times* (London), December 2, 1856.

"The Loss of the *Lyonnais*: The Passenger's Quitting the Sinking Vessel." *Illustrated Times of London*, December 27, 1856.

"Loss of the *Lyonnais*: Sailing of the *Marion* in Search of Survivors of the Wreck." *New York Herald*, November 17, 1856.

"The Loss of the *Lyonnais*: Statement of One of the Survivors—the Rescue of the Third Mate's Party." *New York Times*, February 7, 1857.

"Loss of the Ship *Ocean Queen* with One Hundred Lives." *London Observer*, June 22, 1856.

"Loss of the Steamship *Arctic*." *Baltimore Sun*, October 13, 1854.

"Loss of the Steamship *Philadelphia* and Preservation of 450 Lives." *Hull Packet and East Riding Times* (Hull, UK), September 29, 1854.

"Lost." *Charleston Daily Courier* (Charleston, SC), December 29, 1856.

"The Lost *Lyonnais*." *Poughkeepsie Journal* (Poughkeepsie, NY), March 7, 1857.

"The Lost *Lyonnais* and Her Boat." *Brooklyn Evening Star*, December 16, 1856.

"The Lost Steamer *Lyonnais*." *Baltimore Sun*, December 15, 1856.

"The Lost Steamer *Lyonnais*." *Hudson Daily Star*, January 30, 1857.

"The *Lyonnais*." *New York Tribune*, December 15, 1856.

"The *Lyonnais*." *New York Tribune*, December 29, 1856.

"The *Lyonnais*—Interesting Details." *Augusta Chronicle* (Augusta, GA), November 20, 1856.

"The *Lyonnais* Collision." *Brooklyn Daily Eagle*, November 17, 1856.

"The *Lyonnais* Disaster." *Buffalo Morning Express and Illustrated Buffalo Express* (Buffalo, NY), November 20, 1856.

Bibliography

"The *Lyonnais* Disaster—Seizure." *Boston Evening Transcript*, March 18, 1857.

"Marine Affairs: The *Lyonnais*." *New York Tribune*, December 29, 1856.

"Marine and Island Insurance: The Sun Mutual Insurance Company of New York." *Baltimore Daily Exchange*, December 10, 1858.

"Marine Items: *Le Lyonnais*." *New York Times*, December 30, 1856.

"Marine List." *Daily Morning News* (Savannah, GA), December 10, 1856.

"Maritime Intelligence." *New York Daily Herald*, December 10, 1856.

Marraro, Howard R. "Spezia: American Naval Base, 1848–68." *Military Affairs* 7, no. 4 (1943): 202–08.

"Married." *Mexico Weekly Ledger* (Mexico, MO), September 5, 1889.

"Marseilles." *New York Herald*, February 25, 1858.

"Memoranda." *Charleston Daily Courier* (Charleston, SC), February 10, 1859.

"Memoranda." *Charleston Daily Courier* (Charleston, SC), May 24, 1856.

"Memoranda." *Daily Morning News* (Savannah, GA), December 5, 1856.

"Memoranda." *Daily Morning News* (Savannah, GA), June 8, 1858.

"Memoranda." *New York Times*, October 29, 1856.

"Memoranda." *Portland Daily Press* (Portland, ME), April 17, 1884.

"Memoranda." *Portland Daily Press* (Portland, ME), April 19, 1884.

"Merchant's Exchange." *Portland Daily Press* (Portland, ME), September 2, 1884.

"Mexico and the United States." *Daily News* (London), August 30, 1847.

"Miscellaneous." *New York Daily Herald*, January 19, 1848.

"The Missing *City of Glasgow* Steamer." *Sheffield and Rotherham Independent* (Sheffield, UK), May 13, 1854.

"Missing Clipper Ships *Ocean* and *Driver*—Lists of Their Officers and Passengers." *Western Reserve Chronicle* (Warren, OH), August 13, 1856.

"The Missing Steamer *Lyonnais*." *New York Times*, December 11, 1856.

"The Missing Steamer *Lyonnais*: One of Her Boats Picked Up by Liverpool Packet Ship." *Buffalo Morning Express and Courier* (Buffalo, NY), December 13, 1856.

"The Missing Steamer *Pacific*." *Liverpool Mercury*, July 26, 1861.

"Missing Vessel." *Bangor Whig and Courier* (Bangor, ME), December 19, 1842.

Mitchell, H. H., T. S. Hamilton, F. R. Steggerda, and H. W. Bean. "The Chemical Composition of the Adult Human Body and Its Bearing on the Biochemistry of Growth." *Journal of Biological Chemistry* 158, no. 3 (1945): 625–37.

"Moderation of Jonathan." *Morning Chronicle* (London), June 14, 1858.

"More Survivors of *Le Lyonnais*." *Daily Telegraph* (London), February 18, 1857.

"Mr. Buchanan Elected President." *The Guardian* (London), November 17, 1856.

"Musical." *New York Times*, May 13, 1854.

Nautical Magazine and Naval Chronicle for 1842: A Journal of Papers and Subjects Connected with Maritime Affairs. London: Simpkin, Marshall, 1842.

"Naval. Etc. from Rio de Janeiro." *Washington Union* (Washington, DC), March 7, 1846.

"New Line of Packets between Liverpool and New York." *The Guardian* (London), November 26, 1836.

"New Orleans." *Charleston Mercury News* (Charleston, SC), April 28, 1845.

"New York Chamber of Commerce." *Detroit Free Press*, February 20, 1858.

"New York Jan 23." *New York Herald*, January 27, 1855.

Noet, Laurent. "Le grand oeuvre architectural de Maupas: La Préfecture des Bouches-du-Rhône." *Histoire, économie & société* 34, no. 2 (2015): 88–101.

"No Tiding of the *Lyonnais*." *Centennial of Freedom*, December 2, 1856.

"Obituary." *Belfast Republican Journal* (Belfast, ME), September 13, 1900.

"Obituary: Gen. George W. Morgan." *Standard Union* (Cleveland, OH), July 27, 1893.

"The Ocean Steamer: Crossing the Atlantic in Early Steamships." *Harper's New Monthly Magazine* 243, no. 41 (July 1870).

"The Officers of the *Lyonnais*." *Morning Chronicle* (London), December 2, 1856.

"The Officers of the *Lyonnais*." *The Times* (London), December 1, 1856.

"One of the Brothers Gauthier." *Belfast Republican Journal* (Belfast, ME), April 23, 1858.

"On the Beginning of Transatlantic Steamship Service." *Bulletin of the Business Historical Society* 12, no. 3 (June 1938).

"The Pacific Steamship Company." *New York Herald*, June 29, 1855.

"Parisian Gossip." *Buffalo Commercial* (Buffalo, NY), April 21, 1857.

"The Parisian Trade." *The Times* (London), April 17, 1856.

"Patagonia and the Welsh People." *North Wales Chronicle*, February 26, 1876.

Pruett, Laura Moore. "Porch and Playhouse, Parlor and Performance Hall: Traversing Boundaries in Gottschalk's *The Banjo*." *Journal of the Society for American Music* 11, no. 2 (2017): 155–83.

"Public Meeting." *Belfast Republican Journal* (Belfast, ME), March 5, 1858.

"Reports." *Savannah Georgian and Journal* (Savannah, GA), December 31, 1856.

"Sailed." *Belfast Republican Journal* (Belfast, ME), July 17, 1868.

"Saved from the *Lyonnais*." *Sabbath Recorder* (New York), February 26, 1857.

"Saving Life at Sea—Report of the Select Committee of the House of Commons, 1887." *Nautical Magazine* 56, no. 7 (July 1887): 714–19.

"Schooner *S. E. Meaher*." *Jones Valley Times* (Birmingham, AL), August 4, 1854.

"Schr. *S. E. Meaher*." *New York Tribune*, September 22, 1854.

"The Screw Steam-Ship *City of Glasgow*." *The Standard* (London), August 31, 1854.

"Second Escape of the Bark *Adriatic*." *Harper's Weekly Magazine*, February 27, 1858.

"The Second Ohions." *Washington Union* (Washington, DC), October 11, 1847.

"Senator Sumner's Brother." *Junction City Weekly* (Junction City, KS), June 13, 1874.

Sewell, William H., Jr. "Uneven Development, the Autonomy of Politics, and the Dockworkers of Nineteenth-Century Marseille." *American Historical Review* 93, no. 3 (1988): 604–37. https://doi.org/10.2307/1868104.

"Ship Building in Alabama." *Sumter County Whig* (Livingston, AL), November 16, 1852.

"Ship News." *Belfast Republican Journal* (Belfast, ME), June 11, 1858.

"Shipping Record." *Daily Morning News* (Savannah, GA), December 5, 1857.

"Shipwreck of Frightful Sufferings." *Cambridge Chronicle and University Journal* (Cambridge, UK), April 12, 1856.

"The Shipwreck of the *Lyonnais*." *Buffalo Courier* (Buffalo, NY), April 24, 1857.

"Shipwrecks and Loss of Life and Awful Sufferings among Icebergs." *Hull Packet and East Riding Times* (East Yorkshire, UK), April 11, 1856.

"Shocking Loss of an American Steamship." *Bury and Norwich Post* (Bury, UK), November 6, 1866.

"Spanish Steamers from Liverpool to Havana." *Manchester Weekly Times and Examiner* (Manchester, UK), October 13, 1855.

"The Spanish Transatlantic Mail Steam Packet Company Now Run Their Magnificent Steamers." *Glasgow Herald* (Glasgow, Scotland), October 12, 1855.

"Statement of Flora Solomon, One of the Female Passengers." *New York Times*, November 18, 1856.

"Steam to Havana—Spanish Steamers from Liverpool to Havana." *The Guardian* (London), October 10, 1855.

"The Sumner Family: The Last in a Series of Remarkable Fatalities." *Kansas Chief* (Troy, KS), April 23, 1874.

"Survivors of the Missouri, Distressing Tales of Their Suffering at Sea." *Chicago Tribune*, November 4, 1872.

"Telegraphic Marine Reports." *New York Herald*, September 7, 1854.

"Terrible Disaster at Sea—Loss of the French Steamer *Le Lyonnais*." *Morning Chronicle* (London), December 2, 1856.

"Terrible Disaster at Sea." *New York Daily Herald*, November 17, 1856.

"Thomas Tileson, Esq." *New York Times*, March 6, 1864.

"Tiding of the *Lyonnais*." *Gazette & Courier* (Greenfield, MA), March 16, 1857.

"To Correspondents." *New York Tribune*, November 17, 1856.

"To Correspondents." *New York Tribune*, November 18, 1856.

"To the Editor of the Herald: Foresheet." *New York Daily Herald*, November 19, 1856.

"Total Loss of the Ship *Van Cappellan*." *The Standard* (London), July 22, 1865.

"Tout ce qui se rattache au naufrage du *Lyonnais*." *Le Propagateur: Journal d'ypres et de l'arrondissement* (Ypres, Belgium), December 10, 1856.

"Two Sailors of the *Lyonnais* Picked Up." *Gazette & Courier* (Greenfield, MA), February 7, 1857.

"The Unfortunate *Adriatic*." *Belfast Republican Journal* (Belfast, ME), October 5, 1860.

"United States: From Our Correspondents." *The Guardian* (London), December 2, 1856.

Vasilaki, Kalliopi. *The Maritime Community of La Ciotat: 1851–1914*. School of Philosophy, Department and History and Sociology, University of Crete, December 1, 2021.

Vovard, Andre. "Un captaine au long cours bourdelais, Pierre-Stanislas Devaulx: Le naufrage du *Lyonnais* (1856)." *Revue économique de Bordeaux*, 1912, 133–43.

"Ward L. Smith . . . *Cape Giradeau Democrat* (Cape Giradeau, MO), December 18, 1897.

"Weekly Summary: Foreign." *Manchester Weekly Times and Examiner* (Manchester, UK), September 20, 1854.

"We Read in the *Courier of Marseilles*." *The Times* (London), May 16, 1856.

"We the Undersigned . . ." *Times Picayune* (New Orleans), December 24, 1851.

"Whaleman." *New York Daily Herald*, February 13, 1846.

"Whalemen." *New York Evening Post*, June 2, 1845.

"The Wrecked Steamer *Lyonnais*—Rescue of the Captain and Fifteen of the Passengers and Crew." *Charleston Daily Courier* (Charleston, SC), December 29, 1856.

"The Wreck of the *Arctic*." *Charleston Daily Courier* (Charleston, SC), October 18, 1854.

"The Wreck of the *Lyonnais*—Statement of Captain Durham." *Baltimore Sun*, November 20, 1856.

"Wreck of the *Lyonnais*: Statement of a Female Passenger." *Hudson Daily Star*, November 18, 1856.

"Wreck of the Steamship *Le Lyonnais*." *Green Mountain. Freeman* (Montpelier, VT), November 27, 1856.

"The Wreck of the Steamship *Le Lyonnais*." *New York Daily Herald*, November 18, 1856.

Online Resources

Better Health Channel. "Hypothermia." Accessed November 11, 2020. https://www.betterhealth.vic.gov.au/health/healthyliving/hypothermia.

Childs, Dan. "Climber Died in a State of Bliss." KTRE Channel 9, December 19, 2006. https://www.ktre.com/story/5833977/climber-died-in-a-state-of-bliss/.

"*Elise* (1835)." Palmer List of Merchant Vessels. December 9, 1997. https://www.oocities.org/mppraetorius/com-el.htm.

Flachmeier, Jeanette H. "Morgan, George Washington." *Handbook of Texas Online*, accessed December 11, 2022. https://www.tshaonline.org/handbook/entries/morgan-george-washington.

Franklin, Harper. "Fashion History Timeline." Fashion Institute of Technology, State University of New York. February 19, 2020. https://fashionhistory.fitnyc.edu/1850–1859/.

Gjenvick-Gjønvik Archives. "Black Ball Line History and Ephemera." Accessed December 19, 2019. https://www.gjenvick.com/OceanTravel/SteamshipLines/BlackBallLine.html.

Globalsecurity.org. "Passenger Ships—19th Century." Accessed November 16, 2020. https://www.globalsecurity.org/military/systems/ship/passenger-19.htm.

"Hamelin, Ferdinand-Alphonse." Senat, un site au service des citoyens. Accessed December 12, 2022. https://www.senat.fr/senateur-2nd-empire/hamelin_ferdinand_alphonse0280e2.html.

"Junk." *New World Encyclopedia*, 2023. https://www.newworldencyclopedia.org/entry/Junk_(ship).

Mackenzie, Gregory J. "Cammell Laird: Shipbuilders of the World at Birkenhead, England by Alex Naughton." *Ahoy—Mac's Web Log*, 2004. http://ahoy.tk-jk.net/macslog/CammelLairdShipbuildersat.html.

Mayo Clinic. "Hypothermia." Accessed November 11, 2020. https://www.mayoclinic.org/diseases-conditions/hypothermia/symptoms-causes/syc-20352682.

"*Mercury* 1851." Palmer List of Merchant Vessels. December 1997. https://www.oocities.org/mppraetorius/com-me.htm.

Penobscot Marine Museum. "Ships and Shipbuilding." Penobscot Marine Museum Education, 2012, https://www.penobscotmarinemuseum.org/pbho-1/ships-shipbuilding/ships-shipbuilding-introduction.

Riebl, Shaun K., and Brenda M. Davy. "The Hydration Equation: Update on Water Balance and Cognitive Performance." *ACSMs Health Fit Journal* 17, no. 6 (2013):21–28. doi:10.1249/FIT.0b013e3182a9570f

Shinabeck, Katie. "History Repeats Itself." *Gibson House Museum Blog*. Gibson House Museum, January 1, 2015. https://thegibsonhousemuseum.blogspot.com/2015/01/history-repeats-itself.html.

The Ship List. "The Fleets: Compagnie Generale des Paquebots Transatlantiques/French Line." February 6, 2005. http://www.theshipslist.com/ships/lines/french2.shtml.

Vida Maritima. "Zangroniz hermanos y el vapor *Habana*." June 14, 2015. https://vidamaritima.com/2015/06/zangroniz-hermanos-y-el-vapor-habana/.

Von Earl of Cruise. "Transatlantic–Ocean Steamship Navigation Company, New York, 1846–1857." July 6, 2017. https://earlofcruise.blogspot.com/2017/07/transatlantic-ocean-steam-navigation.html.

Index

Abaellino, 236
Acadia, (steamship), 33
Acadia, (barque), 180
Aicard, Albert, 188, 199, 201, 203, 205–07, 308
Album Regio, 59, 168–69
Alexander, Samuel, 299
Allen, Frederick Slocum, 223
Alma, 42–3
Amable, 25
Amity, 27
Ancien Port, Old Port, 210
Andrea Doria, 323–24, 332–34
Andrew Foster, 292
Andrew Jackson, 273
Arabia, 55
Arago, 42
Archimedes, 34–5
Arctic, 20, 24, 33, 119–120, 189, 289–90
Argonaut, 284
Atlantic, 33
Atlas, 304
Ayuruoca, 316–17

○ ○ ○

Babcock, Major Samuel, 281
Bailey, Julia Strong, 53, 79–80, 166
Bailey, Leonard, 166
Bailey, Senator Theodoros, 53
Bailey, Theodore Armstrong, 53, 59, 79–80, 166
Baltic, 33
Baltimore Board of Trade, 293
Bangor, Maine, 92, 180, 194, 284
"Banjo Dance," 63
Barcelona; *Barcelone* (steamship), 39–40, 42, 47, 294–95
Barcelona, Spain, 265, 267, 308
Barclay, Captain Thomas, 53
Barclay Catherine, 53, 164–68
Bassford, Francis Louis, 62–3, 165
Bassford, Margaret Clayton, 62–3, 72, 167
Bassford, Thomas Franklin, 62–4, 169–170
Battle of Bomarsund, 94–5
Battle of Sebastopol, 95, 204
Baumstarck, Gustave, 79, 96
Beaugrand, Captain Charles "Chas," 59, 74, 78–9, 166

Beauty, 167
Behar, 295
Belfast Republican Journal, 153, 155–57, 160–61, 207, 276, 307
Belfast, Maine, 91–3, 153–54, 157, 179–81, 184–85, 191, 193–95, 198–99, 201, 205, 247, 275–77, 285, 298–99, 301–306, 329–30
Bellet, Ernestine, 89, 95, 110, 132, 151, 173
Benet, Louis, 182–83
Benso, Count Camillo; Count of Cavour, 257–58
Bentham, Samuel, 87
Besson, Prefect Olympe, 242–44, 253, 257–58
Betty Kratzer, 301
Bienaimée, Pierre, 66–7, 71–2, 82, 128, 151
"Bignores Polka," 63
Birkenhead, 37–8, 314, 319
Birkenhead, HMS *Birkenhead*, 38
Birkenhead Iron Works, 37
Black Ball Line, 27–8, 274
Black River Conference; Black River Mission, 37–8
Black Sea, 95, 204, 237–39
Black Warrior, 58–9
Blake, 122
Bloomersdijk, 315
Bonaparte, Louis Napoléon III; Napoléon III, 26, 43, 172, 187, 204, 209, 242–43, 257, 286, 296
Borg, Louis, 172
Boston Board of Trade, 271, 279
Boston Daily Courier; *Boston Courier*, 284, 290
Bostone Evening Traveler; *Boston Traveler*, 156, 160
Bouches-du-Rhône, 242
Boyd & Hincken, 174
Brazillero, 234–36
Britannia, 33
North American Royal Mail Steam Packet Company, 32
British Board of Trade, 50, 271
British Merchant Shipping Act of 1854, 292
Briton's Pride, 118
Brooklyn Daily Eagle, 155
Brower, John Henry; J.H. Brower & Company, 271–273, 292
Brown, Henry Collins, 272–73

Brunel, Isambard Kingdom, 30-2, 34-5, 38, 87
Buchanon, President James, 187, 278, 284, 290-91, 293, 296
Burlingame, Congressman Anson, 287, 292
Burroughs, Congressman Silas, 280

○ ○ ○

C. Durham & Company, 298
Cadix; *Cadiz*, 39-40, 42-3, 46, 294, 337, 344
Cadiz, Spain, 294
Cairo, Illinois, 303
Caledonia, 33
Cambridge (barque), 145
Cambridge, Massachusetts, 163
Canadian Steamship Navigation Company, 38-9
Cantua Gréard, Marie Delphine, 25
Carondelet Marine Ways, 303
Carter & Company; Carter Shipyard, 91-2, 181, 185, 193
Carter, Columbia Perkins, 91-3, 181, 193-94, 205, 276, 330
Casey, Henry, 208
Castine, Maine, 184
Cauvin, Alexis, 65-6, 82, 95-6, 128, 137-39, 147, 151, 172, 191, 197-98
Cayolle, 113-14, 145
Cedas, 113-15, 117, 141-45
Chaintal de Laloubie, Catherine Jeanne Felicita, 25
Chas. L. Mashall Line, 17
China, 295
Christian Knudsen, 315
City of Glasgow, 35, 38, 118-19
City of Manchester, 295
City of Philadelphia, 119
Civil War (American), 38, 53, 90, 163, 209, 240, 273, 297, 302-03, 340
Clappier, 192, 257, 260
Clarin, Dr. Jean, 24, 112
Cleaver, Martin, 319
Clemson, Louisiana, 305, 307
Cleopatra, 39
Cleveland, Henry Russell, 163
Clingman, Congressman Thomas, 280
Clotilda, 236, 301-302
Cocagne, Reverend John B., 57-9
Colby, Captain Edward, 180
Collins Line, 29-30, 32-6, 55, 120, 189, 290
Collins, Edward Knight, 29-30, 32-6, 273
Columbus, 29
Columbus, Christopher, 87
Compagnie des Messageries Nationales, 183
Congress; United State Congress, 270-71, 274, 278-80, 285, 288, 290, 297
Constantinople, Turkey, 238-39
Contract, 32

Columbia (Cunard steamship), 33
Columbia; USS *Columbia* (frigate), 231, 234
Cora, 305
Costa Rica, 60-1, 133
Courier, 27
Crawford, Thomas, 62-2
Crimea, 96, 135
Crimean War, 20, 33, 38, 42-3, 81, 94, 204, 237, 257, 307
Critchley, MacDonald, 103-04
Crittendon, 231-32
Cunard, Line, 22, 32-3, 35-6, 55
Cunard, Samuel, 32-3, 35
Czar, 240, 302

○ ○ ○

D'anna, David, 333
Danube River, 237-39
De Eulate, Antonia, 58, 168
De Eulate, Don Jose, 58, 168
De Eulate, Manuel, 58
De Gama, Vasco, 87
de Landaluze, Patricio, 170
de Tounardre, E., 202
De Zangroniz, Ramon, 39-41
Dehon, Theodore, 273-74
Dellamere, Anne, 33
Democrat, 91
Desfour, Third Engineer, 65-7, 76, 82, 128, 151-52, 174
Devaulx, Captain Pierre Stanislas, 24-6, 61-2, 68, 71-80, 82-4, 94, 96-8, 112-13, 156-57, 160, 166, 191, 197-98, 200, 203, 205, 294
Devaulx, Jena-Baptiste, 25
Devaulx, Stenio, 26, 295
Diaz y de Comas, Don Vincente, 59, 168-69
Domenigo, Mr., 82, 128, 151, 173
Donn, Andrew, 322, 326-27, 336, 339-40, 343-45, 347, 349
Dover; HMS *Dover*, 38
Dramatic Line, 29-30
du Montholon, Charles Marquis, 172
Dublic, Julius, 65-6, 75, 82, 96, 110, 128, 138-39, 147-48, 151, 171-72
Dublot, Rene, 79-80, 83
Duke De Braganza, 123
Dummer, Cora Adelaide, 54, 62
Dummer. Francis E., 54, 62
Dundas, James Whitney Dean, 204
Durham, Captain George Anson, 179, 193
Durham, Captain John Sr., 92-3, 179-81, 194, 275-76
Durham, Charles, 92, 154, 179, 193-95, 284, 298-99, 305-06
Durham, Eunice, 179, 193, 305, 331
Durham, James Monroe, 179, 193

Durham, John Sergeant, 179, 181, 193
Durham, Mary Anna, 306
Durham, Sarah E., 306
Durham, William, 179, 193

⊙ ⊙ ⊙

Eads, James Buchanan, 303
Eerie, 39
Elise (Bremen-bound), 149–150
Elise (New York-bound), 149–150, 153, 164–65, 171–73
Elizabeth, 165
Elizabeth Dennison, 274–75
Elliott, Captain David, 236
Ellora, 46, 295–96
Ericsson, John, 34–5, 38
Essex (Captain Ray), 144–45
Essex (Durham), 180
Evening Star, 104
Eyebolt, 157, 159–161

⊙ ⊙ ⊙

Father François, 82, 126–131, 174
Fawcett & Company, 47
Felton, Cornelius, 163–64
Five of Clubs, 163
Flambeau; USS *Flambeau*, 301
Fleet Marina, 339
Florence Nightingale, 104
Flying Cloud, 272
Flying Dutchman, 169–170, 284
Flying Scud, 90
Fort Pulaski, 281
Fort Saint-Jean, 210, 246
Fort Saint-Nicolas, 246
Foster, Captain William, 302
Foster, Captain (*Marion*), 174
Foster, J. T., 236
Foucault, Michel, 52
Fouriere, Victor, 244
Franco-Américaine, 18, 20, 22, 37, 41–5, 4, 51, 54–5, 61, 150, 165, 173–74, 188, 191–92, 199, 201–03, 206–07, 209, 212, 257, 272, 294–95, 347
François Arago, 42
Franklin, 42, 119, 289
Fredericktown, Missouri, 307
Froelich, Augustus, 60
Fulton, 42–3

⊙ ⊙ ⊙

G.B. Lamer, 121
Galatz, 237–39
Gallia, 33
Garcia y Grinda, Captain, 40
Gatto, Steve, 315–17, 323

Gauthier Fréres & Company; Gauthier, Claude-Antoine & Jacques-Victor, 36–7, 41–3, 188, 201, 208, 212, 243, 260, 277–78, 294, 297, 299
Gazielle, 250–51, 257
Geddes, New York, 216–17, 303
General Marshall, 180, 304
Genoa, Italy, 252, 254, 257, 260–61
Georges Bank, 321, 325, 332, 336–37, 339
Germania, 120
Gibraltar, 301, 304
Gibraltar, Spain, 260, 274, 276
Gibson, Catherine Hammond, 54, 165
Gibson, Charles, 54, 165
Gibson, John Sr., 54
Gibson, John Gardiner Jr., 54, 165
Gigneux, Chief Engineer, 71–2, 74
Gloucester Customs Exchange; Gloucester Customhouse, 162, 191, 206–07
Gloucester, Massachusetts, 152–55, 157, 159–162, 165, 174, 183, 191, 206–07, 243, 285, 299
Goodwin, Captain Albert G., 224–26, 228–32, 236
Gottschalk, Louis Morceau, 63–4
Great Britain, 35, 38, 87
Great Western, 30–3
Great Western Steamship Company, 30
Grinnell, Minturn & Company; Grinnell, Moses H., 272–73
Grove Cemetery, 193, 304, 306, 330
Guilbert fils, Nantes, 42

⊙ ⊙ ⊙

Habana, 39–40, 54, 295
Hamelin, Ferdinand-Alphonse, 203–05, 257
Hamelin, Jacques Felix Emmanuel 203–04
Hant, Stanislas Ferriere, 25
Harriet Martha, 180
Harvey Birch, 273
Havana, Cuba, 39–40, 48, 59, 79, 294
Havener, J., 92
Henry Clay, 273
Higginson, Henry Lee, 55
Hillard, George, 163–64
Home Wrecker, 315
Howe, Stanley Gridley, 61–2
Humboldt, 42, 289
Hunt, Dana C., 221, 231, 232–34
Huron, 39

⊙ ⊙ ⊙

Imperial Court of Aix; Court of Aix, 202, 205, 207–09, 257, 261, 286
Imperial Order of the Legion of Honor; Legion of Honor, 158, 172, 191
Inman Lines, 35–6, 39, 118–19

Inman, William, 35–6
Irish Inland Lakes Steam Navigation Company, 37
Irving, John C., 196

◦ ◦ ◦

J.W. Elwell, 237
Jacquard, 42
James Miller, 304
James Monroe, 27
Java, 25
Jeddo, 55
John Blyth & Company, 295
John Gilpin, 301
John Rutledge, 104, 124
John Sidney, 304
Johnson, Horatio H., 276
Joliette Port, 210, 262
Jordan, Dr. Charles A., 284
Joste (sailor), 82, 95, 128, 151

◦ ◦ ◦

Kavanaugh, Governor Edward 235
Koller, William, 191, 197–98, 206
Kozak, Garry, 317, 327, 343

◦ ◦ ◦

L'Aigle, 94–5
La Ciotat, France, 93, 162, 182–87, 189, 201, 203, 285
La Luna, 248, 267
LaDuke, Sharon, 216
Laird & Company; Laird & Sons, 34, 37–42, 45–7, 50, 55, 295, 347
Laird, John, 37–9
Laird, William, 37
Lambert (the baker), 82, 99, 128, 151
Laura Russ, 301
Lawrence, Captain, 133–34
Le Chacal, 250–51, 253, 257–59, 264, 277, 283
Le Franc Comtois, 39, 42–3, 47
Le Havre, France, 19–21, 26, 28, 42–3, 51, 58, 64, 121, 166, 174–76, 184, 191, 199, 274, 294
Lee, Robert E., 305–06
Leese, R. H., 255–56, 258–60, 262
LeFevre, George Shaw, 50
Leguit, 114, 117, 141–42
Leviathan, 284
London Guardian, The, 37, 161–62
Long, Colonel William, 258, 283
Longfellow, Henry Wadsworth, 53, 163–64, 167
Low, Abiel Albert, 273–74
Lucania, 22
Lysander, New York, 216–19, 299

◦ ◦ ◦

Madison County Democrat, 306
Magellan, Ferdinand, 87
Malabar, 181, 194, 299
Marguery (avoué), 206
Marie, 59, 79
Marion, 173–74
Marshall, Benjamin, 27
Marshall, Captain Charles, 273–74, 278
Marshall, Congressman Humphrey, 278
Martha Hill, 193–94
Martin and Blohorn & Cavagna, 261
Martin, Captain John Stephen, 188–89, 202, 213, 240, 261–64, 284, 299, 301
Mary Farrow, 180
Mason, Powell, 55
Masons, 238
Mathieu, Jean-Marie, 67, 69
Matthews, Alice Irene, 304
Mauritius Campaign, 204
Mazraani, Joe, 313–21, 323–29, 334–50
Meaher, Augustine, 306
Meaher, James, 235–37
Meaher, Captain Timothy, 235–37, 240, 301–02, 306
Mercury, 174–75, 191
Meridian Star, 346
Merle, François, 334, 337
Mersey River, 37–8, 51
Midway; USS *Midway*, 328
Mills, Edward, 42
Millson, Congressman John, 302
Mintell, Kurt, 313, 334, 339–41, 343–47, 349
Missouri, 105
Mitchell, Lieutenant Joseph, 303
Mobile, Alabama, 234–37, 299, 302–03, 319
Mocquard, Jean François Constant, 26
Mogador, 95
Monitor; USS *Monitor*, 38, 340
Moore, George, 153–55, 276
Morgan, Colonel George Washington, 186–88, 205, 209–10, 240, 262, 284, 299, 308
Mound City Marine & Railway Shipyard, 303
Moyer, John, 323
Moyers, Harold, 317
Murphy; USS *Murphy*, 333

◦ ◦ ◦

Napier, Robert; Napier & Sons, 32–3
Napoleon, 181
Ned White, 304
Neilson, A. B., 273–74
Neilson, Captain Adolph, 150, 164, 171
Neptune, 17, 166–67
Nestor, Fabian, 71, 75–6, 78, 82, 128, 151
New Bedford, Massachusetts, 53, 104, 219–21, 223, 226, 273, 302, 321, 325, 332, 335, 338–39, 350

Newcastle City, 316, 345
New York & Havre Steamship Navigation Company, 42
New York Chamber of Commerce 270–74, 277–79, 288–94
New York Herald, 29, 161, 173–74
New York Times, 166, 205, 211, 279
Nordenholt, Captain George, 149–150
Nouvelle Gabrielle, 25
Nouvelle Louise, 25
Nye, Captain Ezra, 104–05, 120
Nye, Thomas, 273

○ ○ ○

Ocean Queen, 121
Ocean Steam Navigation Company, 42
Ocean Wave, 304
Ontario, 39
Oran, Missouri, 305–06
Oriline St. John, 235
Orissa, 296
Osbourne, Ella Nancy, 185
Ottawa, 180

○ ○ ○

Pacific (sailing vessel), 27
Pacific (steamship), 120, 123–24, 273
Pacific Mail Steamship Company, 274
Packer, Tom, 315–17, 323, 338, 340–41, 343, 345–47, 349
Palmer, Andrew Thatcher, 276
Paquebots Transatlantiques; "Transatlantic General Steam Packet Company," 41–2
Patagonia, Argentina; Patagonia, Chile, 229
Patterson & Carter, 92, 194, 290, 301
Peabody, Captain Enoch, 17–8, 166, 168
Pearce, Elizabeth Parrot, 299
Peck, Bob, 319
Peninsular & Oriental Steam Navigating Company; P&O, 22, 45–6, 55, 295–96
Penobscot Bay, Maine, 90–2, 184–85
Perkins, Stephen, 55
Perit, Pelatiah, 272–73, 293–94
Persia, 22, 33, 58–9
"Phantom Ship," 63
Philadelphie, 42
Phillips, Congressman Henry, 280
Poirier Guynet, Emma, 20
Poirier, Edmund; Poirier, Edward, 20, 61, 155, 171
Poirreaux, Victor, 71, 82, 128, 151, 174
Pook, Samuel L.; Pook's gunboats, 303
Princeton; USS *Princeton*, 38
Providence, Rhode Island, 308, 310–11
Python, 205

○ ○ ○

Quaker City, 59
Quest, 315, 320

○ ○ ○

Rainbow, 34
Ray, Captain, 144–45
Red Jacket, 90
Red Star Line, 28
Rennie & Sons, 34, 47, 343
Rennie, George, 34
Ringbolt, 157
Rio de Janeiro, Brazil, 26, 43, 51, 90, 144–46, 231, 234, 316
Robert F. Stockton, 34, 38
Robert Menzies & Sons, 31
Roger B. Taney, 240, 302
Rogers, George H., 155
Romain (stoker), 113–14, 145
Rooney, Pat, 316
Roussel, Pierre, 67, 78, 81–2, 167
Russ, James A., 301

○ ○ ○

Sagaland, 316
Saint Mary, 133
Salisbury, 180
Sarah E. Meaher; S.E. Meaher, 213, 236–40, 244, 265–67, 269, 274, 299–303
Sarah Sands, 39
Savannah, Georgia, 93, 154, 162, 180–183, 195, 276–86, 291, 294, 298–99, 308
Schedel, George, 60–1, 80–4, 95–8, 109–111, 127, 132–140, 146, 149–151, 166, 176, 205
Schedel, Mrs., 60–1, 132, 140, 151
Sellitti, Rudolph, 328, 329, 332–33, 346, 351
Shammer, 180
Sharpe, Captain, 176
Sheard, Brad, 317
Sheridan, 29
Siam, 181, 299
Simon, Rick, 326, 334, 338
Sirius, 31–2
Smith, Catherine Vrooman, 216
Smith & Stewart Lumber Dealers, 303
Smith, John T., 154–55
Smith, Junius, 31
Smith, Noah Hudson, 216
Smith, William Wallace, 299, 303
Solomon, Flora, 54, 62, 72–3, 75, 80, 82, 95, 97, 99, 110–11, 127, 130–31, 134, 147–48, 151, 166–68, 171–73
Southern Republic, 240
Spaniard; the Spaniard, 126, 130–31, 174

Spanish Transatlantic Mail Steam Packet Company, "Spanish Transatlantic," 39–42, 46–7, 54
Spezia, Italy; Spezia, Sardinia, 252–55, 257–62, 269, 277, 283
Spofford, Paul N., 274
Spofford, Tileston & Company of New York, 274
St. Amand, Joe, 326
St. Denis, 121, 123
St. George Steam Packet Company, 31
Stephano, 315
Stetson, Captain Thomas, 175
Stockholm, 323, 333, 335
Stockton, Captain Robert F., 34
Strathdene, 315
Strickler, Van, 332, 350
Strong, Jeannette Amy, 53, 80
Sulina, Wallachia, 238–39
Sumner, Captain Albert, 53, 61–2, 74, 78–80, 166–68
Sumner, Charles Pinckney, 53
Sumner, Senator Charles, 53, 163–68
Sun Mutual Fire Insurance Company of New York, 274
Swallowtail Lines, 28, 272–73
"Sweet Lady Do Not Stay," 63
Swift & Allen, 218–21, 223
Swift, Jireh, 223

◦ ◦ ◦

Takakjian, Eric, 9–10, 313–21, 323–27, 329, 334–36, 339–41, 343–47, 349–50
Taylor, Congressman Miles, 277–79, 291
Tedeschi, Anthony, 317
Thillaye, Stanislas, 65–7, 76, 82, 128, 151–52, 171
Thombs, Captain Joseph Shaw, 184–86, 188, 191, 197–98, 243, 244–46, 249, 254, 269, 300–01, 303–06, 308
Thombs, Charles E., 301
Thombs, Charles R., 184
Thompson, Jerimiah, 27
Thourel, (avocat), 206–07
Tileston, Thomas, 273–74
Tillman, Samuel, 224–25
Titanic, 119
Tongard, 113–17, 141–45

Tonquin, 181, 193
Topliff, 179–80
Toulon, France, 182–83, 254, 257
Tuscaloosa, 220–21, 224–25, 229–31, 300
Tuscarora, 292–93
Twain, Mark, 33
Tybee Island Light, 281

U-53, 315, 321, 323–24
U-550, 317, 324, 327
Unicorn, 32
Union, 42
Upper Steamboat Wharf, 92, 181, 194, 330

◦ ◦ ◦

Van Capellan, 125
van der Decken, Hendrick, 169
Venus, 203
Vesta, 20, 169, 189, 289
Vidal, Captain Emile, 202
Vigo, 39–40, 43, 47, 54–5, 172, 174, 295

◦ ◦ ◦

Waldo County, Maine, 92, 179
Warrer, Thomas, 191, 197–98
Waters, Mary C., 235
Waverly, 236
Webster, Daniel, 30
Western Chief, 276
West Point, 315
Whitehead, Tim, 337, 339–41, 343–47, 349
Whittaker, Paul, 316, 338
Widow; the widow, 219–20, 224
William Bradstreet, 235
William G. Jones Jr., 235
William Hallett, 236
William L. Burroughs, 166
Williams, Anna, 299
Woodlawn Cemetery, 307, 327
Wording, Captain Charles H., 276
Wyandot, 193

◦ ◦ ◦

Zangroniz Brothers and Company, 39–41
Zone, 263